# Education
## An Introduction

## 4th Edition

David G. Armstrong
Texas A&M University

Kenneth T. Henson
Eastern Kentucky University

Tom V. Savage
California State University, Fullerton

Macmillan Publishing Company
New York
Maxwell Macmillan Canada
Toronto
Maxwell Macmillan International
New York   Oxford   Singapore   Sydney

Cover art: Hans Hofmann (1880-1966). *Rhapsody*. Oil on canvas. The Metropolitan Museum of Art, Gift of Renate Hofmann, 1975. (1975.323)
Editor: Robert Miller
Developmental Editor: Molly Kyle
Production Editor: Mary Irvin
Artist: Jane Lopez
Art Coordinator: Peter A. Robison
Photo Editor: Anne Vega
Cover Designer: Robert Vega
Production Buyer: Pamela D. Bennett
Electronic Text Management: Ben Ko, Marilyn Wilson Phelps


This book was set in Transitional 511 by Macmillan Publishing Company and was printed and bound by R. R. Donnelley/Indiana. The cover was printed by Phoenix Color Corp.

Photo credits: Courtesy of IBM: 3. National Education Association/Joe DiDio: 13, 243. Robert Finken: 14, 111, 166, 193, 223, 282, 301, 364, 408, 468, 483. Andy Brunk: 37, 163, 179, 306, 326, 349, 376. Ulrike Welsch: 44, 143, 252, 272, 338, 403, 421. Culver Pictures, Inc.: 57, 73, 76, 93, 122. Bettman Archive: 90, 197. UPI/Bettman Newsphotos: 154, 431. Gale Zucker: 205, 219, 355. Jean-Claude LeJeune: 239. Mark Madden/KS Studios: 385. Richard B. Levine: 426. Macmillan Publishing Company: 467. Red Morgan/Time Magazine: 491.

Macmillan Publishing Company
866 Third Avenue
New York, New York 10022

Maxwell Macmillan Canada, Inc.
1200 Eglinton Avenue East, Suite 200
Don Mills, Ontario M3C 3N1

Library of Congress Cataloging-in-Publication Data
Armstrong, David G.
Education: an introduction/David G. Armstrong, Kenneth T. Henson, Tom V. Savage.—4th ed.
p. cm.
Includes bibliographical references and index.
ISBN 0-02-304151-X
1. Teaching—Vocational guidance—United States. 2. Education-Study and teaching—United States. 3. Public schools—United States. I. Henson, Kenneth T. II. Savage, Tom V. III. Title.
LB1775.A665 1993
371'.01' 0973—dc20                                                                                  92-12494
                                                                                                          CIP

Printing: 1 2 3 4 5 6 7 8 9  Year: 2 3 4 5

# Preface

$D$o you like change? Do you thrive on controversy? Are you willing to try something different? If your answers are "yes," you'll feel right at home in the field of education. After a decade of rhetoric, the engine of reform has left the station. Precedent-shattering ideas are moving from the drawing board to be tested in the hard crucible of reality. Here are some examples you may have read about.

- The state of Oregon is abandoning the traditional high school. At the end of the 10th grade, students will receive a certificate of mastery based on what they have learned. For the last two years of school, they will either be tracked into a college preparatory program or placed into an intensive vocational training program. Among other things, the plan is intended to better prepare noncollege-bound students for the workplace. In part, this improvement is expected to result from a plan to extend the school year by the year 2010 to 220 days a year from its present level of 175 days.

- The Golden Rule Insurance Company, headquartered in Illinois, has begun a pilot program to pay the tuition for poor students who wish to attend private schools. The idea is to let children of impoverished parents in the major urban areas escape poor central-city schools. If these economically-deprived young people achieve at higher levels in the private schools, there may be an incentive for states to provide school funds directly to parents (who might be allowed to spend them in schools of their choice) rather than to school districts. Supporters of the Golden Rule approach feel this competition might lead to improvements in the quality of educational services being delivered by the public schools.

- Potential benefits of year-round schooling have been discussed by some educators for years. One stumbling block to establishment of such programs has been parental resistance. Moton Elementary School in New Orleans has overcome this resistance. It has instituted an 11-month school year, the longest public school calendar in the United States. And it has done so with the enthusiastic support of the parents. Their support has little to do with learning benefits of a longer year that have long been claimed by some professional educators. Rather, they have discovered that the school is a much safer place for their children to be than in the dangerous low-income housing projects surrounding the school. Perhaps safety, rather than academic concerns, will encourage the spread of longer school years in the nation's cities.

This is an exciting time for educators everywhere. Newcomers will find much to challenge them. Not every new idea they will confront will have merit. But what is certain is that there will *be* suggestions for change. As professionals, teachers must be prepared to analyze proposals that could profoundly affect how they discharge their responsibilities. We believe decision making to be the heart of the teacher's role. We have written this book to help newcomers understand the intellectual roots of the profession, the research base on which curriculum and instruction rests, and some issues that have implications for policy and practice.

New teachers face many challenges. Among them are those related to influencing policy decisions; motivating learners; responding to individual differences; implementing new technologies; managing learning environments; selecting and organizing content; working with administrators, counselors, and other teachers; pursuing professional development opportunities; and operating within legal and ethical guidelines. This text prepares teachers to meet these obligations knowledgeably and confidently.

*Education: An Introduction* has been used successfully in undergraduate and graduate courses. It is designed for use in introduction to education classes, introduction to teaching classes, general education classes, foundations of education classes, issues in education classes, and problems in education classes. The content can serve as a source for inservice work with teachers and as a valuable professional reference for the career teacher.

The fourth edition contains much new content, including:

- examples of classroom observation instruments and instructions for their use
- a new chapter on the sociology of education
- a new chapter on multicultural and gender-equity education
- a new chapter on educational innovations
- a new chapter on school and school-district organization and personnel (including role descriptions of many categories of professional and nonprofessional employees in education)

- greatly expanded treatment of gifted and talented students
- extensive treatment of President Bush's AMERICA 2000 education reform proposals
- updated treatment of educational applications of technology
- expanded coverage of specialty organizations in the chapter on teachers' professional groups
- case studies to accompany every chapter
- selected findings from educational research as boxes in each chapter
- extensive updating of content in all chapters from the previous edition

Each chapter in the fourth edition of *Education: An Introduction* includes:

- *Objectives* to help focus attention on key chapter content.
- *Focus Questions* to provide students with conceptual anchors as they work through the material.
- *Introductions* to establish a clear context for the content to follow.
- *Boxes* that raise important issues for student comment and consideration.
- *Figures* to display statistical and other graphical information.
- *What the Experts Say* to raise student's awareness of what researchers have had to say about important educational issues.
- *Case Studies* to highlight critical issues and give students opportunities to develop their analytical powers.
- *Summary Tables* to recapitulate key chapter points.
- *Key Ideas in Summary* to review critical aspects of chapter content succinctly and efficiently.
- *Review and Discussion Questions* to provide students with opportunities to check their own learning and extend their thinking powers.
- *Ideas for Field Experiences, Projects, and Enrichment* to suggest opportunities for students to engage in learning activities involving extensions and applications of chapter content.
- *Supplementary Reading* to suggest titles of books and articles containing information to enrich student understanding of chapter content.
- *References* to indicate to students where they might find some of the original materials consulted by the authors.

Continuing the pattern established in previous editions of *Education: An Introduction*, an instructor's guide has been prepared. It has been completely revised for this edition and includes:

- overviews of the chapter content
- alternative ideas for sequencing courses using this text
- suggested activities

- a collection of questions suitable for quizzes and tests, with accompanying keys.

The test items are also available in a computerized format for use with Macintosh and IBM and IBM-compatible computers.

We believe teachers should design their own courses and not be bound by the order of presentation of chapters in their textbooks. We also feel that this is how instructors should use our book. We have organized the book in a way that makes sense to us, but we recognize that others will want to follow a different sequence of chapters, and we encourage them to do so. Chapters have been written so that each is "free standing"; that is, no chapter is a prerequisite to understanding content introduced in another.

In particular, we would like to point out that information regarding classroom observation instruments is included in the last part of Chapter 11, "Effective Teaching Practices." We placed these materials here because the behaviors that the instrument focus on are those that researchers have found to be effective. It was our intentions to establish a rationale for the importance of these behaviors before introducing the related observation instruments.

We realize that many instructors may assign their students to do classroom observations very early in the term. If this is the case, we encourage an early introduction of the observation instruments, even though the text does not deal with them early on.

In preparing this text, we decided to organize content under six major headings. These section headings establish a general context for the related chapters. Because we feel future teachers are interested in some important "here-and-now" issues, we begin the book with a section titled, "Challenges and Changes," The first chapter introduces a selection of important issues facing educators today. The second takes a more detailed look at several innovations, paying particular attention to how these innovations are affecting different groups.

The second section, "Foundations," is designed to develop learners' understanding of the intellectual underpinnings of education. The first chapter develops themes related to the international roots of American education. The second picks up the historical story of education as it developed in colonial America and, later, within the United States. The third chapter introduces some philosophical perspectives as they relate to education. The final chapter in this section introduces issues associated with the sociology of education.

The third section, "Learners," provides students with an overview of young people in the school today. The first chapter sketches a profile of the range of learners in the schools, with particular attention to characteristics of young people in different age groups. The second chapter provides detailed information about the changing demographic characteristics of the schools, particularly regarding the rapidly increasing numbers of learners from minority cultural and ethnic groups. This chapter also introduces issues associated with gender equity. The final chapter in this section focuses on characteristics of learners with disabilities and learners who are gifted and talented.

The fourth section, "Profession and Teaching," includes chapters addressing issues having to do with teachers' organizations and with various dimensions of teachers' classroom teaching responsibility. The first chapter introduces both general teachers' organizations and specialty teachers' organizations. The second chapter introduces findings of research that has pinpointed practices associated with effective teaching practices. The third chapter draws together information related to practices associated with sound management and discipline practices. The final chapter provides specific examples of how some schools are utilizing new technologies to improve their programs.

The fifth section, "Schools," focuses on school characteristics related to administration, staffing, programming, and delivery of quality services to learners. The first chapter describes basic organizational patterns and introduces both professional and nonprofessional people who play important roles in the schools today. The second chapter centers on the academic programs of elementary and high schools, with particular attention to basic patterns. The final chapter introduces characteristics researchers have found to be associated with effective schools.

The final section, "Legal Relationships," includes three chapters. The first centers on the changing legal relationships among federal, state, and local school authorities. The second chapter emphasizes legal issues affecting teachers' professional lives. Issues such as academic freedom, copyright law, and teachers' private lives are addressed. The final chapter centers on laws and court decisions related to rights and responsibilities of school learners.

*Education: An Introduction* is a comprehensive treatment of education and teaching. It provides a solid grounding in the intellectual foundations of the field, results of research, and current issues. We have provided many opportunities for users of the book to study, reflect, analyze, and decide. We think the book will develop your decision-making skills. This is something we value. And we hope it is something you as future teachers will prize, as well. Good luck!

Let's conclude with a recognition of some incredibly patient and tolerant people who helped with the development of the fourth edition of *Education: An Introduction.* We would like to thank Mary Lee Batesko, Georgian Court College; Myra J. Baughman, Pacific Lutheran University; Frank P. Bazeli, Illinois University; Carlos F. Diaz, Florida Atlantic University; Dwight Hare, Mississippi State University; David S. Huseman, Butler County Community College; Alan Pardoen, Potsdam State University; Ann F. Reitzammer, University of Alabama at Birmingham; Vera Lynn Sheets, Union College (Kentucky); John A. Stirton, San Joaquin Delta Community College; Maryjane Tomcala, East Texas State University; and Mary Louise Wilson, Southern University—Shreveport. The developmental editor for this project, Molly Kyle, gave long hours to this project, and her suggestions added immeasurably to the substance and coherence of the final version. Thanks, too, to our long-time New York Macmillan editor, Robert Miller, for his continued support. Finally, our wives deserve special thanks for their support while we were working on this revision.

D.G.A.
K.T.H.
T.V.S.

# Brief Contents

# Contents

# List of Cases

# What the Experts Say

# Education
## An Introduction

# Section 1

# Challenges and Changes

## Overview

What is *right* with our schools? Even asking such a question catches many by surprise. For a decade, we have heard little but complaints about our schools. Are things as bad as has been reported? Not at all. Can the schools be better? Yes they can.

Gerald Bracey (1991), a research and evaluation director in a Colorado school district, has identified some overlooked pluses of our educational system. He notes that:

- A higher percentage of young people are completing high school than ever before.

- Unlike many other countries, the United States has an educational system that allows young people who drop out of school to complete high school equivalency programs and go on to colleges and universities.

- Standardized test scores, after falling in the 1960s and 1970s, have begun to rise. By the late 1980s, some were at all-time highs.

- Today's learners are exposed to much more sophisticated content in schools than were their parents.

- We spend a smaller proportion of our gross national product on education today than we did in 1970. Thus, the argument that we are spending more on education and getting less is not correct.

- Fully 30 to 40 percent of all articles in the world's scientific journals are the work of Americans, most of whom attended public schools.*

*Gerald W. Bracey, "The Straight Story about the Education Our Kids Are Getting," *The Washington Post*, 13–19 May 1991, 23–24, national weekly edition.

The condition of public education is not nearly so bleak as it is sometimes depicted. In our quest for educational excellence, we need to remember that there is good as well as bad in our present system. Educational improvement means making adjustments to a scheme that already does some things well.

Content in Section I provides answers to questions that are often asked by people who seek to make American schools even better. Among these questions are:

- What kinds of demands are being placed on schools today?
- What are some specific problem areas facing educators at the present time?
- What are some innovations that have been adopted for the purpose of improving education?
- How successful have such innovations been?

Discussion related to these questions is introduced in two unit chapters:

Chapter 1: Challenges Facing Today's Schools
Chapter 2: Innovations

# Chapter 1

# Challenges Facing Today's Schools

## Objectives

This chapter provides information to help the reader to

- identify some challenges facing today's schools.
- identify several different and potentially conflicting purposes of education.
- suggest how an understanding of educational foundations can contribute to an understanding of issues related to public schools and teaching.
- explain why it is difficult to get consensus regarding characteristics of good schools and school programs.

# Focus Questions

1. What are challenges facing professional educators as the beginning of the 21st century approaches?
2. How can a given teacher be doing an "excellent" job in the eyes of some people and an "inadequate" job in the eyes of others?
3. How much emphasis should schools place on the notion of education for intellectual attainment?
4. What arguments do proponents of the concept of education for citizenship make to establish the importance of this perspective?
5. What are some concerns of those people who want schools to pay more attention to vocational education?
6. What are some examples of school programs that have been developed in response to pressures to pay more attention to learners' individual development?
7. What are some key concerns of educational sociologists, educational historians, and educational psychologists?
8. In what ways can a comprehension of educational foundations help teachers understand decisions that are made regarding school policies?

•••••••••••••••••••••••••••••••

# Introduction

As the 21st century approaches, schools are being challenged by many serious problems. Demands on educators to produce graduates who can move smoothly into the demanding world of highly technological workplaces are increasing. Unfavorable comparisons between performance levels of learners in the United States and those in other countries are putting pressure on legislatures. Increasing numbers of learners are coming from economically impoverished backgrounds. Ethnic and cultural minority learners, whose perspectives may differ from those of many of their teachers, are representing larger and larger percentages of the total school population. In short, people preparing to become teachers today are seeking entrance to an extraordinarily challenging professional world.

## Challenges Facing Today's Educators

Suspicions that our schools are not as good as they should be have led to much speculation about what might be done to correct this problem. Critics of present practices have raised many important issues. As we in education prepare to take action to make schools better, we will have to develop reasoned responses to questions such as these:

- How can public confidence in the schools be restored?
- How can schools be restructured to become more effective?
- How can adequate finances for schools be provided?
- How can needs of an increasingly diverse learner population be met?
- How can curricula be revised to reflect present and future realities?
- How can new technologies be incorporated into school programs?
- How can the quality of teaching be improved?
- How can teachers better deal with unmotivated learners?

## Restoring Public Confidence

Many observers of education believe that public confidence in our schools is lower today than it has been in the past. Newspaper stories about marginally competent teachers have led some people to doubt the intellectual credibility of teachers in general. Growing interest in the home school movement (parents teaching their children at home rather than sending them to school) is symptomatic of some people's lack of confidence in schools and teachers.

On the positive side, academic standards for prospective teachers have become stiffer in recent years. Much effort has gone into the development of better teacher preparation programs. There has been some recognition, too, that salaries and other teaching conditions must be improved if quality people are to be attracted to and retained in the profession. In addition, a growing body of research is beginning to identify characteristics of schools that are doing a good job of educating the learners they serve. (For detailed information regarding what researchers have found about characteristics of these schools, see Chapter 16.)

Box 1–1 discusses the issue of public opinion.

## Restructuring Schools

*Restructuring schools* refers to the idea that a comprehensive review and overhaul of traditional administrative arrangements is needed (Raywid, 1990). Traditional assumptions related to such issues as the relative authority held by administrators, teachers, and parents are being challenged. For example, new, evolving administrative arrangements seem to feature more decentralized decision making and more sharing of power. (For an extended discussion of restructuring, see Chapter 2.)

## Financing Education

Most money to support public schools comes from state governments and local taxing authorities; relatively little financial support comes from the federal government. Often, states provide a certain minimum level of support to each of their school districts. Local officials frequently have the authority to raise additional revenue from local sources to support school programs. Frequently, a tax on real property (land, houses, and other buildings) is the source of local revenues for schools. This means that serious efforts to improve finances for schools often require increases in property tax rates. As a result, school board members and other local educational policymakers often find their budgetary actions to be closely scrutinized by individuals and groups concerned about possible increases in tax rates.

## BOX 1–1
# QUALITY OF THE SCHOOLS

Public opinion surveys regularly find that people rate their local schools higher than they rate schools in general. This may result from media coverage that highlights exceptionally bad school situations, or it may simply be a matter of people being more willing to regard what they know well as "good" and to hold what they do not know as well as "suspect" or "bad." Other explanations might also explain our tendency to look kindly at our own local schools.

### What Do You Think?

1. In your opinion, what were the best features of the schools you attended?
2. In general, do you believe that your teachers were competent?
3. What were some weaknesses in the schools you attended?
4. Think about some criticisms you have heard about schools in general. Could any of them have been fairly applied to any of the schools you attended?

For many years, individual school districts differed greatly from one another in terms of the amount of tax money they had available to support their educational programs. Though state governments tried to provide funds to offset glaring discrepancies in the wealth of individual school districts, districts with an abundance of valuable taxable property still tended to have much more money with which to work than less affluent districts. This reality resulted in great discrepancies in the quality of educational programming available to learners from district to district.

The courts increasingly have become willing to declare unconstitutional and discriminatory those systems of finance that gave some districts much more money than others to spend on education. In responding to such court decisions, it is probable that efforts will be more frequently directed at providing additional money for "have not" districts rather than at taking money away from "have" districts. This may mean a general increase in state taxes—a situation that will put public education in direct competition with other state functions that rely on tax dollars for their funds (Pipho, 1990). (Some additional discussion of the issue of school financing can be found in Chapters 14 and 17.)

## Increasing Diversity of the Learner Population

The diversity of the learner population in schools has increased dramatically over the past few decades (Grant and Secada, 1990)—large numbers of learners from racial, ethnic, and language minorities are now enrolled in public schools. At the same time

*We are pleased to have with us today, Representative Smith, who will bring us up-to-date on his effort to build a consensus in support of the proposed educational improvement package.*
Courtesy of Ford Button.

the learner population is becoming increasingly diverse, the teacher population is becoming more homogeneous (particularly more white and more female) (Grant and Secada, 1990). Sensitizing teachers, most of whom come from the majority white group, to special perspectives of learners who come from different backgrounds is an important priority for educational leaders today. (For more information regarding diversity in today's schools, see Chapters 6, 7, and 8.)

## Modernizing the Curriculum

In every setting, the force of tradition is strong. Many courses offered in today's schools differ little from those taught to learners a generation ago, yet our society has undergone profound changes. A challenge for educators as they look to the year 2000 and beyond is to devise programs that accommodate new knowledge and prepare learners for the world they will encounter as adults. Our schools can ill afford to educate for obsolescence. (For more information on issues related to curricular patterns, see Chapters 2, 13, 15, and 17.)

## Implementing New Technologies

Schools have been much slower than businesses and governmental agencies to take advantage of modern electronic technologies (Mecklenburger, 1990). Part of the difficulty has been financial—instead of making a broad-scale commitment to implementing new technologies, schools have too often attempted to do the job in a piecemeal fashion. This has not allowed for the kinds of complex interconnections among technological devices needed to maximize the advantages of these exciting new systems. Schools are almost certain to face pressures in the years ahead to use technology more effectively. Moves in this direction may lead to new ideas about school and the proper roles of teachers, learners, and parents. (Some examples of innovative technologies that are being implemented by schools today are discussed in Chapter 13.)

## Improving Content Teaching

A growing body of literature has identified many characteristics of teachers who are able to successfully transmit knowledge to their learners. Regrettably, much of this information is not known to many of today's teachers. Some experts have speculated that there is a lag of nearly 10 years between the discovery of new information and its broad-scale use. At the present time, efforts are under way to reduce this lag time and increase the nation's teachers' awareness of recent instructional practices that have proved to be effective. (Research related to effective teaching is cited in Chapter 11. Chapter 11 also provides guidelines for using practical classroom observation techniques to gather data about behaviors of teachers and learners in the classroom.)

## Motivating Learners

It is common for teachers to report that large numbers of their learners appear to be uninterested in what goes on in school, and that some of them seem downright hostile. In part, schools are being affected by intractable social problems such as substance abuse and violence. Some children attending school have suffered brain damage because of their mothers' drug use during pregnancy. Even learners without these problems sometimes see little point in a school program that seems unconnected to the world they will face as adults. Developing worthwhile educational programs and selling them to learners seem certain to be high-priority concerns of educators for years to come. The accompanying What the Experts Say examines one such program.

---

WHAT THE EXPERTS SAY

## What accounts for academic success?
### Varying views of learners in different age groups

Teachers often try to motivate their learners to work hard. Their view is that hard work is a variable that bears a clear relationship to achievement. Merlin C. Wittrock (1986) reviewed a large number of studies that focused on learners' thought processes. He uncovered some work by researcher John G. Nicholls that suggested younger learners may not have established the connection between effort and achievement.

Nicholls found that 6-year-olds frequently see little difference among the concepts of effort, basic ability, and achievement. High achievement is something that "just happens" to smart people. Or, looked at in a different way, smart people just naturally work hard. Children at about age 7 or 8 are able to distinguish among these concepts, but they tend to disregard ability as a factor in achievement. Achievement is seen as something that will come to all who put out a high level of effort. An appreciation of the role of ability in achievement begins to appear in children between ages 9 and 11, but during this phase many children believe that hard work is a certain indicator of ability. It is only at about age 11 that children really become able to clearly separate the ideas of effort and ability.

---

Source: M. C. Wittrock, "Students' Thought Processes," in M. C. Wittrock (ed.), *Handbook of Research on Teaching,* 3rd ed. (New York: Macmillan Publishing Company, 1986), 297–314.

---

Responses to these important issues will vary, because there is no consensus regarding how the school, as an institution, should handle them. What we need to understand is that the level of educational excellence we get is a result of a political compromise between the excellence our society *says* it wants and the excellence our society is actually *willing to pay for*. The nature of this compromise at any given time is a result of conflicts between people and groups having quite different views.

For example, many purposes of schooling have been identified (preparing people for jobs, preparing people to be "good" citizens, preparing people to add to the store of the world's knowledge, and so forth). Individual groups think that some of these purposes are much more important than others. These groups, in turn, are often faced with arguments put forward by other groups who believe in quite different purposes. We educators live in a professional world that calls on us to contend with diverse opinions regarding what schools should do.

Should our schools be primarily directed toward teaching academic content? To what extent should they be expected to confront serious social problems such as sub-

**BOX 1–2**
## FACING THE CHALLENGE

The complex issues facing today's educators sometimes discourage people who are thinking about entering the profession. On the bright side, educators have always had to confront problems. History suggests that difficulties that appear overwhelmingly complex today will somehow be resolved sooner or later.

*What Do You Think?*

1. Which of the challenges facing educators do you believe will be the most difficult to resolve?
2. Which one will be easiest to overcome?
3. Which challenges can be most directly influenced by the actions of teachers?
4. Which challenges will require actions of people other than teachers? Which persons or groups will be most influential in bringing about a resolution of these problems?
5. How do you personally react to the challenges introduced in this chapter? Do any of them discourage you from pursuing a program leading to certification as a teacher?

stance abuse? How much time should schools spend in preparing learners for specific vocations? Different groups of citizens have developed very different answers to these questions, and Box 1–2 addresses the educators' perspective. The next section elaborates on some broad purposes of education that provide a useful context for thought about some present debates concerning educational priorities.

## Purposes of Education

Much of the debate about education concerns divergent ideas about what schools should be accomplishing. Only limited amounts of funds are available to support education; hence, it is necessary for priorities to be established. In the effort to establish these priorities, different perspectives regarding what the schools should do come to light. Though perspectives reflect a number of subtle shadings, most of them can be organized under one of these four basic perspectives:

- education for intellectual attainment
- education for citizenship
- education for vocational preparation
- education for individual development

Box 1–3 addresses considerations related to these perspectives.

## BOX 1–3
# EMPHASES OF THE SCHOOL PROGRAM

Most school programs include some elements of (1) education for intellectual attainment, (2) education for citizenship, (3) education for vocational preparation, and (4) education for individual development. The relative emphasis given to each of these perspectives varies from school to school.

***What Do You Think?***
1. What would you say was the most important of these four perspectives in the schools you attended?
2. What specific courses offered in your high school were consistent with each of these perspectives?
3. Which perspective do you see as receiving the most attention today? What would happen if a school's entire program were revised to reflect only this perspective?
4. Some people suggest that separate kinds of high schools should be created with individual emphases on (*a*) intellectual attainment and (*b*) vocational preparation. What is your reaction to this idea?

## Education for Intellectual Attainment

Helping learners to develop intellectually has long been recognized as an important purpose of schooling. Very few people argue against the idea that teachers have an important responsibility to develop learners' intellects. However, there is debate about how this is to be done. Additionally, there is dispute about the relative importance of the school's role as an agency to promote learners' intellectual growth.

In recent years, American students' poor showings on international learner achievement tests have led some critics to charge that American schools deserve a failing grade. Other observers contend that these tests measure only the ability to recall isolated bits of information, and fail to assess more sophisticated thinking abilities. Unless tests are developed that compare relative abilities of American and foreign learners to engage in these higher-level thinking skills, it may be premature to suggest that American schools are less effective than those in other countries.

In summary, the view is widely held that schools have an important responsibility to develop learners' intellects. Further, many people consider it to be the single most important responsibility of the school. Debates related to this perspective tend not to focus on the appropriateness of the objective so much as on issues related to how it should be achieved.

## Education for Citizenship

Education for citizenship has long been recognized as an important purpose of education. The ancient Greek philosopher Aristotle believed that the success of governments depended on the quality of education provided to the young. In the early days of our own country, Thomas Jefferson commented that, "If a nation expects to be ignorant and free, in a state of civilization, it expects what never was and never will be" (Jefferson, reported in Ford, 1893; p. 221).

The famous American historian Henry Steel Commager stated that the first duty of our schools is to develop an enlightened citizenry that will allow the great American experiment in self-government to work (Commager, 1976). In the same work, Commager went on to suggest that education for citizenship is necessary to build a sense of national unity.

Some people who are strongly committed to the school's role as a developer of citizenship have argued that this responsibility has not been discharged well in recent years. They cite lack of respect for public officials and diminished feelings of national pride as evidence that schools have not been adequately teaching citizenship. But others see citizenship in a broader context, arguing that education for good citizenship

These young people are learning something about community helpers and about how technology helps improve our lives.

properly should be directed at developing in learners a healthy skepticism about traditional values and practices. Individuals with this point of view have been less quick to challenge what schools are doing in the area of citizenship. (For more information on the role of schools as transmitters of perspectives, see Chapter 6.)

## Education for Vocational Preparation

Many Americans support the perspective of education for vocational preparation. Some critics of our schools have taken particular aim at the schools' alleged failure to adequately prepare learners for the world of work. For example, some business leaders point to the expensive training programs private firms have been forced to develop as evidence that schools have not been preparing learners to perform well in today's complex workplaces.

Not all Americans agree that schools should devote scarce resources to supporting vocational programs. Some feel that workplaces change too quickly for schools to keep up. Others say vocational preparation is important and that schools should pay more attention to preparing young people for their future occupational roles.

How much emphasis schools should put on preparing learners for specific occupational roles has engendered heated debate. On the one hand, a number of supporters of vocational programs have pointed out that many learners are destined to enter the workplace upon high school graduation, and that traditional academic subject instruction has failed to meet their needs. On the other hand, some critics contend that a heavy emphasis on vocational training does not make sense, pointing out that vocational programs carry within them the danger of preparing individuals with obsolete skills. It is better, they contend, to provide learners with a sound general academic education and then allow employers to provide job-specific training when these young people enter the work force.

## Education for Individual Development

The idea that schools should provide learning experiences that allow learners to maximize their individual potentials has enjoyed a long tradition of support. This emphasis draws on a core American value that emphasizes the worth and dignity of the individual. During the 1960s and 1970s, proponents of this perspective were particularly successful in securing the passage of several laws that sought to make educational programs more responsive to individual needs. Among them were laws that called for special programs to be established for physically challenged learners and for bilingual learners.

More recently, support for expanding programs designed to accommodate individual differences has not been so strong. Beginning in the 1980s and continuing into the 1990s, public concern for the quality of programs offered at individual schools led to great emphasis on standardized test scores. Such tests presume that populations of learners have experienced basically the same instructional program, and hence the growth of interest in standardized testing has been a force acting against expansion of programs designed to respond to individual learner differences.

The diversity of perspectives regarding what schools should emphasize continues to pose challenges for educators. The case study titled "Why Aren't They Pleased?" highlights this point.

---

CASE STUDY

## *Why aren't they pleased?*

**My name is Jan Kim**. I'm about eight months through my second year of teaching at Centennial Junior High School. My major responsibility is directing the school orchestra and teaching orchestra classes. For the most part, I have had a great experience.

Last month, I took my students on a two-day trip to the state orchestra competition. It was held in the state capital, about 100 miles away. My students raised money for the trip, and we had plenty of parents along to help. My people had really worked hard for this contest experience, and I was absolutely thrilled when we received a 1 rating, the highest awarded in our state.

As soon as the award ceremony was over, I hurried back to the hotel and called my principal. She was delighted at the good news. Centennial's orchestra had never before received such a high rating. In fact, the principal was so excited that she immediately called the superintendent. It turns out that our superintendent has been concerned for some time that our district's music program was not as strong as it should be, and the news about our 1 rating was very welcome.

A few days after I returned to school, I got a nice letter from the superintendent congratulating me and all of the kids in the orchestra for their hard work. The letter went on to invite me to a school board meeting where I was to receive some public congratulations for the honor brought to the district by our orchestra's high rating. The school board meeting was last night.

It was fairly late into the evening when the board president asked me to stand. Some very nice words were said about what had been accomplished by the Centennial orchestra kids, and some warm comments were made to me about how much the district appreciated what I had accomplished in just two years in the district. At the conclusion of these remarks, each member of the school board came over to shake my hand. I felt I had arrived at some kind of professional pinnacle.

The next item on the agenda was an open forum for citizens' comments. The first speaker deflated my fine feelings in a hurry. He said that the school district was spending entirely too much money on frivolous nonacademic subjects, such as music. He said that he was "sick and tired" of not being able to hire high school graduates who could write a grammatical sentence or make accurate change. He indicated that the two days my orchestra kids had spent participating in the state contest had robbed them of two days of serious instruction in English and mathematics. He went on to say that until the world begins caring as much about a person's ability to fiddle as about writing and computing, we should forget about wasting money on music. Four or five people actually applauded these remarks.

I left the meeting in a very depressed state. I have worked so hard this year. And now I've just found out that there are some people who think my entire function is unnecessary. I have a really bad taste in my mouth about this. I just don't know what I'm going to do.

*How is it possible for a teacher who has been recognized for excellence to have the worth of what he or she has been doing so bitterly challenged? What do you think Jan Kim should do next? Do the school principal and the superintendent have roles to play here? If so, what are they? What advice would you give to this teacher? Do you think other teachers have faced similar circumstances? If you know of any particular instances, how did these teachers resolve their difficulties?*

## Foundations of Education

To develop insights regarding problems facing educators today and to further the search for solutions, newcomers to the profession need an understanding of the important social, historical, and political forces that influence our schools. These educational foundations provide a basic underlying structure for the differing views people have regarding the purposes of schooling.

The study of educational foundations inevitably leads to the conclusion that school programs are shaped not by consensus, but by working majorities. Priorities endorsed by today's majority may be rejected by tomorrow's. Many changes in our schools are not instituted because of their intrinsic merits; rather, they come about as a result of the development of a coalition of supporters that has been able to sway the opinions of a majority (often a narrow one) of educational decision makers.

Some subjects generally considered to be among the foundations of education include the following:

- history of education
- philosophy of education
- sociology of education
- educational psychology
- educational curriculum and instruction
- legal subjects in education

Each of these subjects will now be addressed.

## History of Education

The current structure of public education did not come about because a group of experts sat down and began working with a blank slate—present patterns have been greatly influenced by historical developments. School practices that may appear to have come about for no particular reason frequently are legacies of important historic needs.

For example, why does American history continue to be widely taught at grade eight? Today, when the vast majority of learners go on to high school, other content logically could be taught at this grade level. The original decision to place an American history course at this grade level was made at a time when few learners attended school beyond the eighth grade. It was an attempt to teach as many of them as possible something about their national heritage. (More detailed information related to the history of education is presented in Chapters 3 and 4.)

## Philosophy of Education

Many debates about education are really debates among people who have different educational philosophies. Hence an understanding of various philosophical positions is important. The criteria people apply in judging the merit of a given school program reflect their philosophies. If people are ignorant of the philosophical orientation that undergirds a particular argument, they may find it difficult to respond in a way that makes sense to those who support the argument.

Differences in educational philosophies are reflected in many ways. School programs that emphasize developing learners' general thinking skills (as opposed to their mastering particular items of information) reflect a specific philosophic orientation. Supporters of this view contend that specific knowledge is transitory and that, over time, it makes more sense to teach general thinking skills. A contending view is reflected in vocational programs that emphasize preparing learners for specific jobs—the assumption here is that particular items of content are important and should be emphasized in the school program.

The issue of philosophy comes into play, too, in discussions of the adequacy of American schools as compared to those in other nations. In this country, there is broad support for an egalitarian perspective suggesting that as many learners as possible should be kept in school for as long as possible. In some other nations, a more elitist view is supported that has resulted in school systems that shunt large numbers of less academically able learners out of formal schools and into vocational training programs. As a result, secondary schools in these nations enroll a much smaller percentage of the total population of teenagers than do American schools. The philosophic difference that accounts for this very different makeup of student bodies in American and some foreign secondary schools may explain some standardized test performance discrepancies between our students and theirs.

Differences in philosophical perspectives result in different prescriptions for what needs to be done to "make our schools better." (Descriptions of several important perspectives associated with the philosophy of education are included in Chapter 5.)

## Sociology of Education

Schools are an integral part of a society's culture. Through formal institutions of education, designated professionals (teachers) are charged with transmitting elements of the cultural heritage to the young. The sociology of education is concerned with how schools go about this business of cultural transmission.

There are important place-to-place differences in school programs that reflect expectations of the local community. For example, courses that focus on agriculture are offered in some rural areas, whereas school programs in music, painting, and other fine arts-related subjects receive substantial financial support in communities whose citizens are greatly interested in those areas. An understanding of how the priorities of groups influence schools is an important concern of the sociology of education. (Some key ideas from educational sociology are introduced in Chapter 6.)

## Educational Psychology

Educational psychologists, particularly those interested in how young people learn, are not in agreement as to how content should be organized and presented in the school. Some learning theorists place heavy emphasis on patterns of learners' development and suggest that some learning experiences must be deferred until learners have reached certain maturational levels. Others downplay the importance of maturation and suggest that there is no predictable relationship between maturational levels and the kinds of content young people are capable of learning.

Another argument within the community of educational psychologists concerns whether it is better to organize learning in small pieces or in larger blocks. Partisans of each view have very different ideas about how content should be organized and presented to learners. Teachers are more effective when they understand the specific learning theory orientation of those who developed their instructional programs. (Chapters 7 and 12 provide additional information derived from educational psychology.)

### Educational Curriculum and Instruction

Schools transmit content. This content is organized and packaged in a number of different ways. There are important place-to-place differences in content as well as place-to-place similarities. Teachers must be conversant with such important issues as what is taught, who decides what is taught, and how are programs organized. (Curricular and instructional issues receive more extensive treatment in Chapters 11, 12, and 15.)

The *curriculum* is an overall operational plan for a school program. What goes on each day in the classroom is *instruction*. There are many instructional approaches, and each has its special strengths and limitations. Familiarity with a broad array of instructional techniques helps teachers select approaches that maximize the ability of young people to learn in their classrooms.

### Legal Issues in Education

Many topics are included under this heading. First, the legal bases for public schooling—including such issues as state and local financial support, prescribed courses, and standards for teachers—help define the context within which teachers work. In recent years, many new regulations and much litigation have set important limits on what schools, teachers, and learners can legally do. Issues such as teachers' potential legal liability and learners' rights and responsibilities have drawn considerable attention. Some familiarity with legal dimensions of education is expected of today's teachers. (Discussion of legal issues can be found in Chapters 17, 18, and 19.)

· · · · · · · · · · · · · · · · · · · · · · · · · · · ·

# Key Ideas in Summary

- Prospective teachers are preparing for entry into a profession facing many pressures. Among these pressures are demands that schools do something about unfavorable performance comparisons between American and foreign learners, respond to calls from business leaders for more technically adept workers, and deal with strains associated with the need to prepare instruction designs to meet the unique needs of learners from diverse ethnic, cultural, and language groups.

- Among important challenges facing educators are those related to (1) restoring public confidence, (2) restructuring schools, (3) financing education, (4) dealing with an increasingly diverse learner population, (5) modernizing the curriculum, (6) implementing new technologies, (7) improving content teaching, and (8) motivating learners.

- First-year teachers are often unsettled by criticisms they encounter, even when they are convinced they are doing a highly professional job. Often criticism results when certain unhappy school patrons use criteria to measure "excellence" different from those many teachers might apply. To understand critics'

**Table 1–1**
Summary table: Challenges facing today's schools

| Topic | Key Points |
|---|---|
| Examples of challenges for educators | Among these are (1) demands for schools to produce graduates who can function effectively in a work environment that, increasingly, requires employees who have high degrees of technological literacy; (2) calls for schools to produce learners who can score higher on international comparison tests; and (3) needs associated with a learner population that is increasingly drawn from impoverished sectors of the population and from ethnic and cultural minorities. |
| Tasks for educators | These are diverse. Among them are (1) restoring public confidence in schools, (2) restructuring the schools (challenging basic assumptions about how schools are organized and administered), (3) seeking adequate levels of funding, (4) developing programs responsive to needs of an increasingly diverse population of learners, (5) modernizing the curriculum, (6) improving content teaching, and (7) motivating learners. |
| Purposes of education<br>• Intellectual attainment | This purpose focuses on the role of the school as a promoter of learners' intellectual growth. |
| • Development of citizenship | This purpose focuses on the need of schools to develop individuals who will be committed to basic national values and who will be thinking people capable of weighing alternatives and making rational decisions. |
| • Vocational preparation | This purpose focuses on the need for schools to prepare learners for the workplace. Critics of schools have been especially concerned that some schools may not be giving learners the kinds of technical training they need to be effective members of the work force. |
| • Individual development | This purpose focuses on the need to maximize the potential of each learner by providing school experiences fitted to individual needs, abilities, and aspirations. |

| Topic | Key Points |
|---|---|
| **Foundations of education** | |
| • History of education | Educational history explains the origins of many present-day educational practices. For example, the tradition of teaching a course in U.S. history at grade 8 began at a time when this was the terminal grade for most students. Educators felt these learners, who were about to leave school for the "real world," needed a final course emphasizing their American heritage. |
| • Philosophy of education | Arguments about educational policies often result from differing philosophical perspectives. People with different philosophical views do not define educational excellence in the same ways. Hence, an understanding of educational philosophy can help educators understand individual disputants' points of view in debates over the appropriate ways to approach curricula and teaching. |
| • Sociology of education | Institutions and groups affect educational programming. Educators must understand their impact if they are to have a sophisticated grasp of priorities as reflected in patterns of school organization, patterns of relationships among different categories of people involved in education, and patterns of learning experiences delivered to pupils and students. These are matters studied by experts on the sociology of education. |
| • Educational curriculum and instruction | The curriculum (the general organizational scheme for school programs) and instructional practices give individual schools their unique atmospheres. Federal, state, and local regulations provide some school-to-school commonalities; however, individual school leaders and teachers retain much discretionary authority over what is taught and how it is taught. |
| **Legal issues** | Educational programs are governed by many regulations. Authority is exercised, in varying degrees, by national, state, and local authorities. Laws, official policies, and common law precedents influence what teachers and learners can do. Today, teachers are expected to have some familiarity with legal issues pertaining to their profession. |

perspectives, it is a good idea for prospective teachers to be familiar with alternative views regarding the proper purposes of education.

- There has always been a strong contingent in this country supporting the view that the school's most important mission is to teach academic content to learners. Some critics of present practices are so committed to this education-for-intellectual-attainment perspective that they strongly resist diversions of school funds to support programs supporting any other educational focuses.

- Proponents of education for citizenship believe that a commitment to the nation's values is essential for the preservation of our way of life. They believe that school programs dedicated to promoting behaviors associated with responsible citizenship provide a kind of social glue that binds our society together.

- Supporters of vocational programs suggest that our schools should do more to prepare learners for the kinds of roles they will be expected to discharge once they join the work force. These people tend to criticize many present school practices for not being connected closely enough to the employment world learners will join after their school years are over.

- Education for individual development is another perspective regarding what schools should do. Supporters of this view believe strongly that school programs should be made as responsive as possible to special needs of individual learners. Laws mandating programs for physically challenged learners and bilingual learners reflect legislative victories for partisans of this point of view.

- Approved school programs result when coalitions of committed individuals manage to sway opinions of educational decision makers. To appreciate how such decisions are made, an understanding of certain educational foundations is essential. Subjects often included among these educational foundations are (1) sociology of education, (2) history of education, (3) educational psychology, (4) philosophy of education, (5) educational curriculum and instruction, and (6) legal issues in education.

## Review and Discussion Questions

1. What are some general challenges facing educators today?
2. What is meant by the phrase "restructuring schools?"
3. Why have schools been slower than businesses and governmental agencies to take advantage of modern technologies?
4. What are some general perspectives regarding the purposes of education?
5. How is it possible for an educational practice many people consider to be good to be seen as inappropriate by others?

6. In the future, would you expect there to be more or less emphasis on vocational preparation of learners?

7. What are some of the foundations of education?

8. What is meant by the statement that "school programs are shaped not by consensus, but rather by working majorities"?

9. What are some ways educational philosophies influence what goes on in schools?

10. What are some general kinds of legal issues with which teachers need to be familiar?

......................................

# Ideas for Field Experiences, Projects, and Enrichment

1. Much is being written today about the idea of restructuring schools. Organize a group of three or four people to research this issue. You can locate some articles on this topic in professional journals. (Consult the *Education Index* and/or ask your instructor for appropriate titles.) Then present your findings to the class in the form of a symposium.

2. Interview a local school official (perhaps a director of instruction or an assistant superintendent for instruction) about proposals that have been made in the past five years regarding new courses or programs. Try to determine these proposals' relative emphases on (*a*) education for intellectual attainment, (*b*) education for citizenship, (*c*) education for vocational preparation, and (*d*) education for individual attainment. Present your findings to your class in the form of an oral report.

3. Some people argue that, by design, our school system attempts to maximize the development of *all* learners. Others contend that, again by design, our school system attempts to maximize the development of only *some* learners. Organize a debate on this topic: "Resolved that our schools are deliberately organized with a view to preventing *every* student from maximizing his or her potential."

4. Read several articles from professional journals on a controversial topic related to public education. (Journals such as *Phi Delta Kappan* and *Educational Leadership* often publish such articles, and your course instructor may be able to suggest some other journals you might wish to look at.) Do people on various sides of the issue you have selected have a common view regarding characteristics of a "good" school or school program? If not, to what extent do their differences reflect varying philosophical perspectives? (As an aid to understanding various philosophical perspectives, you might wish to look ahead to Chapter 5.)

5. Write a position paper on the topic "characteristics of a good school." Turn it in to your instructor, and then discuss your perspectives with others in the class who have written papers on the same topic.

······························

# Supplementary Reading

Chiarelott, L., L. Davidman, and K. Ryan. *Lenses on Teaching: Developing Perspectives on Classroom Life*. New York: Holt, Rinehart, and Winston, 1990.

Levinson, E. "Will Technology Transform Education, or Will the Schools Co-opt Technology?" *Phi Delta Kappan* (October 1990): 121–26.

Stanfield II, J. "American Business People and the Ambivalent Transformation of Racially Segregated Public Schools." *Phi Delta Kappan* (September 1990): 63–67.

Webb, R., and R. Sherman. *Schooling and Society*. 2nd ed. New York: Macmillan Publishing Company, 1989.

······························

# References

Commager, H. S. *The People and Their Schools*. Bloomington, IN: Phi Delta Kappa Educational Foundation, 1976.

Ford, L., ed. *The Writings of Thomas Jefferson*. Vol. 2. New York: G.P. Putnam's, 1893.

Grant, C. A. and W. G. Secada. "Preparing Teachers for Diversity." In R. Houston, ed. *Handbook of Research on Teacher Education*. New York: Macmillan Publishing Company, 1990, 403–422.

Mecklenburger, J. A. "Educational Technology Is Not Enough." *Phi Delta Kappan* (October 1990): 105–08.

Pipho, C. "Taxes and Tempers." *Phi Delta Kappan* (September 1990): 6–7.

Raywid, M. A. "The Evolving Effort to Improve Schools: Pseudo Reform, Incremental Reform, and Restructuring." *Phi Delta Kappan* (October 1983): 139–43.

Wittrock, M. C. "Students' Thought Processes." In M. C. Wittrock, ed. *Handbook of Research on Teaching*. 3rd ed. New York: Macmillan Publishing Company, 1986, 297–314.

# Chapter 2

# Innovations

· · · · · · · · · · · · · · · · · · · · · · · · · · · · · · · · · · · · · ·

## Objectives

This chapter provides information to help the reader to

- recognize that individual innovations affect different people in different ways.
- describe a systematic procedure for analyzing the impact of a given innovation on different groups.
- recognize some forces that lead to the adoption of innovations.
- identify examples of innovations that are being tried in various places today.
- point out basic characteristics of selected school innovations.

# Focus Questions

1. Why has there always been a great deal of interest in the United States in educational innovations?
2. What are some examples of how different groups of people are affected in different ways by a common innovation?
3. What are some examples of innovations that have been recommended to improve American education?
4. Why is it that a common innovation is not always implemented in the same way in different places?
5. What are some issues that need to be addressed by administrators when they introduce innovations affecting teachers?
6. If parents had the right to choose the schools their children would attend, what criteria would they most likely apply when making their choices?
7. What are some arguments for and against the idea of year-round education?
8. How might present roles of principals, parents, and teachers change in a school district that decided to decentralize decision making?

• • • • • • • • • • • • • • • • • • • • • • • • • •

# Introduction

Education has always had a love affair with innovations. This tradition has intensified in recent years as pressures on schools to "do better" have spawned dozens of ideas. For example, in April 1991 the U.S. Department of Education released *America 2000: An Education Strategy*. This report specified five key goals for improving our system of education, asserting that by the year 2000:

- All children in America will start school ready to learn.
- The high school graduation rate will increase to at least 90 percent.
- American students will leave grades 4, 8, and 12 having demonstrated competency in such subject matter as English, mathematics, science, history, and geography; and every school in America will ensure that all students learn to use their minds well, so they may be prepared for responsible citizenship, further learning, and productive employment in our modern society.
- U.S. students will be first in the world in science and mathematics achievement.
- Every adult American will be literate and will possess the knowledge and skills necessary to compete in a global economy and exercise the rights and responsibilities of citizenship.
- Every school in America will be free of drugs and violence and will offer a disciplined environment conducive to learning.*

These proposals and others that have been developed to provide guidelines for school improvement imply a need for change. Perception of a need to "do better" spawns educational innovations. A willingness to innovate is a strength of the American education system. It reflects an assumption that even intractable problems *can* be resolved and that good programs can be made even better.

Proposed innovations are often complex. When they are adopted, they may create new and unanticipated difficulties. Further, innovations often affect different people in different ways. This helps explain why a given innovation may draw rave reviews from some people and ridicule from others (see What the Experts Say).

---

WHAT THE EXPERTS SAY

*What can be done to ensure that innovations make a difference?*

Schools are not bashful about trying new approaches. Some critics, including Larry Cuban (1986) and Robert E. Slavin (1989), contend that the enthusiasm for educational innovation has produced few enduring changes. These critics note that innovative practices follow a relatively predictable cycle. At first the innovation is endorsed as a novel solution to a pressing educational problem. Next, it is adopted by a small number of

---

*America 2000: An Education Strategy* (Washington, DC: U.S. Department of Education, 1991), 61–65.

progressive school districts. Then, the innovation garners more publicity and is implemented in many more districts. Eventually, glimmers of initial dissatisfaction begin to be voiced in a few isolated areas. In time, there are calls for widespread evaluation of the innovation. More often than not, these evaluations reveal that the innovation is delivering much less than its early promoters had promised. Numbers of districts using the innovation begin to decline.

Robert Slavin (1989) argues this dismal pattern often results because school districts fail to insist on solid research evidence supporting the effectiveness of innovations *before* they are implemented. He notes that school districts, in their eagerness to respond to pressing problems, have been too willing to endorse an innovation simply on the strength of promotional claims of its initial developers. Often years pass before serious evaluations begin.

Slavin proposes that three specific steps be taken to change this situation. First, he recommends that the federal government set up an innovation evaluation information clearinghouse. This would facilitate sharing of evaluation information among the nation's school districts. Second, he proposes that federal funding of innovations include money to support top-quality evaluation systems (including use of control groups assurances that common objectives are being pursued by both experimental and control groups, and provisions calling for evaluations to occur under realistic conditions). Finally, he supports the establishment of independent evaluation laboratories that would be specifically charged with evaluating the effectiveness of innovations and disseminating the results.

## Groups That Might Be Influenced by an Innovation

Innovations have both planned and unplanned consequences. For example, suppose a school adopts an innovative scheme that eliminates all textbooks. When this innovation is implemented, learners will read only material printed out in their classroom via a computer. The computer will have all of the material from traditional texts in its memory, and teachers will be encouraged to create individual texts of their own on the computer, featuring material suited for the particular needs of individual students.

In thinking about the probable consequences of a given innovation, it is well to consider its impact on groups including:

- learners
- school administrators
- teachers
- parents
- representatives of the larger community

For example, one side effect of this arrangement will be a reduction in income flowing to people who produce and sell traditional textbooks. (Certainly there will be other side effects as well.)

## Impact on Learners

Most school innovations seek to improve the conditions under which young people learn. These conditions relate to such things as organization of materials, emphases on particular subjects, social organization of schools and classrooms, utilization of new technologies, and consideration of individual learning styles. Change always requires some adjustment. Some learners may initially feel resentment when confronted with new and unfamiliar approaches.

## Impact on School Administrators

Many changes affect decisions that are the responsibility of principals and other school administrators. For example, innovations changing traditional attendance boundaries or rearranging the school day so that not all learners follow the same schedule might require changes in arrival and departure times of buses. Certain kinds of mandated learning resources might require diversion of funds from one account to another. Maintenance schedules could be affected. Principals could even find increasing demands on their time, as community groups and parents ask them to make presentations explaining changes.

## Impact on Teachers

Innovations may require teachers to work in unfamiliar ways. In making efforts to integrate content from several disciplines, they may be confronted with massive course development responsibilities. They could be called upon to plan and implement cooperative learning activities and other content-delivery techniques with which they have had little prior experience. A few teachers may have to adjust psychologically to the suggestion that what they have been doing previously has not been effective enough.

## Impact on Parents

Innovations may affect parents in several ways. Some parents may be unsettled by innovations that seem to mark a significant departure from the kinds of practices they remember from their own school days. A lack of familiarity may breed some suspicions about "what the schools are up to." Changes involving attendance patterns and school schedules can influence family life, particularly when parents are obligated to meet school schedules that are at odds with their own employment schedules. Parents may be confronted with choices regarding the schools their children attend and the kinds of programs they follow that they have never previously had to make. In some instances, they may be asked to play substantive roles in making decisions about school curricula.

## Impact on the Larger Community

Influences of innovations on the larger community represent both side and direct effects of changes in school practices. For example, a change in school schedules that would allow some high school students to go to school from 1:00 P.M. to 8:00 P.M. rather than from 8:00 A.M. to 3:00 (or 4:00) P.M. might result in swarms of students strolling through local shopping centers in the morning hours. Innovations featuring emphases on new technologies might result in tax increases to support equipment purchases.

*Our architect has come up with an interesting innovation in building design that might create an atmosphere in which students could achieve excellence.*
Courtesy of Ford Button.

Outreach programs might require local businesses and governmental offices to set up more internship programs designed to give learners a feel for the professional work-place.

## Innovations in Schools Today

Some innovations have been tried in large numbers of places, while others are unique to individual school districts and even to individual schools. This pattern is not surprising. Schools throughout the country share certain similarities, including some common problems. It is only natural that some new ideas that address such widespread problems have been widely adopted. On the other hand, individual communities and schools have important unique qualities, and some innovations have been established in response to local needs. Such innovations generally do not attract the attention of schools in other areas that have different characteristics and problems.

Innovations that have been tried in various schools over a period even as short as 10 years are far too numerous to list in their entirety. A sampling would include team teaching, flexible class scheduling, open-space learning environments, schools without walls, voucher systems, various computer-assisted learning approaches, nongraded elementary schools, continuous progress learning, site-based management, year-round schools, in-school daycare for children of high school students, and restructuring schools.

The remainder of this chapter will introduce four innovative practices—school choice, restructuring schools, peer coaching, and year-round education—which are attracting interest at the present time. These innovations focus on quite different aspects of the overall school program. They have been selected to illustrate the diverse nature of innovations that have been designed to improve our schools.

Descriptions of these innovations focus on their *general* features. For many innovations, there is no universally agreed-upon list of defining characteristics. Hence, several school districts that claim to be implementing a common innovation may not, in fact, be doing precisely the same thing.

In analyzing innovations, it is useful to consider their influence on various constituencies. Innovations rarely affect all people in the same ways. The innovations discussed in this chapter will be described in terms of their varying impacts on different groups.

## School Choice

Traditionally, school districts have established attendance boundaries. Learners living within a given school's boundary lines have been obligated to attend that school. At one time, attendance boundaries of a school encompassed a region surrounding the school building. Efforts to provide more racial and ethnic balance among learners within schools have led to the abandonment of these neighborhood attendance boundaries in some areas, particularly in the nation's larger cities. Note, though, that while some schools may now garner students from areas that are not physically close to the school, for the most part learners are still required to attend the school within whose attendance boundaries they live.

Critics suggest that this traditional attendance system does little to encourage schools to become better. Mandatory attendance boundaries guarantee each school a supply of learners. The criteria by which schools get their money from state governments are based for the most part on the number of learners they enroll. Since attendance boundaries guarantee a steady supply of learners, even schools that deliver inadequate instructional services face little financial pressure from the state to improve.

Advocates of school choice suggest that by giving learners the right to attend the schools of their parents' choice, pressures will be placed on all schools to do better. According to this argument, parents will tend to enroll their children in "good" schools. More state money will flow to these schools, thus encouraging them to develop even more effective programs. Similarly, "poor" schools will lose money, which will provide an incentive for administrators of these schools to take actions to improve their programs. If these administrators are successful, learners will be attracted back to these schools. If unsuccessful, extremely poor schools, over time, will be forced to shut down. Hence, it is argued, school choice will improve the overall quality of education in all of the schools.

Several issues continue to be debated among proponents of school choice. One of them has to do with the question of range of choices. Are learners to be free to attend any school within (1) a district, (2) a number of contiguous districts, (3) the boundaries of a given state, or (4) the boundaries of several states? Another question centers on the worth of this innovation to learners living in isolated rural areas, who would have to be transported many miles to reach a school outside of their normal attendance area. Educational policymakers in several states are wrestling with these and other concerns. At the present time, the school-choice innovation continues to be widely discussed by professional educators throughout the nation.

## Impact on Learners

Theoretically, school choice should help all learners because of financial incentives for all schools to improve their programs. However, some differences among individual schools are likely to remain. Certainly this innovation, even if it delivers all the promised benefits, will not guarantee an education of similarly high quality to all learners.

The school-choice innovation depends on the willingness of parents and learners to seek enrollment in schools outside of their traditional attendance zones. This may create a hardship on learners in terms of time required to travel to school. Also, traditional athletic and social allegiances may have to be modified. Additionally, financial restraints may make it difficult or nearly impossible for some learners to take advantage of the opportunity to move to better schools outside of their traditional boundaries. For example, their parents may lack automobiles to transport them, they may not have sufficient money to take advantage of buses or other public transportation opportunites, or these schools may be too far away from after-school jobs.

## Impact on School Administrators

By design, school choice places pressure on school administrators to see to it that quality instruction takes place in their individual institutions. There is a presumption that good instruction will enhance the reputation of a school, a good reputation will draw more learners, and more learners will bring more educational support money from the state. Hence, this innovation may result in administrators monitoring teachers' performance levels more carefully. Similarly, it may cause them to pay more attention to the quality of teachers hired to fill vacancies. Because public perceptions of a school's quality sometimes rest on published achievement test scores, principals may play a very active role in encouraging instructional practices that promise to make these scores higher. Finally, principals may feel it necessary to organize elaborate public relations operations in order to sell the public on the quality of programs offered by their schools.

## Impact on Teachers

Giving people a choice of schools is designed to encourage quality instruction. Principals will be encouraging teachers to do their best. Because of the threat of a school's funding being cut if learners choose to enroll elsewhere, teachers may do a better job of teaching simply to avoid the possibility of being laid off (something that could happen if a school's enrollment dropped precipitously).

Also, teachers may sense themselves forced to provide instruction that will produce good short-term results, particularly in terms of learners' scores on standardized achievement tests. Some teachers may feel that this situation restricts their options in an unprofessional way, suspecting that they are being forced to "teach to the test."

Finally, many teachers have been trained to think of themselves as cooperative rather than competitive professionals. Some of them may find it difficult to accommodate to a world in which their relative merit may be measured in terms of their ability to be perceived as better than teachers in another school.

## Impact on Parents

To achieve its objectives, school choice requires parents to become informed about the quality of education available in different schools. It presumes that parents can recognize qualitative differences among schools, and it assumes that they will choose to enroll learners in schools that offer "better" programs. If special money is not provided for transportation of learners to schools that may be a significant distance from where they live, parents may be obliged to arrange transportation on their own, which will inevitably involve additional expense.

Another issue is related to time. Because school programs will be expected to change in response to pressures brought about by this innovation, parents will need to keep informed from year to year about the relative qualities of programs offered in different schools. This might require them to visit numerous schools, read extensively, and talk regularly with people who have information about changes in programs.

A third issue involves logistics. It may be that school A has better programs in grades K to 3, while school B has better programs in grades 4 to 6. Parents with some children in the early grades and some in the upper grades might face the possibility of sending some of their children to one school and others to another. Such a decision would present them with two sets of parents' association meetings to attend, and possibly even different school calendars.

## Impact on the Larger Community

If school choice works out as its supporters predict, an overall increase in the quality of schools might result. The general community would benefit in two ways. First, school graduates would be more knowledgeable, and in time the whole society would benefit from the higher levels of productivity that tend to be associated with a better-educated work force. Second, school programs might become more cost effective. This would be a result of administrators' efforts to use available resources to maximize academic achievement to achieve the desired reputation for their institution as a good school.

## School Choice: Present Status

School choice continues to be a hotly debated topic. Early attempts at implementation have had inconclusive results. For example, in Minnesota, where parents are permitted to enroll their children in any school in the state, few parents have taken advantage of this option. Some seem to have been motivated by factors other than the academic reputation of the schools. For example, several children have been enrolled in schools that are closer to their parents' places of employment than the schools they

BOX 2–1
## SCHOOL CHOICE: SOCKING IT TO THE POOR ONE MORE TIME?

A citizen recently made these comments when testifying before a state committee considering legislation that would allow citizens to send their children to any school of their choice within the state:

> As usual, good intentions are behind proposed legislation that will have very bad, very unintended side effects. How much *real* freedom of school choice will there be for low-income families? How are they going to get their children to distant 'good' schools? This plan is going to draw middle class and well-to-do parents and their children away from schools needing the most help. So-called 'poor' schools increasingly will enroll learners from low-income families. The school choice scheme is beautifully, albeit unintentionally, designed to keep children from low-income families from breaking out of poverty's vicious cycle.

### What Do You Think?
1. What are your general reactions to this testimony?
2. What modifications to school-choice plans might be made to better serve the interests of children from low-income families?
3. The school-choice proposal presumes that the threat of loss of state support money will spur administrators and teachers to improve the quality of their schools. How valid is this assumption?

traditionally attended. In a few instances, secondary school students have enrolled in schools where they believe their chances of making the varsity hockey team to be better than at their old school.

Critics of school choice argue that the scheme may act to widen differences between children from upper middle class and wealthy homes as compared with those from poorer families (see Box 2–1). The expense and time required to get children to distant "good" schools may cut off change of school as a legitimate option for children from low-income households.

Supporters of school choice argue that critics are quibbling over side issues that can be addressed if there are serious attempts to implement the innovation. They note that transportation and other costs that may inhibit parents' selection of distant schools for their children may have to be borne by taxpayers. They suggest, too, that initial efforts at implementing the proposal have not gone on long enough for parents to become sophisticated consumers of information about the relative academic quality of schools. In time, supporters believe, parents will demand more information about the quality of programs offered by individual schools. When this happens, pressures will mount to improve school programs everywhere.

## Restructuring Schools

Proponents of restructuring schools argue that present organizational and administrative characteristics stifle attempts to improve education. They suggest that American education has become too centralized. Policies and even suggested teaching procedures often are proposed by legislators, school board members, and others who are far removed from the actual setting where instruction is delivered to students. This arrangement gets in the way of efforts of dedicated administrators and teachers who sincerely wish to improve the quality of learning experiences provided to children in the school.

The restructuring-of-the-schools movement seeks to place more decision-making power at the level where instructional services are being delivered. The concept of restructuring schools goes forward under a number of labels—sometimes it is referred to as "site-based management"; "teacher empowerment" also embodies many concepts associated with the general effort to restructure schools. By whatever name it is known, restructuring schools is directed at giving those individuals held accountable for the quality of school programs the power they need to shape programs to meet the unique needs of the learners they serve.

Proponents of restructuring schools would limit centralized authorities such as legislatures, state boards of education, and local school boards to making only broad policy statements about education. Designing programs consistent with these policies would be left to decision makers actively involved with the local institution. Many discussions of restructuring schools emphasize the importance of sharing decision-making power with several constituencies. Programs, for example, might be designed by a consensus of a group including teachers, administrators, parents, child development specialists, and selected representatives of the community. Supporters of restructuring schools argue that it makes little sense to hold local administrators and teachers responsible for the quality of educational services unless they also are given real power to change what they are doing. This kind of empowerment is central to the restructuring-schools innovation.

## Impact on Learners

The impact of restructuring schools on learners is supposed to be a positive one. A basic purpose of the innovation is to develop programs that serve learners' needs more adequately. Placing broad-ranging decision authority into the hands of local administrators, teachers, parents, and others is supposed to result in school experiences that are well-suited to the characteristics of the learners who are served. If the innovation operates as it is supposed to, learners may be exposed to programs that are well-adapted to their needs.

The idea of restructuring the schools exacts a price, however, for yielding broad decision-making powers to local people—these individuals are expected to produce. The accountability dimension of restructuring schools may help learners by quickly drawing negative attention to unsuccessful programs. In theory, at least, these programs will be able to be quickly modified, as decision makers will not be required to deal with a distant bureaucracy to obtain permission to make needed changes.

Members of this school staff are discussing a transition to a site-based management plan, which would place greater decision-making power in the hands of teachers actually delivering instructional services.

## Impact on School Administrators

Restructuring schools is an innovation that both gives and removes power from school administrators. On the one hand, the innovation awards great decision-making authority to the individual institutions where administrators work, thus removing much of the red tape that working with distant educational bureaucracies traditionally has entailed. On the other hand, restructuring schools implies a sharing of authority with other people. The innovation assumes that the best educational programming results when teachers, parents, and others join with administrators to design learning experiences well-suited to children who attend the school. A building principal must accept the idea that his or her voice will be but one of many that will be heard as program alternatives are considered (see Box 2–2 for two views of this issue). The principal must be willing to stand behind programs that have been jointly planned by people representing several important local constituencies.

## Impact on Teachers

Restructuring the schools is an innovation that asks teachers to be more than deliverers of instruction—they are expected to play active roles in planning educational programs. In addition, they have to accept being held accountable for the actual learning

BOX 2–2
# IS SHARED AUTHORITY GOOD OR BAD?

The question has arisen as to whether the shared authority that goes along with restructuring schools is good or bad for principals. Two principals with different views on this matter recently had this exchange:

Principal A:    I was trained to be a leader. I know how to work with people, solicit their reactions, and forge a consensus. I also am willing to be held accountable for my decisions. *But,* I do so only out of a recognition that any decision I make, in the final analysis, is *my* decision. I don't want to become a spokesperson for a group. If that's what it is going to mean to be a principal, I don't want the job.

Principal B:    I like being part of a decision-making group. In fact, I sense that my own power grows when decisions are made by groups representing teachers, parents, and citizens. I am more than happy about being held accountable for these decisions, because I know I have teachers, parents, and influential community leaders solidly behind me. I mean, this structure makes the school really theirs. They have a vested interest in making the thing work.

*What Do You Think?*
1. Can a principal be a real leader and, at the same time, be part of a collective decision-making team?
2. Is it right to expect a principal to be accountable for decisions when he or she has not been directly responsible for making them?
3. What are your general reactions to the positions taken by principals A and B?

of the young people they teach. This acceptance of accountability is a price teachers must pay for the authority they gain when they become part of the decision-making team that designs the school program.

This innovation may require teachers to see themselves in new ways. Traditionally, there has been a hierarchy in schools, featuring school administrators at the top and teachers in subordinate roles. Restructuring the schools presumes an equality among teachers, administrators, parents, and other members of the school management team.

## Impact on Parents

Restructuring the schools promises to give parents more direct control over the education of their children. As active members of a school management team, they will play a direct role in shaping the instructional programs to which their sons and daughters will be exposed. The innovation may require them to become much more informed than many parents currently are about schools and schooling. The innovation has the potential to build a strong base of parental support for school programs. This is likely to occur because parents may sense that their opinions have a real opportunity to be reflected in school programs and policies.

## Impact on the Larger Community

Restructuring schools may generate broad-based community support for schools. When significant authority for developing school programs is vested in a group of people representing a broad range of professional and community interests, the programs developed should reflect some sensitivity to local priorities. Responsiveness of school programs to local values should reduce criticism of schools and engender support for local administrators and teachers.

## Restructuring Schools: Present Status

Restructuring schools continues to be a hot topic wherever educational issues are debated. Concerns about the quality of American schools are widespread. The view that "something must be done" has elicited a commitment from politicians, business leaders, and many other thoughtful members of our national community to actually *do* something. The logic of placing more responsibility at the local school level is appealing. It recognizes important place-to-place differences among learner populations. Also, it suggests that professionals and others at the local level are in the best position to make responsible decisions about what is good for the learners served in their local schools. It is consistent with a long-standing tradition favoring local control of education.

In practice, restructuring schools has not always worked out as promoters of the innovation suggested it might. For example, in some large metropolitan areas where the innovation has been tried, shared decision-making authority has led to angry conflicts among parents representing the interests of different ethnic and racial groups. Additionally, teachers, parents, and other members of school-management teams have sometimes had difficulty in grasping the complexity of school budgets. And, as in all arenas, it is difficult for management teams representing different groups to come to a consensus regarding what should be done.

Supporters of restructuring schools suggest that these difficulties by no means undermine the worth of the innovation. Shared management, they argue, is a new idea, and once people become more familiar with it, some problems experienced by early adopters of this approach will disappear. At this time, it is fair to say that despite difficulties that have surfaced in some communities that have actually adopted the innovation, interest in restructuring schools remains high.

## Peer Coaching

Peer coaching is an innovation designed to build teachers' confidence in using new instructional procedures in their individual classrooms. It is directed primarily at experienced teachers. According to Larry Barber, the director of the Phi Delta Kappa Center on Evaluation, Development, and Research, peer coaching is defined as "the assistance that one teacher provides to another in the development of teaching skills, strategies, or techniques" (Strother, 1989, p. 824).

Peer coaching has a research base that supports its effectiveness. Researchers Bruce Joyce and Beverly Showers found that many teachers who were introduced to new instructional techniques through various in-service activities tended to have difficulty incorporating these new techniques into their own teaching. Peer coaching was found to make them more confident about the new techniques, which resulted in greater use of these procedures in the classroom (Joyce and Showers, 1982).

The "peer" component of peer coaching is important—it implies that the person providing information and feedback to the teacher is a fellow teacher. The peer coach is someone who is familiar with the new technique or method. He or she observes the teacher being coached and provides helpful suggestions regarding how the procedure should be implemented. But note that the peer coach acts as a professional supporter, not as an evaluator. The credibility of this person as a peer who plays no role in the evaluation of the target teacher's overall performance has been thought to contribute to the success of the innovation. This chapter's Case Study examines the possible conflicts that may arise when the peer coach is also a teacher's evaluator.

---

CASE STUDY

## *Is my peer coach really my peer?*

**Stanley Lacasse is a first-year teacher at Martin Luther King Elementary School**. He is one of four fourth grade teachers in the building. The school is organized in such a way that there is one grade-level leader for each grade. Sharon McPhee, who has been teaching in the school for 12 years, is Stanley's grade-level leader.

Recently, Stanley and other fourth grade teachers in the district attended a two-day in-service session on "cooperative learning." Sharon McPhee, who has been using cooperative learning techniques in her own classroom for many years, arranged to bring the workshop to the district. The workshop was well-planned and effectively delivered by some excellent teachers from a neighboring school district. Stanley and other teachers in his school were quite impressed. They were particularly receptive because presenters were real teachers who taught children in their own schools every day.

Based on generally favorable reactions from all of the fourth grade teachers in the school, Duwayne Johnson, the principal at Martin Luther King, has decided to support a recommendation from Sharon McPhee that cooperative learning techniques be used by all fourth grade teachers there.

Duwayne Johnson is a strong believer in peer coaching and he appreciates the enthusiasm of the fourth grade teachers who attended the cooperative learning workshop. But he also believes that people who are new to cooperative learning will be more inclined to implement the approach properly if they are coached by someone who is familiar with it. He has decided to appoint Sharon McPhee to serve as a peer coach for the fourth grade teachers in his school.

Stanley Lacasse is very enthusiastic about implementing cooperative learning. He also feels that his relationship with Sharon McPhee is quite good. But he is bothered by the principal's decision to appoint her as a peer coach. As grade-level leader for the fourth grade, Sharon McPhee is responsible for writing evaluation reports on all fourth grade teachers, and especially detailed reports are required on all new teachers. Stanley feels that any inadequacies Sharon McPhee observes when he is trying to implement cooperative learning may well end up in a report on the principal's desk. Though Sharon has assured all of the teachers that her role as peer coach will be to help and support them when they start using cooperative learning, Stanley is still worried that some negative comments might find their way to the principal.

*How realistic are Stanley's concerns? Should the principal have appointed Sharon McPhee to be the peer coach? What alternative approaches might have been taken to help the fourth grade teachers become more proficient in the use of cooperative learning? What should Stanley do now?*

The best peer coaching programs are characterized by several important characteristics. First of all, the target teachers themselves need to volunteer for the program and request that a peer coach be assigned to them. Second, the peer coaching must be conducted in as nonthreatening and supportive a manner as possible. Third, the program must enjoy widespread administrative support at the school and district level. Fourth, there needs to be general support for the program from all teachers, including those who never personally choose to participate. Finally, there must be a clear understanding that reactions from peer coaches to their target teachers will be confidential and, especially, that they will never be used as part of formal teacher evaluations (Strother, 1989). Box 2–3 presents two teachers' views on peer coaching.

## Impact on Learners

Peer coaching has the potential to influence learners in a positive manner. They will feel the impact of the innovation in terms of their exposure to instructional techniques that their teacher may not have felt comfortable using before receiving the support of his or her peer coach. Peer coaching may well broaden a given teacher's repertoire of instructional skills. This opens up the possibility of more variety in daily lessons, which often improves learners' interest. Hence, enhanced learner motivation may be an indirect result of a teacher's agreement to participate in a peer coaching program.

Learners may have to adjust to the occasional presence of another teacher in their classroom. The peer coach will be visiting from time to time to observe the target teacher. However, visits from principals, student teacher supervisors, and others are fairly common in all classrooms, and hence it is unlikely that learners will be particularly bothered by an occasional peer coach visit.

## Impact on School Administrators

Peer coaching, for some administrators at least, requires rethinking about leadership roles. For this innovation to succeed, responsibility for instructional leadership must be assumed by teachers (the peer coaches). An administrator adopting this innovation must be secure, willing to acknowledge the expertise of certain teachers as

BOX 2–3
# PEER COACHING: FOR AND AGAINST

Two teachers recently discussed their differing reactions to peer coaching:

Teacher A: Peer coaching is the best thing that has happened to teachers in this district. For the first time, administrators are taking our professionalism seriously. We are being asked about instructional techniques that have a solid research base. Individuals in the district with expertise in these techniques are being encouraged to coach others in their use. The credibility these teachers have with other teachers is what makes the program work. The teachers in this district know that the peer coaches have been in the trenches, and thus they are willing to listen and learn. This is making everybody more professional.

Teacher B: The idea of peer teaching is great. I'm all for anything that gives teachers some status, particularly among administrators. But I'm a bit suspicious about the selection of the peer coaches. I see a lot of the "old boy" and "old girl" network at play here—principals are selecting their friends to be peer coaches. Despite all the rhetoric to the contrary, I think some of these peer coaches are funneling information back to the principal about the performance levels of teachers who are being coached. It seems to me that peer coaching is little more than a beautiful cover for a spy operation for administrators.

*What Do You Think?*
1. What are the strong and weak points of the perspectives presented by teacher A?
2. What are the strong and weak points of the perspectives presented by teacher B?
3. What safeguards need to be included in a peer coaching program to avoid negative results?

instructional leaders and to allow them to work directly with the target teachers who agree to participate.

Administrators must agree to support the program. For example, this means that they must agree to treat peer coaching as a nurturing, supportive, instructional-improvement program rather than as a vehicle for gathering information that can be used to make evaluative judgments about teachers.

Peer coaching takes time. Teachers who serve as coaches must make multiple visits to the classrooms of their target teachers, and are obligated to meet with them to discuss what has happened, provide support, and make suggestions. These duties require administrative arrangements that will allow the peer coaches to discharge these responsibilities—administrators must devise ways for covering some of the peer coaches' classes to provide them with the necessary opportunities.

## Impact on Teachers

Peer coaching is an innovation that has the potential to enhance teachers' images of themselves as professionals. Responsibility for instructional improvement is placed on the teachers themselves, not on central office curriculum specialists, administrators, nor colleges and universities.

Individuals who are coached may experience an increase in their confidence to use a wider range of procedures more effectively. When this occurs, their sense of efficacy as teachers is likely to be enhanced. There are also benefits that may accrue to the peer coaches—they may develop a broader view of themselves as professionals as they come to appreciate the benefits for learners that can result when the teachers they have coached begin to implement new techniques successfully.

## Impact on Parents

Peer coaching is an innovation that may be invisible to many parents. Few parents pay much attention to in-service efforts directed at teachers. Peer coaching, though, may have some important indirect influences on parents. In part, these benefits may accrue in terms of their children's improved attitudes toward the school program. To illustrate: many peer coaching programs seek to increase the number of instructional approaches available to teachers. Teachers who have been coached may introduce more variety into their lessons than those who have not been exposed to this kind of professional development program. Learners may thus enjoy classes more and complain less to parents about what is going on at school.

It is possible that school districts may require some extra funding to implement a large-scale peer coaching program, because of the need to free up coaches to visit their target teachers' classes. One administrative response might be to hire substitute teachers to cover some classes taught by peer coaches. Conceivably, payment for these substitutes could result in a need for additional school tax revenues. But this may not necessarily be the case. Existing revenue sources may be sufficient to fund peer coaching programs, or clever administrators may find ways to free up teachers for coaching duties that do not require additional funds.

## Impact on the Larger Community

Peer coaching programs tend to have little immediate impact on the larger community. As is the case with many parents, large numbers of people in the larger community pay little attention to staff-development programs in our schools. One indirect impact of this innovation on the larger community might be possible (though certainly not inevitable) increases in taxes to fund the peer coaching programs.

An important indirect benefit of peer coaching to the total community may be in its potential to reduce rates of teaching-staff turnover in local schools. Successful peer coaching programs enhance teachers' feeling of confidence. Confident teachers feel good about what they do, and are much less likely to leave the profession than teachers

This teacher is working as a peer coach with a colleague. Peer coaching is a teacher-to-teacher approach designed to improve the quality of classroom instruction.

who feel less secure about their work in the classroom. Confident teachers with long-term commitment to local schools provide valuable assistance in developing and delivering curricula that are effective with learners. It is very difficult to build quality programs when rates of teaching-staff turnover are high.

## Peer Coaching: Present Status

Peer coaching began to attract serious attention in the early and mid-1980s. The innovation has a relatively solid research base supporting its use. Its emphasis on placing increasing responsibility on teachers for monitoring and improving the quality of their own profession is consistent with present trends. From the perspective of the early 1990s, it seems safe to suggest that the innovation will continue to attract attention for some time to come.

## Year-round Education

For its supporters, the term *year-round education* has proved troublesome. To some people, the name seems to imply that children will be in school all of the time. This misconception may stem from citizens' focusing on schools in other countries where learners spend more days in school than American children do. For example, in Japan learners spend well over 200 days in school each year; in this country, most schools are in session about 180 days.

While a few year-round programs have attempted to add more required school days, the vast majority of year-round schools have simply reconfigured the school calendar. Typically this has been done with a view to eliminating the traditional long summer vacation and replacing it with a number of shorter breaks scattered throughout the school year. Some supporters of year-round education have even considered the possibility of presenting the innovation to the public under the name *multiple-vacation calendar,* a description that quite accurately denotes what most of these programs provide.

Supporters of year-round education feel that a reconfigured school calendar will provide learners with a more continuous learning experience. A number of benefits are thought to be associated with the innovation. One benefit speaks to educators in this country who have long been concerned about the learning loss that occurs during the three-month summer break. In traditional schools, teachers respond to this situation by reteaching in September much of the content that was taught at the end of the previous school year. Proponents of year-round education argue that shorter breaks away from school will diminish the learning-loss problem and allow teachers to spend less time reviewing what has already been taught.

Year-round education has also been promoted, on cost-effectiveness grounds, by the idea of using school buildings all year long. It is possible to organize schedules in such a way that individual buildings can serve a larger total number of students than is possible during a nine-month school year. This may save taxpayers money in that new schools will not have to be constructed so frequently.

Schools employing year-round education have developed many different calendar patterns. One of the most popular schemes divides the school year into four instructional segments of 45 weekdays each and four vacation periods of 15 weekdays each. This often is called a *45/15 calendar.* Where this calendar is in use, it is often the practice to divide learners into four groups, or tracks. During a given 45-day instructional period, three of the four tracks will be in school, and one will be on vacation. Since only 75 percent of the total group of learners will be in school at one time, it is possible under this arrangement for one building to serve a larger total group of learners than would be possible under a traditional nine-month calendar, where all learners would be in school at the same time. An example of a 45/15 calendar with four tracks is illustrated in Figure 2–1.

The 45/15 scheme is by no means the only year-round education calendar that has been adopted. Among other alternatives have been these schemes:

- 60/15, featuring three 60-weekday periods of instruction, each of which is followed by 15 weekdays of vacation;
- 90/30, featuring two 90-weekday periods of instruction, each of which is followed by 30 weekdays of vacation;
- 30/10, featuring six 30-weekday periods of instruction, each of which is followed by 10 weekdays of vacation.

Many of these calendars are set up to allow for a somewhat longer vacation sometime during the June through August period and a traditional winter break beginning in the latter part of December.

## Impact on Learners

This innovation is designed to help learners progress more smoothly through academic content. Short breaks do not seriously interrupt the flow of the instructional program. The forgetting that occurs over the traditional long summer break should be less of a problem.

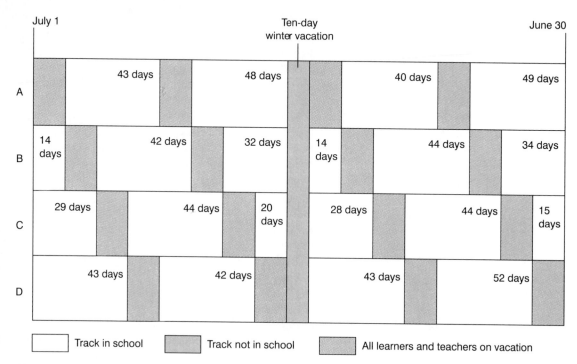

**Figure 2–1**
A year-round education plan based on a 45/15 calendar and four tracks

Relatively frequent breaks give learners something to look forward to. They have opportunities to be intellectually refreshed, and their attitudes toward school should be more positive. In support of this claim, adopters of year-round education have reported lowered levels of school vandalism (Conroe Independent School District, 1989).

Another benefit to learners is that examination anxiety may be somewhat reduced. Because periods when school is in session are shorter on this plan than on a traditional school calendar, tests tend to cover smaller quantities of material. As a result, review becomes a less burdensome activity. This may result in better learner test performances.

One possibly negative aspect of this innovation is that scheduling of traditional summer activities may need to be modified. For example, instead of attending extended summer camp sessions, learners may find themselves having to adjust to recreational opportunities organized around shorter periods of time (to conform with their shorter between-term breaks).

## Impact on School Administrators

Since this innovation is new to most parents, school administrators must spend a great deal of time explaining and justifying it. Because of the need to win broad parental and community support, they often find it necessary to create and work closely with broad-based, year-round school advisory groups.

Scheduling of maintenance has to be adjusted. In schools that follow a traditional nine-month calendar, much maintenance work is done during the summer. Since learners are in school all through the year in a year-round program, maintenance activities need to be scheduled at various times through the year. In this case it may be necessary to increase the amount of maintenance work done at night, when learners and teachers are out of the building.

Developing attendance schedules for individual learners may require more time, particularly in year-round programs where students are assigned to several tracks. (For an example of such a calendar, see Figure 2–1.) To the extent possible, administrators try to place all children from a single family on the same track so that their vacation and in-school schedules will be the same.

## Impact on Teachers

This innovation has the potential to reduce teachers' feelings of burnout—the frequent breaks during the year provide opportunities to rest, relax, and regenerate energy levels. Teachers may also find themselves better able to plan ways to meet the needs of individual learners. In a traditional school calendar, there are no significant breaks from September until late December, and teachers find it difficult to do any unpressured planning during this time. But in a year-round schedule, one or more short breaks occur during this period. Teachers may use some of this break time to reflect on their learners and plan subsequent instruction to better respond to their special characteristics.

One negative aspect of this innovation is that until more schools adopt year-round calendars, teachers may have to spend extra time adapting textbooks and other learning resources as many commercially prepared materials have been developed on the assumption that they will be used in nine-month instructional programs. If large numbers of schools were to switch to year-round education, commercial materials manufacturers would probably respond with items geared to the new time configurations. Until this happens, though, teachers in year-round programs will need to spend additional time adapting materials to the particular calendar in use at their school.

Another potential problem that teachers in such programs may face concern pursuing advanced degree work at colleges and universities. Many master's degree programs in education, for example, are planned on the assumption that teachers will be available to go to school during the summer months. Again, if large numbers of schools were to adopt year-round schedules, colleges and universities would be almost certain to accommodate these changes by scheduling courses at times when teachers could attend.

## Impact on Parents

Under this innovation, parents must adjust to a different school calendar than the one they followed when they were young. Children will be home for extended periods at several times during the school year, which may influence vacation plans. Some parents may take positive views of the new flexibility that year-round school calendars provide in terms of scheduling family vacations. On the other hand, others may be unhappy that their children will not be free to participate in a long family vacation during the three summer months.

Childcare services for children of working parents will need to be arranged for times when learners are not in school. If larger numbers of schools adopt a year-round program this will not prove a problem, though, as providers of such services will be likely to arrange for service during the multiple vacation periods occurring throughout the year.

Theoretically, parents may face problems if some of their children are attending a school on a year-round calendar and others are attending a school on a traditional nine-month calendar. In practice, though, administrators in school districts with year-round programs work hard to ensure that all children in a single family are on a common school calendar.

Parents often complain that their children are very bored by the time school begins in the fall. This situation may be remedied when a year-round calendar is followed, because individual vacation periods are shorter. Parents, too, may find that their children complain less about school when it is in session. Supporters of year-round education contend that children in such programs enjoy school more than children in traditional nine-month schools (Loyd, 1991).

## Impact on the Larger Community

Year-round programs, particularly those featuring tracks similar to the plan depicted in Figure 2–1, may hold down school construction costs. A larger number of learners may be able to be accommodated in existing buildings, and thus the community might not need to raise funds for new structures.

There may be other, somewhat intangible benefits to the community. If, as a result of shortened vacation periods, teachers are able to spend less time reviewing previously taught material, learners should be exposed to more content. The end result will be better-prepared school graduates. An improvement of the total "intellectual capital" of the area's learners, over time, should improve the quality of life for the whole community.

If teachers in year-round programs suffer less career burnout than teachers in nine-month schools, staff turnover rates may go down. This would result in a stability of instructional staffs. This kind of stability is important to the development and maintenance of school quality, and when schools are good, the entire community benefits.

## Year-round Education: Present Status

There continues to be much interest in year-round education. Year-round calendars have been implemented by hundreds of schools. Currently, the innovation is most common in western parts of the country—states such as California, Utah, Colorado, and Texas have pioneered various models of year-round education. There is a large and active national professional association, the National Association for Year-Round Education, that acts as a source of basic information and as an idea exchange network for districts interested in the innovation. All signs point to increasing national interest in year-round education during the 1990s.

**Table 2–1**
Summary table: Innovations

| Topic | Key Points |
|---|---|
| General impact of innovations in our schools | Innovations affect different groups in different ways. For example, innovations have varied impacts on learners, administrators, parents, teachers, and members of the larger community. |
| School choice | This innovation centers on the idea that parents should be able to send learners to schools of the parents own choosing, unrestricted by attendance boundaries tied to places of residence. Supporters of this policy argue that it would act to improve the quality of the schools. Critics contend that this would not be the case and that needs of some learners would not be served well by this innovation. |
| Restructuring schools | Supporters of this innovation contend that many of today's education problems can be attributed to administrative control that is too centralized. They advocate placing more decision-making power at the levels where the decisions must be implemented. They want to give local parents, teachers, and administrators a larger voice in how programs are planned and delivered in individual schools. Implementation of this innovation means new and unfamiliar roles for parents, teachers, and local administrators. Some critics point out that restructuring efforts do not always work out as planned. Shared decision making sometimes leads to angry conflicts among individuals trying to promote interests of specific groups. Some decision makers may not have the expertise needed to understand questions associated with complex school budgets. |

**Table 2–1**
*continued*

| Topic | Key Points |
|---|---|
| Peer coaching | This innovation seeks to build teachers' confidence in using new instructional procedures. It involves providing assistance or coaching to a teacher unfamiliar with an approach by a teacher well-versed in its use. Because this is a teacher-to-teacher approach, supporters feel that change is promoted in a nonthreatening way. Some critics are not convinced that peer coaches will avoid making negative comments to administrators about some of the people with whom they are working. |
| Year-round education | Despite its name, this innovation is not a proposal to keep the schools in session all the time. In most of its versions, the idea is to create a new school calendar that better distributes the 180 or 190 days in the school year throughout the calendar year. In part, there is an effort to do something about the traditional three-month summer vacation, when learners forget much of what they have learned. Many year-round calendars make it possible to serve a larger total number of learners in a given building, because some learners will be on vacation at all times during the calendar year. Year-round calendars fly in the face of much educational tradition. For example, career enhancement programs for teachers presume that they will be free to attend universities during the summer months, and many textbooks presume a traditional nine-month school year. Despite the difficulties involved in challenging years of tradition, year-round calendars are increasing in popularity. |

..................................

# Key Ideas in Summary

- Schools have had a long tradition of encouraging the adoption of innovations. The predisposition to try something new, in part, suggests a view that educational problems are capable of being solved. This attitude is a reflection of optimism on the part of those who care about the quality of school programs. A recent example of an effort to identify problems and propose solutions is *America 2000: An Education Strategy,* a report released by the U.S. Department of Education in April 1991.

- Innovations are often designed to accomplish a specific purpose. However, as they are implemented, they sometimes have unintended side effects. In assessing the immediate or potential impacts of an innovation, it is wise to consider how the change might affect (1) learners, (2) school administrators, (3) teachers, (4) parents, and (5) members of the larger community.

- The general worth of a given innovation is difficult to assess. In part, this is because there often is little agreement about the defining characteristics of an individual innovation. For example, two school districts might commit to an innovative practice that both call "site-based management" and yet be doing very different things.

- Numbers of innovations that have been tried are too large to allow for development of a comprehensive list. Some innovative practices that have been adopted in large numbers of school districts at one time or another include team teaching, flexible class scheduling, open-space learning environments, nongraded elementary schools, continuous progress learning, site-based management, year-round education, in-school daycare for children of learners and site-based management.

- Proponents of school choice suggest that schools will be prodded to become better if parents are free to send their children to any school they choose. By abandoning the practice of requiring learners to attend schools based on their places of residence, the practice of school choice is supposed to result in attracting more learners to the "good" schools. As a result, administrators in schools that are perceived as poor are expected to take action to improve the situation. Improvement, if successful, will attract students back to these schools. According to supporters of school choice, the net effect of all this will be an improvement in the general quality of all schools.

- Supporters of restructuring schools see highly centralized and bureaucratic organizational and administrative structures as the main causes of poor schools. Though recommended approaches vary, a common suggestion is for new administrative arrangements that will place more decision-making power at the level where instructional services are being delivered. The idea is to give people in the individual schools the authority to make decisions, and then hold them rigorously accountable for the quality of programs they deliver. Many discussions of restructuring schools emphasize the importance of sharing decision-making power among school administrators, teachers, parents, child-development specialists, and selected representatives of the local community.

• Peer coaching is a staff-development innovation. It features the use of teachers as mentors who work with other teachers to help them successfully implement effective instructional approaches. The idea is to broaden the repertoire of effective instructional procedures of individual classroom teachers. Some research supports the view that new techniques are more likely to become a permanent part of a teacher's repertoire when peer coaching reinforces the general in-service sessions that introduce the basic steps of the techniques. Peer coaching is completely independent from teacher evaluation. Successful programs must enjoy broad teacher support, and individuals must volunteer to participate in the program, not be assigned to do so. To permit coaches the time to follow through the process, peer coaching programs require a strong commitment from school administrators to juggling the coaches' existing responsibilities.

• *Year-round education* is a name given to a number of proposals to change the traditional school calendar. Usually, the term does not imply an actual increase in the total number of instructional days learners experience in a typical year; in most year-round programs, learners spend about the same amount of time, approximately 180 days, in school as in a traditional, nine-month school program. What is different is the way the instructional days are scattered throughout the year. Year-round programs tend to do away with the three-month summer vacation, providing instead a number of shorter breaks throughout the school year. One popular year-round calendar features four instructional periods of 45 weekdays each, with four intervening vacation times of 15 weekdays each. By reducing the length of time learners are out of school, learners experience less "forgetting time." Hence, teachers can spend less time reviewing old material before introducing new content. Year-round calendars are said to have a number of other advantages. Among them are (1) increased levels of learner motivation, (2) opportunities for families to take vacations at several times during the year, (3) more learners can be served in a building during a given 12-month period, and (4) learners' overall achievement levels may go up. There are also problems that have to be addressed when year-round calendars are considered. Among them are (1) many commercial materials, such as textbooks, assume a traditional nine-month school year, (2) building maintenance schedules must be rearranged because teachers and learners are in the building during the summer months, when much heavy maintenance has traditionally been done, (3) parents have not experienced this kind of a school calendar and may assume that children will be available for extended out-of-town travel during the summer months, (4) different children in the same family may attend schools with different calendars, and (5) many graduate programs for teachers presume that they will be available to take courses during the months of June, July, and August.

......................................

# Review and Discussion Questions

1. Is American education's "love affair" with innovations an indictment of our schools, or is it an indication of our belief that educational problems can be solved?

2. Are all groups affected in the same way by a given educational innovation?

3. What are some examples of educational innovations?

4. If we read that two different school districts have decided to implement a year-round education calendar, would we expect this year-round program to be designed the same way in the two districts? Why or why not?

5. Who are some groups that might be affected when a school district adopts an educational innovation?

6. If a school administrator announced at a faculty meeting that the superintendent had decreed that a peer coaching program was to be implemented and that every teacher was expected to volunteer, how do you suppose teachers might react? Would there be a better way to introduce such a program?

7. If parents were given the option of sending their children to any school in their state, on what bases do you think they might make their selections?

8. How do you feel about the argument that school-choice programs will tend to make schools better over time?

9. What are some arguments for and against the idea of year-round education? What are your personal reactions to this idea?

10. Suppose a school district decided to decentralize decision making in its schools as part of a restructuring process. What are some changes that might occur in traditional roles of principals, parents, and teachers?

......................................

# Ideas for Field Experiences, Projects, and Enrichment

1. Select an innovation (team teaching, site-based management, programmed learning, computer-assisted instruction, modular scheduling, and schools without walls are possibilities you might wish to consider—ask your instructor

about others), and then assess the possible implications of a decision to adopt this innovation for (*a*) learners, (*b*) school administrators, (*c*) teachers, (*d*) parents, and (*e*) the larger community. If appropriate, note both potential positive and negative effects of the innovation for each of these groups.

2. Many alternative calendars have been proposed (and implemented) by school districts interested in year-round education. With a team of about four people, identify three or more of these schemes. Organize information in chart form, and share your findings with others in your class.

3. Review the text discussion on year-round education and organize a classroom debate on this topic:

    "Resolved that benefits accruing from a decision to operate all schools on a year-round calendar more than compensate for any disadvantages."

4. Suppose a state decreed that parents could send their children to any school within that state. With three or four other students, organize a symposium to present to your class on this general topic: "School Choice: Its Probable Effects on (*a*) Learners in Small Towns and Isolated Rural Areas, (*b*) Learners in Homes with Incomes Below the Poverty Level, (*c*) Learners with Parents Who Are College Graduates, (*d*) Learners from Families that Make a High Priority of School Team Sports Participation, and (*e*) Learners from Homes in the Affluent Suburbs."

5. Interview two or more teachers who have been teaching for 10 or more years. Ask them to comment on innovations that have been proposed during the years they have been teaching. What innovations did they find beneficial? Which ones did they find unsuccessful? At this point in their careers, what is their general attitude toward innovations? How did they come to feel this way? Report your findings to members of your class.

• • • • • • • • • • • • • • • • • • • • • • • • •

# Supplementary Reading

Center on Evaluation, Development, Research. *Year-Round Schools: Do They Make a Difference?* Bloomington, IN: Phi Delta Kappa, 1990.

Chrisco, I. M. "Peer Assistance Works." *Educational Leadership* (May 1989): 31–32.

Cuban, L. *Teachers and Machines: The Classroom Use of Technology Since 1920.* New York: Teachers College Press, 1986.

Leithwood, K. A., and D. J. Montgomery, eds. *Improving Classroom Practice Using Innovation Profiles.* Toronto: Olse Press, 1987.

Lieberman, M. *Privatization and Educational Choice.* New York: St. Martin's Press, 1989.

Paulu, N. *Improving Schools and Empowering Parents: A Report Based on Choice in Education*. Washington, DC: U.S. Department of Education, Office of Educational Research and Improvement, 1989.

Slavin, R. "PET and the Pendulum: Faddism in Education and How to Stop It." *Educational Leadership* (June 1989): 752–58.

• • • • • • • • • • • • • • • • • • • • • • • • • • • •

# References

*America 2000: An Education Strategy*. Washington, DC: U.S. Department of Education, 1991.

Conroe Independent School District. *Year-Round Education*. Conroe, TX: Conroe Independent School District, 1989.

Cuban, L. *Teachers and Machines: The Classroom Use of Technology Since 1920*. New York: Teachers College Press, 1986.

Joyce, R., and B. Showers. "The Coaching of Teaching." *Educational Leadership* (October 1982): 4–8, 10.

Loyd, C. R. *A Study to Determine the Effects of Year-Round Education on the Retention of Learning by Sixth Grade Students*. Unpublished Doctoral Dissertation, College Station, Texas: Texas A&M University, 1991.

Slavin, R. "PET and the Pendulum: Faddism in Education and How to Stop It." *Educational Leadership* (June 1989): 752–58.

Strother, D. B. "Peer Coaching for Teachers: Opening Classroom Doors." *Phi Delta Kappan* (June 1989): 824–27.

# Section 2

# Foundations

In early 1991, the Bush administration released *America 2000: An Education Strategy.**** This booklet put forward several ideas for improving the nation's educational system, including:

- creation of a National Goals Panel to develop standards for what learners should know in English, mathematics, science, history, and geography.

- development of a voluntary national assessment system to see how well learners are meeting standards established by the National Goals Panel.

- establishment of at least 535 "New American Schools" that will break away from traditional school calendars, schedules, and staffing patterns, but will operate at costs not exceeding those of conventional schools.

- establishment of academies in each state to provide teachers with in-depth training in the five core subjects.

- provision of a financial arrangement that will allow parents to choose which schools their children will attend, whether public or private.

Are these ideas good or bad? Initial reactions have been mixed. Some people argue that these changes are right on target and are precisely the prescription for improving American education. Others retort that these ideas are cosmetic sideshows that fail to address the basic problems facing our schools. The discussion continues.

*America 2000: An Education Strategy. Washington, DC: U.S. Department of Education, 1990.

People who take sides in these kinds of improvement-of-education debates have arrived at personal answers to questions such as these:

- What is the nature of the government's responsibility for educating our young people?
- How should learners be treated in school?
- What kinds of content should be taught?
- What should be the most important lessons that children take away from their experiences in school?
- How do different groups perceive the educational enterprise?

Different people respond to these questions in different ways. In part, answers depend on how individuals interpret our educational traditions and the particular philosophical stances with which they identify. To understand where contending parties are coming from in improvement-of-education arguments, some perspectives from educational history, philosophy, and sociology are useful. The four chapters in this section explore these areas. They are:

Chapter 3: International Roots
Chapter 4: History of American Education
Chapter 5: Philosophies of Education
Chapter 6: Sociology of Education

# Chapter 3

# International Roots

## Objectives

This chapter provides information to help the reader to

- identify some educational legacies from the ancient Sumerian, Egyptian, and Hebrew civilizations;
- summarize the beliefs of key educational thinkers from ancient Greece and Rome;
- describe the general development of educational practices in the Middle Ages;
- suggest some lingering influences on education of the Renaissance and the Reformation;
- identify positions taken by some important thinkers who addressed educational issues in the seventeenth, eighteenth, and nineteenth centuries.

1. What are several practices developed among the ancient Sumerians, Egyptians, and Hebrews that continue to be reflected in some schools?
2. Why were instructional programs in ancient Sparta and Athens so different?
3. Who were some of the leading educational thinkers of ancient Greece and Rome, and what were some of their views?
4. What were some differences in what were considered to be the major purposes of education in the Middle Ages and in the Renaissance?
5. Why did many Reformation leaders promote the idea that as many people as possible should be taught to read?
6. What were some of Pestalozzi's and Comenius's lasting contributions to educational thought?
7. In what ways have today's schools been influenced by seventeenth, eighteenth, and nineteenth century educational thought?

# Introduction

Many present ideas about education and schooling are not new. The sources of these historical residues are varied—some of them have even come down to us from practices of preliterate people who lived thousands of years ago.

Because many of the first formal educational institutions in the part of the globe we now know as the United States came from Europe, many current American educational practices can be traced to European roots. This by no means suggests that educational ideas developed in Asia, Africa, the Pacific Island Region, and among indigenous American peoples are less worthy; it simply attests to the importance attached to education by populations who came to North America from Europe, and to their success in transplanting many European educational ideas to North America.

Information presented here about the international roots of American education represents only a selection of what might have been included. This chapter highlights only a few of the societies and individuals whose work and thought provide a historic backdrop for the development of education in the United States. Specific periods that are discussed include the following:

- Ancient Middle Eastern civilizations
- Ancient Greece and Rome
- The Middle Ages, Renaissance, and Reformation
- The Seventeenth, eighteenth, and nineteenth centuries

## Ancient Middle Eastern Civilizations

About 5,000 B.C., towns and small cities began to develop in the low-lying plain between the Tigris and Euphrates rivers in an area sometimes referred to as *Mesopotamia.* (Today this area is part of Iraq.) One of the great civilizations of Mesopotamia was Sumer, established about 3,000 B.C. The Sumerians are perhaps best known for creating the world's first system of writing. They also established a huge empire and had a well-developed commercial system. In Sumerian society, it was highly important for large numbers of people to know how to keep good commercial records.

Another ancient river civilization, that of the Egyptians, developed along the banks of the Nile, about 5,000 B.C. The Egyptians were very much concerned about the afterlife. As a result, priests were influential, and they played an important role in ancient Egyptian education.

The Hebrews, another Middle Eastern group, became especially interested in education during the period of the Babylonian captivity in the sixth century (Butts, 1955), although they almost lost their identity as a people during this period. Centers of worship were centers of both education and religion.

The institution of the school traces back to these ancient civilizations, particularly to Sumer. The Sumerians developed an instructional theory for teaching young people the difficult Sumerian writing system—progress from the simple concepts to the more complex. This simple-to-complex approach still plays a role in today's instructional planning.

Both the Sumerians and the Hebrews were quick to discipline learners who did not work diligently on assigned academic tasks. This association between discipline and learning persisted throughout much of education's history. Indeed, some modern critics of our schools charge that one of education's problems is that discipline has become too relaxed.

Teachers in these ancient civilizations emphasized mastery of a limited amount of basic content. Learners were required to do a good deal of memory work and drill (see Box 3–1). This general approach continues today, particularly when the instructional focus is on basic skills, including writing and simple computation.

## Ancient Greece and Rome

Greece was settled between 1,500 and 2,000 B.C. by people who entered the peninsula from the north. Greece is very mountainous, and settlements developed in valleys and pockets between the mountains. Land communication among these settlements was difficult because of the terrain. Settlements tended to develop into politically independent city-states that were physically isolated from one another. Two of the most important city-states were Athens and Sparta. Greek civilization fell to the Romans in 146 B.C.

Ancient Rome began as a monarchy during the sixth century B.C. At various times through Rome's history, it was a republic, a dictatorship, and a powerful empire. The Roman Empire in the west ended in 476 A.D.

---

BOX 3–1
# ROTE LEARNING: SOME ISSUES TO THINK ABOUT

The ancient Egyptians required students to memorize things and to reproduce what they had learned precisely as it was taught. Educators call this *rote learning*. There used to be much more rote learning in American schools than there is today. For example, children in schools used to be required to memorize numerous poems.

*What Do You Think?*
1. Would rote learning work better in a traditional society with little generation-to-generation change or in a society with much generation-to-generation change?
2. What possible value might there be in rote learning?
3. Under a rote learning system, what kinds of learners would likely be designated as the best? Would this group vary in any way from those we might designate as the best learners in our schools today?
4. In general, how would you react to a proposal calling for a great increase in rote learning in our schools?

## Ancient Greece

In the period before the fifth century B.C., Greek education was vastly different in the two city-states of Sparta and Athens. Sparta was a military state that prepared its young people to live and die as fighters; Athens sought to prepare young people to be politically contributing citizens. Education in early Sparta and early Athens could not have been more different.

Spartan education sought to wash out all traces of learners' individualism. The object was to produce someone who was totally obedient and loyal to the state. Through education, the individual was trained to fight for the state with unquestioned loyalty to the commander.

Early Athenian education sought to prepare young people to be citizen decision makers. Though not all people in Athens were citizens (some were slaves, for example), relatively large numbers of Athenians participated in making political decisions. Education for young people under the age of 16 was left to the discretion (and the income) of the individual family. All schools for these young people were private. State-supported education was available only for young people who were at least 16 years old (Cordasco, 1976).

Beginning about 430 B.C., a group of teachers known as *Sophists* appeared. The Sophists originally came to Athens from colonies in Athenean Greece. Many conservatives in Athens felt the Sophists to be dangerous. This was because of their heavy emphasis on individualism and their rejection of the idea that any truths were absolute. In particular, critics feared that ideas of the Sophists would undermine in the young any sense of obligation to serve the interests of the state.

*Some Important Thinkers.*    One person who challenged the Sophists was *Socrates* (469–399 B.C.). He applauded the idea that reason should guide decision making but, unlike the Sophists, held that there were some universal truths. Socrates argued his case from the principle that "knowledge is virtue," which he regarded as an unchallengeable axiom. Among Socrates's contributions to education was the view that "education has for its immediate objective the development of thought, not the imparting of knowledge" (Cordasco, 1976, p. 7).

*Plato* (427–347 B.C.) described a view of an idealized society in *The Republic*. In this work, he described a scheme of education designed to help people prepare for the social roles for which they were best suited. Education was directed toward both the promotion of individual happiness and the development of a just government. Plato believed that for future leaders, school subjects were not important so much for their specific content as for their capacity to enhance general thinking abilities.

*Aristotle* (384–322 B.C.) believed that learning begins with perceptual information that comes to an individual through his or her senses. The mental image of an object is the beginning point of knowledge. Aristotle recognized the importance of teaching learners that categories of objects have certain similar characteristics. In modern parlance, we call these categories *concepts*. Aristotle developed elaborate schemes for classifying knowledge. In time, these became the bases for dividing information into separate subject areas.

*Legacies for the Present.*    Many traces of Greek educational ideas remain in our schools today. Ancient Sparta and Athens both embraced the idea that physical aspects of educa-

*"Makes you wonder what Socrates would have thought, doesn't it?"*
Courtesy of Ford Button.

tion were important. The Athenians placed great stock in the idea of educating for individual development, which is central to present-day American education. The Athenian commitment to education for citizenship continues to be very much with us. In addition, systematic learning, concept learning, and knowledge classification, whose origins can be traced back to ancient Greece, are all features of present-day educational programs.

## Ancient Rome

Ancient Rome lasted for about 1200 years. Although no one knows the precise date, by tradition the city of Rome traces its beginning to the year 753 B.C. Roman education was much influenced by Greece, particularly after Greece fell under Roman control. Greek slaves were brought to Rome, and many of them worked as teachers. Reactions of Rome's leaders to these Greeks were sometimes positive, sometimes negative.

In the early days of Rome, imitation was the most commonly used method of instruction (Wilds and Lottich, 1964). Even individuals who had learned to read were required to do much memory work, often "encouraged" to do so by the threat of harsh physical discipline. In Rome, fathers had absolute power over their children—they could even kill them if they so chose.

In later years, Roman education placed more emphasis on the development of writing and speaking skills in addition to reading skills. The teacher gave learners exercises to copy. The learners marked responses on wax tablets with a stylus. There was a strong emphasis on development of a particular style of public speaking. To develop this skill, learners were drilled on specific aspects of speechmaking, including logical organization. Harsh discipline continued to be important, even though some reformers, such as Quintilian (discussed below), opposed it.

*Some Important Thinkers.*    The importance of developing speaking abilities was a special concern of *Cicero* (106–43 B.C.). He wanted learners to develop into citizens who were capable of participating effectively in public policy debates. He saw the study of the humanities as the best preparation for a life of public service.

*Quintilian* (35–95 A.D.) made many important contributions to Roman educational thought. He believed that education should be oriented toward the practical needs of learners. It should be directed toward life as it *is,* not to an imaginary life as envisioned by some philosophers. To accomplish this purpose, Quintilian admonished teachers to carefully note characteristics of individual learners with a view to developing programs responsive to their needs.

Quintilian believed learners should study Greek before Latin, feeling that the process of learning a foreign language first would facilitate their mastery of their own language. Quintilian opposed the brutal punishments that were a common feature of most Roman schools of his day. He believed that decent treatment of learners would lead to better levels of achievement.

Quintilian was also interested in whether it was better to educate learners alone in their individual homes or in groups in classrooms. He concluded that it was better to bring learners together in classrooms because, in groups, individuals tended to motivate one another (Meyer, 1965). Quintilian was among the first to note that individuals gain important insights from their associations with one another in school as well as from their exposure to lessons taught by the teacher.

*Legacies for the Present.*    The values of ancient Rome parallel many present-day American values. The Romans prized the practical over the theoretical, and their educational arrangements reflected this orientation. The view that education should prepare learners for the real world is a priority of many Americans.

The common Roman view (Quintilian being an exception) that learning best results from strict discipline has many present-day American adherents. On the other hand, other Americans follow Quintilian's lead in suggesting that learning is promoted when there are warm, unthreatening relationships between teachers and learners.

Quintilian's work regarding the importance of individual differences and the socializing function of the school is reflected in much present-day educational thought (See Box 3–2). His contention that the study of a foreign language provides a good foundation for mastering one's native tongue is also still around, albeit as a widely debated proposition.

Cicero's emphasis on the humanities is also currently being debated, as reflected in the arguments of many groups who wish to restrict the range of school subjects to

BOX 3–2
# WHICH IS BETTER—LEARNING ALONE OR LEARNING IN A GROUP?

The important Roman educational thinker, Quintilian, had strong feelings about where learning should occur. He believed that it should take place in a classroom, where a number of learners are under the supervision of a teacher. He felt that this group setting had advantages over a situation that featured only a single learner working alone with a tutor.

*What Do You Think?*

1. What are some advantages that might result from an instructional situation featuring only a single learner working with a teacher?
2. Would you imagine that motivation might be more of a problem for a teacher working with only a single learner than for one with a whole class? Why or why not?
3. What is your general reaction to Quintilian's argument that it is better for learning to occur in a group setting rather than in a one-on-one teacher-and-learner situation?

"needed essentials." But the Roman view that education should prepare learners for responsible citizenship would probably be supported by a huge majority of contemporary Americans.

## The Middle Ages, Renaissance, and Reformation

Greek and Roman education focused on gaining an understanding of the world through the application of reason and logic; education in the Middle Ages emphasized knowledge through religious faith. With the spread of the influence of Christianity, writings of the "pagan" Greeks and Romans became suspect. A church council held at Carthage in 401 A.D. went so far as to declare that even members of the clergy should not read the old Greek and Roman authors (Meyer, 1965).

These attempts at suppression succeeded in making Greek and Roman learning accessible to only a few, usually people who worked or studied in monasteries, cathedrals, or other Christian centers. It was not until the Renaissance, a thousand years after the meeting at Carthage, that large numbers of people again came to know the writers and thinkers of ancient Greece and Rome.

### The Middle Ages

The Middle Ages lasted approximately from the middle of the fifth century A.D. to the middle of the fifteenth century A.D. It was a period when the Roman Catholic

Church exercised an extraordinary influence. The education of those few people to whom it was available went forward under the auspices of the church. Subject matter was checked carefully for the purpose of eliminating "pagan" content, such as references to the Greek and Roman gods.

Over time, there developed at the cathedral schools and monasteries a program of study that has come to be identified as the "seven liberal arts." These were divided into two groups, known as the *Trivium* and the *Quadrivium*. The Trivium included the study of (1) grammar, (2) rhetoric, and (3) dialectic; the Quadrivium included (4) arithmetic, (5) geometry, (6) astronomy, and (7) music. Most cathedral schools and monasteries taught only the Trivium, although some offered one or two of the courses associated with the Quadrivium. Only a few cathedral schools and monasteries offered the entire Quadrivium along with the Trivium.

In the later Middle Ages, beginning about the eleventh century, there was a movement to develop learners' rational thinking powers so that they would be able to build a logical case in support of their commitment to the Christian faith. This movement was known as *Scholasticism*. The Scholastics produced many books that were highly intellectual in nature. (However, relatively few learners read them.) One result of the Scholastics' emphasis on rigorous intellectual debate was the foundation of universities, which slowly began to appear in the twelfth and thirteenth centuries. But even as late as 1500, there were only 79 universities in all of Europe (Cordasco, 1976).

*Some Important Thinkers.*    Alcuin (734–804), a prolific writer, was a chief adviser to Charlemagne. One of his lasting contributions was his strong support for intellectual study as an important complement to a religious education. Alcuin's work helped to broaden the curriculum of church-supported schools to include more than just religious instruction. Alcuin argued that both intellectual and religious education were needed if learners were to experience moral growth.

*Saint Thomas Aquinas* (about 1225–1274), an Italian, was the most famous of the Scholastics. He was brilliantly grounded in all seven of the liberal arts. Aquinas developed a persuasive synthesis of intellectual thinking and religious faith. He argued that each operates according to its own rules—principles of verification that apply to intellectual debate do not apply to religious faith, and some elements of faith cannot be proved by reason alone.

Aquinas' work suggested that Greek culture and its emphasis on the development of the intellect did have its place in education. He helped make studying the writings of "pagan" authors acceptable to audiences who, before his time, had felt that such works were totally lacking in merit.

*Legacies for the Present.*    As stated earlier, most responsibility for education during the Middle Ages was assumed by religious institutions. This idea that religious bodies have a responsibility to provide a secular as well as religious education continues to be reflected today in thousands of parochial school classrooms.

Throughout the Middle Ages, learners at cathedral schools, monasteries, and universities were taught to read and write Latin and, in some instances, Greek. For centuries thereafter, there was a presumption that an educated person ought to be able to read and write at least Latin, if not both. Even today, some people argue that mastery of these languages is imperative to anyone who hopes to become "truly educated."

The strong continuing tradition of the liberal arts has its foundations in the Trivium and Quadrivium of the Middle Ages. Some people even today believe that our schools should deal with no other subjects.

The establishment of universities as centers of learning began during the Middle Ages. Academic gowns, certain traditional ceremonies, and other conventions of present-day university life owe their origins to the universities of the late Middle Ages.

## The Renaissance and Reformation

The Renaissance and Reformation are closely related periods. The Renaissance began in the fourteenth century and extended into the sixteenth. The Reformation occurred during the sixteenth century.

The Renaissance began in Italy during the latter part of the fourteenth century. During this period, there was a rediscovery of the writings of the ancient Greeks and Romans. Scholars became interested in locating and preserving manuscripts of the great writers of these ancient worlds. Also, there was a tremendous resurgence of interest in the study of ancient Greek, a language that had been almost unknown at the beginning of the Renaissance.

During the early Italian Renaissance, much emphasis was placed on the worth of "individuals" as opposed to that of "authorities." Later, there was a movement to slavishly imitate certain people from the ancient world whose works were particularly admired. Cicero especially was held up as a stylistic model.

The Renaissance taking place in Europe north of Italy placed less emphasis on individual development, instead concentrating on social reform. One view that flowed out of this stream of Renaissance thought was that much social and religious evil resulted from ignorance. This belief provided the fuel for a great expansion of educational activity.

In the sixteenth century, the social reform impetus of northern Europe gave rise to the Reformation, a revolt against the authority of the Roman Catholic Church. Initially, the Reformation, in keeping with Renaissance traditions, emphasized individuals' rights to apply their own reason to theological issues. (In time, though, some organized Protestant groups began endorsing certain "preferred" views.) An especially important educational outcome of the Reformation was the insistence that all people be taught to read so they could apply their own intellectual powers to the holy scriptures.

Education during the Renaissance placed a heavy emphasis on the liberal arts. These tended to be defined rather narrowly as the literature and language of ancient Greece and Rome (Cordasco, 1976). As time went on, however, more attention was spent on having learners master the rudiments of the ancient languages than on encouraging them to think about implications of the ideas contained in the writings.

The Reformation resulted in a huge increase in the demand for education. Leaders argued that every effort should be made to teach as many people as possible to read the Bible. This objective envisioned an enormous increase in the numbers of people to be educated. It gave impetus to the establishment of elementary schools that would be available to all children, not just favored males (see the accompanying What the Experts Say).

## What Can Females Learn?

Today, most educated people probably would respond to this question with "Anything that males can learn!" Until recently, however, this might not have been the automatic answer. Even into our own century, some people were convinced that females were simply "unsuited" to master certain educational subjects. In some places, this view persists even today.

A group of scholars organized by L. Glenn Smith (1984) found that concerns about alleged intellectual limitations of females can be traced back for centuries. Around the year 1800, it was commonly believed that women lacked the physical stamina necessary to succeed at the study of complicated subjects, such as mathematics. Requiring females to do so, it was thought, might well result in their suffering nervous breakdowns.

Much earlier, during the late Middle Ages, the prevailing view was that women were totally inferior to men. Although this was the prevailing view, not all women subscribed to it willingly. Smith and his scholars describe a Venetian, one Christine de Pisan, who lived in the late fourteenth and early fifteenth centuries and actively contested the idea that men were superior to women. For example, she went after a famous male author who, after spending many pages suggesting that women were stupid, went on at great length to elaborate numerous stratagems a man could use to seduce virgins. Why, Christine de Pisan wondered, must such complex plans be developed to accomplish this objective if women were indeed so stupid?

Many authorities were outraged that such a question should even be asked by a woman. But Christine de Pisan won some converts, even among males—the chancellor of the University of Paris became one of her champions. Christine de Pisan's writing helped draw attention to the question of the accuracy of roles ascribed to females. Concerns about gender equity continue today. (More information about this topic is provided in Chapter 8.)

Source: L. Glenn Smith et al., "Christine de Pisan," *Lives in Education* (Ames, IA: Educational Studies Press, 1984), 88–94.

*Some Important Thinkers.*    *Erasmus* (1466–1536) of Rotterdam was the most influential Renaissance figure in terms of impact on education. He was an indefatigable scholar who roamed over much of Europe spreading his ideas. He wrote sparingly, but his works enjoyed an enormous audience for the time. His most ambitious undertaking was a Greek–Latin version of the New Testament. Another of Erasmus's works was the *Colloquies,* a textbook that transmitted serious thought along with many humorous remarks. The latter feature made the book very popular among learners. In a third work, *Liberal Education of Children,* Erasmus emphasized the importance of encouraging learners to study the classics. He also pointed out the importance of educationally related games. Additionally, Erasmus advocated the civilized treatment of learners, emphasizing their individual differences. Erasmus believed that the ultimate purpose of education was to create a "good" person.

*John Calvin* (1509–1564), an important figure in the Reformation, established a school in Geneva. Calvin's school introduced learners to some study of texts written by ancient Greek and Roman authors, but its main purpose was to provide religious training.

*Martin Luther* (1483–1546) worked hard to remove education from the control of the church. He advocated establishment of schools by governments, and is closely associated with the pervading ideas of universal education and compulsory school attendance.

*Philip Melanchthon* (1497–1560) was a leader in the effort to establish schools in parts of Germany where large numbers of people had embraced Lutheranism. His work helped to establish the principle of government support for public education. Though Melanchthon himself favored that instruction take place in Latin, eventually many government schools began to teach in the local languages.

*Legacies for the Present.*     The Renaissance and the Reformation established some patterns that continue to be reflected in American education. The focus of the early Renaissance on individual development is perfectly compatible with views of many present-day educators. For example, the beliefs of some Renaissance leaders (such as Erasmus) that individual differences are important and learners should be treated humanely continue to be endorsed.

The eventual Renaissance shift from a heavy emphasis on individualism to a narrower view regarding what is "proper" has parallels in today's educational settings. Debates continue regarding the appropriate weighting of (1) a desire to allow each person to develop in his or her own way and (2) a social need to have people commit to a limited number of core values.

The Reformation view that all should be educated spawned the idea that schooling should be compulsory. This position continues as a major theme in educational thought today (although, as shown in Box 3–3, not all people agree with the idea).

## The Seventeenth, Eighteenth, and Nineteenth Centuries

During the 1500s, some thinkers became increasingly satisfied with the view that learners should model their thinking, speaking, and writing on patterns established by key figures in ancient Greece and Rome. But the late 1500s and most of the 1600s were years of political upheaval in Europe. Frequent wars and bitter divisions suggested that the Greek idea of humanistic interpersonal relations was far from reality. In the seventeenth century, there was a move to attune education more closely to practical needs of learners.

In the eighteenth century, a tidal wave of intellectual opposition to perceived abuses of political and religious authorities spawned an interest in the development of more balanced relationships between governments and the governed. In education, this resulted in an increasing availability of education to children of the middle classes. Education was seen as a means of giving middle-class people the knowledge and skills needed to restrain the excesses of constituted authority. Government support for mass education increased throughout the nineteenth century as political influence was asserted by the middle class as well as by less economically advantaged people.

BOX 3–3

## COMPULSORY EDUCATION: AN "ERODER" OF EDUCATIONAL STANDARDS?

The following information was taken from a lengthy letter to the editor of a major metropolitan newspaper:

> Our teachers cannot do the kind of job they need to do when they have so many unmotivated, untalented students in their classes. If they are still having to teach basic reading and writing skills, how can teachers introduce the kind of sophisticated concepts that our brighter students deserve?
>
> We need to think about undesirable side effects of our policy of keeping students in school as long as possible. Some constructive weeding might result in a more productive academic garden.

*What Do You Think?*
1. What is the basic argument made by the writer?
2. What might be some consequences if the local school board took action to implement a policy consistent with this person's ideas?
3. How do you react to the writer's comments?

## The Seventeenth Century

In the seventeenth century, there was a new appreciation for education directed toward practical ends, leading to a revolt against the idea that book learning was a worthy objective in and of itself. Political unrest of the time led to a suspicion that long-trusted "authorities" had planted false knowledge. Increasingly, there was a tendency to assess the worth of learning in terms of examinations of evidence and practical utility.

Although he wrote in the sixteenth century, Nicolaus Copernicus (1473–1543) had a great influence on seventeenth century thought. Copernicus suggested that the sun, not the earth, was the center of the universe. This astonishing contention drew the wrath of traditional thinkers, especially church leaders. In time, though, observational evidence by Galileo and others confirmed its accuracy. This helped to establish the idea that truth could be challenged and modified through observation and the rational weighing of evidence.

This view that truth was not a given but could be created and supported by empirical evidence was strongly supported by the work of Francis Bacon (1561–1626). Bacon is regarded as the father of *inductive learning*—the idea that general principles can be developed after a careful study of available evidence. His work had an important influence on others who were rejecting "given" truths and demanding an education that applied thought to practical problems.

*Some Important Thinkers.*    *Richard Mulcaster* (1530–1611) served for many years as a public school headmaster in England, and had some extraordinarily modern views about education. He believed that education should be closely tied to the needs of modern living. He had the then-revolutionary idea that education should be made available to all young people and that it should be paid for with public funds. And as a great lover of the English language, he encouraged the use of English as the language of instruction in his country, instead of the customary Latin. Mulcaster also proposed that extremely able people should be recruited as teachers and that special colleges should be established to train them. In these and many of his other ideas, Mulcaster's thinking was centuries ahead of what was then reality.

*John Milton* (1608–1674) is better known as an English writer than as an educational leader. Nevertheless, his experiences as a tutor led him to volunteer some views on educational reform. Specifically, he was interested in improving schooling for upper-class youths.

Milton contended that too much time was wasted in the study of a few ancient Greek and Latin works. He advocated a much broader bill of fare. In the realm of languages, he suggested that, in addition to Greek and Latin, students learn Hebrew, Chaldean, Syriac, and, time permitting, Italian. He proposed that other subjects be studied along with these languages.

To accompany this heavy academic load, Milton recommended a healthy dose of physical training. He was especially enamored of riding horses and wrestling. To soothe the spirits after rigorous physical and mental exercise, Milton prescribed quiet listening to organ music.

*John Locke* (1632–1704), an English philosopher, greatly influenced both education and politics. His educational views were directed at improvement of schooling for children of the upper classes. Locke contended that there are no ideas that are innate—a person comes into the world with his or her mind a *tabula rasa,* a blank slate. For Locke, the only source of knowledge was human experience as perceived through the senses.

Locke stressed the importance of physical education and good hygiene, noting the connection between robust health and proper development of the mind. He also believed that school subjects should be oriented around "useful information." This implied a need for a sound foundation in the learner's native language, including the development of good reading, writing, and speaking skills.

Perhaps the most lasting legacy of seventeenth-century educational thought comes to us from the work of *John Amos Comenius* (1592–1670). Comenius, a Moravian (Moravia is part of today's Czechoslovakia), argued that if the purpose of education was to prepare people for happiness, then it should logically be extended to all people. He proposed a compulsory system of education that called for at least six years of formal schooling for everyone. He argued for a school that would encourage children to observe the world and learn through the senses. Comenius was a strong advocate of the concept of learning by doing. The school was to be a pleasant place that featured pictures on the walls inside and a recreational space outside. Children were to be treated humanely.

Comenius proposed a sequential educational system. The first six years of a child's life were to be spent at home, which he referred to as the *Mother School.* The second six years, required of all, would occur in the *Vernacular School,* where instruction was to be provided in the native language. The Vernacular School was to be the only formal school attended by most young people. A few bright students would go on to the *Latin School.* Talented graduates of the Latin School would continue their training at the university level.

*Legacies for the Present.*    Concerns of many leading seventeenth-century reformers centered around the question of whether education should be directed toward purely intellectual ends or toward more practical ends. This question is still being debated.

The view that education ought to be available to a high percentage of the population was widely promoted by seventeenth-century educational thinkers. Though this reform was not implemented widely at the time, today it has become a fundamental commitment of educators everywhere. The same can be said of the position that governments have an obligation to pay for schooling. This idea also can be traced to the beliefs of many seventeenth-century educational thinkers.

Comenius's notion of a system of interrelated schools has been widely implemented. Mulcaster's arguments for special training of teachers provided part of the intellectual base that led to the establishment of institutions that, over time, grew into today's schools and colleges of education.

## The Eighteenth Century

During the eighteenth century, national governments grew stronger. There were attempts to install national systems of education. In part, these enterprises were directed at producing citizens who were capable of playing leadership roles in government and managing economic enterprises of various kinds. The century produced a number of notable educational thinkers. Some of them were very much out of the mainstream of eighteenth century thought, and their influences were reflected in educational practices that often did not become common until many years after their deaths.

*Some Important Thinkers.*    Perhaps the century's leading educational theorist was the Swiss–French philosopher, *Jean Jacques Rousseau* (1712–1778). Rousseau's best-known educational treatise is his book *Emile,* which focuses on the education of a young man, named Emile, from birth to early adulthood. Rousseau wished to demonstrate how, under perfect conditions, a person might be educated to an ideal state.

Rousseau believed that at birth people were basically good. It was only after exposure to corrupting influences of the world that they might become bad. Rousseau's position was contrary to the prevailing view that people were naturally bad and that an important function of education was the suppression of these innate evil tendencies. Rousseau's work suggested that there was no need for harsh and prescriptive educational programs; instead, he believed, educators should allow learners' basically good natural tendencies to unfold.

*Johann Heinrich Pestalozzi* (1746–1827) was a Swiss educational reformer. He discussed many of his educational theories in his book *How Gertrude Teaches Her Children,* published in 1802. Like Rousseau, Pestalozzi believed that education should serve the naturally developing nature of the individual child. In Pestalozzi's view, how-

The 19th century Swiss–French philosopher Jean Jacques Rousseau believed people were born good and kind without need or impulse to hurt, but that living together in society corrupts people by bringing out their aggression and selfishness. He believed educators should strive to help young people develop their natural goodness.

ever, education had the purpose not only of developing each person but also of improving society.

Pestalozzi was a strong believer in learning through the senses. His learners were encouraged to begin by observing isolated phenomena and then gradually work themselves to the point of developing exploratory generalizations.

Pestalozzi hoped to replicate the warm, caring atmosphere of the home in school classrooms. His schools and methods were greatly admired. Many aspiring teachers from Europe and elsewhere visited his schools to study and copy his methods.

*Legacies for the Present.*    The heavy emphasis of eighteenth-century educational reformers on learning through the senses still pervades the field of education. The modern view that each learner is unique and has special strengths to be developed by the schools is compatible with the thought of Rousseau, and the idea that schools and education can cure social problems, an idea strongly promoted by Pestalozzi, is with us still. Also, today's teachers endorse the use of visual supplements to prose materials and the development of lessons to sharpen learners' observational powers. Both of these ideas had support among some important eighteenth-century educational thinkers. This chapter's Case Study discusses some of these eighteenth-century beliefs.

CASE STUDY

## *The Wild Boy of Southern France**

**In 1797, some farmers in southern France reported to the authorities that they had spotted a naked boy hurrying through the woods.** In time, authorities caught the boy. Newspaper readers were astounded to learn that he went about on all fours, made grunting sounds, and liked to sway from side to side like a nervous animal. He was thought to be about 12 years old.

The boy was taken in by Dr. Jean-Marc-Gaspard Itard. Among other things, Dr. Itard wanted to find out whether a person who had lacked the sensory stimulation that comes from contact with other human beings could learn. Dr. Itard worked with the boy for four years, and he kept a diary in which he recorded his observations. He developed an imaginative instructional program that was designed to develop the boy's social and oral-language skills.

The boy never progressed as far as Dr. Itard had hoped. He did learn how to identify a few words and phrases, but he never learned to speak. However, the significance of Dr. Itard's work is not so much in the relative success of his experiment but that he undertook it at all. His work challenged a prevailing myth that a totally ignorant person simply could not learn. Itard refused to take the myth as gospel and was willing to suspend judgment while he gathered and studied evidence.

Although it was limited, the progress the boy made suggested that even people with severe disabilities can learn. Dr. Itard's efforts hinted at the wisdom of providing learning experiences for people who are physically or mentally disabled. Previously, such people had been assumed to be incapable of profiting from any kind of formal instruction.

*Do society's expectations regarding what kinds of people can learn continue to influence the kinds of instructional programs made available to certain people? If so, can you cite some examples? Are prior experiences of today's learners ever a barrier to their continued learning? Dr. Itard's work raises questions about the relative impact on learning of (1) innate ability, (2) the nature of the learner's home and family environment, and (3) the nature of instructional experiences provided to the learner. In your view, what is the relative importance of each of these three variables?*

*For additional information about this case, see L. Glenn Smith et al., *Lives in Education* (Ames, IA: Educational Studies Press, 1984), 170–171.

## The Nineteenth Century

The industrial revolution, with its roots in the eighteenth century, became an explosive force in the nineteenth century. Revolutions and reforms in the 1830s resulted in a tremendous expansion in the power of the middle class. Subsequent revolutions in 1848 greatly expanded the political influence of working-class people. A basic theme in nineteenth-century Europe was the increasing democratization of political life.

The trend toward extending political power to an ever-larger portion of the population influenced education. During this century, the principle of government support of at least some education for all children became widespread.

*Some Important Thinkers.*    During the nineteenth century, there was great interest in the psychology of learning. *Johann Friedrich Herbart* (1776–1841), a German, developed a theory of learning known as *apperception.* According to Herbart's theory, learning occurred when ideas already in the brain came into contact with new information. Herbart believed that if there was some consistency between what was already in the brain and new information, the probability was high that the new information would be absorbed. When this occurred, the new information would be added to the brain's store of knowledge.

Herbart's theory clearly suggested the need for teachers to provide learners with new information that had some logical relationship to what they had learned previously. His theory provided an impetus for the idea of examining, or diagnosing, learners to find out what they already knew before exposing them to new information. Since different learners knew different things, the idea of diagnosis led naturally to the view that instruction should be individualized.

Herbart proposed a five-part plan for teaching that included these steps:

- preparation
- presentation
- association (tying new information to old)
- generalization (encouraging learners to state broad explanatory principles in their own words)
- application

These five steps became parts of lesson plans that were provided to people who were beginning to teach. These steps, sometimes under different names, continue to be found in many lesson plans today.

Another German, *Friedrich Froebel* (1782–1852), is best remembered as the "father of the kindergarten." He emphasized the importance of creativity, motor-skill development, group participation, and individual expression. Froebel's kindergarten also provided experiences designed to improve young learners' observational and conceptual powers. None of this was done in a heavy-handed manner; Froebel believed that the kindergarten should be a joyous experience for learners that included music, pleasant physical activities, and work with fascinating objects.

*Legacies for the Present.*    In the nineteenth century, there was a movement to make elementary-level schooling mandatory for all children and to provide government support for schools. The tradition of free, government-supported schools for all learners continues. The trend has been extended in the twentieth century to include government support for free secondary-level education as well.

The interest in the psychology of learning that began in earnest in the nineteenth century accelerated in the twentieth. Today a broad base of learning theory and research supports educational practice. This body of knowledge owes its existence, in

Friedrich Froebel is remembered as the "father of the kindergarten." This early kindergarten is an example of many that were established as a result of his work.

part, to the nineteenth-century recognition that an issue such as how people learn was worthy of serious study.

The thousands of kindergartens in existence today are monuments to the work of Froebel. In a broader sense, educational leaders of the nineteenth century encouraged practical responses to concerns of early educational thinkers that learners have a variety of needs. Kindergartens, schools for learners interested in pursuing careers in industrial trades, and other special-purpose institutions began to appear in the nineteenth century. Present-day American "magnet schools," which feature emphases on specific subjects, illustrate a continuing educational interest in serving learners' diverse needs and interests.

Information presented about all of these important historical roots represents only a selection of a few highlights from many centuries of educational histories. In considering periods of time as long as centuries, it is important to remember that, as in our own time, not all people were in agreement about either education's ends or its means. This point must be borne in mind as you review the summary chart presented in Table 3–1. For example, though some Romans, Quintilian among them, believed in treating learners humanely, certainly others were just as committed to the idea that harsh punishment and learning went hand in hand. Frequently, people who initiated new educational ideas were far out of the educational mainstreams of their own time. Often it fell to later generations to appreciate the merit of arguments that were little prized by contemporaries of the educational thinkers who created them.

## Key Ideas in Summary

- Early educational systems developed among the ancient Sumerians, Egyptians, and Hebrews. Among legacies of these early educational efforts are the ideas that learning should progress from the simple to the complex, discipline is closely associated with learning, and memory work is important.

- Two quite different education systems developed in the ancient Greek city-states of Athens and Sparta. The Athenians attempted to teach their young people to become citizen decision makers. The Spartans tried to eliminate individualistic tendencies and train young people to obey military leaders without questioning authority. Physical education was important in both Athens and Sparta.

- Roman education placed importance on the development of reading, writing, and speaking skills. There was an emphasis on the practical as opposed to the purely theoretical side of education. Though most Roman educators felt that discipline should be harsh, some thinkers, notably Quintilian, made a case for treating learners sensitively and humanely. There was an intent in Roman education to prepare learners for responsible citizenship.

- During the Middle Ages, most responsibility for education of Europeans was assumed by the Roman Catholic Church, although few people were lucky enough to receive any education at all. Such schooling as did take place occurred in cathedrals, monasteries, and universities. (Universities first appeared during this period.) The curriculum consisted of some, and in a few cases all seven, of the liberal arts. Learners were taught to read Latin and, sometimes, Greek.

- The early Renaissance placed a heavy emphasis on the development of the individual. This focus continues to be evidenced in American education today. Subsequently, many Reformation leaders placed a high priority on a literate public who could read the Bible. This view resulted in support for compulsory education that would be made available to an increasingly broad spectrum of the population.

**TABLE 3–1**
Summary Table: International Roots

| Feature | Earliest Source(s) |
|---|---|
| Simple-to-complex organization of lessons | Ancient Sumerians |
| Emphasis on memory and drill as aids to learning | Ancient Sumerians, Hebrews, Egyptians |
| Emphasis on physical education | Ancient Greeks |
| Education for individual development | Ancient Greeks; Renaissance; Reformation; seventeenth, eighteenth, nineteenth centuries |
| Emphasis on education for citizenship | Ancient Greeks |
| Emphasis on systematic learning, concept learning, classification of knowledge | Ancient Greeks |
| Emphasis on practical rather than theoretical content | Ancient Romans |
| Treating learners humanely | Ancient Romans |
| Emphasis on humanities | Ancient Romans |
| Establishment of tradition of parochial schools | Middle Ages |
| Identification of the seven liberal arts | Middle Ages |
| Beginnings of ideas of compulsory education | Renaissance and Reformation |
| View that governments should pay for education | Seventeenth century |
| Idea of interlocking system of elementary, secondary, and higher education | Seventeenth century |
| View that a high percentage of the total population should be educated | Seventeenth century |
| Importance of learning through the senses | Eighteenth century |
| Importance of visual aids to learning | Eighteenth century |
| Kindergartens | Nineteenth century |
| Interest in the psychology of learning as a serious area of study | Nineteenth century |

- In the seventeenth century, many educational thinkers promoted the view that education should be directed toward practical ends. Increasingly, scholars believed that "truth" could be established through rational consideration of evidence.

- As national governments grew stronger during the eighteenth century, there were attempts to establish national systems of education. The view that much learning occurs through utilization of all of the senses was promoted by a number of eighteenth-century thinkers. Additionally, the importance of individual differences increasingly came to be appreciated during this century.

- During the nineteenth century, elementary education became mandatory in many places. Increasingly it was expected that governments would pay for this education. Later, governments came to be expected to support secondary education as well. Kindergartens developed in the nineteenth century, and many specialty schools, particularly those focusing on vocational preparation, came into existence.

- Many of today's educational practices are not new. They are contemporary reflections of responses to educational issues that, in some cases, have been debated for centuries.

## Review and Discussion Questions

1. Why do you think the Sumerians found it necessary to establish schools? Couldn't parents simply have taught their learners at home?

2. What problems do you think might have faced a young person from Sparta who was educated according to the scheme followed in Athens instead of the one typically followed in Sparta? Do you think schools today must be concerned about the "fit" of their programs to the expectations of society?

3. What are some features of present-day American education that are consistent with what was either practiced in ancient Rome or recommended by certain thinkers from ancient Rome?

4. What are some conflicts between educational views of the Middle Ages and those of the Renaissance?

5. An important view of many thinkers in northern Europe during the Renaissance was that important social problems could be solved through education. To what extent is solving social problems still considered to be a responsibility of the school? Can you cite examples to support your case?

6. Many Reformation-era leaders favored programs that would greatly increase the numbers of people who could read. What kinds of arguments do you suppose might have been made by people who opposed this idea?

7. What are some present-day educational practices that are consistent with the ideas of seventeenth-century educational thinker John Amos Comenius?

8. The eighteenth-century philosopher Jean Jacques Rousseau believed that people were naturally good. Do present school practices operate on the assumption that people are basically good or on the assumption that they are basically bad?

9. Several nineteenth-century educational developments are still reflected in American schools. Which of these developments do you regard as most important, and why?

10. There is little question that many present-day school practices trace their roots to innovations and perspectives developed centuries ago. Do these traditions inhibit the ability of our schools to respond to changing conditions? Why or why not?

. . . . . . . . . . . . . . . . . . . . . . . . . . . . . . .

# Ideas for Field Experiences, Projects, and Enrichment

1. The ancient Sumerians were a fascinating people. With their commitment to meticulous recordkeeping, they probably would have eagerly embraced computers had they been available at the time. Do some background reading on Sumerian education and prepare a brief oral report for the class, focusing on the kinds of things that a young Sumerian would have been expected to learn. Are there any similarities between the Sumerian curriculum and the curricula in our schools today?

2. Throughout the history of education there have been bitter debates between people who have suggested that schools should help individuals develop beliefs of their own and people who have suggested that schools should try to make all learners commit to certain values held by the larger society. What do you see as the appropriate balance between education for individual development and education to promote shared social values? Organize your thoughts in the form of a position paper, and present it to your course instructor for review.

3. In the Middle Ages, many people in charge of teaching the young felt that certain kinds of information had to be kept secret. For example, information about the "pagan" religious practices of the ancient Greeks and Romans was considered particularly dangerous. Do we face any similar situations in education today? Together with several other people from your class, organize a symposium on the topic, "What Learners Should *Not* Learn in School."

4. Today, many states have regulations requiring the kinds of subjects that learners must study. In some places, high school graduation requirements are quite

rigid. Ask your course instructor to help you identify some regulations in your state that specify what learners must study. Then, do some additional reading about the views of Jean Jacques Rousseau. Make an oral presentation to the class in which you, while role playing Rousseau, comment on the worth or desirability of those state regulations that apply to all learners.

5. Many lingering influences from seventeenth-, eighteenth-, and nineteenth-century schools remain in our schools today. As you look ahead to schools in the first quarter of the twenty-first century, which of these influences will weaken? Which will stay about the same? Which will grow stronger? Prepare a chart that summarizes your speculations, and then share it with your class as you briefly summarize your position.

## Supplementary Reading

Bonner, S. F. *Education in Ancient Rome.* London: Methuen, 1977.
Butler, H. E., trans. *Quintilian as Educator.* New York: Twayne Publishers, 1974.
Meyer, A. E. *Grandmasters of Educational Thought.* New York: McGraw-Hill, 1975.
Rothman, E. P. *Foundations of Education.* New York: McGraw-Hill, 1989.
Shapiro, M. S. *Child's Garden: The Kindergarten Movement from Froebel to Dewey.* University Park, PA: Pennsylvania State University Press, 1983.
Silber, K. *Pestalozzi: The Man and His Work.* New York: Schocken Books, 1973.
Smith, G. L., et al. *Lives in Education.* Ames, IA: Educational Studies Press, 1984.

## References

Butts, R. F. *A Cultural History of Western Education.* 2nd ed. New York: McGraw-Hill, 1955.
Cordasco, F. *A Brief History of Education.* Totowa, NJ: Littlefield, Adams, and Company, 1976.
Meyer, A. E. *An Educational History of the Western World.* New York: McGraw-Hill, 1965.
Smith, G. L., et al. *Lives in Education.* Ames, IA: Educational Studies Press, 1984.
Wilds, E. H., and K. V. Lottich. *The Foundations of Modern Education.* 3rd ed. New York: Holt, Rinehart and Winston, 1964.

# Chapter 4

# History of American Education

## Objectives

This chapter provides information to help the reader to

- identify several patterns of education as they developed in the New England colonies, the middle colonies, and the southern colonies.
- point out several weaknesses of the Boston Latin Grammar School and the Franklin Academy.
- summarize nineteenth-century developments that contributed to shaping the nature of present-day American education.
- identify the basic principles that helped establish a rationale for the comprehensive high school.
- describe several of Horace Mann's contributions to American education.
- point out examples of John Dewey's influence on American education.

## Focus Questions

1. What are some contributions of the New England Puritans to present-day American education?
2. During the middle and late 1700s, why was there an expansion of interest in extending secondary education to a larger proportion of the population?
3. Why did the high school overtake the academy as the most common type of American secondary school?
4. Why is Horace Mann regarded as such an important figure in the development of American education?
5. What are some developments in the evolution of American education that occurred in the years between the Civil War and the end of the nineteenth century?
6. What arguments were made regarding the most important function of American secondary schools, and how did the comprehensive school seek to reconcile differences of contending parties?
7. What were some of John Dewey's beliefs regarding the kinds of learning that should be emphasized in schools?
8. Why are some critics concerned about the use of IQ scores by public school educators?
9. What was the impact on public school programs of the Soviet launch of *Sputnik*, and for how long did programs introduced in response to this event continue to enjoy widespread support?
10. Why have some critics of junior high schools felt that these institutions fail to serve needs of 11- to 14-year-olds as well as middle schools do?

11. What are some criticisms of American public education that have been made since the early 1980s?

..............................

# Introduction

A study of the history of American education reveals that at different times people have had vastly different expectations of what educators should emphasize. Varying expectations have led to quite different views regarding characteristics of a "good" school.

Differing patterns of educational development over time have resulted in many answers to these key questions:

- What is the most important purpose of education?
- Who is to be educated?
- What are learners expected to take away from their educational experiences?
- How are learners to be educated?

In the sections that follow, think about how these questions might have been addressed at different periods in our history. An understanding of changing perspectives on these issues can provide a foundation for understanding positions in today's debates about educational policies and practices.

## Colonial Period to 1800
## The New England Colonies

Some familiarity with conditions in sixteenth- and seventeenth-century England is helpful in understanding the nature of American education as it developed in New England during the colonial period. In England, at that time, there was little room for open discussion of alternatives to the established church, the Church of England. Because it was the official church of the English government, people who espoused religious views in opposition to those of the Church of England were viewed by governmental officials as disloyal not only to the church, but also to the state. In effect, the Church of England was viewed as an extension of the legal authority of the government. Consequently, religious dissidents were dealt with harshly. The official view was that such people might represent a subversive threat to the power of the crown.

*Views of the Puritans.*   Political problems in England for groups such as the Puritans, who wanted to reform policies of the Church of England, led them to develop an interest in emigrating to the New World. Equally important was their fear of remaining in England and exposing their children to what they considered to be the religious errors of the Church of England. The intransigent Puritans had definite ideas about what religious beliefs and practices should be, and by no means were a tolerant people. (Witness, for example, their persecution of the nonconforming Roger Williams.) Once they left England, those Puritans who settled in New England sought to establish a church and government different from those in England. Their belief that their own church and government were more consistent with the Bible's teachings had important educational implications.

The Puritans saw the Bible as the source of all wisdom. As a result, they placed a high priority on developing an educational system that would enable large numbers of people to read "God's Holy Word." The Bible, as the Puritans interpreted it, outlined a specific type of preferred government for both church and state. This contrasted importantly with practices in England, where authority in the Church of England was highly centralized and few decisions were left to the discretion of members of individual churches. The Puritans, however, believed that the Bible promoted a different organizational structure. In their view, power should be exercised by local church congregations, and the Puritans' churches in Massachusetts reflected this pattern. Such beliefs also helped establish the more general principle of local control over civil as well as religious affairs. It was out of this context that the tradition of local control of education evolved.

*New England School Legislation.*    Concern for education in Massachusetts was demonstrated early in our history, in the Massachusetts School Law of 1642. This law charged local magistrates with the responsibility of ensuring that parents would not neglect the education of their children. Although the law itself did not provide for the establishment of schools, it did require that children attend schools. It represented the first attempt in America to make school attendance compulsory. Reflecting the local-control tradition, this law placed responsibility for enforcement at the local rather than the state level.

The law of 1642 was extended by the famous "Old Deluder Satan Act" of 1647. The name was derived from wording in the act that promoted education as a buffer against Satan's wiles. The law required every town of 50 or more families to hire a teacher of reading or writing. The teacher was to be paid by either the community or parents of the learners. This act represented an early legislative attempt to establish the principle of public responsibility for education.

During the seventeenth century, concern for publicly supported education referred only to the very basic education of young children; few learners attended secondary schools. However, small numbers of secondary schools did come into being during the seventeenth century. One of the most famous of them was the Boston Latin Grammar School, founded in 1635. This school had a specific purpose: preparation of boys for Harvard. The curriculum consisted of difficult academic subjects including Latin, Greek, and theology (see Box 4–1).

## The Middle Colonies

Most Puritan settlers of New England came from an area in eastern England known as *East Anglia.* It was in this part of the country that opposition to the Church of England was strongest. Many of these Puritan settlers came to the New World during the period 1629-1641 (Fischer, 1989).

People who settled the middle colonies of New York, New Jersey, Delaware, and Pennsylvania came from different places than the Puritans and were also a more diverse group. Some of these settlers were descendants of the Dutch and Swedes who

BOX 4–1
## EARLY SCHOOLS: SOME "WHAT IF" QUESTIONS

The Boston Latin Grammar School was established to teach traditional classical subjects to sons of well-to-do families. Latin, Greek, and theological studies were emphasized. No attention was paid to subjects of a more practical nature, as they were not seen as necessary for an "educated" person. Suppose that when American education became free and public, the model the schools followed had been the Boston Latin Grammar School.

*What Do You Think?*
1. What kinds of courses would you expect to find in high schools today?
2. How would learners in these schools react to their curriculum?
3. What differences in entertainment (perhaps in television and films) would you expect in a society educated in a school system that reflected the values of the Boston Latin Grammar School?
4. How would you feel personally about a public school system consistent with the Boston Latin Grammar School?
5. Have we emphasized practical and vocational education too much in this country? Why or why not?

• • • • • • • • • • • • • • • • • • • • • • • • • • • • • • • • • • • • • • • • • • • • • • • • • • • • • • • • • •

originally occupied parts of New York. Many English Quakers came during the 50 years between 1675 and 1725, and a majority of them settled in Pennsylvania. These immigrants came mostly from the north Midlands of England and Wales, an area completely different from the East Anglia homeland of many of the Puritans. Western and frontier areas of the middle colonies were largely settled by people originally from the north of England, Scotland, and Ireland, during a period extending approximately from 1717 to 1775 (Fischer, 1989).

Not surprisingly, given the mixed origins of the population, patterns of schooling in the middle colonies were varied. For example, merchants in New York sponsored private schools that emphasized commercial subjects thought necessary for young people who would play future roles in business and trade. In contrast, the Pennsylvania Quakers maintained schools that were open to all children. These Quaker schools were notable for their willingness to recognize the educational needs and rights of African-Americans, Native Americans, and other groups that usually were not encouraged (and often, not allowed) to go to school.

*The Franklin Academy.*    Benjamin Franklin was among the first to give American education a practical orientation. In his 1749 work *Proposals Relating to the Youth of Pennsylvania,* Franklin proposed a new kind of school, oriented to the "real" world, that would be free of all religious ties. Two years later, he established the Franklin Academy, an institution that was nonsectarian and offered such practical subjects as mathematics, astronomy, navigation, and bookkeeping. By the end of the Revolutionary War, the Franklin Academy had replaced the Boston Latin Grammar School as the most important secondary school in America. Students at the Franklin Academy were able to make some choices about their course of study, thus setting the pattern of elective courses common in high schools today.

For all its strengths, relatively few learners attended the Franklin Academy. It was a private school, and tuition was beyond the means of most families. But the establishment of the Franklin Academy directed a great deal of attention to the importance of secondary education. This interest was reflected in the subsequent establishment of many other private academies.

*Contributions of the Academies.*    The private academies popularized the idea that secondary education had something important to offer, and they laid the foundation for public support of secondary schools. Collectively, the academies helped establish these important precedents for American education:

- American education would have a strong orientation toward the practical rather than the purely intellectual or theoretical.
- American education would be nonsectarian.
- American education would feature diverse course offerings.

## The Southern Colonies

A revolution in England in the late 1640s resulted in victory for the side supporting Parliament and the Puritans against the King and the established Church of England. King Charles I was executed and for a dozen years England existed as a Puritan-controlled commonwealth, governed for much of this time by Oliver Cromwell as Lord Protector. This was an especially dangerous period for large land owners, members of the nobility, and others who had supported King Charles and wanted the monarchy restored (something that was finally achieved in 1660 when Charles II assumed the throne). Because of dangers in England, many supporters of the King's cause migrated to the New World, often settling in the southern colonies of Maryland, Virginia, North Carolina, South Carolina, and Georgia. Large numbers of these settlers came from the southeastern part of England, an area different from both the East Anglian homeland of the Puritans and the north Midland, north English, Scottish, and Irish homelands of most of those who settled the middle colonies (Fischer, 1989).

Settlement in the southern colonies was distributed along rivers. There were few towns, and families tended to be separated by considerable distances. Under these conditions, it was difficult to gather sufficient numbers of children in one place to establish schools. Wealthy families hired tutors for their children. People in these colonies continued to identify very strongly with upper-class English values, and they often sent their sons to England to be educated in English schools. Education in these colonies was generally restricted to children of wealthy landowners; little schooling was available for those from less affluent families.

## Education From 1800 to the Civil War

During the first 20 years of the nineteenth century, few educational innovations were introduced. American society was consumed with challenges such as settling the nation and providing workers for the nation's growing industries. There was more interest in getting young people into the work force than in providing them with opportunities for extensive education. Schooling beyond rudimentary elementary instruction was generally available only to children of families who were able to pay for this privilege and who did not need the income that a young person could generate. Proposals for an education system that was universal and free were only just beginning to be discussed. (See the accompanying Case Study for a discussion of one radical approach to life that did emerge during this period—in the Fruitlands experiment.)

------

CASE STUDY

## *Bronson Alcott's Fruitlands*

**Amos Bronson Alcott, the distinguished American philosopher, educator, and writer, lived from 1799 to 1888.** Alcott had many intellectual enthusiasms. Among them was his admiration of the Greek philosopher Pythagoras, who placed high stock on the importance of personal purity and simplicity as necessary prerequisites of worthy living. Alcott was very interested in helping people become "better." He was convinced that reform of social evils (slavery, for example) could not occur unless individual human beings were uplifted to higher moral levels.

In 1844, Alcott secured modest financial backing and, with an intellectual comrade, Charles Lane, purchased a farm in rural Massachusetts. He proposed to establish an environment that would embody principles of living to nurture the spiritual and moral uplifting of residents. Alcott and Lane called their community "Fruitlands," in recognition that fruit would be the primary food staple of the community. Alcott had hoped that many people would be attracted to live there, but at its height, no more than 14 people were in residence (including children). This lot included an interesting cast of eccentrics, among them a barrelmaker who was a sometime inmate of an insane asylum and who insisted on being called "Wood Abraham." Also in residence was Sam Bower, a former member of an English nudist group. And especially memorable was Samuel Larned, a veteran of other experimental communities, who had earlier distinguished himself by living for a year entirely on crackers and then for a second year entirely on apples.

The Fruitlanders were convinced that human slavery existed largely because of people's insensitivity to other, less obvious forms of slavery. They went so far as to suggest that farm animals were the unwitting servants of their masters. Though the Fruitlanders did initially bring in a horse to assist with plowing, they soon abandoned this deviation from their principles and took to using hand spades to cultivate their garden areas.

Even the source of fabric for clothing was considered in light of its relationship to slavery. Cotton was rejected as a textile on the basis that it existed only because of slave labor in the cotton fields. Wool, of course, came from human enslavement of sheep, and also was rejected as a material to cloak a Fruitlander. After lengthy deliberations, it was decided that only linen clothing would be worn. Shoes presented an even bigger problem, and the Fruitlanders did some experimenting with canvas. The evidence is unclear on this point, but suspicions are that the Fruitlanders eventually bent their principles and continued to wear leather shoes, even though they resulted from the "murder" of captive cattle.

The foods of the Fruitlanders were simple. Tea, coffee, molasses, and rice were proscribed because they were believed to be produced by slave labor, and milk was forbidden as a product that was available to human beings only from enslaved cows. Hence water was the Fruitlanders' only beverage. For food, the Fruitlanders grew basic crops such as potatoes, corn, and beans. Their diet featured these simple foods accompanied by plain bread.

Bathing outdoors with cold water was also part of the regimen at Fruitlands. This practice was simply part of a prescription for living that featured simple dress, lodging, and food. The organizers of the Fruitlands experiment believed that a combination of hard work and an unpretentious lifestyle would bring the intellectual, physical, and emotional aspects of the human being into harmony. This would result in a better person, and a community of better persons would lead to a better world.

For a variety of reasons, the Fruitlands experiment failed. The community ceased to exist in January 1845, about seven months after it had begun. Part of the problem was that Bronson Alcott and Charles Lane spent a great deal of time away from Fruitlands, talking to outsiders rather than personally engaging in the hard physical work on the farm. Their frequent absences placed an overwhelming burden of work on the others in the community, particularly on Bronson Alcott's wife. Certainly, too, many outsiders found the prospect of affiliating with a group that advocated outside cold-water bathing, handwork with spade and shovel, and a diet of plain food washed down only with water to be less than alluring. New members simply did not materialize.

*Fruitlands had been established by individuals strongly committed to the view that the environment is all-important in shaping the individual. Is this view still held today? Can you cite some examples? Do we have any schools today that have been set up to shield learners from the "evils" of the world? How would you assess the success of such efforts? Would people today be more inclined to move to Fruitlands than they were in the 1840s? Why or why not?*

## The Birth of the High School

In the early nineteenth century, only a few students attended secondary schools. The most popular secondary school continued to be the academy, which responded well to an American educational bias in favor of preparing learners for practical problem solving and work rather than for a life of scholarship. Many new academies came into being during the first half of the nineteenth century. By 1850, when the number of academies reached its peak, over six thousand were in operation (Barry, 1961).

Although the academies were highly regarded, they had an important drawback—overwhelmingly, they were private, tuition-charging institutions. This limited their learner population, as only young people from families that were relatively well off could attend. Gradually, people became convinced that larger numbers of young people than were being accommodated by the private academies could profit from secondary-level education. This recognition led to support for a new institution, the public high school.

The first public high school, the Boston English Classical School, was established in 1821. The school's courses closely paralleled the practical curriculum of most academies. But the idea of public high schools did not catch on quickly; in 1860, there were only 40 in the entire country (Barry, 1961). It was not until 1900 that the number of public high schools surpassed the number of academies that had existed in 1850 (Barry, 1961).

## The Contributions of Horace Mann

During the 1820s, Horace Mann began to make his views known. Mann, elected to the Massachusetts legislature in 1827, was an eloquent speaker who took up the cause of the "common school," one for the average American. Mann's mission was to convince taxpayers that it was in their own interest to support the establishment of a system of public education. He pointed out that public schools would turn out educated young people whose skills would ultimately result in improved living standards for all. In Mann's view, the school was a springboard for opportunity. It was an institution capable of equalizing differences among people from different social classes.

Horace Mann helped convince American taxpayers that it was in their best interests to support public schools.

Mann's arguments were persuasive. In 1837, Massachusetts established a State Board of Education. Horace Mann gave up his career in politics to become its first secretary. In time, Mann's views attracted attention of people throughout the entire country.

In addition to his interest in encouraging people to get behind the idea of publicly supported schools, Mann also recognized the importance of improving teachers' qualifications. In response to this concern, the nation's first normal school (an institution specifically designed to train people to teach) was established in 1839. In the beginning, these normal schools provided only one or two years of formal education for those wishing to become teachers. Their importance was in the precedent they set for formalizing the education of future teachers. (See the accompanying What the Experts Say for a discussion of the related issue of teacher certification.) Many of today's institutions that offer undergraduate and graduate study in a variety of disciplines began life as normal schools.

---

WHAT THE EXPERTS SAY

## Certifying teachers: An innovation that was slow to take root

Horace Mann was a strong believer in normal schools, institutions specifically designed to prepare people to teach in public schools. The first one was established in 1839. Though many people supported the logic of providing special training for teachers and certifying them before they were allowed to work, these innovations were very slow to be adopted. Stringent certification requirements did not become really universal until the 1930s and 1940s.

Educational historian James Bowen (1981) notes that all the states had normal schools by the year 1900, but few required their teachers to be graduates of these institutions. The state with the strictest regulations regarding teachers' entry into the profession was Massachusetts, which required teachers to have a high school diploma and two years of formal teacher training. Every other state had less stringent requirements.

Even as late as 1921, only four states required prospective teachers to have completed formal training programs. In that year, there were 14 states where people could qualify for a teaching credential with no more training than four years of high school, and some of these 14 states required teachers to have only an eighth grade education. In fact, in 1921 there were 31 states with *no* official academic requirements for awarding a teaching credential (Bowen, 1981, p. 433).

---

Prompted by Mann's work, public schools began to be established throughout the country. By 1860, 50.6 percent of the nation's children were enrolled in public school programs (U.S. Department of Commerce, *Historical Statistics of the United States*, 1975, p. 370). A majority of states had formalized the development of free school systems, including elementary schools, secondary schools, and public universities. In 1867, a National Department of Education was established as part of the federal government. By the late 1860s, many of the basic patterns of American education were in place. That these patterns continue is a tribute to the vision, patience, and political skills of Horace Mann.

## Education from the Civil War to 1900

The post-Civil War years were characterized by unparalleled industrial growth. Technological innovations reduced the need for unskilled labor. The resulting demand for workers who had knowledge that was of value in the workplace intensified interest in the vocational-preparation function of education.

## Serving Immigrants and Financing Secondary Schools

Huge numbers of immigrants entered the United States during this period. These people needed both useful work skills and an orientation to the values of their new country. These needs placed new demands on educators, and there was a great increase in the number of schools. The schools these young people attended were eager to "Americanize" newcomers, and many immigrant learners were exposed to school programs that made light or even fun of their native cultures and languages. There can be no doubt that American public schools exacted a psychological toll on many of the immigrant children who came into the country during this period.

In the realm of school financing, the famous Kalamazoo case (*Stuart* v. *School District No. 1 of the Village of Kalamazoo*, 30 Mich. 69 [1874]) resulted in a ruling that the state legislature had the right to pass laws levying taxes for the support of *both* elementary and secondary schools. This established a legal precedent for public funding of secondary schools. As a result, there was a dramatic increase in the total number of schools and in the total number of learners who were enrolled, as districts began to build large numbers of secondary schools. Because of a widespread desire to provide older learners with "useful" educational experiences, many secondary schools broadened their curricula to include more practical, work-related subjects.

## Influences of Professional Organizations

Organizational activity among teachers increased during this period. Prior to 1900, organizations that were the forerunners of today's American Federation of Teachers and National Education Association were established (see Chapter 10 for some more detailed information). Reports of such groups as the NEA's Committee of Ten and the Committee on College Entrance Requirements began to influence public school curricula. In the last decade of the nineteenth century, these groups, while acknowledging that schools should provide some services to learners with varied academic and career goals, nevertheless suggested that preparation for college and university study was the primary purpose of high schools. This orientation represented a temporary reversal of a century-long trend to view secondary education as a provider of more practical kinds of learning experiences.

## Twentieth-century Education to World War II

During the first two decades of the twentieth century, the conflict between those who viewed the high school as an institution to serve college-bound learners and those who viewed it as an institution to prepare young people for the workplace was resolved

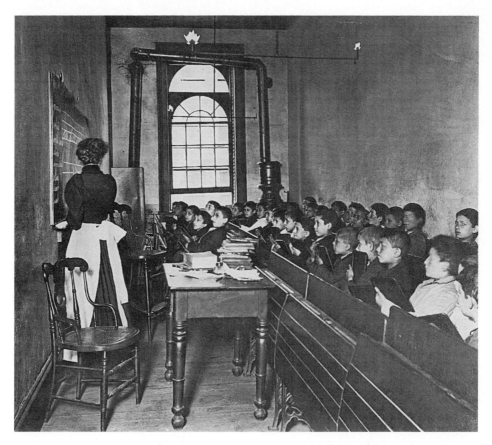

Interiors of many elementary schools in the late 19th century were very plain. Note the total absence of decoration in this classroom.

by a compromise. This compromise was a new view of the high school as a "comprehensive" institution. The comprehensive high school was seen as an institution that would include curricula directed at providing both academic and work-oriented instruction. Debate about how much weight should be given to each of these emphases continues even today.

Toward the end of the nineteenth century, there was a recognition that many of the increasing numbers of learners who were entering high schools were having difficulty doing the required work. Some individuals who studied this problem concluded that something needed to be done to ease learners' transition from elementary schools to high schools. A new institution that came to be known as the *junior high school* was the proposed solution.

The first junior high school was established in Berkeley, California, in 1909. The Berkeley school district developed a 6-3-3 plan of school organization that, in time, came to be widely copied elsewhere (Popper, 1967). The first six grades comprised the elementary program, the next three grades the junior high school program, and the final three years the senior high school program.

Numbers of public schools and learners attending them increased tremendously during the first four decades of the twentieth century. Schooling became almost universal during this period. In 1900, only 50.5 percent of young people in the 5- to 20-year-old age group were in school, but by 1940, 74.8 percent of this age group were enrolled (U.S. Department of Commerce, *Historical Statistics of the United States,* 1975, pp. 369–70). Given the tremendous growth in the total U.S. population between 1900 and 1940, these figures indicate that millions more children were served by schools in 1940 than in 1900.

## The Work of John Dewey

An individual who had a tremendous influence on education during this period was John Dewey (1859–1952). His work continues to affect educational thought and practice.

Dewey viewed education as a process through which young people are brought to fully participate in society. He saw the primary goal of education as that of promoting growth and development of the individual. Hence, school should not set out to serve the goals of society (e.g., turning out electrical engineers if the society is short of them) at the cost of overlooking the unique needs of individual learners. Schools, Dewey believed, should produce secure human beings who leave school committed to their own continuing self-education.

Dewey believed that every learner actively attempts to explore and understand the environment. If this is so, Dewey argued, learners need intellectual tools that they can use to make sound judgments about those things they encounter. They need to be familiar with thinking processes that can be applied to any unfamiliar situation. Dewey maintained that it was much more important for learners to master systematic thinking processes than to know specific items of information—thinking processes can be applied universally, but a specific item of information often has little value beyond the context in which it is learned.

The thought process that Dewey felt learners should master was the scientific problem-solving method. Familiarity with this method, Dewey felt, would give young people confidence in their abilities to develop rational responses to dilemmas they would face throughout their lives. Interest in teaching problem-solving techniques and a commitment to responding to individual differences still feature prominently in American schools today.

## The Testing Movement

Schools today also continue to be influenced by an early twentieth-century movement that first developed in France. Education in France became compulsory in 1904. At that time, a special commission was established there to identify those young people who might benefit from regular instruction in public schools and those who would be better off in special classes. To help with this identification, in 1905 Alfred Binet and his associates developed a test, called the intelligence quotient (IQ) test, that was designed to predict learners' likelihood of success in regular school classrooms. Soon educators from other countries, including the United States, were seeking information about ways to measure intelligence. It is interesting that a test designed to predict school success was viewed almost immediately as a test of intelligence. The presumption was that the school program had been designed so that the most intelligent would do the best. (Today, this idea is debated. Some people, for example, argue that the "most intelligent" learners resist school rules and procedures and do not do well.)

The testing movement in the United States grew during World War I. The military needed a system that could be used to identify individuals who would be suited to a variety of necessary tasks. Intelligence tests were developed that were believed to provide information that could be used to classify individuals by intelligence. At the time they were initially developed, few people doubted that the scores yielded by these tests represented a highly reliable measure of intelligence.

Some of these early intelligence tests were given to European immigrants. Immigrants from western Europe did better than immigrants from eastern Europe. (This was hardly a surprising development, in that most tests were developed by western Europeans or Americans trained by western Europeans.) There is some evidence that congressional passage of laws restricting numbers of immigrants from eastern Europe resulted from dissemination of these score differences. This might be one of the first examples of the cultural bias that can be embedded within tests of this sort.

During and after World War I, the testing movement was embraced by educators. It became common for learners to be classified and counseled into certain courses on the basis of their IQ scores. There is evidence that some teachers' patterns of interaction with individual learners were affected by their perception of these learners' intelligence as revealed by IQ scores.

In recent years, use of intelligence tests, particularly paper-and-pencil, group intelligence tests, has been challenged. The issue of cultural bias has been raised by African-Americans, Hispanics, and other minorities. Some people have argued that a factor as broad and diffuse as intelligence cannot possibly be measured by a single test. There have been situations in which perfectly normal young people have been assigned to institutions for the mentally retarded on the basis of a faulty IQ score obtained from a group intelligence test. The debate about intelligence testing continues. Although we are far from a consensus on this issue, it is generally fair to say that educators are becoming increasingly hesitant to predict the educational futures of young people on the basis of a single measure such as an IQ score.

## The Cardinal Principles

As special circumstances and needs associated with the wartime situation expanded interest in the testing movement, during the World War I years people also became concerned about education's more general purposes. In particular, the war's last year, 1918, was a landmark one for education. In this year, the National Education Association's Commission on the Reorganization of Secondary Education identified seven specific goals for the public schools. These seven goals came to be known as education's "Cardinal Principles." They included:

- health
- command of fundamental processes
- worthy home membership
- vocational preparation
- citizenship
- worthy use of leisure time
- ethical character*

These principles laid the groundwork for the comprehensive high school. They implied that secondary schools should have a broader purpose than simply preparing learners for colleges and universities. In time, publication of the Cardinal Principles led to an expansion of course offerings in high schools. By no means, however, did all high schools give equal emphasis to each of the many subjects that came to be offered; in many, considerable attention (critics would say too much attention) continued to be given to college and university preparatory courses (see Box 4–2).

Changes in the schools wrought by both attention to the Cardinal Principles and actions taken by groups looking for a more practical emphasis in the curriculum suggested that more and more people were viewing education as a necessity for all young people. Compulsory attendance laws became common during the first two decades of the twentieth century. Increasingly, learners were being required to stay in school until they turned 16.

In the 1920s and 1930s, the influence of those who wanted schools to respond humanely to the needs and interests of individual learners was strong. The term *progressive education movement* has been applied to the general program of people who sought these goals. Supporters of the progressive education movement drew inspiration from the work of John Dewey. For example, the installation of counseling programs in schools, which developed at an especially rapid rate during the 1930s, represented a logical extension of Dewey's concern for individual development.

## American Education After World War II

After World War II, the progressive education movement developed into a loosely knit group of people who supported school practices that came to be known as *life-adjustment education.* In some of its more extreme forms, life-adjustment education programs seemed to encourage learners to do whatever they pleased. Systematic attention to intellectual rigor or subject matter was avoided. Critics of such programs suggested that learners were being shortchanged by schools that failed to provide needed understandings and skills. These critics attracted many supporters, and by the middle 1950s, support for life-adjustment education had greatly diminished.

### *Sputnik* and "Rigor"

Rarely can change in education (or, indeed, in other social institutions) be attributed to a single event. But in the fall of 1957, the Soviet Union's launching of the first

---

*Commission on Reorganization of Secondary Education, *Cardinal Principles of Secondary Education* (Washington, DC: U.S. Government Printing Office, 1918).

BOX 4–2
# THE CARDINAL PRINCIPLES AND SECONDARY EDUCATION TODAY

The seven Cardinal Principles of secondary education of 1918 suggested that secondary schools should devote attention to each of these areas:

- health
- command of fundamental processes
- worthy home membership
- vocational preparation
- citizenship
- worthy use of leisure time
- ethical character

### *What Do You Think?*

1. Which of these principles received *most* attention in the high school you attended? Which received *least?* Why?
2. Suppose a decision were made requiring a high school to develop a curriculum that gave equal weight to each of these principles. What courses would be included? How would people in the local community react? In particular, how would people with great political influence react?
3. Which of these principles are most important to you? Do you think your personal ranking is similar or different to how most others would rank them?

• • • • • • • • • • • • • • • • • • • • • • • • • • • • • • • • • • • • • • • • • • • • • • • • • • • • •

earth satellite, *Sputnik,* so changed the public's perception of education's role that many subsequent alterations in school curricula can be traced back to this single, seminal event. *Sputnik* shocked the nation by challenging America's presumed technological supremacy. Those people looking for an explanation placed a great deal of blame on public education. Large audiences listened sympathetically to critics who told them that American schools had gone soft and that instruction in subject-matter content compared unfavorably with that provided to learners in other countries. Instruction in the sciences was identified as a particularly weak area of the curriculum.

Reacting to pressures to "do something" about the schools, in 1958 the federal government passed the National Defense Education Act. This legislation provided federal funds to improve the quality of education. Large-scale curriculum reform projects were launched, first in mathematics and the sciences and later in the social sciences. Special summer workshops designed to upgrade teachers' skills were held on college campuses across the nation. There was a massive effort to improve the quality of textbooks and other instructional materials. People carried high hopes that this revolution in American school programming could be carried to a successful conclusion.

## Cultural Change and Education in the 1960s

Though the curriculum reform movement of the 1960s did result in important changes, the modifications fell well short of the expectations of many who had supported passage of the National Defense Education Act. Teachers who attended summer programs became proficient in the use of new techniques and materials, but only a small minority of all teachers participated in such programs. Others who did not take part found themselves ill at ease with many of the new programs, and a majority of teachers continued doing things much as they had always done them.

Another problem involved the new instructional materials themselves. Many were developed by subject-matter experts who had little experience working with public school learners. Consequently, some of the new materials were written at reading levels that were too difficult for many learners. Further, the issue of motivation was not attended to well—a lot of young people were simply not interested in some of the new instructional materials.

Probably the changing national culture of the 1960s did more than anything else to subvert those changes being pushed by people who wanted to introduce more "intellectual rigor" into school programs. With growing discontent over official policies toward Vietnam and frustrations of minorities in the nation's large cities, the ground was not fertile for changes that appeared to critics to be an effort to push "establishment" values on the young. Increasingly, young people questioned the relevance of school curricula that seemed to favor esoteric intellectual subjects rather than topics of more immediate personal concern.

## Junior High School versus Middle School

After World War II, concerns increased about the junior high school as an institution. Many people had originally hoped that junior high schools would be particularly sensitive to the emotional and developmental needs of early adolescents. Over time, however, a majority of junior high schools came to be organized as academic preparatory institutions for the high schools. Middle schools have grown tremendously in popularity; today there are more middle schools than there are high schools.

The middle school movement began to attract supporters during the 1960s. This interest continued throughout the 1970s, 1980s, and on into the 1990s. Individual middle schools often have one of several different grade-level organizational patterns. Generally, a middle school has three to five grades, which almost always includes grades 6 and 7 (Lounsbury and Vars, 1978). The National Middle School Association and other supporters of middle schools emphasize programs that are sensitive to the special characteristics of learners in the 11-to-14 age group. Today, middle schools are beginning to displace junior high schools as the dominant school type for learners between their elementary and high school years.

## School Reform Efforts Since the 1980s

Beginning in the early 1980s, concerns about the quality of American schools led to a period of intense public scrutiny of school programs. There were concerns about the sophistication of thinking being developed by school programs, the readiness of

*". . . and the reason we have summer vacation is so you can go home to help with the crops."*
Courtesy of Ford Button.

graduates to assume jobs requiring ever-more-complex levels of technical proficiency, general reading and writing abilities of learners, patterns of scores on academic achievement tests, and unfavorable achievement comparisons between American learners and those in other nations.

A number of major themes have appeared consistently in recommendations to improve the schools that have been broadly circulated during the past 10 years. There has been a frequent call for school programs to become more rigorous. At the high school level, this recommendation has sometimes taken the form of a proposal to reduce numbers of electives and to require all learners to take a common core of content drawn from the academic disciplines.

Recommendations have also addressed the issue of teacher quality. There have been suggestions of various ways to attract brighter, more committed people to teaching and to improve the duration and quality of their preparation (Holmes Group, 1986). Further, there has been a recognition that quality people will not remain in the profession unless there are also efforts to improve teachers' working conditions (e.g., salaries, giving teachers more power to make decisions about how they discharge their responsibilities, etc.).

The issue of school administrative organization has also been addressed. There have been recommendations to decrease sizes of schools to allow for more personal attention to learners. There have also been suggestions that principals spend more time in their role as instructional leaders than in their role as business managers. Additionally, there have been proposals to lengthen the school year to make it conform more to those in countries where learners are doing better on content-achievement tests than are learners in the United States.

In short, the past decade has witnessed an unprecedented public interest in education. Increasing numbers of people have become convinced that in the quality of our schools lies the quality of our nation's future. Spirited discussions about how to maintain and improve school quality seem certain to feature prominently in our national life for the remainder of the century (see Box 4–3).

BOX 4–3

# THE FUTURE OF AMERICAN EDUCATION

Some people argue that our schools demand too little of learners. These critics contend that today's programs tap only a fraction of the learners' intellectual power, and they want curricula revised to provide for more academic rigor.

Other people contend that the basic problem of the schools is that they fail to pay enough attention to differences among learners. They suggest that, in a culture claiming to prize individualism, schools reward only those learners who conform. As a result, our educational system fails to nurture the creative talents of many young people.

*What Do You Think?*
1. Do you think our schools demand too little of learners? How would you go about determining an appropriate level of expectations?
2. Suppose school authorities decreed that teachers' only obligations were to transmit rigorous subject matter to learners. How would today's practices change? What would be the reaction of learners, parents, and other community members?
3. Are schools oppressive places? Can you cite examples of instances when very bright learners have been so turned off that they have performed at only minimal levels?
4. Is it possible for schools to be both intellectually challenging *and* sensitive to individual learner differences?

**TABLE 4–1**
Summary Table: History of American Education

| Period | Key Developments |
|---|---|
| Colonial period to 1800 | • Principle of local control of education established |
| | • Development of idea of compulsory attendance |
| | • Required schooling restricted to basic instruction of young children |
| | • Limited secondary and advanced education; focus was largely on classical studies |
| | • Development of interest in practical learning |
| | • New academies developed to provide secondary education |
| | • Secondary education remained private |
| | • Development of idea of providing some electives to secondary school students |
| 1800 to Civil War | • First public high school appeared, but private academies continued to be the most popular form of secondary school |
| | • Work of Horace Mann helped to establish publicly supported elementary schools throughout the country |
| | • First special teacher-training institutions appeared |
| Civil War to 1900 | • Principle of public financing of secondary schools established |
| | • Teachers' professional groups began to be organized |
| | • Debates began regarding whether schooling should be directed toward intellectual or vocational outcomes |

**TABLE 4–1**
*continued*

| Topic | Key Developments |
|---|---|
| 1900 to World War II | • Introduction of testing, particularly of intelligence (IQ) testing |
| | • Comprehensive high school was developed—a compromise institution serving many educational purposes at the same time |
| | • First junior high schools appeared |
| | • Cardinal Principles of education introduced |
| | • School counseling programs appeared in large numbers, especially during the 1930s |
| Post-World War II | • Life-adjustment education developed after World War II; lost popularity in early 1950s |
| | • *Sputnik* launch prompted emphasis on rigorous academic subjects, particularly mathematics and science |
| | • In 1960s, changing national values resulted in educational emphases on personal development of learners |
| | • Middle schools began to appear; junior high schools declined in popularity |
| | • Major reform efforts began in the 1980s that pursued multiple objectives such as improving technical competence of graduates, improving performance levels on standardized tests, increasing the rigor of school programs, and upgrading proficiency levels of teachers and administrators |

········ · · · · · · · · · · · · · · · · · · · ·

# Key Ideas in Summary

- The Puritans who came to New England during the colonial period were motivated by the desires to reform policies of the Church of England and raise their children in an environment free from "religious error." They hoped to establish a society consistent with the Bible's teaching. Among other things, this implied a society of people capable of reading the Bible, and hence there was an interest in teaching a large proportion of the population to read.

- Settlers in the middle colonies tended to come from the north Midlands of England and Wales, the north of England, and Scotland and Ireland. They were more diverse than were the early settlers of New England. In New York, many early private schools sought to prepare young people for commercial careers. In Pennsylvania, the Quakers established schools that were open to all children.

- Many early settlers of the southern colonies were supporters of King Charles I, who was defeated by the forces of Parliament in the late 1640s. It became dangerous for these people to stay in England, and many sought safety in the New World. Settlement patterns in the southern colonies were along the region's many rivers. Because there were few towns and cities, it was difficult for children to be brought together in sufficient numbers to support a school. Wealthy individuals hired tutors to educate their children, and some people sent their children to England for at least part of their education. Little schooling was available to children whose families were not prosperous.

- The first high school was established in Boston in 1821. Unlike academies, which were mostly private institutions, most high schools were publicly supported. At first, the growth of high schools proceeded slowly. For example, in 1860 there were only 40 high schools in the entire country.

- Horace Mann championed the "common school" in the 1820s and 1830s. Mann strongly believed that it was in the taxpayers' interest to support the establishment of a strong system of public education. He saw the schools as a way of equalizing differences among people from different social classes, and of contributing to the economic growth of the country. He also promoted the development of formal institutions, normal schools, to prepare teachers. Mann's work was very influential in promoting the establishment of public school systems throughout the nation.

- The post-Civil War period featured many changes in education. The famous Kalamazoo case established a legal precedent for public support of secondary as well as elementary education. As well, teachers started to organize in professional associations. Additionally, the large numbers of immigrants entering the public schools challenged educators to develop programs responsive to their needs and to needs of American employers. But toward the end of the nineteenth century, some people argued in favor of narrowing the purpose of the school to provide a stronger focus on preparation for advanced study in colleges and universities.

- During the first 20 years of the twentieth century, one conflict regarding the purpose of the American high school was resolved—arguments between those seeing high schools as college-preparatory institutions and those regarding them as vocational-preparatory institutions were accommodated in a new view of the high school as a "comprehensive" institution, one having multiple objectives.

- John Dewey had a significant influence on twentieth-century American education. Dewey believed that education should primarily focus on the development of the individual. He was especially interested in providing learners with the kinds of problem-solving abilities they would need to successfully confront the challenges they would face throughout their lives.

- The testing movement, originating in France and developing rapidly during World War I, led to American schools' extensive use of intelligence testing of learners by the second and third decades of the twentieth century. In recent years, much skepticism has been generated regarding the idea that an IQ represents an accurate measure of something as complex and sophisticated as human intelligence.

- After World War II, there was interest in life-adjustment education. Critics felt that this view of education encouraged learners to do only what pleased them and that school programs lacked needed intellectual substance. By the 1950s, much enthusiasm for life-adjustment education had faded.

- In the late 1950s, following the launch of the earth satellite, *Sputnik*, and continuing into the very early 1960s, there was a push to place heavier emphasis in schools on challenging academic content. There were particular efforts to strengthen programs in mathematics and the sciences. As public disaffection with the nation's Vietnam policy increased, suspicions began to be directed at leaders of many public institutions, including the schools. In time, these suspicions led to widespread rejection of narrow school programs with strong focuses on traditional academic subjects; increasingly, young people questioned the relevance of such programs.

- Beginning in the 1960s, concerns about junior high schools prompted a great deal of interest in middle schools. This interest continues to the present time. Supporters of middle schools believe that their programs tend to be more responsive than junior high school programs to special needs of learners in the 11-to-14 age group.

- Beginning in the 1980s, a large number of proposals to reform the schools were made. These were prompted by concerns about the intellectual levels of school graduates, unfavorable achievement comparisons between American and foreign learners, and perceived learner deficiencies in such key areas as reading and writing. There were also concerns about the quality of the teaching force. These reform proposals focused public attention on the schools, and that attention continues today.

# Review and Discussion Questions

1. What were some educational implications of the colonial Puritans' beliefs?

2. In what ways were people who settled the middle colonies different from many of those who settled in New England, and what impact did these differences have on education in the two areas?

3. What were some patterns of education in the southern colonies?

4. What are some lasting contributions to American education made by the academies?

5. What were some of Horace Mann's contributions to the development of American education?

6. How might you explain why Americans endorsed publicly supported elementary schools long before they were willing to endorse publicly supported secondary schools?

7. What are some challenges that faced educators in the United States from the Civil War to the beginning of the twentieth century?

8. Why do you think American educators were so quick to use intelligence tests in schools once such tests became available?

9. Today, some critics of schools argue that curricula should place heavier emphases on training learners with the specific technical skills they will need when they enter the workplace. How do you think John Dewey might have responded to this opinion?

10. In what ways are criticisms of schools at the time when *Sputnik* was launched similar and different from criticisms of schools today?

# Ideas for Field Experiences, Projects, and Enrichment

1. Fruitlands was one of a number of experimental communities established in the United States during the nineteenth century; New Harmony and Brook Farm were among the others. Many of these communities had definite ideas about how children should be educated. Do some background reading on these communities, and prepare an oral report on each one's educational practices.

2. Many of today's inquiry teaching techniques are based on a model of thinking set forth by John Dewey. Read John Dewey's *How We Think* (see the refer-

ences at the end of the chapter), and prepare a chart illustrating the steps in the thinking process that Dewey describes.

3. What should be the *most important* function of the school: transmitting academic knowledge to the young, facilitating their individual personal development, or preparing young people for the workplace? Organize a symposium in which one person takes a stand in favor of each position. Follow this presentation with a general class discussion.

4. In the years following the launch of *Sputnik*, many people argued that American schools should place heavier emphasis on teaching rigorous academic content. Years later, many of the reform reports of the early and middle 1980s made similar suggestions. Review some of the criticisms of schools (and accompanying suggestions for improvement) made after *Sputnik* was launched. Then review some criticisms (and accompanying suggestions for improvement) contained in reform reports issued during the 1980s. Prepare a report in which you note similarities and differences in the recommendations made during the two periods.

5. Some people argue that the comprehensive high school has outlived its usefulness. They suggest that it would be better to have separate schools for separate purposes. For example, some high schools might be exclusively dedicated to the traditional academic subjects, and others might be totally oriented toward vocational preparation. Organize a debate on this topic: "Has the Comprehensive High School Outlived its Usefulness?"

· · · · · · · · · · · · · · · · · · · · · · · · · ·

# Supplementary Reading

Bowen, J. *A History of Western Education.* Vol. III, *The Modern West, Europe, and the New World.* New York: St. Martin's Press, 1981.

Cremin, L. A. *American Education: The Metropolitan Experience, 1876–1980.* New York: Harper and Row, 1988.

Dahlstrand, F. C. *Amos Bronson Alcott.* East Brunswick, NJ: Associated University Presses, 1982.

Dewey, J. *How We Think.* Boston: D.C. Heath, 1910.

Filler, L., ed. *Horace Mann on the Crisis in Education.* Lanham, MD: University Press of America, 1983.

Kliebard, H. M. *The Struggle for the American Curriculum, 1893–1958.* Boston: Routledge and Kegan Paul, 1986.

Sears, C. E. *Bronson Alcott's Fruitlands.* Philadelphia: Porcupine Press, 1975.

Spring, J. *The American School, 1642–1990: Varieties of Historical Interpretations of the Foundation and Development of American Education.* New York: Longman, 1990.

. . . . . . . . . . . . . . . . . . . . . . . . . . . .

# References

Barry, T. N. "Origin and Development of the American Public High School in the 19th Century." Ph.D. diss., Stanford University, 1961.

Bowen, J. *A History of Western Education.* Vol. III, *The Modern West, Europe, and the New World.* New York: St. Martin's Press, 1981.

Dewey, J. *How We Think.* Boston: D.C. Heath, 1910.

Fischer, D. H. *Albion's Seed.* New York: Oxford University Press, 1989.

The Holmes Group. *Tomorrow's Teachers.* East Lansing, MI: The Holmes Group, 1986.

Lounsbury, J. H. and G.E. Vars. *Curriculum for the Middle Years.* New York: Harper & Row, 1978.

Popper, S. H. *The American Middle School: An Organizational Analysis.* Waltham, MA: Blaisdell Publishing Company, 1967.

*Stuart* v. *School District No. 1 of the Village of Kalamazoo,* 30 Mich. 69 (1874).

U.S. Department of Commerce. *Historical Statistics of the United States, Colonial Times to 1970: Part I.* Washington, DC: Bureau of the Census, 1975.

# Chapter 5

# Philosophies of Education

· · · · · · · · · · · · · · · · · · · · · · · · · · · · · · · · · · · · · · · · · · · · ·

## Objectives

This chapter provides information to help the reader to

- describe reasons teachers should know something about philosophies of education.
- identify some metaphysical issues that influence educational practice.
- list epistemological questions of importance to teachers.
- describe how axiology influences teaching.
- point out how knowledge of logic can be useful to teachers.
- suggest differences among alternative philosophical systems.
- recognize differences in philosophical perspectives as they are reflected in educational practices.
- take a stand on educational issues based on a personal philosophy.

# Focus Questions

1. How are philosophical issues relevant for teachers?
2. What are some basic metaphysical questions?
3. How do "hard" and "soft" subjects differ in terms of epistemology?
4. What are two basic types of logic, and how does each relate to teaching methods?
5. How do idealists and realists differ?
6. What has been the impact of pragmatism on American education?
7. For progressives, what are the characteristics of the ideal "educated person?"
8. Which is the dominant philosophical perspective in American education?
9. For perennialists, what are the characteristics of the ideal "educated person?"
10. What would be a teacher's role in a school operated according to a reconstructionist perspective?

..............................

# Introduction

The school board meeting had begun quietly enough. Reports on building mainte-nance had been received, and a few contracts for minor repairs were approved. The superintendent was authorized to begin a search for a new personnel director. But then something happened that turned a placid (some might say boring) meeting into an emotional firestorm.

It all started when the associate superintendent for curriculum reported learner results on a battery of recently administered standardized tests—the scores were lower than they had been in previous years. This revelation prompted some initial discussion among members of the board. The debate really grew heated when the board invited comment from members of the public who were in attendance at the meeting.

The first speaker identified himself as a member of the taxpayers' league. He noted that the decline in scores represented "yet another instance" of public money being used for unproductive purposes. The teachers, he pointed out, were simply "not get-ting the job done." "My people," he went on to say, "want to be sure somebody is watching the store. Who is responsible for seeing that teachers actually teach what they're supposed to teach? Is this person really holding our children's teachers to account? Certainly these dismal test results suggest otherwise."

These remarks were accompanied by approving nods by some others in the audi-ence. One of these people jumped to his feet when the first speaker had finished. Picking up on the same theme, he pointed out that when he was in school, young peo-ple had certain facts they had to memorize, "or else." "It is obvious," he noted, "that young people are naturally lazy and won't work unless they are expected to. We need to quit coddling these kids. If we have to, we should get out the paddle, get these kids some good textbooks, and not let up on them until they *know* this important material." He concluded by pointing out that the curriculum had been "softened" by the intro-duction of too many electives, and that learners were being denied the "important dis-cipline" of exposure to subjects that they initially might not find either interesting or easy. Many people in the audience applauded these remarks—but not everybody.

Shaking her head in disagreement, a woman in the front row stood and was recog-nized. She began by agreeing that "something is wrong with our schools." But her pre-scription for change was quite different from those suggested by the previous speakers. "The real problem is not with *how* the learners are taught, but with *what* they are taught. For one thing, there are too many vocational courses. We shouldn't be using valuable school time to prepare students for jobs. What we need is more emphasis on the classics. Whatever happened to the humanities? We want people who can *think*, not people who only know how to change an oil filter." These remarks drew scattered applause and an "Absolutely!" or two, but a larger number of people were heard to make such remarks as "impractical," "ivory-tower stuff," and "irrelevant."

Next, a man stood up and shocked the crowd into an attentive silence with his observation that "test scores are meaningless and people should stop worrying about such trivial matters. Tests," he pointed out, "do nothing but ask kids to regurgitate iso-lated facts. Who in this room can name the capital of every state? Does anyone feel seriously handicapped by the inability to do it? Then why should we get upset about scores on tests that feature questions about matters that are equally unimportant?" The speaker went on to suggest that, because of rapid change, most textbook knowledge is obsolete. "What the schools need to do," he asserted, "is to help young people accommodate to change. They need to learn that what we have today is not what we will have tomorrow. They need to think about shaping our tomorrows. And the way to do this is *not* to cram irrelevant facts down their throats."

These comments elicited cheers from some in the audience, but others stood up and started shouting counterarguments. Individual board members looked very uncomfortable. Finally, the chair of the board seized her heavy gavel and began beating furiously on the lectern. The superintendent looked tired and defeated. How could anyone administer a school district when there were so many conflicting views about what should be done?

For a prospective teacher, how relevant is this scene from the board meeting? *Very* relevant. Teachers must make decisions about the content to be taught, and deciding what is to be taught requires them to respond to an important philosophical question: What knowledge is worth knowing?

A second consideration is that teachers, by definition, work with learners. How individual teachers interact with learners depends on their general philosophical positions regarding the nature of human beings. Are they basically good, or basically evil? Teachers who see people as basically good work with their learners in ways that differ from those who see people as basically bad.

A third variable that teachers must deal with is their individual understanding of what conduct is "moral" or "right." Teachers differ in terms of how they believe moral behavior should be determined. Some make the judgment through intuition, others rely on situational variables, and still others use some objective measures.

Still another factor that distinguishes individual teachers is their view of what constitutes "correct thinking" on philosophical questions regarding rules of inference and consistency. For example, how are conclusions to be defended? Is intuition enough, or must there be some reliance on evidence? If so, what kinds of evidence are appropriate, and how must evidence be organized?

Teachers have to understand that different people (including themselves) perceive the nature of the world and knowledge in many ways. An understanding of different perspectives helps teachers to maintain open lines of communication with others. When teachers fail to consider that others may see the world in a way different from their own, they may not understand why some people oppose school programs that, to the teachers, seem to make perfectly good sense.

Everything teachers do in schools is supported by a given set of assumptions. Often these assumptions have been little noticed, but today, given increasing public interest in what is taught in our schools, certain people are challenging some traditional school practices. These challenges are also an attack of the assumptions upon which these practices are based. Thus teachers need to recognize not only the assumptions supporting today's school practices, but also those assumptions supporting the positions of people who favor changing what we are doing now.

In short, teachers need to be able to defend what they are doing. They need a philosophical base from which to operate, and they need some grasp of the philosophi-

Teachers' individual assumptions about what constitutes good education often leads to serious discussion when curriculum changes are being considered.

cal foundations on which their critics are building their own arguments. As a beginning, prospective teachers might review some of the categories of questions that must be answered as they begin working out their own philosophies of education (as the speakers in Box 5–1 have already done). These categories are introduced in the sections that follow.

## Metaphysics (or Ontology)

*Metaphysics* is concerned with the nature of reality. Questions in this category cannot be answered by application of the scientific method, as they tend to be speculative and focus on such issues as the nature of cause-and-effect relationships. For example, do cause and effect exist in reality, or are they simply a creation of our mind? Is there a purpose to the universe, or is life basically meaningless? Are humans essentially spiritual beings, or are they creatures that exist in a particular time and space with no meaning beyond self? Is there a set of constant and unchanging principles that guides the operation of things and, therefore, can be discovered? Is reality a constantly changing entity that is always relative, thus rendering any search for truth fruitless?

BOX 5–1

# PURPOSES OF SCHOOLING AND TEACHERS' ATTITUDES

Speaker A:    Schools should follow a business model. Specific information should be identified for learners to acquire, and teachers should be held accountable for teaching this material. Schools and teachers should be rated in terms of their efficiency in transmitting this information to learners. Also, rewards should go to administrators and teachers in schools that accomplish this in a cost-effective way.

Speaker B:    Schools should prepare learners to move immediately into the workplace. Graduates should be able to make change, keep accurate records, and perform basic skills associated with the occupations of their choice. Businesses should not have to do the schools' work for them. Young people should be prepared and ready to do meaningful work beginning with their first day on the job.

Speaker C:    Schools should teach young people mathematics, sciences, literature, history, and foreign languages. Most other subjects should be eliminated. Because our society changes so rapidly, it is important that the essential "truths" of these traditional disciplines be mastered. Armed with the kinds of thinking abilities that come from an understanding of these subjects, young people will have something to hang on to as they adapt to societal change.

Speaker D:    Our society is filled with injustices. Schools should teach young people to transform society to make it more sensitive to individual differences and needs. Courses should prepare learners to be politically active citizens who are eager and willing to challenge existing economic and social practices.

### What Do You Think?

1. What basic differences do you note among the positions taken by these speakers?
2. If you were a school board member, how would you respond to each of these opinions in an open meeting?
3. Which of these positions is closest to your own? Most distant?
4. What is your own view about the "proper" function of our schools?

As stated before, all of these questions are metaphysical—obviously, we cannot conduct experiments to test our answers to them against scientific evidence. To some people, these questions may seem very abstract and hopelessly remote from the everyday world of the teacher, but such is not the case. Consider, for example, that in recent years some critics have argued that the primary purpose of education is to help learners achieve "happiness." This implies that "happiness" has been identified as an answer to a metaphysical question about what the central purpose of life ought to be. Given this orientation, some critics of more traditional school practices have suggested that there is no subject matter worth knowing that is not of clear and pressing interest to the individual learner. Therefore, it has been suggested that schools should permit learners to determine what they will study and that, above all, the schools should provide for learners' freedom and individual choice.

Those people advocating such practices have made a number of philosophical assumptions about reality. They reject the idea that known principles exist which explain reality, and that these should be mastered by all learners. Furthermore, they perceive human beings to be essentially good and trustworthy. Basic to this position is an assumption that if people are given freedom, they will intuitively do what is "good."

Another group of parents and citizens whom teachers frequently encounter are convinced that there are certain unchanging principles that should be taught to learners. These people tend to believe that individual experience is an unreliable guide to "proper" action. They reject the idea that people intuitively choose what is "best." In their view, teachers must exert control to ensure that learners do the "right" thing. This position, too, derives from a metaphysical stance about the nature of human beings.

Many divisive issues in education *are* divisive because people have arrived at different answers to basic metaphysical questions. Teachers who are familiar with the nature of metaphysical questions—and more particularly with the reality that answers to such questions cannot be tested against scientific evidence—are better prepared to understand the assumptions supporting views about school practices that differ from their own. Teachers with these insights know when an argument is based on metaphysics (and cannot, therefore, be proved with evidence) and when an argument is not (and thus can be challenged or defended with evidence).

## Epistemology

A second major category of philosophical questions is *Epistemology*. Epistemological questions are concerned with the nature of knowledge. Since educators are interested in the discovery and transmission of information, teachers have a special need to know about this category. Answers to epistemological questions provide a rationale for selecting material that is worth transmitting to learners.

One of the basic epistemological questions is whether accurate knowledge about reality is possible. Some people maintain that there is no possibility of obtaining knowledge about ultimate reality. Others counter that it is possible to identify a set of principles that represents true knowledge. Still others argue that there are no principles that are true under all sets of conditions, but there is knowledge that is true in certain circumstances. (Stated another way, what these people contend is that knowledge functions in a particular situation, and all we can know is what is "functional.")

Another fundamental epistemological question centers on what might be described as the ways of knowing and the reliability of these ways. Basically, the issue involves whether knowledge comes from revelation, authority, intuition, the senses, or reason or experimentation. Today, many people have a bias favoring the position that knowledge comes from scientific experimentation. Indeed, among some people, this idea is so firmly rooted that they cannot even imagine it being challenged. But even these people sometimes take actions based only on intuition—they do something just because they "feel" it is right.

Some people have religious convictions that lead them to include revelation as a source of knowledge. While this view has not been widely endorsed, there are instances of pressures being brought on schools by individuals who subscribe to it. For example, some groups have pushed hard for high school biology programs that present the view of creation as revealed in the Book of Genesis as an alternative to Darwinian natural selection.

People in many other world cultures place a lower premium on scientific experimentation than we do. Because of differences in views regarding how knowledge is best acquired, we often find it hard to understand the perspectives of people living in unfamiliar cultural settings. It is particularly important for teachers to help learners appreciate how people in different cultures view the world. When learners lack such understandings, they may conclude that practices of other peoples are strange or even funny. An important objective of the school program is to help learners understand that they see the world through some "cultural blinders" of their own. Learners must come to recognize that there is nothing correct in any absolute sense in the way we think knowledge is best acquired. Our views, to a large measure, are simply reflections of how our culture has decided to view reality (Oliver and Gersham, 1989).

Teachers' approaches to teaching content say a good deal about their own answers to epistemological questions. For example, a teacher who insists that learners master basic facts and principles operates on the assumption that there is such a thing as true knowledge. Other teachers, who are more interested in teaching the processes of learning, imply that there is no ultimate truth and that it is better for young people to master problem-solving skills that can be applied to diverse situations.

Some school subjects feature instructional practices that are derived from differing conclusions regarding the source of knowledge. For example, instruction in the humanities frequently is premised on the assumption that knowledge results at least as much from intuition, feeling, and reason as from scientific experimentation. Critics who do not understand the appropriateness of an approach to truth through any process except scientific experimentation have sometimes labeled the humanities as "soft" subjects; that is, they are "soft" compared with the "hard" sciences that rely more heavily on scientific experimentation.

The labels *hard* and *soft* have nothing to do with the difficulty of the subjects. Rather, they relate to the sources of knowledge deemed appropriate within each discipline. Debates over the worthiness of "soft" subjects and "hard" subjects have important curricular implications. For example, if it is decided that only scientifically verifiable knowledge is important, then there will be a much heavier emphasis on the sciences than on the humanities. On the other hand, if other sources of knowledge are considered important, humanities-oriented courses will probably receive a heavy emphasis.

## Axiology

Should teachers stress the acquisition of knowledge or the moral and character development of their learners? Is there a standard of moral behavior that teachers should emphasize? These questions relate to the nature of values and ethics, and within the general area of *axiology*.

One important axiological concern focuses on the issue of whether life is worth living. What is the nature of existence? Does life have any meaning? Answers to these questions, particularly as they are developed by learners, are of interest to teachers. For example, the rate of suicide among young people in our society suggests that many of them have concluded that life has no meaning (or at least not a meaning worth living for).

Drug problems in schools can be tied to the issue of the value and worth of life. Many people who use drugs are convinced that the highest good amounts to seeking immediate pleasure and living for the moment. In traditional philosophy, such attitudes collectively are referred to as *hedonism*. Though many learners would be unable to define this term, their actions suggest that hedonism represents their basic philosophy of life.

Hedonism is only one perspective that results from a consideration of axiological questions. Another perspective takes the optimistic view that life is absolutely worth living over the long term and that the highest good involves something other than short-term pleasure. For example, a lot of individuals see the highest good as self-realization or self-perfection—many star athletes in the schools have this orientation, and social reformers of all kinds who believe in the perfectibility of the human condition also reflect this general position.

Some people find life's purpose through religion. They accept the view that there is an ultimate purpose to life and that every human being has a divine reason for being. They see the highest good being served in the effort to understand God's will and in the attempt to meet God's expectations.

An important axiological question of a different kind concerns the nature of "right" conduct. How should a person behave? What is moral behavior? How does a person know when he or she is doing the right thing? In answering these questions, some argue that there are universal principles or guidelines that can be followed. For example, there are people who cite the Ten Commandments as an example of a universal guide to appropriate behavior. But others reject the idea that there are guidelines that fit every set of circumstances. They contend that "appropriateness" of behavior is situation-specific. An example of this occurred during the late 1960s, when some people argued that America's fight against Hitler during World War II was moral but that America's participation in the Vietnam War was not.

Teachers often find themselves faced with the need to help learners make value choices. Additionally, teachers must also make value judgments of their own as they attempt to make decisions about such things as the appropriateness of learners' behavior and the evaluation of programs. The frequent need for them to make value decisions underscores the need for teachers to have some familiarity with axiology.

## Logic

The science of exact thought is a subfield of philosophy known as *logic*. Logic deals with the relationships between ideas and with the procedures used to differentiate between valid thinking and fallacious thinking.

There are several reasons that a knowledge of logic is important for teachers. First, logic helps them to communicate more effectively by encouraging a careful, systematic arrangement of thoughts. Second, logic helps them to evaluate the consistency of learners' reasoning. Third, logic helps them assess the faculty adequacy and the reliability of new information they encounter.

There are two basic types of logic, *deductive* logic and *inductive* logic. Deductive logic begins with a general conclusion and then elucidates this conclusion by citing examples and particulars that logically flow from it. Inductive logic begins with particulars. Reasoning focuses on these particulars and leads to a general conclusion that explains them.

The choice of a deductive or an inductive approach has implications for how teachers organize and present materials. When a deductive approach is selected, great care must be taken to ensure that learners acquire a solid grasp of the major principle or idea before the teacher moves on to illustrate it through the use of examples. A choice of an inductive approach requires the teacher to locate a large number of examples before instruction can begin. Further, these examples must be selected with great care—it is essential that they accurately represent the larger principle that, it is hoped, learners will come to understand.

There has been much professional discussion about the relative effectiveness of deductive and inductive instruction. Research suggests that neither approach is demonstrably superior to the other. The key issue seems to be how the teacher takes learners through a lesson, regardless of whether it is organized deductively or inductively. Clever teachers who help their learners grasp relationships among ideas and distinguish between valid and invalid arguments find that their learners do well regardless of whether content is sequenced deductively or inductively. (See the accompanying What the Experts Say for a broader view of the role of philosophical questions in the classroom.)

---

WHAT THE EXPERTS SAY

## *Should school learners be introduced to philosophy?*

Some experts believe that basic philosophical questions should be taught to children even in the elementary school grades (Oliver and Gersham, 1989; Gray, 1984). They cite several reasons to support their position. First, an understanding of alternative ways of looking at the world promotes multicultural understanding. Learners who understand that there are no simple, agreed-upon answers to many important human questions are likely to develop an appreciation for the perspectives of people who have developed their own, different responses to these issues.

Second, even young people are bombarded by conflicting messages from the media and other sources. They need ways of evaluating the many claims of truth, logic, and value that confront them in their daily lives. An introduction to philosophy can provide them with the tools to make sense out of this confusing welter of claims.

## Basic Philosophies

For centuries, great thinkers have grappled with questions associated with metaphysics, epistemology, axiology, and logic. Several systems of philosophy have developed out of their quests for answers. Some of these philosophical systems have ancient roots; others are of relatively recent origin. Among the basic philosophical systems with important implications for education are the following:

- idealism
- realism
- pragmatism
- existentialism

See Box 5–2 for some important questions to consider about these basic philosophies.

## Idealism

*Idealism*, one of the oldest philosophical systems, has its roots in the thinking of Plato. For the idealist, the ultimate reality is not to be found in the material world we know through the senses. Rather, it exists in the mental world of ideas or ideals. What we see in the material world is simply a representation of the true reality that exists only as an intangible, idealized state.

The idealist believes in the existence of universal truths and values. Human beings are thought to be capable of attaining some understanding of these principles. An important task of education is to bring these ideas to a conscious level. A basic familiar-

---

BOX 5–2
# IDENTIFYING A PERSONAL PHILOSOPHY

Four basic philosophies of education are introduced in this chapter. As you continue to work toward the development of a philosophical position of your own, it is important to think about some important questions.

### What Do You Think?

1. Which of the basic philosophies is most consistent with your beliefs? Which points of this philosophy do you find most appealing? Are there some points with which you disagree?
2. With which of the basic philosophies do you disagree the most? What are your specific points of disagreement?
3. What does your philosophical position tell you about your own attitudes toward life? Toward others? Toward education?
4. What are some implications of your beliefs for your role as a teacher?

ity with the cultural heritage of humankind is thought to be useful to people as they seek to develop more complete understandings of the ultimate verities.

In education, individuals who have associated their thinking with the idealist position often strongly endorse curricula that emphasize philosophy, theology, literature, and the other liberal arts. These are seen as key disciplines that can help learners develop insights regarding important universal truths and values. Debates in education often involve conflicts between people who subscribe to idealism and other people who are committed to different philosophical positions.

## Realism

*Realists* agree with idealists on several points. For example, realists and idealists agree that people should seek after truth. They also agree that there is rationality in the universe. However, realism and idealism have very different positions regarding the nature of ultimate reality. Idealists focus on an intangible world of ideas; realists believe that there is a tangible world of things that exists quite apart from any ideas about them. For realists, the test for truth is whether a given idea about the world corresponds with what can be verified tangibly through the senses (Kelley, 1986).

In realism, the ultimate value is rational behavior. This is behavior that conforms to theories that have been validated through the use of observation and other human perceptual activities. With regard to education, realists believe that certain kinds of knowledge ought to be regarded as fundamental. They place particular emphasis on subjects that help people classify and make rational judgments about what they observe in the world around them. Subjects such as science and mathematics have often been cited as being particularly well-suited to developing these competencies in learners (Martin, 1969).

The realists' belief in the importance of rational organizational schemes has tended to support school programs that emphasize separate subject areas rather than interdisciplinary programs. For realists, there is merit in learning the basic organizational patterns of the sciences, history, and other disciplines. This kind of outcome may be lost in interdisciplinary programs, in which learners are not exposed to the organizational features of the separate subjects.

The scientific method of thinking receives a great deal of emphasis in many school programs, which is consistent with realism. Modifying learner behaviors through careful observation and the application of behavior-modification techniques represents another example of realism at work in the schools.

## Pragmatism

*Pragmatism* does not share the conviction of idealism and realism that there is important, unchanging knowledge to be learned. Instead, pragmatism emphasizes the changing nature of the universe. Truth and values are the result of evolving human experience. Humans are not born with any inherent knowledge, universal truths, or values; rather, they have the necessary physical and mental capabilities to participate in the world around them and obtain knowledge that has individual relevance and meaning. Obtaining knowledge and truth is not a matter of learning what others have discovered—it is a matter of discovering for oneself. The pragmatist develops new knowledge by solving problems as they arise through interaction with the environment.

The test of truth for the pragmatist is that of consequences. The basic value question for the pragmatist is "What is it good for?" Information is considered to be an important tool that helps individuals obtain what ends they desire and to achieve progress. Values are viewed as relative to circumstances. Thus it is necessary for individuals to engage in a continual testing of the appropriateness of their value assumptions.

Pragmatism has had an important influence on American education. Much of its influence stems from the work of John Dewey. Dewey was one of the commanding figures in education who subscribed to pragmatism. He emphasized the importance of experience as a teacher and the need to help learners develop problem-solving skills. (For more on the work and beliefs of John Dewey, see Chapter 4.)

Pragmatists believe that learners who become good problem solvers will be able to respond and adapt to the changing conditions they will confront throughout their lives. School programs that provide learners with practice in working with problems common to their own experiences are thought to facilitate the development of problem-solving skills. Pragmatists believe that many school subjects can be used to provide learners with these kinds of experiences (Bayles, 1966).

## Existentialism

*Existentialism,* a philosophical position of relatively recent origin, is difficult to characterize in general terms. Many individuals associated with the existentialist position reject the view that existentialism is an all-embracing philosophical position with widely agreed-upon tenets. However, one theme that runs through most descriptions of existentialism is that people come into this world facing only one ultimate constraint, the inevitability of their own death, and in all other areas they should have freedom to make choices and identify their own reasons for existing.

Existentialism suggests that individuals do not fit into any grand design of God or nature. People are viewed as being born into a world devoid of any universal meaning. They are challenged to create personal meanings of their own design (Morris, 1966).

It is fair to say that existentialism has influenced education less than the other basic philosophies. In part this may be true because schools, as institutions designed to provide at least some common experiences to learners, promote goals that are inconsistent with the existentialists' commitment to personal freedom. Learner-designed programs and other courses that seek to maximize personal choice are examples of school-based offerings that have been influenced by the existential perspective.

## Educational Applications of Philosophical Ideas

Each philosophy reflects thinking about the meaning of life. Education comprises an important part of human experience. Educational applications of questions associated with the basic philosophies have led to the development of perspectives concerning schools and learning. The influence of several basic philosophies can often be detected in each of these schools of thought. The following educational applications of philosophical ideas are introduced in this section:

- progressivism
- essentialism
- perennialism
- reconstructionism

See Box 5–3 for some questions pertaining to these applications.

## Progressivism

*Progressivism,* as applied to education, has its roots in the work of John Dewey (1902, 1910, 1916, 1923, 1938) and in the spirit of progress that characterized the close of the nineteenth century and the beginning years of the twentieth. Progressivism emphasizes change as the essence of reality. It views knowledge as a tentative view that may explain present reality adequately but has no claim to being true forever. Reality is seen as undergoing continuous change.

Progressives view an educated person as someone who has the insights needed to adapt to change. They believe that schools should teach learners how to solve problems and inquire about their natural and social environments. Since there are no unchanging truths that must be taught, knowledge that is of value is that which can help people think about and respond to problems associated with their need to adjust to change.

Progressives view human beings as basically good. They believe that people who are free to choose generally will select a course of action that is best for them. Applied to schools, this perspective suggests that learners be given some choices regarding what and how they will study.

Some principles of education that are consistent with progressivism include:

---

BOX 5–3
# PHILOSOPHY AND EDUCATIONAL ISSUES

After you read about progressivism, essentialism, perennialism, and reconstructionism, respond to the following questions.

### *What Do You Think?*

1. Reflect on your own experiences in school. Which of these applications seemed to have been most influential in shaping your school's program? Can you recall some elements from your school's program that reflected each of these applications?
2. Which of these applications is most consistent with your own beliefs about the purpose of education, the nature of the curriculum, the role of the teacher, and the role of the learner?
3. List some current criticisms of schools. Which of the four applications are reflected in each of the criticisms? How would you respond to each criticism?

John Dewey, one of the giants of American educational thought, developed much of the intellectual foundation for progressivism.

- Direct experience with the environment is the best stimulus for learning.
- Reliance on authoritarian textbooks and methods of teaching are inappropriate for the education of free people.
- Teachers should be instructional managers who establish the learning environment, ask stimulating questions, and guide learners' interests in productive directions.
- Individuals need to learn how to inquire about their environment.
- Schools should not be isolated from the social world outside of the school.

Dewey did not object to the introduction of new content to learners. However, he believed that the content should be presented so that the interest of the learner was stimulated through an interaction with the environment. Dewey recommended that subject matter be organized in ways that would take advantage of learners' interests. By using personal interests as a point of reference, teachers could impart valuable problem-solving skills to learners.

Some of the later progressives went far beyond Dewey's ideas to suggest that the entire scholastic program should consist only of what the learners wanted to study. When putting this theory to practice in some of their classrooms, the learners pursued activities of doubtful significance. For example, a class might study Native Americans by building a paper teepee in the room and by eating the foods the early Native Americans were supposed to have eaten. In some of these programs, there was an assumption that the experience was the thing.

Some of the more irresponsible applications of progressive principles led some critics to allege that the entire progressive education movement was anti-intellectual. Though Dewey and other leading progressives clearly acknowledged the importance of sound academic content, the entire progressive movement was tainted by critics' concerns about what was going on in some experience-is-the-thing classrooms. Consequently, since the end of World War II there has been an increasing reluctance among educators to identify themselves publicly as "progressives."

## Essentialism

*Essentialism* began as an organized tradition in education in the 1930s. It owes much to the work of William C. Bagley (1938). Essentialism began as a reaction against some of the more extreme variants of progressivism. The essentialist positions are tied to the philosophy of realism with a dash of idealism.

Essentialism is based on several important propositions. First, the school program should not be diluted by any trivial and nonessential courses. Second, the academic rigor of American education is threatened by many of the perspectives of the progressives. Third, schools should not lose sight of their fundamental purpose—the provision of sound practical and intellectual training.

Essentialists hold that there is a core of knowledge and skills that should be taught to all learners. This common core includes those subjects that are essential for preparing a person to function as a productive adult in society. For example, the basic subjects of reading, writing, and arithmetic should form the core of content taught at the elementary level. At the secondary level, science, mathematics, English, and history would be among the core requirements. Essentialists perceive serious knowledge as residing primarily in the sciences and the technical fields. Vocational subjects are also favored because they meet the important criterion of usefulness.

In this perspective, the arts and humanities are fine for personal pleasure, but are generally not considered as among those essentials that are needed for a learner to become a useful adult. Many essentialists view these subjects as frills and, when budgets are tight, suggest that they should be the first cut. Essentialists argue that the schools should not waste time dealing with topics that are of little practical utility.

Essentialists believe that the primary role of the teacher is to impart information to learners. For their part, learners are expected to learn and retain this factual information. Teacher-centered techniques, such as the lecture, are favored, as are any new technologies that are thought to be capable of transmitting new information quickly and efficiently.

Essentialists tend to believe that people are not basically good, and that individuals who are left to their own devices will not develop the habits and knowledge necessary for them to become good people. Therefore, the authority of the teacher, hard work, and discipline are important values for the essentialist. Because essentialists believe that character development is important and that teachers instruct by example, they are convinced that the character and habits of the teacher must be above reproach.

Essentialism reflects the hard-work and "can-do" spirit of Americans. These perspectives can be traced to the earliest days of our country. Recall, for example, that Benjamin Franklin was interested in making the school a "more practical" place. Current trends suggest that the essentialist position continues to be a potent force in American education.

## Perennialism

*Perennialism* views truth as unchanging, or perennial. Perennialists such as Mortimer Adler (1982), Arthur Bestor (1955), and Robert Hutchins (1936) have contended that education should focus on the search for and dissemination of these unchanging principles. Though perennialists grant that changing times bring some surface-level alterations in the problems that people face, they feel that the real substance of our lives remains unchanged over generations. Furthermore, they believe that the experiences of human beings through the centuries have established which truths are worth knowing.

*"Utterly fascinating. And just which philosophical tradition is the source of your 'clownology' approach?"*
Courtesy of Ford Button.

Perennialists believe that western society lost its way several centuries ago. They decry what they see as a trend to rely too much on experimental science and technology and thus ignore enduring truths. They argue that the growing status of scientific experimentation has led to a denial of the power and importance of human reason.

Perennialists favor schools that develop the intellect of all learners and prepare them for life. This preparation is best accomplished when individuals have mastered the truths discovered through the centuries. Such wisdom is seen as important regardless of the career or vocation an individual ultimately chooses to follow.

Because the perennialist views knowledge as consisting of unified and unchanging principles, the emphasis of essentialism on separate subjects and on the learning and retention of factual information is soundly condemned. The separate subjects that the perennialist might support are those that are broadly defined as the classical liberal arts. The perennialist points out that what the essentialist considers "essential" is constantly changing. Therefore, a school program's focus on the essentials runs the risk of teaching learners information that, in time, will have little relevance for their lives.

Perennialists are particularly vocal in their opposition to vocational training in the schools. They believe that vocational education represents a sellout of the true educational purposes of the school to the narrow interests of business and government. This concern is directed not only at public schools, but at colleges and universities as well.

Perennialists believe that higher education has developed entirely inappropriate emphases on developing students' research skills and on preparing them for future careers. In the eyes of perennialists, courses with these emphases divert students away from a "genuine education" that would emphasize a mastery of lasting truth. If they could, perennialists would ban all research and practical training from colleges and universities and turn these responsibilities over to technical institutes.

The perennialist shares with the essentialist the idea that the primary goal of education is to develop the intellect. However, in the perennialist view learners should pursue truth for its own sake, not because it happens to be useful for some vocation. This pursuit of truth can best be accomplished through the study of the great literary works of civilization. Perennialists are especially attracted to courses in the humanities and literature. These classics are viewed as important because they deal with universal issues and themes that are as contemporary today as when they were written.

One branch of perennialism is relevant to some current debate about school curricula. Supporters of this variant of perennialism contend that universal truths flow from God. Therefore, they see education as distorted and incomplete unless theology and religious instruction accompany the study of other topics. The protests of some religious groups about schools and schooling are manifestations of this branch of perennialism.

## Reconstructionism

Similar to the perennialists, *reconstructionists* believe that society has lost its way. A classic work laying out the basic position of reconstructionism is George Counts's 1932 work, *Dare the Schools Build a New Social Order?*

Whereas perennialists seek answers from the past, reconstructionists propose to build a whole new social order. They see the aim of the school as an important catalyst in the effort to improve the human condition through reform.

For reconstructionists, the legitimate goal of education is to promote a critical appraisal of all elements of society. As a result of schooling, individuals should be in control of their own destinies and capable of promoting social reform. Reconstructionists favor curricula that emphasize the importance of creating a world of economic abundance, equality, fairness, and democratic decision making. They see this social reconstruction as necessary for the survival of humankind. Reconstructionists favor a school program that focuses on the ills of society and awakens individuals' consciousness about social problems. They believe that students need to be taught to critically analyze all aspects of life and learn to question rather than accept the pronouncements of those who hold political power. The reconstructionist curriculum draws heavily from the insights of the behavioral sciences, which reconstructionists believe can be used as the basis for creating a society where individuals can attain their fullest potentials.

Teachers have a direct and important role to play in the education program of the reconstructionist. Their role is not to transmit knowledge, but instead to raise issues and direct learners to relevant resources. There is an emphasis on active participation by the learners. Ideally, the classroom enacts the values of equality and social justice. Teachers seek to create a classroom environment that mirrors the kind of just society that the reconstructionists seek.

## Philosophy and Educational Issues

Controversy results when individuals with different philosophies make recommendations about educational programs (as shown in this chapter's Case Study). This controversy is often unsettling for the teacher who fails to understand that there are important differences in what various people see as the purpose of the school. Many of the current issues facing our schools regarding teaching religion, censoring textbooks, relying heavily on standardized testing of students and teachers, and selecting curriculum content have their roots in philosophy.

---

CASE STUDY

*Conflicting philosophies can spell trouble*

**Roberto Lopez really likes the sixth graders he teaches.** He feels that he is connecting with them as individuals, and many parents have praised him for his work. Roberto believes strongly that learners have to be actively involved if they are to take much away from their work at school. He has developed a series of lessons built around the interests of the people in his class. Many of these lessons feature challenging problem-solving activities. Roberto finds little need for the textbooks and prepackaged unit plans that were given to him at the beginning of the year.

If someone would have asked him before yesterday how things were going, Roberto would have said, "Great!" But after this morning's visit from Ms. Fifer, the school principal, this sunny vision has been clouded. Ms. Fifer commented that the kinds of lessons he was using were of "little value" because they had little substance and strayed too far from the prescribed curriculum. The prescribed curriculum, Ms. Fifer pointed out, contained "tried and true" information that every learner ought to master. In short, virtually everything Ms. Fifer said suggested to Roberto that he was doing a very poor job in the classroom. He is quite upset at this unanticipated reaction to his teaching.

*What do you see as the major problem in this situation? What philosophical orientation does Roberto Lopez seem to have? How does this compare to Ms. Fifer's? What do you think ought to be done? What does this situation suggest to you as you think about your own future as a teacher?*

In reality, educational programs result from compromises among various philosophical positions. An observation of the current educational scene reveals some elements of essentialism, some of progressivism, some of perennialism, and some of reconstructionism. An understanding of the basic positions associated with these perspectives can contribute to the development of a more adequate grasp of what divides the contending parties.

# Key Ideas in Summary

- Behind every teaching method and every plan for organizing a school is a set of assumptions. When teachers understand these assumptions, they are in a better position to defend what they are doing and to understand the sources of criticism leveled at their educational practices.

- *Metaphysics* deals with the nature of reality. Answers to metaphysical questions have implications for the identification of educational goals, the selection of appropriate content, and the formation of attitudes regarding the general nature of learners.

- *Epistemology* is concerned with the nature of knowledge. It has relevance for such educational issues as determining the types of knowledge to be taught and deciding upon the reliability of alternative ways of knowing content.

- *Axiology* deals with the nature of values. It has implications for education in terms of how teaching relates to character development, morality, and the formation of personal values. Axiological questions focus on such issues as the purpose of life and the characteristics of right conduct.

- *Logic* centers on the clarity of thought and on relationships among ideas. It provides people with a process they can use to make clear distinctions between valid and fallacious thinking. For this reason, educators should be concerned that their learners develop a solid grounding in logical thinking.

- *Idealism* is one of the oldest philosophies. It holds that the ultimate reality is in the world of ideas. There is a universal set of truths that can be discovered through use of the intellect.

**Table 5–1**
Summary Table: Philosophies of Education

| Major Topics | Characteristics |
|---|---|
| Kinds of philosophical questions | |
| • Metaphysical | Concern the nature of reality |
| • Epistemological | Concern the nature of knowledge |
| • Axiological | Concern values and ethics |
| • Logical | Concern the relationship between ideas and the procedures used to distinguish between valid and fallacious thinking |
| Basic philosophies | |
| • Idealism | Reality is not to be found in the material world but instead in the mental world of ideas or ideals |
| • Realism | Reality is the tangible world that can be perceived directly through the senses |
| • Pragmatism | Reality changes; truth is temporary, and it is found by examining evidence relevant to a particular situation |
| • Existentialism | The universe lacks any grand design or purpose; each person must determine his or her own reason for existing |
| Educational applications of philosophical ideas | |
| • Progressivism | Knowledge is tentative; schools should teach problem-solving skills to learners so that they can adapt to change |
| • Essentialism | Schools should provide sound, practical training that will help learners become employed, contributing citizens; trivial and nonessential courses should be eliminated |
| • Perennialism | Truth is unchanging; universal principles have been known for centuries; traditional knowledge should be transmitted by schools, chiefly through the classics and the liberal arts |
| • Reconstructionism | Society is in desperate need of reform; learners should be trained to be reform-minded political and social activists; schools should place a heavy emphasis on the social sciences |

- *Realism* emphasizes that the material universe represents the ultimate reality. What people should do is study this material universe with a view to making sense out of the patterns they observe. For the realist, ideas are merely shadows of reality; the real test for truth is the extent to which these ideas correspond with what exists in the material world.

- *Pragmatism* does not accept the existence of universal truths or principles. The appropriateness of any action should be judged by its consequences, which may vary with time and circumstances. For the pragmatist, experimentation is the best approach to gain knowledge. All knowledge should be regarded as tentative and should be readily modified as new information becomes available.

- *Existentialism* contends that, beyond the certainty of one's ultimate death, there are no universal truths. There is no overall order or purpose to life. People must find their own meaning for existing. Personal freedom is a dominant theme in existentialist thought—each person must come to understand that he or she bears a personal responsibility for shaping the nature of his or her life.

- *Progressivism* has important ties to pragmatism. Progressives hold that knowledge is ever-changing and that the best approach to acquiring it is to actively involve learners with the environment. Scientific experimentation is considered the most reliable way to acquire new knowledge. Progressives want learners to master the processes of scientific thinking so that they will apply these tested problem-solving techniques to any new situations they encounter. Such skills are believed to be important aids in accommodating change.

- *Essentialism* is a perspective that holds a dominant position in American education. Essentialism focuses on the identification of information that is thought essential for a person to become a productive member of society. There is a heavy emphasis on useful information. Essentialists expect teachers to transmit knowledge to learners in an orderly and efficient manner.

- *Perennialism* represents something of a protest against both progressivism and essentialism. Perennialists hold that there are a number of universal principles that need to be mastered by all learners. They believe that western society has strayed away from a focus on these universal truths and has become irresponsibly devoted to experimentation and technology. Perennialists believe that the focus of school study should be the classics, including writings of the ancients and other great works of philosophy and literature. The perennialist believes that insights revealed in these works are as relevant today as they were when first set down.

- *Reconstructionism* holds that the role of the school is to teach learners how to make a new social order. Reconstructionists emphasize the importance of questioning present practices and developing learners' abilities to think critically about social issues. The role of content for the reconstructionist is to inform learners about issues and help them choose courses of action that will lead to social improvement.

## Review and Discussion Questions

1. What are some concerns of metaphysics?
2. What are some examples of positions that can be taken in answering basic epistemological questions?
3. What do you think most Americans have concluded regarding (*a*) appropriate sources of knowledge and (*b*) how knowledge should be verified?
4. An acceptance of which sort of philosophical ideas is implied by a teacher's decision to emphasize problem-solving in his or her lessons?
5. What are some contemporary issues in education that are related to axiological questions?
6. How does inductive logic differ from deductive logic?
7. Which educational practices might win support from someone strongly attracted to realism?
8. What are some instructional emphases that would be supported by people identifying with progressivism?
9. According to essentialists, what should be the major purposes of education and the schools?
10. What differences might you expect in (*a*) a school with a faculty and administration totally committed to perennialism and (*b*) a school with a faculty and administration totally committed to reconstructionism?

## Ideas for Field Experiences, Projects, and Enrichment

1. In recent years, many proposals to reform the schools have been put forward and widely reported in professional education journals and general-circulation magazines and newspapers. Read an article that outlines specific ideas suggested in one of these major reform proposals, and identify the specific philosophical orientation that seems to be reflected in each idea. Prepare this information for presentation to your class in the form of an oral report.

2. Observe teacher behavior in two or more classrooms. Tie the individual instructional practices you observe to some of the philosophical perspectives introduced in this chapter. Share your information with others in the class. As a class group, identify some of the philosophical perspectives that you reported were most frequently observed in the classrooms.

3. Interview a school principal about his or her views regarding the characteristics of the ideal teacher. In a short paper, identify the philosophical perspectives that the principal seems to have preferred in this ideal teacher. What kinds of instructional practices would you expect this principal to praise? Which kinds might receive less favorable comment from the principal?

4. In a short paper, describe what you consider an ideal school curriculum. Be sure to identify those subjects that should receive greatest emphasis. You also might wish to include your views regarding subjects that should receive little emphasis or should not be taught at all. In the concluding portion of your paper, identify the philosophical assumptions that undergird the curriculum you describe.

5. Invite a school district curriculum director to visit your class. Ask this person to explain a typical elementary school course of study and a typical high school course of study in his or her district. As a follow-up to this presentation, participate in a class discussion focusing on philosophical assumptions that seem to support the described courses of study in this district.

· · · · · · · · · · · · · · · · · · · · · · · · · · · ·

# Supplementary Reading

Bigge, M. *Educational Philosophies for Teachers.* Columbus, OH: Merrill, 1982.

Cremin, L. *The Transformation of the School: Progressivism in American Education, 1876–1957.* New York: Knopf, 1961.

Gray, J. *Re-Thinking American Education: A Philosophy of Teaching and Learning.* 2d ed. Middletown, CT: Wesleyan University Press, 1984.

Gutek, G. *Philosophical and Ideological Perspectives on Education.* Englewood Cliffs, NJ: Prentice Hall, 1988.

Kneller, G. F. *Movements of Thought in Modern Education.* New York: Wiley, 1984.

Lipman, M., and A. Sharp, eds. *Growing Up with Philosophy.* Philadelphia: Temple University Press, 1978.

Ornstein, A. C., and D. U. Levine. *An Introduction to the Foundations of Education.* 3d ed. Boston: Houghton Mifflin, 1985.

Power, E. J. *Philosophy of Education.* Englewood Cliffs, NJ: Prentice Hall, 1982.

· · · · · · · · · · · · · · · · · · · · · · · · · · · ·

# References

Adler, M. *The Paideia Proposal.* New York: Macmillan, 1982.

Bagley, W. C. "An Essentialist's Platform for the Advancement of American Education." *Educational Administration and Supervision* (April 1938): 241–56.

Bayles, E. *Pragmatism in Education.* New York: Harper and Row, 1966.

Bestor, A. *The Restoration of Learning.* New York: Knopf, 1955.

Counts, G. S. *Dare the Schools Build a New Social Order?* New York: John Day, 1932.

Dewey, J. *The Child and The Curriculum.* Chicago: University of Chicago Press, 1902.

Dewey, J. *Democracy and Education.* New York: Macmillan, 1916.

Dewey, J. *Experience and Education.* New York: Macmillan, 1938.

Dewey, J. *How We Think.* Boston: D.C. Heath, 1910.

Dewey, J. *The School and Society.* Chicago: University of Chicago Press, 1923.

Gray, J. *Re-Thinking American Education: A Philosophy of Teaching and Learning.* 2d ed. Middletown, CT: Wesleyan University Press, 1984.

Hutchins, R. M. *The Higher Learning in America.* New Haven, CT: Yale University Press, 1936.

Kelley, E. *The Evidence of the Senses: A Realist Theory of Perception.* Baton Rouge, LA: Louisiana State University Press, 1986.

Martin, W. *Realism in Education.* New York: Harper and Row, 1969.

Morris, V. C. *Existentialism in Education.* New York: Harper and Row, 1966.

Oliver, D., and K. Gersham. *Education, Modernity, and Fractured Meaning.* Albany, NY: State University of New York Press, 1989.

# Chapter 6

# Sociology of Education

· · · · · · · · · · · · · · · · · · · · · · · · · · · · · · · · · · · · · ·

## Objectives

This chapter provides information to help the reader

- distinguish among perspectives of people subscribing to the functionalist, economic-class conflict, and status-group conflict positions.
- explain various roles played by schools as institutions.
- describe in-school and out-of-school roles of teachers and potential conflicts between and among roles.
- point out alternative ways individual learners may react to the school program.
- suggest potential sources of conflict between views promoted in school programs and those espoused in learners' homes, ethnic and cultural groups, and religious and social groups.

# Focus Questions

1. What are some examples of issues that interest educational sociologists?
2. What are some assumptions of people who subscribe to the functionalist position?
3. What are the basic positions of individuals committed to (*a*) the economic-class conflict position and (*b*) the status-group conflict position?
4. How are changes in school programs explained by people who are committed to (*a*) the economic-class conflict position and to (*b*) the status-group conflict position?
5. What are some roles that schools play as institutions?
6. What are some contrasting responsibilities teachers must discharge in their roles as school professionals?
7. In what ways might teachers' out-of-school and in-school roles and responsibilities conflict?
8. What are some different ways individual learners react to the school program?
9. What kinds of role conflicts are experienced by some learners as a result of their family, ethnic and cultural group, or religious or social group membership?
10. How can teachers help learners maintain a commitment to the school program even when some content seems at odds with values espoused by the learners' families and other groups to which they belong?

• • • • • • • • • • • • • • • • • • • • • • • • • • •

# Introduction

The learning and behavior patterns of young people have many bases. Certainly the prescribed school curriculum has some influence, but so do learners' families, friends, and the cultural and ethnic groups to which they belong. These social factors often shape young people's reactions to school programs (Webb and Sherman, 1989). The relative importance of the school curriculum and outside influences has prompted interest in such questions as:

- Whose interests do schools serve?
- What functions are fulfilled by schools?
- What are the various roles teachers play?
- How do families, ethnicity, and groups influence learners' reactions to schools?

Educational sociologists are interested in how groups influence individual learners and how the school, as an institution, functions in a society where not all groups share common values. Different sociologists have developed some quite different perspectives on the nature of the school as an institution and on the kinds of people who most benefit from school programs.

## School Programs: Three Sociological Perspectives

The nature and impact of school programs can be looked at from a number of viewpoints. Three perspectives that different educational sociologists have used are:

- the functionalist position
- the economic-class conflict position
- the status-group conflict position

## The Functionalist Position

Functionalists see society as sharing a common set of values. Over time, these values have led to the development of institutions such as schools, families, governmental entities, and religious bodies. Each of these institutions has a specialized responsibility or function. Performance of these functions helps maintain the society. In the functionalist view, society in its present form is worth maintaining, because people in society share more common values than values that might lead to conflict and discord. This harmonious social order deserves to be saved and passed on intact from generation to generation.

In our society, schools have come to discharge responsibilities that once were taken care of by families. This is particularly true in the area of preparing young people for the workplace. Today, most work is performed away from the home. Additionally, skills needed have become so specialized that parents are no longer able to prepare their children for their future vocational roles. The role of families has become limited to providing for children's emotional and psychological needs; preparation for economic life has more and more been turned over to specialists in the schools.

Talcott Parsons (1959), a leading American functionalist, saw the school as an agency with a responsibility for providing our society with trained workers. In the functionalist view, all learners have the ability to profit from programs offered by the school. Those who will get the best jobs are those learners who, by virtue of their individual abilities and effort, take full advantage of what schools have to offer. There is an assumption that economic rewards will be distributed on the basis of individual merit, and that the school provides equal opportunities for all (Dougherty and Hammack, 1990).

The functionalist view has been very popular. It suggests that the school, by training people for occupations needed by the society as a whole, will provide the conditions for economic growth. Economic growth, in turn, will yield benefits that will improve the lives of everyone in the society. The potential for economic growth provides a rationale for expanding educational services. Functionalists argue that this expansion will benefit disadvantaged as well as advantaged groups.

The functionalist position assumes that once a school structure is in place that can provide learners with the information they will need as adults, all learners will have the potential to derive maximum benefits from school programs. Critics have argued that functionalism fails to attend to important differences among groups of learners in the school. They argue that school programs often do not serve interests of all learners equally well.

## The Economic-Class Conflict Position

Adherents of the economic-class conflict position reject functionalism's premise that there exists within society a broad consensus on basic values. Rather than viewed as a calm and homogeneous community of people sharing common commitments, society is better thought of as a battleground where contesting groups strive for supremacy. In these conflicts, there are winners and losers. As applied to school programs, the economic-class conflict perspective suggests that there is competition for the benefits that schools have to offer, and that more economically powerful groups see to it that school advantages flow to their children. This results in fewer educational advantages for less economically powerful groups.

Historically, the economic-class conflict position stems from the work of Karl Marx and Friedrich Engels. Marx and Engels argued that the class struggle features a conflict between a capitalist class that controls the means of economic production and a working class forced to serve the capitalists. This situation produces a condition of tension that leads to a continuing confrontation between the two groups.

As applied to present-day education, the economic-class conflict position has led to two somewhat different interpretations: (1) the class reproduction view and (2) the class conflict view (Dougherty and Hammack, 1990). People who support the class reproduction point of view argue that expansion of school programs has been motivated by capitalists' desires to serve the needs of their own class. Such supporters point to efforts to infuse computer technology, advanced mathematics, and similar content into the school as evidence of an attempt to skew school programs to meet the needs of future owners and managers. Attempts to upgrade vocational skills are portrayed as efforts of the managerial and ownership class to ensure a steady supply of trained workers.

Supporters of the class conflict view argue that educational change has not come about as a result of capitalists seeking to shape school programs to serve their own interest; rather, such changes have occurred because economically disadvantaged groups have expressed their unhappiness with existing practices. These groups have challenged the adequacy of existing school practices, and the conflict they have initiated has led to many changes in school programs favored by such economically disadvantaged groups as females and ethnic minorities.

Critics of the economic-class conflict position suggest that its supporters place too much emphasis on economic status of groups as an explanation for changes in school programs. They point out that many Americans have little personal sense of membership in a particular economic class. For example, recent national elections have witnessed large numbers of people with relatively modest incomes identifying with the same Republican candidates that large business interests have strongly supported. Further, there is evidence that many learners who come from working-class families do acquire the education necessary to move into managerial and executive positions. Though social mobility is not guaranteed by access to schooling, it is not so uncommon an occurrence as might be suggested by supporters of the economic-class conflict position.

## The Status-Group Conflict Position

The economic-class conflict position suggests that social status and power are a function of economics. The status-group conflict position derives from the thought of the German sociologist Max Weber, who proposed that change results from conflicts among competing groups (Dougherty and Hammack, 1990). This position proposes that economic conditions alone are too narrow a basis for determining individual or group status. Status instead is awarded to influential leaders in social organizations, governmental organizations, religious organizations, and other groups. These status groups serve the interests of their members. In doing so, they often come into conflict with one another. Thus, according to the status-group conflict position, it is conflict among these diverse status groups that best explains why educational changes occur.

Supporters of the status-group conflict position suggest that school programs have many characteristics that are the result of efforts of specific groups to advance their own interests. It has been suggested that the organization of school knowledge into separate subject areas and the division of the school day into time periods is a reflection of industrial managers' desires to familiarize learners with the working environment of an industrial culture (with its departmentalized functions, systematic planning, and careful attention to time schedules) (Khumar, 1989). Another view is that physical education programs have been supported by military leaders who are interested in having available for service people who are in good physical condition. Student government and other school groups that require learners to work on committees and engage in problem solving have been seen as schemes to familiarize young people with the roles of government officials and to prepare some of them for future employment in government service. Finally, pressures on schools to hire teachers representing a cross-section of ethnic groups have been thought to result, in part, from interests of ethnic minorities to retain their special identities and to apprise others of their particular perspectives.

Critics of the status-group conflict position contend that its adherents overemphasize conflict as the primary determinant of the character of school programs. These critics acknowledge that there are differences among groups and that these differences frequently lead to disputes. They accept, too, that these conflicts may influence school programs. But they also continue to argue for the importance of some shared national values that cut across individual groups. The critics maintain that these shared values, as well as between-group conflict, influence what goes on in our schools.

The varying perspectives of people committed to the functionalist position, the economic-class conflict position, and the status-group conflict position look at efforts to change school programs very differently (see Box 6–1). For functionalists, disagreements about present school programs are viewed as arguments within a basically warm and harmonious family whose members are trying to define a common ground that all can support. Changes are adopted out of a conviction that they will be helpful to the entire society. The basic question they ask is "Is this change consistent with broadly held values and is it designed to benefit all learners?"

People who are committed to either of the two conflict positions take a different view. They look for potential winners and losers when proposals are put forward to change school programs. They do not see discussions of school program reform as efforts

---

## BOX 6–1
## ADVANCED CALCULUS: WHO WILL BENEFIT?

A reader recently wrote these comments in a letter to the editor of a local newspaper:

Our school board has done it again. Now we are to be treated to a high school curriculum featuring a spanking new advanced calculus course. We already have a regular calculus course which, according to my calculations, serves a grand total of 10 percent of the high school population. This advanced calculus offering will be taken just by a select few who do well in the regular calculus course.

Why are we committing scarce district funds to support a program that will benefit a tiny fraction of our students? I think I know the answer, and I don't like it. The well-heeled families who have a lot of political stroke around here want their kids to have an extra edge when they head off to the engineering programs in the prestigious private colleges and universities. As for the other kids—the vast majority, I might add—well, too bad. The school district won't have money this year to take care of their needs.

*What Do You Think?*

1. Are these comments most consistent with the functionalist position or with one of the conflict positions?
2. What arguments might you make to attack the position taken by this writer? To add further support to it?
3. What are your personal reactions to this point of view?

to achieve a society-wide consensus. Instead, such talks are viewed as a part of a recurring pattern of conflict among groups—a pattern that almost always results in individual decisions benefiting some groups more than others. A major objective of conflict-position partisans is to expose to public view the likely consequences of a proposed school policy for members of individual groups. They see the debate as being properly focused on the question "Will this policy benefit the groups that deserve to benefit from it?"

The functionalist position and the conflict positions often lead people to quite different conclusions about what schools are doing. For example, a functionalist might view a high school curriculum featuring many electives as a positive indicator of a program responsive to learners' varying interests and needs. But a person committed to one of the conflict positions might see the very same curriculum as a clever device that powerful interest groups use to direct learners from non-influential groups into courses that fail to prepare them for well-paid, high-status jobs.

## Roles of Schools

As important social institutions, schools play many roles. Among them are roles associated with:

- transmission of the general culture
- transmission of knowledge
- preparation for the workplace
- promotion of social and group relationships
- encouragement of social change

## Transmission of the General Culture

Schools act to transmit certain values, beliefs, and norms to learners. These perspectives are broadly endorsed by our society, but this does not mean that all individuals and groups subscribe to every value, belief, and norm that is explicitly or implicitly included in our school programs. Discussions about the extent of the school's responsibilities for shaping learners' attitudes sometimes lead to acrimonious debates regarding the proper limits of the school's socialization responsibilities.

Part of the difficulty stems from the school's standing as just one of several influences on learners' values. Families also greatly affect learners' patterns of behavior and thinking. This is especially true of younger children, but families have an impact on older learners as well. Social groups, churches, friends, and other sources of influence also help shape the perspectives of young people. The accompanying What the Experts Say illustrates cultural influences on textbooks in India and Canada.

Some school activities undertaken by educators to socialize the young are more controversial than others. It has generally been recognized that schools have a special responsibility to prepare young people for the workplace (Goslin, 1990). Few families and other groups in our society have the expertise needed to perform this role. On the other hand, school programs that are related to personal behavior (e.g., sex education) often bring protests from people who suggest that the school is improperly infringing on the prerogatives of the family (or some other institution or group).

## *Cultural influences on school learning materials*

Cultural perspectives influence the content of school programs. In this connection, educational sociologist Krishna Khumar (1989) has pointed out that ". . . the curriculum is not just a logical packaging of facts, but rather a reorganization of available knowledge from a certain perspective" (p. 69).

To illustrate this point, Khumar compared depictions of children in texts used in India and Canada by learners in grades 4 through 6. He found that many more children were included in stories in the Canadian texts than in the Indian texts. Further, the children in the Canadian texts were portrayed as engaged in more creative and imaginative activities than those in the Indian texts.

Khumar attributed the relatively infrequent occurrence of children as characters and their relative passivity to the Indian cultural context. He pointed out that because of the very high death rate among young children in India, not much "personhood" is attached to them. Consequently, not much thought is given to special characteristics of children. In Indian society, as in the Indian texts, the social world is very much dominated by adults.

On the other hand, survival rates of children in Canada are high. There, children are perceived as people of consequence in their own right. It is only natural, then, that they play more active roles in stories included in Canadian school texts.

Source: Krishna Khumar, *Social Character of Learning* (New Delhi, India: Sage Publications India Pvt. Ltd., 1989).

### Transmission of Knowledge

Schools have an obligation to transmit specialized knowledge, particularly academic knowledge, to learners. The quantity and sophistication of knowledge needed by young people today goes beyond the limits of what most of their parents know. Educators in the school are expected to draw on their expertise and transmit specialized information to learners.

The quantity of knowledge and time limitations prevent schools from teaching *everything*. The adopted curriculum functions as a screen or filter that allows only a limited amount of information to be included in the school program. As a result, sometimes groups challenge the adequacy of certain aspects of the adopted curriculum.

For example, some educators who note that Hispanics in just a few years will become the nation's most numerous minority group wonder about the traditional east-to-west presentation of U.S. history in the schools. For many years, the settlement and development of the United States has been described in terms of a wave of migration from the Atlantic coast to the Pacific coast. Given this pattern of course organization, it has been hard for teachers to include information about contributions of Hispanics, a group who have gradually occupied the country from south to north. It may be that, in the future, consideration will be given to presenting the country's settlement in terms of both an east-to-west and a south-to-north pattern.

Sometimes, too, specific learning materials transmit a lesson suggesting that members of certain groups are less worthy than members of other groups. A prominent educational psychologist from India, Krishna Khumar (1989), describes a widely used school story about a wealthy merchant who listens to the complaints of a poor worker that his life is worthless. The wealthy merchant offers to buy one of the poor worker's eyes for a small price. The worker rejects the initial offer but continues to negotiate with the rich merchant, who gradually increases his offer to the princely sum of 100,000 rupees. At this point, the poor worker realizes that he does have value and thanks the merchant for providing him with this insight (but still rejects the offer).

There are several messages in this story that some groups might find objectionable. For example, it seems to imply that wealth, wisdom, and virtue go together. It also suggests that the poor should follow the ideas of the rich. The subtext of the tale might be summarized as "Don't rock the boat, but appreciate what you have, even if you're poor."

## Preparation for the Workplace

The economic existence of every society depends on the availability of people to perform the kinds of work that need to be done. The various jobs that must be performed require enormously different levels of expertise. One of the functions of the school as an institution is to prepare new people to take on these diverse job roles. In a sense, the school performs a sorting function. As learners progress through school programs, they develop varying levels of expertise that help qualify them for some positions and eliminate them from positions requiring different kinds of understandings and talents.

Some occupational roles carry with them more prestige and, often, higher levels of remuneration than others. School programs that help people prepare for these valued occupational roles are often academically rigorous. For example, young people preparing to pursue careers in engineering often take intellectually challenging mathematics courses. The difficulty of some of these courses, in theory, ensures that competent people will enter advanced engineering curricula. It also ensures that numbers of potential engineers will not be too high and that many individuals who might be attracted to engineering early in their school years will subsequently be diverted into other career paths.

Controversy sometimes accompanies decisions that direct individual learners toward courses of study related to preparation for particular careers. For example, there may be concerns that learners from some groups (e.g., young people from economically impoverished households or from certain ethnic and minority groups) are being directed away from the courses of study that lead to high-prestige occupations. Today, schools are under increasing pressure to demonstrate an absence of bias in their procedures of assigning individuals to particular courses.

## Promotion of Social and Group Relationships

The school provides a setting that fosters the development of learners' social and group skills. This is done both by design and as a side effect of the special environment of the school setting. Deliberate attempts to help learners develop a sense of identity with the entire group of individuals enrolled in their school include such recurring activities as pep assemblies and athletic contests (Bernstein, 1977).

Does a student with AIDS have a right to continue with his or her education? These parents are picketing in front of the school board offices to keep AIDS-infected students out of their neighborhood school.

Learners who strongly identify with their school are thought to have a more positive attitude toward teachers, other learners, and the entire educational enterprise. At the same time, this kind of group identification stands as a proxy for what many learners will be encouraged to promote as adult employees of businesses and government agencies and as members of religious groups and other organizations.

There are official clubs and organizations in most schools, and there are especially large numbers of them in secondary schools. Learners who participate in these groups gain experience in working with others inside the individual organizations and, to some extent, in working and competing with outside groups (for meeting space, limited financial resources, and so forth). For example, organizations not formally sponsored by the school sometimes make arrangements to use school facilities when classes are not in session (such organizations might include scouting groups, church youth groups, and junior branches of fraternal organizations). Learners derive benefits from their association with these groups in the same way they profit from participation in school-sponsored organizations.

In addition to providing a setting within which different learner organizations flourish, schools also provide a context for helping young people learn socially appropriate patterns of interpersonal relations. A school brings large numbers of young people together in a common place. It provides a laboratory for the development of many kinds of acceptable person-to-person behavior patterns. For example, school classes include a variety of individuals. In these classes, learners meet people from social, ethnic, and cultural backgrounds that may be different from their own. Also, male–female relationships begin to develop as young people mature. Some school functions— dances, for example—are specifically designed to support socially acceptable ways of developing such relationships. In summary, the school teaches much to learners beyond the prescribed academic curriculum. It encourages the development of social behaviors that will be useful to them as adults (see Box 6–2).

### Encouragement of Social Change

Schools are often regarded as agencies of social improvement. This is particularly true when the public is greatly concerned about specific social problems (Goslin, 1990). Faith in better education as a curative agent is widespread. Few politicians miss opportunities to speak about their intentions to "reduce the crime rate," "effect a reduction in the number of alcoholics," "diminish the use of illegal drugs," or "reduce promiscuity and teenage pregnancies" through the institution of "sound educational programs."

The view that schools can function as powerful social reform agents appeals to some educators, but others question this view. Critics point out that schools themselves

---

BOX 6–2

## WHAT DID YOU LEARN IN SCHOOL OUTSIDE OF THE CLASSROOM?

Schools teach many things that are not part of the academic curriculum. Think about clubs, organizations, and other activities that were conducted under the auspices of the schools you attended. Try to identify at least six things you learned in these settings that have proved useful to you later in your life.

1. _____

2. _____

3. _____

4. _____

5. _____

6. _____

are part of the larger society that has spawned these problems. For this reason, these critics doubt that changes in school programs will have meaningful results because of the absence of changes in society as a whole.

When policymakers ask schools to take on challenges such as "diminishing the rate of drug use," there is a good chance that even well-intentioned efforts of educators will fail. If this happens, schools are likely to receive undeserved blame from people who have placed too much faith in their schools' curative powers. This can lead to an erosion of support for more traditional school functions, such as transmitting academic knowledge to learners.

Despite concerns that have been raised about the appropriateness of asking schools to solve intractable social problems, the belief that education is a potent reform agent has wide support. It is quite probable that political leaders will continue to look on the schools as important institutional players in efforts to cure society's ills.

When we speak of the role of the school, we are really making a shorthand statement about the net impact of actions of all the individuals who interact within the school. These individuals include administrators, counselors, teachers, learners, custodians, school nurses, cafeteria and kitchen workers, and secretaries. All have important roles to play, but because they represent such a large majority, teachers and learners play especially important roles in the educational enterprise. The remainder of this chapter will examine these roles in depth.

## Roles of Teachers

Teachers play many roles. Duties associated with one role may conflict with those associated with another. The need to balance competing role responsibilities contributes to the complexity of teaching. Among teachers' diverse obligations are:

- instructional responsibilities
- counseling responsibilities
- administrative responsibilities
- curriculum development responsibilities
- professional development responsibilities
- public relations responsibilities
- nonschool-related responsibilities

## Instructional Responsibilities

Without instruction, there would be no schools. This function is universally regarded as a critical obligation that the school, as an institution, must discharge. Though the mix of other teacher responsibilities varies from school to school, it is fair to say that all classroom teachers share a common duty to provide instruction.

In years gone by, *teaching* was sometimes viewed as synonymous with *telling*, and the teacher was seen as a dispenser of knowledge. Today, teachers are often considered not exclusive sources of information but instructional managers. Teachers who function as instructional managers work to establish an environment in which learning can take place. In planning learning experiences, teachers attend to such tasks as:

- determining objectives
- diagnosing learners
- selecting and implementing instructional procedures
- assessing learners' progress

*Determining Objectives.*    This task involves identifying what learners will be able to do as a consequence of instruction. The learning objective becomes a target that the teacher uses in selecting learning resources and instructional techniques that will help learners to demonstrate the desired behavior at the conclusion of the instructional sequence.

*Diagnosing Learners.*    Learners in our classrooms are becoming increasingly diverse. The purpose of instructional diagnosis is to gather information about each learner for the purpose of designing an instructional program suitable for his or her needs. Information about prior learning, reading and computational skills, general interests, learning style, and other areas help teachers to design lessons that help young people to experience success. Success builds learner confidence and leads to more positive attitudes about the teacher and the school (Good and Brophy, 1991).

*Selecting and Implementing Instructional Procedures.*    Teachers are expected to be familiar with a variety of instructional procedures. They must know strengths and weaknesses of approaches such as class discussion, simulation, team learning, cooperative learning, independent study, brainstorming, lecture, and debate. One of teachers' important responsibilities is to select and implement techniques that are consistent with diagnosed needs and that are appropriate given identified learning objectives.

*Assessing Learners' Progress.*    Teachers are responsible for assessing learners' progress. *Formative evaluation* occurs as part of the ongoing instructional process. It is designed to provide feedback to learners as they are beginning to work with new material. *Summative evaluation* occurs at the end of an instructional sequence, and is designed to provide information about what learners have retained from their exposure to the content that has been taught.

Some assessment involves use of formal tests that feature multiple choice, essay, true–false, matching, and completion questions. At other times, teachers rely on personal observation; individual teacher–learner conferences; and models, papers, special projects, and other "products" of learning.

Assessment information serves two important purposes. First, it gives an indication of how well individuals have mastered the content that has been introduced. Second, it provides the teacher with useful information about strengths and weaknesses of the instructional program.

## Counseling Responsibilities

Though most schools today have professional counselors, they often must spend much of their time working with learners who are experiencing particularly difficult personal problems and, thus, simply do not have time to work closely with every learner. Further, most learners do not know counselors as well as they know their teachers. As a result, it is common for teachers to be approached by individuals seeking advice about personal difficulties. Sometimes teachers can help, but other times they find it prudent to refer the learner to a counselor or to some other trained specialist.

Teachers who are good at discharging the counseling function help learners live and behave in constructive and satisfying ways. Many young people in school have not learned how to set and achieve goals. Teachers can help learners set personal objectives and identify what they must do to achieve them. When this happens, learners often develop behavior patterns that lead to success, and the success reinforces the behavior patterns that led to it. It can greatly improve learners' levels of achievement and their attitudes toward school.

To be successful in discharging the counseling function, teachers must be mature, personally secure people. An emotionally crippled teacher is in no position to help young people with serious problems. If the goal is to produce confident, self-assured learners, teachers must exemplify these attributes themselves.

## Administrative Responsibilities

It is common for teachers to comment that the administrative aspects of teaching are among their least enjoyable duties. Many complain that so much time is spent on paperwork that more important activities, such as preparing for lessons and working with individual learners, is neglected. Evidence indicates that teachers' paperwork load has increased in recent years. In part, this has resulted from accountability requirements imposed by state and federal educational authorities.

Much of the paperwork teachers deal with is internal to the school. Schedules must be developed. Learner records must be kept. Materials have to be ordered. Requests for films and other materials have to be filed. Attendance forms must be completed. Notes have to be recorded from school committee meetings. Though such tasks often are not particularly interesting or satisfying, teachers perform them to keep the school program functioning smoothly.

Maintenance of accurate attendance records is an especially important responsibility. In many states, school districts receive money from the state based on the number of learners in attendance. School districts have a heavy financial interest in seeing to it that reliable records document the number of learners that have been claimed for purposes of securing state funds. The teacher's daily attendance record often is a vital component of this documentation.

In addition to attendance, teachers maintain records of learners' academic progress. This information is used as a basis for grading. Good documentation can provide support for teachers who find learners or their parents challenging a grade that has been awarded. Courts generally have been reluctant to overturn grades when teachers have maintained good records of learner performance to support their grading decisions.

## Curriculum Development Responsibilities

It is common for teachers to participate in curriculum revision efforts. In larger districts, teachers frequently serve on curriculum committees that may include other teachers, several curriculum specialists, and one or two administrators.

Curriculum work often imposes burdens on teachers' time. Sometimes curriculum committee meetings are held after school, and occasionally they take place on weekends. After-school meetings are particularly hard on participants who, after having been hard at work all day, find their energy levels at a low ebb. Many who have participated in curriculum development under these conditions report that creative ideas come slowly when group members are tired. Where money is available, districts hire some teachers to prepare curricula during the summer months. Often this arrangement works well. Participants are able to concentrate all of their energies on this task, and they can start on it at the beginning of the day when they are alert and rested.

It is common for new teachers who are assigned to curriculum committees to feel unqualified for this responsibility. In their preparation programs, new teachers usually learn much more about basic instructional procedures than about curriculum design, and often have to learn many of the aspects of curriculum design on the job.

Teachers who develop an interest in curriculum may take in-service and summer courses to enrich their understanding of the field. Those who have an enthusiasm for and a proficiency in curriculum preparation often derive a great deal of satisfaction when, at the end of a complex curriculum project, they are able to implement new programs and materials in their own classrooms.

## Professional Development Responsibilities

Preparation for teaching does not end with the award of an initial teaching certificate. Unique demands of the particular setting where a teacher works often lead the teacher to seek additional training. Even teachers who have been in the field for many years find themselves confronted from time to time with situations that challenge their present levels of expertise.

In some parts of the country, teachers must take supplementary courses every few years to keep their teaching certificate valid. Other areas require courses for teachers wanting special certificates to gain additional professional authority. Traditionally, teachers have sought professional growth by taking college and university courses, either during the summer months or at night during the school year. Additional development opportunities are offered and staffed by school districts and other educational agencies.

In addition to taking courses, many teachers extend their expertise by reading professional books and journals. Almost all subject-matter areas have large professional organizations that print journals featuring articles of interest to their members. Articles appearing in these journals (and in other journals as well) are listed in the *Education Index*, found in many public libraries as well as in nearly all college and university libraries.

## Public Relations Responsibilities

Teachers can have a positive influence on how citizens view the quality of education in a district. This is particularly true of parents. Parents' views tend to be favorable when communication between themselves and their children's teachers is open and positive.

Sometimes prospective teachers who were raised in communities that took a great interest in their schools find it difficult to imagine groups of parents who are not active supporters of the school, but this kind of support is by no means universal. In an inner-city area of a large west-coast city where one of the authors once taught, the school administration commissioned a study of perceptions of city agencies and institutions. The survey revealed that parents and others in the community viewed the school as an institution second only to the police department as a potential threat to their lifestyle.

Parent–teacher organizations encourage comfortable communication between teachers and parents. A limitation of these groups, however, is that many parents do not attend the meetings. As a result, it is not always clear that the group of generally supportive parents who become involved truly represent the feelings of other parents and of the community as a whole.

Some school districts encourage teachers to visit learners' homes. A variant of this procedure features a neighborhood meeting in the home of a parent, where a few other parents are invited to meet informally with several teachers and administrators.

For all the efforts to encourage teacher–parent communication, many parents never hear from a teacher unless their child is having or causing a problem. Given this pattern, it is not surprising that a note or a call from the school often results in initial anxiety ("What has he or she done *this* time?"). To break the expectation that a message from a teacher means bad news, many districts encourage teachers to call parents when their children have done some exceptionally good work in school. This practice can generate a tremendous amount of positive support for the school.

In addition to various kinds of formal contacts, teachers frequently communicate informally with parents. For example, comments written on learners' papers are often read by parents. If the teacher's comments are insensitive or contain grammatical errors, the parents may develop negative feelings about the teacher and the school. These informal communication links often are parents' only connection with the school. Consequently, teacher comments on any materials learners are likely to take home need to be prepared sensitively and carefully.

## Nonschool-Related Responsibilities

Teachers have commitments and interests beyond those reflected in what they do at school.* These obligations impose responsibilities that, in many cases, must be managed in tandem with their professional roles as teachers. Conflicting responsibilities have the potential to produce stress. For example, many teachers must make difficult decisions about how much time they should devote to meeting the needs of their family members and how much they should devote to preparing lessons and correcting papers.

Teachers are bright people with diverse interests. Often they are active in religious groups, political parties, local governments, and social and fraternal organizations. As articulate, well-educated people, it is not uncommon for them to be tapped for leadership responsibilities. Many of these commitments can be extremely time consuming.

---

*Interestingly, many very young elementary children do not know this. Often they think the teacher lives and even sleeps at the school, and frequently express surprise when they meet their teacher in a supermarket or in some other out-of-school location.

Teachers' private, nonprofessional lives have both positive and negative influences on their roles as educators. Frequently, experiences with their own families give them insights that are useful in working with learners who are experiencing problems. Active involvement in groups and organizations broaden their interests and improve their abilities to work well with many different kinds of people. The exposure they get in the general community may result in better community appreciation for teachers and the schools.

On the other hand, the many obligations imposed by various aspects of teachers' nonprofessional lives can absorb tremendous quantities of emotional energy. Too many outside interests can undercut teachers' ability to discharge their professional responsibilities effectively.

Most teachers are aware of potential conflicts that can result between their professional and nonprofessional duties. They work throughout their careers to allocate their time in a reasonable way among the various people and groups competing for their attention.

## Learners' Perceptions and Roles

Though learners share many common school experiences, they do not all perceive them the same way. Educational sociologists sometimes find it useful to develop classifications of learners based on their reactions to school programs (Bernstein, 1977). Learners can be viewed as falling into one of these four categories:

- high adaptors
- estranged learners
- irrelevant perceivers
- alienated learners

Figure 6–1 depicts the dominating characteristics of these categories.

*High adaptors* are learners who believe that the content of the school program is important and who experience success in their classes. They sense a good fit between the agenda of the school and their personal hopes and aspirations (and those of their families; friends; and social, religious, and ethnic groups). These learners tend to be supportive of teachers and of the school in general.

**Figure 6–1**
Four categories of learner reactions to the school program

|  | Tend to cope with class work successfully | Tend to have great difficulty with class work |
|---|---|---|
| Tend to believe school work is important | High Adaptors | Estranged Learners |
| Tend to believe school work is not important | Irrelevant Perceivers | Alienated Learners |

*Estranged learners* also are convinced of the importance of the school program. However, for intellectual, social, or other reasons, they do not do well in school. They often develop negative self-concepts and worry that their lack of success in school will permanently tag them as losers. These young people often become increasingly disenchanted with school as the years go by, and many of them drop out before graduating from high school.

*Irrelevant Perceivers* are capable of succeeding in school, but they do not see school work as important. They often have personal priorities that they see as little connected to what teachers ask them to do. One of the authors once had a student who was the son of a local wrecking yard owner. By the time he began high school, he had been working for his father for years, was earning good money, and was looking forward to working full time once he completed high school. In general, this student thought teachers were rather a sorry lot who had bizarre interests and did not make enough money to be taken seriously. He did just enough school work to pass and qualify for a diploma.

*Alienated learners* do not see the school program as personally important, and they have not experienced success on those occasions when they have made serious attempts to do the work. Often, alienated learners have little good to say about teachers or schools. They frequently feel trapped in a setting that requires them to do things that they do not see as important, under conditions that do not allow them to succeed. Many of them drop out of school before they graduate, and those who remain in school often experience problems. In classes, their frustration sometimes results in unacceptable behaviors.

In part, differences among learners who are high adaptors, estranged learners, irrelevant perceivers, or alienated learners stem from social influences that have helped shape how they view the world. Like teachers, learners are called upon to play many roles. Perspectives associated with some of these roles may conflict with perspectives connected to others. Difficulties in school are particularly likely to arise when there are conflicts between learners' roles as students and their roles as part of their family, members of particular cultural or ethnic groups, or participants in religious or social organizations.

## Learners as Pupils or Students

The school imposes a certain number of behavior expectations on learners, and many of these are unwritten. One of the most basic of these norms is that learners are expected to accept the authority and direction of the teacher. Though in some cases it is permissible for them to raise questions about minor points of content, learners are generally expected to accept the validity of what they are taught.

Learners must follow guidelines governing such things as when and how they will move from place to place, where they will sit in classrooms, what they must do to complete assigned tasks, when they may eat, when they may leave the classroom, and when they may converse freely with others. Learners who adapt easily to the school environment are those who are able to cope well with many regulations governing their behavior. Some young people are able to do this better than others.

## Learners as Family Members

Learners take on many of the views prevalent among their immediate family. For example, many young people whose parents have a strong commitment to labor unions will themselves hold a similar commitment. Certainly this is not always the case, but often shared family values are passed intact from generation to generation. When values or positions introduced in school content conflict with those of learners' families, learners may lose interest in what they are taught at school. Someone from a home where the union movement is held in high regard may find it hard to accept conclusions presented in an economics textbook written by an author with a strong anti-union view.

Teachers need to be careful in presenting value-laden content to learners. Such content *does* need to be taught, but conclusions need to be identified as representative of a given perspective, not as unalloyed truth. This suggests to the learner that a variety of views, including his or her own, are acceptable. Sensitive and tolerant teachers are able to sustain interests of learners from many different family backgrounds. This is important because young people need to be encouraged to remain open to perspectives they may never have considered before. This chapter's Case Study presents one such situation.

CASE STUDY

## *Dancing into difficulty*

**Kevin Reynolds, a first-year fourth grade teacher, slumped into the faculty lounge couch at the end of the day**. "This," he announced to the two or three old hands who had gathered around the coffee pot, "has been *some* day."

"What's up, Kevin?" The speaker was Ruth Wilson, the school's longtime middle-grades team leader.

"Sit down, Ruth. This is going to take a while."

Ruth took a seat next to Kevin, placed her coffee cup on the adjacent table, and looked up. "OK, Kevin, let's have it."

"You remember when I told you about the folk dancing we did last summer in my physical education methods class?" Kevin began. "Well, it hit me a couple of nights ago that I could tie some folk dancing activities to the new social studies unit we've been studying in my class. I mean, they're always after us to correlate what we're doing in the different subject areas, and this combination seemed a natural."

"Anyway, I did some background checking, got some music, and relearned the steps of four different dances from four different countries. I got the kids into the gym this morning, explained what we were going to do, and taught them the steps. I thought everything was going splendidly. But then, I noticed that I was getting a lot of frowns from Louis."

"So what was that all about?" asked Ruth.

"I really didn't know," Kevin replied. "I didn't let it bother me and kept on giving instruction. Then, I put the music on and told the kids to try it. And at *that* point, all hell broke loose. Louis jumped up on a bench, shook his fist at the other children, and started shouting, 'You're all going to hell!' Some of the other kids were really shaken. In fact, Nellie and Joe spent some time with the counselor after lunch. And that's not the end of it."

"What else happened?" Ruth asked.

"Well, about 2:00 I got a message from the office to call Louis's mother. He'd gone home for lunch and told her the story. I figured that maybe she was going to apologize for his behavior. Was I ever off base on *that* idea. I called her back after school, and she read me the riot act about subjecting her child to immoral activities. She was just livid! She lectured me for 20 minutes on the scriptural basis for her view that dancing was the 'devil's work.' She's coming to see me after school tomorrow. I think I'm in trouble. Got any ideas?"

*What actions do you think Kevin should take? Are there some specific people he should seek advice from? What do you think he should say to Louis's mother? Should he abandon his plan to have his class do the folk dances? What might he do to avoid a similar situation in the future? What would you do if you faced this problem?*

## Learners as Ethnic and Cultural Group Members

The world view that individual learners have is partially conditioned by the ethnic and cultural groups to which they belong. Young people's ethnic or cultural perspectives can affect their receptivity to what is taught in school. To illustrate the point, we might think about a young Native American girl who is taking a junior-level English course in high school. The teacher has asked people in the class to read some of Mark Twain's works. Recently they have been reading *Roughing It*, a novel based on Twain's travels and experiences in the far west. In this novel, Twain describes Native Americans as "prideless beggars" (Twain, 1985, p. 167).

It is doubtful that this girl sees herself, her family, and other Native Americans as "prideless beggars." If the teacher does not take pains to assure members of the class that this phrase represents an isolated statement by one author (who, elsewhere, deals much more fairly with Native Americans) made at a specific time and in a particular historical context, the girl may conclude that what is taught in the course is irrelevant because Twain's conclusion simply does not square with her view of reality. It would be well, too, for the teacher to introduce other materials providing a more positive view of Native Americans and other groups that have not always been treated sensitively by authors writing at times when cultural diversity was less prized than it is today.

## Learners as Members of Religious and Social Organizations

Many school learners are active in religious and social organizations of various kinds. These groups often have strong commitments that are widely shared by their members. Sometimes, these perspectives may conflict with those that learners encounter in school. For example, school counselors and teachers may encourage females to work hard to master mathematics because a good background in mathemat-

Teachers must work sensitively with learners from many cultural and ethnic groups.

ics is needed for many high-paying jobs, while some religious groups might maintain very traditional views regarding the appropriate roles for women. The leaders of religious groups could well object strongly to any actions school people take to promote the idea that women should prepare for employment options that will take them away from their traditional duties as homemakers.

Learners who are members of these groups may find themselves torn between a desire to please their teachers and their desire to please their religious leaders. These kinds of conflicts are common, and teachers need to understand that many learners they serve are under some pressure to do things that may be inconsistent with what teachers and schools believe is best.

## Key Ideas in Summary

- Educational sociologists are interested in, among other things, how groups influence individual learners and how the institution of the school functions in a society where not all groups share a common set of values.

*"That's a fascinating question, Mr. Baines. Do you want me to answer in my role as a Young Republican, a member of the Luther League, a senior scout leader, a member of an upper-middle class family, an aficionado of "heavy metal," a member of the Tom Cruise fan club, or as a captain of our varsity volleyball team?"*
Courtesy of Ford Button.

- People who subscribe to the functionalist position believe that our society is strongly committed to a common set of values and that these values ought to be reflected in school programs. Supporters maintain that when they are, there is every chance that learners will commit to them. It is assumed that school programs framed in light of these common values afford equal access to the benefits of schooling to all young people who attend.

- Supporters of the economic-class conflict position disagree that our society is basically characterized by a common set of values. They argue that different kinds of people have different values and that these differences lead to conflict. In particular, they see conflict between capitalists, who control most of the wealth and the means of production, and workers, who do the bidding of the capitalists. School programs are viewed as being shaped by one of two intentions: (1) schools are designed for the purpose of keeping our economic system going in a form that will maximize capitalists' control and supply adequate numbers of workers to serve as their employees; and (2) school reforms result from conflicts of working-class people who are unhappy with present arrangements and who do not want school programs that assume present economic arrangements will go on forever.

**TABLE 6–1**
Summary table: Sociology of education

| Major Topics | Key Points |
|---|---|
| Interests of educational sociologists | Examples include how groups influence individual learners and how the institution of the school functions in a society where not all groups share common values. |
| Functionalist position | Members of society are seen as sharing a common set of values; hence, society is characterized more by consensus than by conflict. The school is charged with providing society with trained workers. School programs provide equal opportunities for all, and individual merit is what makes for success in school and in life. |
| Economic-class conflict position | There are vast differences among values held by different people. Society is best described as being in a condition of conflict between capitalists and workers. Educational change comes about either because of (1) pressures brought by capitalists to maintain a social order that gives them great advantages or (2) pressures brought by workers who resent present arrangements that seem to deny them the kinds of advantages capitalists enjoy. |
| Status-group conflict position | Society is best thought of as being in a state of conflict among varying status groups and their leaders. Such groups include those associated with organized religion, government, the military, the private sector, and various social and fraternal associations. Educational change results from attempts by individual groups to maximize advantages for their own members. |
| Roles of the school | These include:<br>• transmission of the general culture<br>• dissemination of academic knowledge<br>• preparation for the world of work<br>• promotion of social and group relationships<br>• encouragement of social change |

**TABLE 6–1**
*continued*

| Major Topics | Key Points |
|---|---|
| Roles of teachers | Professional and private roles of teachers may produce stress because of competing demands on their time. Among teachers' professional responsibilities are those associated with:<br>• instruction<br>• counseling<br>• administrative work<br>• curriculum development<br>• professional development<br>• public relations |
| Learners' reactions to school programs | These are diverse. *High adaptors* are learners who believe school learning is important and who do well. *Estranged learners* believe school learning is important, but they do not do well in their classes and often have low self-images. *Irrelevant perceivers* do not think school learning is especially important nor useful and often do just enough to get by. *Alienated learners* do not think school learning is important and do not do very well in their classes. Many alienated learners drop out of school before earning a high school diploma. |
| Learners' roles | Learners play many roles. When there are conflicts between values espoused at school and values espoused by families and other groups to which the learners belong, they may experience stress. Among other things, learners have roles as:<br>• pupils or students<br>• family members<br>• ethnic and cultural group members<br>• religious and social organization members |

- Individuals who are committed to the status-group conflict position also believe that there is more conflict than consensus in our society. They believe that conflict involves more groups than simply capitalists and workers, drawing much of their inspiration from the work of Max Weber, who pointed out that change often results from conflicts among many status groups. Status groups include social, economic, religious, governmental, ethnic and cultural, and other organizations. These groups try to maximize the benefits of their members. In doing so, they often come into conflict with members of other groups. Thus people who support the status-group conflict position believe that educational change comes about as a result of these conflicts. More specifically, changes are made in directions favored by conflict winners.

- As institutions, schools play many roles, including (1) transmitters of the general culture, (2) disseminators of academic knowledge, (3) preparers of learners for the workplace, (4) promoters of social and group relationships, and (5) encouragers of social change.

- Teachers in schools play many roles, including such school-related responsibilities as (1) instruction, (2) counseling, (3) administration, (4) curriculum development, (5) professional development, and (6) public relations. Teachers also have nonschool-related responsibilities. For example, they have family obligations, and they may be active in religious, political, and social organizations. Time constraints put enormous pressures on teachers—they must continually make judgments about how much time should be allocated to the many obligations competing for their attention.

- Not all learners react in the same way to the school program. Individuals classified as *high adaptors* believe the content of the school program to be important and generally experience success in their classes. *Estranged learners* believe the content of the school program is important, but they often develop poor self-images because they experience little success in their classes. *Irrelevant perceivers* are learners who doubt the importance of the school program. They have the ability to succeed, but they commit only marginally to their studies and often their performance levels fall short of their real abilities. *Alienated learners* neither believe in the importance of the school program nor do well in their classes. Many of them drop out of school before they graduate.

- Young people play many roles in addition to those as learners or pupils in school. For example, they are also members of families, ethnic and cultural groups, and religious and social organizations. Perspectives of these groups, particularly when they differ from perspectives reflected in classes, put pressures on learners. They sometimes must make difficult choices between competing sets of values.

. . . . . . . . . . . . . . . . . . . . . . . . . . . . . .

# Review and Discussion Questions

1. What are some basic issues that are of interest to educational sociologists?

2. What are some basic characteristics of the functionalist position?

3. What are some similarities and differences between the economic-class conflict position and the status-group conflict position?

4. In what ways do schools transmit the general culture and disseminate academic knowledge?

5. What are some things schools do to make learners more comfortable in group and social settings?

6. What kinds of roles do teachers play in schools?

7. What are some potential conflicts teachers may face involving their in-school professional roles and their roles as members of families and out-of-school groups and organizations?

8. Why is it that many parents assume the worst when they get a call from the school about their child, and what are some schools doing to change this expectation of bad news?

9. How can learners' roles as members of families, ethnic and cultural groups, and religious and social organizations place pressures on them in their roles as pupils and students in school?

10. What are some things teachers can do to help learners deal with potential conflicts between perspectives reflected in school classes and those characterizing out-of-school groups to which they belong?

. . . . . . . . . . . . . . . . . . . . . . . . . . . .

# Ideas for Field Experiences, Projects, and Enrichment

1. Invite a member of a local school district's central administrative staff to talk to your class about how the district responds to concerns about certain aspects of the curriculum that are raised by outside groups. What kinds of concerns have been raised? Have the outside groups been satisfied with the district's responses? Are new teachers provided with any guidelines for handling complaints from community groups?

2. Interview several teachers about the different kinds of roles they play both in and out of school. Ask them about any problems they face regarding how to

allocate their time. How do they resolve these situations? Prepare a short report to share with others in your class.

3. Are our school programs designed to maximize the development of all learners, or are they designed to benefit a select few? Prepare a paper in which you support one of these two positions. Ask your instructor to comment on what you have written.

4. Ask five or six secondary-level students whether they have ever been told anything at school that conflicts with what they have been told at home. How did they feel when this occurred? What did they do? What did their teacher do? Prepare a short written summary of your interview and share it with others in your class.

5. Alienated learners often reject what schools have to offer, and they usually do not do well in their classes. Along with several others in your class, do some reading on the subject of learner alienation. What are some things the experts see as leading to this condition? What can teachers and other educators do to help young people affected by this condition? Present your findings to your class in the form of a symposium.

## Supplementary Reading

Apple, M., and L. Weis. *Ideology and Practice in Schooling*. Philadelphia: Temple University Press, 1983.

Dougherty, K. J., and F. M. Hammack. *Education and Society: A Reader*. San Diego: Harcourt Brace Jovanovich, 1990.

Edelman, M. *Families in Peril: An Agenda for Social Change*. Cambridge, MA: Harvard University Press, 1987.

King, R. *The Sociology of School Organization*. London: Methuen and Co., Ltd., 1983.

Richardson, J. G., ed. *Handbook of Theory and Research for the Sociology of Education*. New York: Greenwood Press, 1986.

## References

Bernstein, B. B. *Class Codes and Control*. Vol. 3. 2d ed. London: Routledge and Kegan Paul, 1977.

Dougherty, K. J., and F. M. Hammack. *Education and Society: A Reader*. San Diego: Harcourt Brace Jovanovich, 1990.

Good, T. L., and J. E. Brophy. *Looking in Classrooms*. 5th ed. New York: HarperCollins, 1991.

Goslin, D. A. "The Functions of the School in Modern Society." In K. J. Dougherty and F. M. Hammack, eds. *Education and Society: A Reader*. San Diego: Harcourt Brace Jovanovich, 1990, 29–38.

Khumar, K. *Social Character of Learning*. New Delhi, India: Sage Publications India Pvt. Ltd., 1989.

Parsons, T. "School Class as a Social System: Some of Its Functions in American Society." *Harvard Educational Review* (Fall 1959): 297–318.

Twain, M. *Roughing It*. New York: Penguin Books, 1985 (originally published 1872).

Webb, R., and R. Sherman. *Schooling and Society*. 2d ed. New York: Macmillan, 1989.

# Section 3

# Learners

We have been preparing new teachers for many years. One of the most predictable comments we hear from students when they return to the campus after completing student teaching is, "The kids have really changed since *I* was in school."

The accuracy of this view is debatable. For those who have been out of high school for 10 or more years, there are some changes in the demographic makeup of young people in schools. But for more recent graduates, changes have not been significant. If this is true, why do so many returning student teachers persist in their belief that today's school learners are profoundly different?

We think this happens because, for the first time in their lives, student teachers confront the entire spectrum of young people in the schools. During their student teaching term, they deal with everyone who comes to school, not just with those who share similar interests and enthusiasms. This situation is quite different from what these student teachers experienced when they were learners themselves. In those days, they tended to seek out and befriend kindred spirits. Often, they had little contact with learners with different interests, values, abilities, and personal priorities. In their selective remembrance of their school days, many of these young people simply "were not there."

Learners in our schools mirror the diversity of our society. In preparing for a career that requires contact with young people with wildly divergent personalities, interests, and abilities, it is useful to answer questions such as these:

- What are some general characteristics of today's learners?
- What can schools do to ensure that programs adequately serve learners regardless of their cultural or ethnic background and their gender?
- What kinds of disabilities are some learners likely to have, and what are some things teachers can do to help these young people achieve?
- What are some characteristics of gifted learners, and what can the schools do to help them?

Chapters in this section provide answers to these questions. These chapters are:

Chapter 7: Today's Pupils and Students
Chapter 8: Multicultural and Gender Equity Concerns
Chapter 9: Exceptional Learners

# Today's Pupils and Students

## Objectives

This chapter provides information to help the reader to

- recognize the diversity of learners in the schools today.
- identify selected categories of learners likely to be present in many classrooms.
- note some implications for teachers of having to work with learners reflecting such a wide range of individual differences.
- recognize signs that may indicate that a learner has been abused or neglected.
- cite examples of problems that may be encountered by teachers at different grade levels.
- suggest teacher characteristics that seem to be associated with learner success at different grade levels.

1. What are some general characteristics of families of today's school learners?
2. Has poverty among families of the nation's school children become more or less of a problem in recent years?
3. What are some trends in school enrollment of learners from minority groups?
4. Why are educators becoming increasingly concerned about the growing numbers of children in schools whose mothers used crack cocaine during their pregnancies?
5. What are some trends regarding formal education of 3- and 4-year-olds?
6. What is the most common characteristic of learners with disabilities?
7. What are some behavior indicators that may suggest that a learner has been abused or neglected?
8. What are some general characteristics of learners in elementary and middle schools?
9. In what ways are high school learners different from college and university students and adult learners?

# Introduction

"Young people now are really different from what they used to be."

"Young people today are pretty much the same as they have always been."

These two statements are contradictory. Interestingly, both contain elements of truth. Certainly it is true that there have been great changes in the demographic characteristics of learners in the nation's schools. Today, there are more poor children, more learners from ethnic and language minorities, more learners with disabilities, more learners with drug-related impairments, and more very young learners than there used to be.

On the other hand, many basic characteristics of young people have not changed much. As well, many patterns of young people's development have remained relatively constant.

## Some Characteristics of Today's Learners

The diversity of learners always impresses visitors who have not been in a school for a long time. Teachers today are challenged to recognize and respond to common characteristics of young people; at the same time, they must adjust their instruction to meet unique needs of individual learners.

Today's schools encourage learners from varied backgrounds to work together.

## Families of Learners

Television programs sometimes promote an image of a "typical" American family, consisting of a father who is employed, a mother who stays in the family's well-appointed suburban home, and two well-scrubbed children who romp endlessly with the family's shaggy dog. This image, in all its dimensions, never was typical and certainly does not represent today's norm. One study reported that only 4 percent of the nation's households include a father, a nonworking mother, and two children (Mirga, 1986). Most young people in the schools are either children of two parents living together who both work, or they are children of single parents. In the latter situation, the single parent is often a young woman under age 25 (Strong, 1989).

Current family and employment patterns indicate that large numbers of children in the schools spend many hours with babysitters and at daycare centers. The kind of generation-to-generation communication that went on in traditional families happens less frequently today. As a result, teachers often provide social and personal information to learners that, in years gone by, was passed on by parents. Increasingly, the dividing line separating responsibilities of the home and the school is blurring. Box 7–1 poses some interesting questions relating to our society's changing family patterns.

## Poverty and Children

Poverty continues to be a depressing national problem. This condition is particularly widespread among the young. In 1989, children accounted for 39.5 percent of the nation's poor (Reed and Sautter, 1990, p. K3). Percentages of Americans under age 18

---

BOX 7–1
# CHANGES IN AMERICAN FAMILIES

Today, fewer than half of American households include children. The numbers are likely to decrease even more in the future. There is a trend for young people to stay single longer and, of those who do marry, many more are making the decision to have no children.

### What Do You Think?

1. How do you react to the information that fewer than one-half of American families include children? What do you think this figure will be 10 years from now? Why?
2. What are some positive things that might result for education if our society produces fewer children in the years ahead?
3. What are some negative things that might result for education if our society produces fewer children in the years ahead?
4. Overall, do you see more advantages or disadvantages for education if numbers of children in households continue to be relatively small?

living in poverty have generally increased since 1970. In 1970, 14.9 percent of these young people were poor. By 1987, that figure had increased to 20.0 percent (Ogle and Alsalam, 1990, p. 64). In part, this situation reflects a decline in spending on programs designed to help low-income families. From 1980 to 1990, military spending went up 37 percent, but expenditures on all programs directed at assisting low-income families went down by 2 percent (Gough, 1990).

Poverty is unequally distributed among the major racial and ethnic groups in the school. About one white child in seven is poor, four of nine African-American children are poor, and three of eight Hispanic children are poor (Reed and Sautter, 1990). Large numbers of poor children are from families headed by a single female parent who is under 25 years of age, unemployed, and living in a central city (Strong, 1989). Table 7–1 breaks down percentages of children from these ethnic groups living in poverty in female-headed families.

For many reasons, children from economically deprived homes often do not do well in school. Too many of these learners are assigned to special education classes because of cognitive and developmental deficiencies. Many of these problems result because of mothers' inabilities to pay for quality prenatal care (Reed and Sautter, 1990). Also, poor children often do not receive adequate diets, which may affect their performance in school.

Though we are living in the computer age, few computers are found in economically impoverished homes. Many poor families cannot afford newspaper and magazine subscriptions. Poor children are not nearly so likely to observe their parents reading as are children from more affluent homes. When reading is not modeled by adults at home, it is common for learners to place much less value on acquiring good reading skills. This can begin a cycle of failure, because poorly developed reading proficiencies in the early grades almost always lead to poor academic performance in later school years.

Present trends suggest that teachers will be dealing with at least as many learners from economically impoverished backgrounds in the future as they do now. Helping these learners succeed requires careful planning of instructional programs that respond to the special needs of these young people. A failure to attend to these children's special circumstances will place many of them in a situation where failure is a certainty.

**Table 7–1**
Percentages of white, African-American, and Hispanic children under age 18 from families headed by females who are living in poverty: changes from 1975 to 1987.

| Group | 1970 | 1987 |
|---|---|---|
| Whites | 36.6% | 46.0% |
| African-Americans | 60.8 | 79.0 |
| Hispanics | 42.9 | 47.2 |
| All groups combined | 51.4 | 56.7 |

Source: Laurence T. Ogle (ed.) and Nabeel Alsalam (assoc. ed.), *The Condition of Education, 1990,* Vol. 1, *Elementary and Secondary Education* (Washington, DC: National Center for Education Statistics, 1990), 64.

## Minority-Group Children

Minority-group children are becoming a larger proportion of the total school population. By the early 1990s, they accounted for over 30 percent of all young people in school. By 1990, minority-group learners constituted a majority of the learner population in two states, Mississippi and New Mexico. By the mid-1990s, minority-group learners are expected to become majorities in the schools of California and Texas (Marshall, 1990).

From the middle 1970s to the late 1980s, the percentage of learners of Asian descent in the schools increased faster than percentages for any other minority group. Many of these children's parents fled their homelands because of unsettled political and economic conditions. Large numbers of these young people learned to speak another language before they learned English.

Though learners of Asian descent are the fastest-growing minority in the schools, they still account for only about 3 percent of the total school population (Ogle and Alsalam, 1990, p. 62). African-American children, accounting for about 16 percent of the total school population, are more numerous.

The nation's Hispanic population is very large, and is growing much faster than the white or African-American population. Hispanics will soon surpass African-Americans to become the nation's largest minority. Today, Hispanic children account for about 10 percent of the school population (Ogle and Alsalam, 1990, p. 62). Many, though by no means a majority, of Hispanic learners learn to speak Spanish before they master English.

Native Americans (including Alaska natives) comprise about 1 percent of the total learner population. Though overall numbers are relatively small, these young people represent large minorities in schools in parts of such states as Alaska, Arizona, New Mexico, and Oklahoma. Many of these young people do not speak English as a first language, and there are 100 or more Native American languages still spoken by more than 300 tribes (Marshall, 1990, p. 27).

Minority-group students, with the exception of some learners of Asian heritage, often have not adapted well to school programs. For example, scores of African-American and Hispanic learners on standardized tests typically are below those of white children. There is evidence that differences in performance among white, African-American, and Hispanic learners are narrowing (Ogle and Alsalam, 1990). This may suggest that educators are beginning to do a better job of responding to the learning needs of these minority-group learners. (A much more extensive treatment of issues related to ethnic and cultural minorities is provided in Chapter 8.)

## "Crack Babies" as School Learners

*Crack* is a crystallized, smokable derivative of cocaine. It is a drug that started to become widely available only in the mid-1980s. Since that time, its use has skyrocketed. A report issued in 1990 estimated that one million pregnant women were using the drug (Rist, 1990, p. 2).

Before they are born, so-called crack babies suffer developmental damage that affects their central nervous system. This occurs because crack cocaine use results in a diminished supply of oxygen to the placenta's blood vessels. In addition to harming the central nervous system, a pregnant mother's crack cocaine use can also cause physical malformations in the developing child.

Crack-cocaine children began to be old enough to start entering school only in the late 1980s. Few of them are old enough today to be out of the primary grades, but preliminary evidence about their success at school is not encouraging. These young people find it difficult to cope with complex environments that feature many simultaneous stimuli. They tend to be hypersensitive. When confronted with a typical spirited elementary school classroom, many of these children either react aggressively or withdraw completely. They have problems dealing with the many competing demands for their attention.

How many of these children are there? Figures vary widely. A conservative estimate places the annual number of crack cocaine babies being born each year at between 30,000 and 50,000. This figure represents between 1 and 2 percent of all babies born in the United States each year (Rist, 1990, p. 2). Given these numbers, it is clear "that schools need to prepare for a potentially significant influx of children who will have difficulty learning in traditional school settings" (Rist, 1990, p. 3).

The jury is still out on the question of whether crack-cocaine children will improve over time. Some experts believe that school programs sensitive to the unique needs of these young people may help. Crack-cocaine children need classrooms characterized by stability and containing relatively few diverting stimuli. Teachers need to develop strong personal relationships with these young people. There have been recommendations to keep these children with the same teacher over several years to reduce the stress of adjusting to a new adult figure (Rist, 1990). In general, efforts need to be directed toward making classroom life for crack children more predictable and less stressful.

## Very Young Children in the Schools

Today, increasing numbers of mothers have full-time jobs outside the home, and others are either seeking such positions or are involved in education and training activities that occupy much of their time during the day. A side effect of these out-of-the-home activities has been an increasing interest in enrolling young children in educational programs. Because of the expense and uneven quality of private daycare operations, public schools have been under pressure to expand programs available to 3- and 4-year-old children.

Growth of these programs has been dramatic. In 1970, for example, only about 20 percent of these young children were in formal educational programs. By the middle 1980s, this figure had nearly doubled (Stern and Chandler, 1987, p. 62).

Expansion of school programs for young learners has prompted much debate. On the pro side, supporters have cited some research evidence suggesting that early childhood programs can help young children to develop positive self-images and abilities to work productively and harmoniously with others. On the con side, critics have argued that expansion of early childhood programs imposes obligations on schools that properly should be discharged in the home by parents. Forces supporting expansion of school programs seem to be carrying the day, as economic pressures that encourage mothers of young children to work are heavy. The years ahead probably will witness an even greater expansion of school programs for very young learners.

## Learners with Disabilities

In the past, learners with disabilities were often kept away from other children in the schools. This practice was justified by the claim that such learners needed kinds of training that were unavailable to them in the "regular" classroom. Since the mid-1970s, however, this situation has changed. The Education for All Handicapped Children Act (Public Law 94–142) of 1975 (renamed in 1990 the Individuals with Disabilities Education Act) required schools, to the extent possible, to teach learners with disabilities in traditional classrooms.

In part, this federal legislation was the result of concerns that past practices of isolating learners with disabilities were tending to stigmatize them as something less than real learners. Now, during a typical day, teachers may work with learners with a wide variety of disabilities.

Programs for the disabled are directed at learners that comprise about 11 percent of the total school population (Ogle and Alsalam, 1990, p. 46). By far the largest group of learners in this category consists of young people classified as "learning disabled." Other major groups include children who are speech impaired or developmentally disabled (Ogle and Alsalam, 1990). (Additional information about these special young people is provided in Chapter 9.)

## Abused and Neglected Children

Problems of abused and neglected children have attracted public interest for years. For more than a quarter of a century, every state in the country has had laws requiring that those with authority over children, including teachers, report any injury that appears to be nonaccidental (McEvoy, 1990). Because of these concerns, there has been a trend for reported incidents of child abuse to increase in number. In 1972, there were 610,000 reported cases; by 1988, that figure had climbed to 2,200,000 (McEvoy, 1990, p. 248).

Suspected abuse is handled in most communities by Child Protective Services (CPS) (Haase and Kempe, 1991). This organization usually operates within a state or county agency, which might be known as the Department of Social Services, Department of Human Resources, Department of Social Welfare, Department of Public Welfare, or by some other name.

*Physical Abuse.*    Signs of physical abuse may include bruises, welts, burns, bite marks, and other unusual marks on the body, or the learner may be having what seem to be too many accidental injuries at home. The following are some behavioral indicators of physical abuse:

- Learner is hard to get along with and may frequently be in trouble.
- Learner is unusually shy, or too eager to please.
- Learner is frequently late or absent, or comes to school too early and seems reluctant to go home.
- Learner shies away from physical contact with adults.
- Learner seems frightened of parents.

- Learner may seek affection from any adult [adapted from *American Teacher* (December 1989/January 1990), p. 12].

*Neglect.*   Learners who have been neglected at home may show up at school dirty. They may often be without their lunch money. These young people sometimes seem to be more tired than others in the class. They may need glasses and dental care. Their clothing may be unkempt, or they may wear clothes that are inappropriate given prevailing weather conditions. Some of these young people may beg food from their classmates [*American Teacher* (December 1989/January 1990), p. 12].

*Emotional Abuse.*   Often, emotional abuse is reflected in extreme or excessive behavior patterns. Emotionally abused young people may be too compliant and passive; on the other hand, they may be very aggressive. These are some other behavioral indicators of possible emotional abuse:

- Behavior is either too adult-like or too immature, given the learner's age.
- Learner is behind in physical, emotional, and intellectual development [adapted from *American Teacher* (December 1989/January 1990), p. 12].

*Sexual Abuse.*   One indicator of this condition is that a learner's underclothing is torn, stained, or bloody. Or, the learner may experience pain or itching in the genital area [*American Teacher* (December 1989/January 1990)]. Other behavioral indicators of sexual abuse include:

- Learner is very withdrawn, or learner engages in fantasy-like or baby-like behavior.
- Learner has poor relationships with other children.
- Learner engages in delinquent acts or runs away from home.
- Learner says he or she has been sexually assaulted [adapted from *American Teacher* (December 1989/January 1990), p. 12].

Many groups in our society are interested in doing something about abused and neglected children. They recognize that teachers can play an important part by recognizing potential abuse and reporting it to authorities. The two groups listed below will, upon request, send information on how to spot abuse. Write them at these addresses:

The National Center on Child Abuse and Neglect
P.O. Box 1182
Washington, DC 20013

National Committee for the Prevention of Child Abuse
332 S. Michigan Avenue, Suite 1250
Chicago, IL 60604-4357

## Patterns of Children's Development

Ideas about how children develop influence ideas about how they should be educated. Teachers must base their procedures on up-to-date knowledge about human development, not on outdated views. Some perspectives that were very much in vogue at one time seem bizarre to us today.

One early view had it that children were mindless creatures who were incapable of feeling or knowing anything. Interesting ideas about education flowed logically from this idea. For example, any plans to spend money on early childhood education were not well-received, as formal education for very young children was seen as pointless. Adults' roles were limited to meeting children's physical needs and to keeping them out of mischief.

Another historical view held children to be essentially miniature adults. Aside from their small size, children were seen as having adult characteristics, lacking only knowledge and experience. If these could be provided, it was assumed that children would be able to discharge adult roles at a very early age. Learning materials designed for use by adults were seen as perfectly appropriate for children as well. If children failed to learn, this failure was simply attributed to their laziness. The tradition of punishing children for failing to learn comes out of this view of childhood.

Still another historical perspective maintained that children came into the world totally lacking any personalities of their own. They were simply animated clay or putty awaiting appropriate "modeling" by adults. There was an assumption that young people, when appropriately guided, would turn into good citizens. In the schools, this view resulted in educational practices that were planned and delivered exclusively by adults. Children's interests were considered to be of little importance (see Box 7–2).

BOX 7–2
# DENYING THE IMPORTANCE OF LEARNERS' INDIVIDUAL CHARACTERISTICS

Children have not always been viewed the way they are today. At some times in the past, they were seen as totally lacking individual identities. When young people were looked at in this way, it was assumed that teachers would mold young people in ways that would reproduce abilities and attitudes of adults. In her novel *The Prime of Miss Jean Brodie* (1962), Muriel Spark described a teacher who tried to do this and the disastrous results she brought about. You might find this book interesting.

*What Do You Think?*

1. Did you have any teachers who were insensitive to the individual differences of learners? How did people in your classes feel about these teachers?
2. In what ways did these teachers' approaches to teaching differ from those of teachers who seemed more sensitive to special needs of individual learners?
3. How effective were these insensitive teachers in transmitting information to learners in their classes?

Most of these views from history have not stood up well to the rigors of modern scholarship. Today, we know that each child has unique qualities, and that these qualities affect how individual children react to school. Though teaching might be simpler if young people were just so many "lumps of clay," that is just not how it is. Diversity among learners is the reality.

For example, consider the physical characteristics of young people in a typical junior high school classroom. Differences among such individuals are striking. Some of them are small and immature in appearance. Others may be as large and as physically well-developed as the teacher. Some of the boys may even sport mustaches (much to the envy of their smaller, less physically mature classmates). Differences in learners' rates of physical development present problems related not only to their ability to perform physical tasks, but to their psychological development as well.

## Characteristics of Preschool and Kindergarten Children

Children of preschool and kindergarten age are extremely active. They have quite good control of their bodies, and they seem to enjoy activity for its own sake. Because of their frequent bursts of activity, these children need regular rest periods. When rest periods are not provided, the children often become irritable. Emotional outbursts often result when overtired children in this age group encounter even minor frustrations.

At this age, children's large-muscle coordination is better developed than their small-muscle coordination. As a result, tasks that require small-muscle control can be frustrating. Many children in this group have trouble managing shoestrings, buttons, and other fine-motor tasks that older children find easy. Some children in this age group may not yet have fully developed eyes and eye muscles. They may experience difficulty in focusing on small objects and in completing tasks that require good hand–eye coordination.

Boys in this age group tend to be slightly larger in size than girls, but girls are more advanced by almost any other measure that is applied. This is particularly true in the area of fine-motor-skill development. At this age, girls tend to display much better fine-muscle coordination than boys.

Teachers of preschool and kindergarten children must be patient and able to tolerate a lot of activity in the classroom. They must understand that there are certain things children in this age group simply cannot do. They must be prepared to spend time tying shoes, mopping up paint spills, and buttoning coats—and they must do these things with a smile. Children need a lot of affection at this time of their lives.

## Characteristics of Primary Grades Children (Grades 1 to 3)

The high need for physical activity that characteristic of kindergarten children carries through the first year or two of the primary grades. The large muscles still tend to be more fully developed than the small muscles. This large-muscle development gives these children a tremendous confidence in their ability to accomplish certain physical tasks. Many youngsters in this age group develop more confidence in their physical abilities than is warranted. The accident rate among primary grades children is very high.

The early primary grades are difficult for many young people. Many of them still have a high need for activity. This need persists at a time when school programs begin to expect more "in-seat" learning, a clear break from the almost nonstop activity routine of many kindergarten classrooms. When there is too much forced sitting, youngsters in this age group may develop nervous habits such as pencil chewing, fingernail biting, and general fidgeting. These represent attempts of the body to compensate for the lack of the physical activity that it needs.

Typically, handwriting is introduced during this period. Learning how to perform this task can be a trying experience for late-maturing children who may still have very poor control over the small muscles. During this phase, teachers need to be very sensitive in their comments to children regarding their first efforts at cursive writing. If small-muscle development is inadequate, no amount of admonishment will lead to improved writing skills.

The eyes do not fully develop until children are about 8 years old. Hence, many children in the primary grades may experience difficulty when asked to focus on small print or small objects. This situation has important implications for educators. Serious reading instruction ordinarily begins in grade 1. Teachers of these young children need to understand that difficulties experienced by some of their charges may be due to inadequate eye development, and these children may not yet be able to maintain a focus on objects as small as printed words.

When their teachers have been sensitive to their needs, slow-developing children, as their physical development accelerates, generally have little difficulty in catching up to performance levels of learners who have matured earlier. But if insensitive teachers have falsely attributed problems of physically slow-developing learners to laziness, there is a distinct possibility that these children will come to believe they have no potential for success. When learners develop this kind of self-image, it is common for them to stop trying. A pattern of failure established early in their education can follow learners through their remaining years in school.

Primary grades children have a high need for praise and recognition. They want to please the teacher and do well in school. When they get positive recognition from teachers, they tend to blossom. A positive adjustment to school during these years often sets a pattern for success that will persist as they move through the rest of the elementary and secondary school program.

## Characteristics of Upper Elementary Children (Grades 4 to 6)

In grades 4 to 6, most girls and a few boys experience a tremendous growth spurt. It is not uncommon for 11-year-old girls to be taller and heavier than 11-year-old boys. Many girls reach puberty during this period and, especially toward the end of this time, they tend to become very interested in boys. On the other hand, many boys, even at the end of this period of their lives, have little interest in girls.

Friendships tend to divide along sex lines: boys tend to associate with boys, and girls tend to associate with girls. There is a good deal of competition between boys and girls. Insults are a common feature of interactions between groups of boys and groups of girls.

Learners' fine-motor control is generally quite good by the time they reach this stage of development. Many of them develop an interest in applying their new abilities to "make their fingers do what they're supposed to do" by getting involved in crafts, model building, piano playing, and other activities demanding fine-muscle control.

*"My teacher's bucking for your job."*
Courtesy of Ford Button.

Teachers face a different set of challenges in working with children in grades 4 through 6 than do their colleagues who teach primary grades children. Teachers of children in grades 4 and 5 must pay particular attention to motivation. Additionally, they must develop ways of dealing with children's emerging sense of independence.

Many young people in this age group tend to be perfectionists. Frequently, they set unrealistically high standards for themselves. When they fail to perform up to these standards, they may suffer extreme feelings of guilt. Teachers need to be sensitive to these feelings and devise ways of letting these children know that they are developing in a satisfactory way.

Many teachers of grades 4 to 6 derive great pleasure observing their pupils' growing abilities to behave in sophisticated ways. Interests of many learners broaden tremendously during these years. Some of these young people become voracious readers, some develop a great deal of technical expertise about computers, while others develop a surprising depth of knowledge about a wide range of additional topics. At the same time, these children still retain an engaging air of innocence and trust. They tend to be extremely loyal to teachers they like.

Misbehavior problems faced by teachers of children in this age group tend to be more serious than those faced by primary grades teachers. At this time of life, young people increasingly begin to look to their peer group rather than to adults for guidance regarding what is appropriate behavior. This can prove very frustrating for a teacher. For example, the peer group may have decreed that "reading is boring." Given this dictum, the teacher faces a difficult challenge in motivating the class during the reading period. Teachers of children in this age group must become experts in group dynamics and keen observers of individual friendships within their classrooms. Armed with such insights, they can often act to prevent the peer group from taking a negative position on important academic issues.

As is true of teachers working with primary grades children, teachers of children in grades 4 to 6 need a healthy dose of patience. These children often find some school assignments to be frustrating and difficult, and they need positive support from the teacher. Learners in this age group make many mistakes. An understanding teacher allows them the freedom to make mistakes, yet maintains a reasonable and firm set of expectations. In this kind of atmosphere, children can make tremendous personal strides during these years.

## Characteristics of Students in Grades 7 to 9

Many educators consider young people in these grades to be difficult to teach. There is evidence that a certain kind of teacher is needed to be successful with this group. Part of the challenge teachers face has to do with these learners' incredible diversity. There are great differences in maturity levels among learners, and even great day-to-day differences in patterns of behavior of a single student. A given 8th-grader may at one moment be the very image of sophistication and at the next moment little different from a 4th-grader. Learners at this time of their lives swing crazily back and forth between adult and very childish behavior. This chapter's Case Study presents a situation in which a teacher is confronted with a student's potential risk-taking behavior.

CASE STUDY

## *Should Laura Stearns act on what she knows?*

**Laura Stearns is in her mid-50s.** She has been an enthusiastic 8th-grade mathematics teacher at Drake Junior High School for 30 years. She is a high-spirited professional who looks forward to going to work each day. She tells her friends that she "gets pumped up" by her contact with the 13-year-olds who come bouncing and shoving into her classroom each period of the day.

Laura has always taken a sincere personal interest in her students. She feels that her own experience in raising her two children (now both adults, college graduates, and working in other cities) helps her to empathize with what young people go through during the difficult middle school and junior high school years. She is not at all pleased by one problem that has become increasingly serious at her school with each passing year—more and more of the girls are getting pregnant. Last year, it happened to nearly 15 percent of the 8th-graders.

In her role as sponsor of the pep club, Laura overhears lots of casual student conversations. Students also tend to confide in her. She sometimes has commented to her friends that "parents of my kids would blush if they knew what their kids tell me about what goes on at home." Recently, Laura has learned that Sarah McFarland, one of her outstanding math students, has been getting a lot of attention from a boy who is a junior in high school. Sarah talks about the boy constantly and gives other evidence of having developed a very strong emotional attachment to him. Laura suspects that an intimate physical relationship is about to develop. She hopes that it has not yet happened.

Sarah comes from a family with strong middle-class values. Both parents are deeply committed to their church. They have friends who are very much like themselves. In Laura's view, neither parent has any idea about what social pressures come down on students in present-day junior high schools. Their view of the world is very much the one that used to be depicted on the old "Brady Bunch" television program.

Laura is quite certain that any talks Sarah has had with her parents about sex have been very circumspect. She is positive that Sarah's mother would be incredulous at the suggestion that her daughter might be about to engage in an intimate physical relationship with a high school boy.

As a professional educator, Laura Stearns is outraged at the waste of human capital that results when young girls get pregnant and, sometimes, end up quitting school. As a parent, she senses the pain that might come to Sarah's parents should she become pregnant. And, as a realist, Laura recognizes that, despite these negative consequences, pregnancy (or even AIDS) looms as a real possibility for Sarah unless something is done *now*.

*What should Laura do? Should she talk to Sarah's parents? If she does, will they believe her? Will they think her comments an unconscionable intrusion on the family's private business? Should she take it upon herself to provide birth control information to Sarah? Should she counsel Sarah about the need to avoid a physical relationship? Should she involve the school counseling staff? Should other teachers or administrators be brought into the picture? What kinds of actions can be taken that will resolve the problem and still maintain confidentiality? What would you do in this situation?*

During these years, most girls complete their growth spurt. For boys, growth may not be complete until the end of this age range or even later. Nearly all individuals of both sexes will have attained puberty by the end of this period. Young people in this age group tend to be greatly concerned about the physical and psychological changes they are experiencing. Many wonder whether they are developing properly. Some young people become extremely self-conscious during this time of their lives, sometimes feeling as though their every action is being observed and evaluated. For many young people, their middle school/junior high school years are not a particularly comfortable time.

Teachers who experience success with these students understand and are sensitive to the psychological changes that these young people are experiencing. They are tolerant of the acting-out behavior and the occasionally loud, emotional outbursts displayed by students in this age group. Teachers of these grades need to be flexible individuals who can deal with wildly varying emotional, intellectual, and behavioral patterns in their classrooms.

Rates of physical development vary widely among individuals in grades 7 through 9. Eighth graders are a particularly diverse lot—note the differences in height of the students in this picture.

## Characteristics of Students in Grades 10 to 12

Much has been written about learners in this age group. Parents frequently report great difficulty in communicating with their high school-aged children. Students in this age group often are frustrated as they attempt to come to terms with their world. Several factors contribute to their difficulties.

---

WHAT THE EXPERTS SAY

### *Going to school and having a job*

The National Center for Education Statistics reports that a higher percentage of high school students holds down jobs while going to school than was true 20 years ago (Ogle and Alsalam, 1990, p. 159). In 1989, 33.9 percent of the boys had jobs, as compared to 30.9 percent in 1970. For females, the increase was more dramatic. In 1989, 37.2 percent of the girls were employed, as compared to 27.2 percent in 1970. About 3.5 percent of high school boys and about 1.8 percent of high school girls work full time.

As a group, white high school students are much more likely to hold down jobs while in high school than are African-Americans (39.4 percent and 17.8 percent, respectively) (Ogle and Alsalam, 1990, p. 66). In schools enrolling higher percentages of white students, percentages of employed students are often higher than the national 39.4 percent figure for white student employment. One study conducted at a high school in Iowa where many of the students go on to college found that about 60 percent of its students worked (Workman, 1990, p. 630).

There is evidence that school performance of students who work more than 20 hours a week may be affected negatively. Their attendance and grades tend to suffer (Ogle and Alsalam, 1990, p. 66). Some suggest that work-related fatigue may impair abilities of some students to engage in cognitively-challenging academic tasks. Students in countries such as Japan and Sweden, who have performed better on academic performance tests than American students, tend to be much less frequently employed during their high school years than students in this country (Workman, 1990).

One important issue for young people at this time of their lives is their search for personal identity (Erikson, 1982). They are trying to find personal selves that are distinct from those of their parents. They ask themselves questions such as "Who am I?" "Will I be successful?" and "Will I be accepted?" In their attempts to establish their personal identities, young people in this age group often experiment with behaviors that they believe will show the world that they are independent. They seek to become rulers of their environment. At the same time, they desperately look for evidence that others are accepting them as individuals.

A leading learning theorist, David Elkind (1981), has suggested that young people may experience problems as they begin to move into the formal operations (abstract reasoning) stage of their lives. With their newfound ability to think in abstract terms, a number of adolescents concern themselves with abstract notions of self and personal identity. It may be that some adolescents who have developed the ability to view their own identity as an abstract idea are unable to distinguish between what they think about themselves and what others think about them. Elkind (1981) has suggested that this view sometimes takes the form of either (1) an "imaginary audience" or (2) a "personal fable."

Adolescent behavior in response to an imaginary audience results when the adolescents fail to distinguish between their own thoughts about themselves and those held by others. When this happens, they tend to view themselves as perpetually "on stage." They are certain that everybody is carefully scrutinizing their every move. The imaginary-audience concept explains much about the behavior of young people in this age group. Shyness, for example, is a logical result of their feeling that any mistake made in public will be noticed and criticized. The slavish attention to fashion trends results from an expectation that deviations from the expected norm will be noticed and commented on negatively.

In explaining the personal fable, Elkind (1981) has noted that adolescents often become disoriented by the many physical and emotional changes they experience. At the same time, many of them find these changes to be utterly fascinating. Some of them believe that their new feelings are so unusual that no one else has ever experienced them (particularly not parents or teachers). They may believe that they are living out a one-of-a-kind personal fable. Sometimes they keep diaries that are written out of a conviction that future generations will be intensely interested in their "unique" feelings and experiences.

As students in this age group have more and more life experiences, the validity of the imaginary audience and the personal fable is tested against reality. In time, the imaginary audience gives way to the real audience, and the personal fable is adjusted as young people's interactions with others reveal that many others have experienced similar feelings and have had similar opinions.

High school teachers work with students who are capable of quite abstract thinking, yet these students have characteristics that separate them from college and university students and from older adult learners. They have emotional needs that require teachers' attention. Successful high school teachers strike a balance between their concerns for their students' psychological development and their commitment to provide these students with a respectable grounding in the academic subjects of the curriculum.

....................................

## Key Ideas in Summary

- Learners in today's schools make up a very diverse group. Families of typical learners by no means match the traditional family stereotype of an employed father, a mother who stayed at home, and two children. Many families are now headed by a single parent, and large numbers of these single parents are females under 25 years of age.

- Large numbers of children in the school come from families with annual incomes below the federal poverty level. This situation has worsened over the past 20 years. More African-American and Hispanic children come from poor families than do white children. Children from economically impoverished homes often do not perform well in school.

- With each passing year, minority-group children are comprising a larger percentage of the total school population. African-Americans currently represent the largest minority group in the schools, but this situation is changing rapidly—soon Hispanic learners will be more numerous in the nation's schools than African-American learners. Though their numbers continue to be small relative to African-Americans and Hispanics, the numbers of children of Asian descent enrolled in the nation's schools are increasing rapidly. Though Native Americans (including Alaska natives) comprise only about 1 percent of the school population nationally, in some states these children represent quite high percentages of the total school population.

- Children of mothers who used crack cocaine during pregnancy are just starting to enter the schools in large numbers. These children have difficulty handling multiple stimuli. They tend to react to a typical school environment in one of two ways: they either become very hyperactive and difficult to control, or they withdraw completely. Teachers who work with these learners must provide very structured and caring learning environments.

**TABLE 7–2**
Summary table: Today's pupils and students

| Topic | Important Ideas |
|-------|-----------------|
| Learners' families | Today, few families include a father who works and a nonemployed mother who stays home. Most children in the schools are from either single-parent homes or homes where both parents are employed. Pressures on parents' time often results in teachers being called on to provide social and personal information that used to be provided by parents. |
| Poverty | In a recent survey, it was found that children accounted for nearly 40 percent of the nation's poor. Children from ethnic and cultural minorities are particularly likely to be economically impoverished. |
| Minority-group learners | Learners from minority groups are becoming an increasingly larger proportion of the total school population. Hispanic children will soon become the largest minority group in the schools. (Today African-Americans are the largest minority.) Asians are the fastest-growing minority group in the schools. |
| "Crack babies" as school learners | Children whose mothers used crack cocaine during pregnancy are just now entering the schools in large numbers. Many of these children have suffered harm to their central nervous system and may experience difficulty in learning. |
| Very young learners | Larger numbers of 3- and 4-year-olds are being served by public school programs. In part, this trend has been a result of the increase in the number of mothers who have full-time jobs. |
| Learners with disabilities | Since the passage of the Education for All Handicapped Children Act in 1975 (in 1990 renamed the Individuals with Disabilities Education Act), large numbers of learners with various disabilities have spent at least part of each school day in regular school classrooms. These learners account for about 11 percent of the total school population. |
| Abused and neglected children | All states have laws requiring that people who work with children, including teachers, report suspected incidents of abuse and neglect to the proper authorities. In many communities, suspected abuse is handled by Child Protective Service. Kinds of abuse teachers may observe in learners includes (1) physical abuse, (2) neglect, (3) emotional abuse, and (4) sexual abuse. |

**TABLE 7–2**
*continued*

| Topic | Important Ideas |
|---|---|
| Characteristics of preschool and kindergarten children | These learners often enjoy physical activity for its own sake, but they tire easily and need regular rest periods. Because fine-muscle development is not yet complete, these learners often feel frustrated when asked to do things requiring a high degree of coordination. These learners require a lot of affection. |
| Characteristics of primary-grades children | Fine-muscle development is still not complete, and many of these learners are still not well coordinated. They still like a great deal of physical activity and often find it difficult to sit still for long periods of time. Teachers need to be sensitive to the very different rates of physical development of individuals in this age group. |
| Characteristics of upper-elementary children | Many girls and some boys experience a tremendous growth spurt during these years. Friendships tend to divide along sex lines (boys with boys and girls with girls). Fine-muscle control is quite good, and many learners increase confidence in their abilities to do things requiring high levels of coordination. Learners are beginning to develop a strong sense of personal independence, and their teachers must work hard to motivate their interests in school work. Interests of learners broaden greatly during these years. |
| Characteristics of learners in grades 7 to 9 | Diversity among individual learners is particularly pronounced during these years. Many young people in this age group are concerned with the physical and emotional changes they are experiencing. Emotional outbursts at school are common. Teachers of these learners need to be tolerant and flexible people who can deal with the varying emotional, intellectual, and behavioral patterns of their students. |
| Characteristics of learners in grades 10 to 12 | Most learners at this time of their lives are trying to bring their own personal identities into focus. Many of these young people will take on adult thinking and behavior patterns toward the end of this period. Some of them are capable of quite abstract levels of thinking. |

- In the past 20 years, there has been a great increase in the numbers of 3- and 4-year-olds enrolled in school programs. In part, this trend has been spurred by the tendency for more and more mothers to hold down full-time jobs outside the home. Additionally, there have been concerns about the quality and the expense of programs offered by private daycare facilities.

- About 11 percent of learners in the schools are eligible for programs directed toward the disabled. These learners have widely varied characteristics. The largest number of young people receiving these services are classified as "learning disabled." Other large groups within this population are the speech-impaired and developmentally disabled learners.

- Every state has laws requiring teachers to file reports with the appropriate authorities when they observe injuries to children that appear to be nonaccidental. Episodes of child abuse appear to be on the increase. Among categories of abuse are (1) physical abuse, (2) neglect, (3) emotional abuse, and (4) sexual abuse. Teachers are expected to know behavioral indicators of possible abuse.

- Children's general characteristics vary enormously as they progress through the school program. For example, preschool and kindergarten children tend to require high levels of physical activity. Learners in grades 1 to 3 still have underdeveloped fine-motor control, and they are often frustrated by tasks requiring them to manipulate small objects and do detailed work with their hands. In grades 4 to 6, girls are often physically larger than boys. For the most part, friendships among learners in these grade levels do not cross sex lines. There are tremendous differences in the physical development of individual learners in grades 7 to 9. These differences sometimes occasion great personal anxieties on the part of these young people. During grades 10 to 12, many students are engaged in a search for personal identity. By this time in their development, many young people are able to deal with quite abstract levels of thinking.

..............................

# Review and Discussion Questions

1. To what extent does the traditional image of an American family consisting of an employed father, a mother who stays home, and two children reflect today's reality?

2. Has the percentage of young Americans under age 18 who are living in poverty increased or decreased over the past 20 years?

3. What are some problems educators may face as increasing numbers of "crack babies" begin entering the schools?

4. What are some categories of child abuse, and what are some indicators teachers might look for that might suggest a given child is being abused?

5. Is a teacher legally obligated to report suspected abuse?

6. What kinds of behaviors sometimes result when preschool and kindergarten children are not provided with enough physical activity?

7. Some people argue that because of the changing nature of our society, teachers increasingly are expected to take on much of the nurturing function that formerly was taken care of by children's parents. To what extent do you believe this is true? Are teachers prepared to do this? If not, what kinds of additional professional training should they receive?

8. Young people of junior high school age sometimes are considered to be difficult to work with. Is this reputation deserved? Are there special skills that you think teachers assigned to work with young people in this age group should have? If so, what are they?

9. One suggestion for helping "crack children" is to keep the same teacher with them for several years, to reduce the number of changes to which the children will need to adjust. Do you think this would be a good idea for all children in the early years of their schooling?

10. Many students, particularly during the first several years of high school, sense that their every move is being watched and commented upon critically. What kinds of things might you, as a teacher, do to help individual students appreciate that they really are not "under the microscope" and that people, in general, are much more tolerant of their attitudes, opinions, and behaviors than the students might suppose?

. . . . . . . . . . . . . . . . . . . . . . . . . . . .

# Ideas for Field Experiences, Projects, and Enrichment

1. Interview two or more teachers at a grade level you would like to teach (and in your subject area if you are interested in secondary school teaching). Ask them to comment about the family life of learners in their classroom. In particular, seek information about economic status, family values, and the extent to which there is support in the home for what learners are expected to do at school. Share your findings with others in your class as part of a general discussion on the nature of learners in the schools.

2. Review some suggested lessons in a course textbook or a professional journal that are directed toward learners in a grade you would like to teach. Interview a teacher who teaches the kinds of learners for whom the lessons are directed. Are the lessons appropriate for the intellectual and maturity levels of these learners? Do they respond well to the interests of these young people? If the teacher would change anything in the lessons to make them more effective,

what would he or she make different? Prepare a short report of your interview to share with your instructor.

3. Visit a classroom that includes learners from a cross-section of cultural and ethnic groups. Take note of any differences in ways members of different cultural and ethnic groups participate. You might wish to ask the teacher about his or her own observations regarding this issue. Share your findings with others in your class.

4. "Crack children" are just now beginning to enroll in the schools in large numbers. Read some articles in professional journals that focus on these learners, and prepare a short oral report for presentation to your class in which you describe some approaches being tried in various places to help such students better adjust to the demands of school.

5. Invite a panel of three to five middle school and junior high school teachers to visit your class. Ask them to comment on some special challenges of working with learners in this age group, and to suggest aspects of working with these learners that they find to be particularly satisfying.

· · · · · · · · · · · · · · · · · · · · · · · · · ·

# Supplementary Reading

Elkind, D. *All Grown Up and No Place to Go*. Reading, MA: Addison-Wesley, 1984.

Reed, S., and R. C. Sautter. "Children of Poverty: The Status of 12 Million Young Americans." *Phi Delta Kappan* (June 1990): K1–K12.

Rist, M. C. "The Shadow Children: Preparing for the Arrival of Crack Babies in School." *Research Bulletin*. Bloomington, IN: Phi Delta Kappa Center on Evaluation, Development, and Research, July 1990.

Slavin, R., and N. A. Madden. "What Works for Students at Risk: A Research Synthesis." *Educational Leadership* (February 1989): 4–13.

Spark, M. *The Prime of Miss Jean Brodie*. Philadelphia: Lippincott, 1962.

Tucker, F. B., L. A. Becker, and J. A. Sousa. *Characteristics and Identification of Gifted and Talented Students*. 3d ed. Washington, DC: National Education Association Professional Library, 1988.

· · · · · · · · · · · · · · · · · · · · · · · · · ·

# References

Clifford, M. "Students Need Challenge, Not Easy Success." *Educational Leadership* (September 1990): 22–26.

Elkind, D. *Children and Adolescents: Interpretive Essays on Jean Piaget*. 3d ed. New York: Oxford University Press, 1981.

Erikson, E. H. *The Life Cycle Completed: A Review*. New York: Norton, 1982.

Gough, P. B. "Good News/Bad News." *Phi Delta Kappan* (June 1990): 747.

Haase, C. C., and R. S. Kempe. "The School and Protective Services." *Education and Urban Society* (May 1990).

"How to Identify Signs of Abuse." *American Teacher* (December 1989/January 1990): 12.

Marshall, R. C., chair—Quality Education for Minorities Project. *Education That Works: An Action Plan for the Education of Minorities*. Cambridge, MA: Quality Education for Minorities Project, Massachusetts Institute of Technology, 1990.

McEvoy, A. W. "Child Abuse Law and School Policy." *Education and Urban Society* (May 1990): 247–57.

Mirga, T. "Today's Numbers, Tomorrow's Nation." *Education Week* (May 14, 1986): 22.

Ogle, L. T., ed., and N. Alsalam, associate ed. *The Condition of Education: 1990*. Washington, DC: National Center for Education Statistics, 1990.

Reed, S., and R. C. Sautter. "Children of Poverty: The Status of 12 Million Young Americans." *Phi Delta Kappan* (June 1990): K1–K12.

Rist, M. C. "The Shadow Children: Preparing for the Arrival of Crack Babies in School." *Research Bulletin*. Bloomington, IN: Phi Delta Kappa Center on Evaluation, Development, and Research, July 1990.

Slavin, R., and N. A. Madden. "What Works for Students at Risk: A Research Synthesis." *Educational Leadership* (February 1989): 4–13.

Stern, J. D., ed., and M. O. Chandler, associate ed. *The Condition of Education: 1987*. Washington, DC: National Center for Education Statistics, 1987.

Strong, L. "The Best Kids They Have." *Educational Leadership* (February 1989): 79.

Workman, B. "The Teenager and the World of Work: Alienation at West High." *Phi Delta Kappan* (April 1990): 628–31.

# Chapter 8

# Multicultural and Gender Equity Concerns

· · · · · · · · · · · · · · · · · · · · · · · · · · · · · · · ·

## Objectives

This chapter provides information to help the reader

- identify a rationale for paying particular attention to school experiences of minority-group and female learners.
- recognize the changing demographics of the school population and some accompanying implications for educational practices.
- describe some patterns of within-school segregation that persist despite successful attempts to eliminate patterns of within-district segregation.
- point out examples of how school programs of various kinds tend to use race, ethnicity, or gender as criteria for determining the kinds of educational experiences to be provided for a given learner.
- recognize the growing discontinuity between demographic characteristics of teachers and demographic characteristics of learners.
- identify sources of information for materials and programs designed to sensitize teachers to multicultural and gender equity perspectives.

# Focus Questions

1. What are some trends regarding racial characteristics of learners and of teachers?
2. Why is it important for teachers to become sensitive to the cultural backgrounds of learners?
3. How did people who supported the "genetic deficit" view explain academic problems of minorities?
4. What are some factors that continue to result in many schools enrolling disproportionately large numbers of learners from certain cultural and ethnic groups?
5. What is meant by "within-school segregation," and does the term refer to gender as well as racial segregation?
6. What evidence is there that many minority-group learners are not well served by the schools?
7. What problems can result when people are too quick to generalize about characteristics of all members of a given minority?
8. What are some recommendations that have been made to improve the quality of educational services to ethnic and cultural minorities?
9. What are some important features of "Comer-model" schools?
10. What are some special features of high schools that have proved particularly successful in graduating large numbers of students for whom Spanish was their first language?

• • • • • • • • • • • • • • • • • • • • • • • • • •

# Introduction

Teachers entering the profession today are almost certain to encounter many learners who come from ethnic and cultural backgrounds with which the teachers have little familiarity. Our schools have an obligation to serve all who attend, and thus today's teachers must work hard to become sensitive to their learners' backgrounds. Their backgrounds help shape learners' views of the world, and successful lessons take these special perspectives into account. The more teachers who are able to accommodate these differences, the more successful learners will be. Successful learners feel good about themselves and their experiences in schools, and their positive attitudes, in turn, positively reinforce teachers. These teachers find themselves facing fewer discipline problems and gaining confidence as they see young people under their charge profit from their instruction. It is thus to the advantage of both teachers and learners to encourage a multicultural perspective in the schools.

The laudable objective of maximizing each learner's potential has implications not only for how members of diverse ethnic and cultural groups are treated, but also for the issue of gender. Today's adult females are as likely to be employed as are adult males. Women occupy important positions in government, the arts, medicine, law, and the other areas of our society. Female learners have not always had the kinds of educational opportunities that have been available to males, but today's school programs recognize that human capital is a precious resource. Talents of females and members of ethnic and cultural minorities deserve to be fully developed. Society stands to benefit from the potential contributions of citizens who leave school as confident, competent young adults, fully prepared to assume positions of responsibility and leadership.

Changing demographics suggest that we need to pay more attention to familiarizing teachers with multicultural demands than ever before. Educational sociologists Carl Grant and Walter Secada (1990) point out that there is a discontinuity between the characteristics of teachers and learners in the schools. They note that the current population of teachers is predominantly white and female, and it is becoming even more so. More than 85 percent of all teachers are white, and two-thirds are female. By the year 2000, it is estimated that between 30 and 40 percent of learners in the schools will be nonwhite (Grant and Secada, 1990, p. 403). Statistics regarding more current percentages of racial and cultural learners are presented in Figure 8–1.

Teacher preparation programs in colleges and universities have sometimes not done as much as they might have to sensitize future teachers to the growing diversity in the schools. Though many professors of education are well-versed in the professional literature as it relates to disadvantaged groups, few of them are either minority or female (93 percent are white; 70 percent are male) (Grant and Secada, 1990, p. 404). Further, many of them are middle-aged, with public school teaching experience predating the recent changes that have given schools a much more diverse population of learners.

**FIGURE 8–1**
Racial and cultural characteristics of the public schools 1986

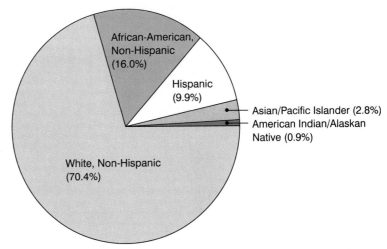

Source: From Laurence T. Ogle, ed., and Nabeel Alsalam, associate ed., *The Condition of Education, 1990,* Vol. 1, *Elementary and Secondary Education* (Washington, DC: National Center for Education Statistics, 1990), 62.

## A Brief History of Attitudes Toward Minority-Group Learners

Educators have long been aware that large numbers of learners from minority groups have not done well in school. An early explanation for this phenomenon was the "genetic deficit" view (Savage and Armstrong, 1992). People who subscribed to this position believed that minority-group learners lacked the necessary intellectual tools to succeed in school. Individuals who accepted this premise were reluctant to divert school resources to improve instructional programs for children who were perceived as incapable of profiting from them.

By the 1960s, the genetic deficit position had given way to a "cultural deficit" view (Erickson, 1987). Those who subscribed to this argument contended that poor school performance could be blamed on the failure of minority-group children's parents to provide an intellectually stimulating home atmosphere that prepared the learners for the expectations of the school. The cultural deficit view seemed to allow schools a way out when confronted with statistics revealing high dropout rates and other evidence of mediocre levels of school performance on the part of minority-group learners. This position permitted blame for these dismal statistics to be placed on learners' homes rather than on the school.

A more recent explanation for the schools' failure to adequately serve needs of minority-group learners has been the "communication process" position (Erickson, 1987). According to this view, language patterns of minority-group learners are substantially different from those of their teachers and majority-group learners; hence, they are not capable of understanding much of what goes on in the classroom. The communication failure accounts for their poor academic performance. This position has been attacked because it fails to explain why some minority-group learners do extremely well in school.

In recent years, professional educators have been downplaying explanations for difficulties of minority-group learners that seem to shift the blame away from the schools. Increasingly, it is argued that school programs have failed to plan seriously for the success of *all* learners (even though educators' rhetoric has espoused this intent for years). Because of this failure, many minority-group learners and their parents may not believe the schools' claims that they are truly interested in promoting the development of each child. To establish credibility, schools must work hard to "avoid instructional practices that undermine learners' self confidence and . . . work hard to [help them] appreciate the social benefits of a culture that encourages diversity" (Savage and Armstrong, 1992).

## Desegregation and Its Influences on Learners

For many years, it was difficult to promote the development of intercultural and interracial sensitivities in the schools because many schools were racially segregated. Then and now, concerns about desegregating schools and promoting more communication among learners from different racial and cultural backgrounds fall into three distinct categories:

1. concerns about ending legal segregation and following court-ordered plans to achieve integration
2. concerns about *within-school* segregation of minority-group learners and females
3. concerns about achievement levels of minority-group learners and females (Simon-McWilliams, 1989)

## Efforts to End Legal Segregation

The 1954 Supreme Court case *Brown* v. *Board of Education* established a legal guideline that led to the dismantling of segregated school systems. However, the effort to achieve a school system featuring a cross-section of students from a wide variety of ethnic and racial backgrounds has been only moderately successful. A key 1974 Supreme Court decision in the case of *Milliken* v. *Bradley* held that courts lacked authority to order busing between districts for the purpose of achieving racial balance in the schools. This has meant that busing has been authorized as an option only within the boundaries of individual school districts.

In districts with homogeneous populations, the *Milliken* v. *Bradley* restriction has made it difficult for school authorities to organize schools that reflect a broad ethnic and racial diversity. For example, the nation's inner cities are becoming increasingly African-American and Hispanic, while the suburbs remain predominantly white. As a result, large numbers of inner-city schools are overwhelmingly African-American, Hispanic, or both African-American and Hispanic. Similarly, many suburban schools are overwhelmingly white. Bates states that "there is evidence that the number of U.S. students attending racially isolated schools is now on the rise" (1990, p. 9).

Today, many learners attend schools with others who are much like themselves. This pattern suggests that they have few opportunities to interact with young people from other cultural and ethnic backgrounds. This means that "blacks, Hispanics, and whites are likely to attend schools that are increasingly unrepresentative of the pluralis-

Perspectives of individuals from different ethnic and cultural backgrounds enrich understandings of all learners.

tic society where they live and work" (Vergon, 1989). Educators continue to be concerned about this situation.

## Within-School Segregation

Even in school districts that have managed to create student bodies that embrace a mixture of learners from different cultural and ethic groups, segregation continues to be a concern. The issue in such places relates not to a legal, physical separation of learners along ethnic or racial lines, but instead a kind of segregation that may result as a consequence of how learners from different groups are assigned to courses.

Within-school segregation of students along cultural, racial, and even gender lines is thought to be particularly serious at the secondary school level. College preparatory courses in many high schools enroll disproportionately high percentages of white students. Remedial courses, on the other hand, frequently have much higher percentages of minority-group students enrolled than these students' numbers within the total school population would seem to warrant.

Male students comprise high percentages of some high school classes. For example, 80 percent of students enrolled in high school physical science classes are male (Simon-McWilliams, 1989). Males are also overrepresented in many special education classes—they are 1.7 times as likely as females to be classified as mentally retarded, trainable mentally retarded, or seriously emotionally disturbed. Minority-group students are 1.6 times as likely as white students to be placed in special education classes (Simon-McWilliams, 1989).

Evidence indicates a relationship between a student's race or ethnic group and his or her likelihood of being suspended from school. Minority-group students are suspended from school at nearly twice the rate of their white counterparts. African-American students are particularly likely to be suspended; their rate of suspension is three times that of white students (Bates, 1990).

Critics of present school practices point out that ability grouping, counseling learners into academic or vocational classes, and so forth have been used to resegregate the schools. They argue that many minority-group students have been assigned to "dead-end" programs on the basis of race rather than on ability levels. One study found differences even in the nature of vocational programs recommended to white students and African-American students—those recommended to whites tended to emphasize business skills and to tie closely to the core academic program, whereas those recommended to African-Americans tended to require their frequent absence from the school building and to feature little systematic contact with the core academic program (Oakes, 1985).

In summary, professionals who are concerned about the issue of within-school segregation are not satisfied with a simple count of the number of learners from various ethnic and racial groups who are enrolled in a given school (see Box 8–1 for one teacher's concerns). They want evidence that there are efforts to serve *all* learners in ways that will maximize their individual development. Further, they argue that learners will not develop multicultural sensitivity and an acceptance for diversity if individual classes within the school resegregate the learner population.

## Concerns about Achievement Levels

This issue ties closely to concerns about within-school segregation. If academic standards in classes to which certain groups of learners have been assigned are not high, it should be no surprise when these learners fare poorly on achievement tests. Many high school students who aspire to continue their education in a college or university take the Scholastic Aptitude Test (SAT). African-American and Hispanic students' scores on these tests have continually lagged behind white students' scores, and females have generally received lower scores than males on the quantitative portion of the SAT. These patterns suggest that the benefits of schooling are not equally accorded to students regardless of their race, ethnicity, or gender.

Generally, more benefits accrue to a learner the longer he or she stays in school. Ideally, there should be no difference in the dropout rates associated with race or ethnicity. This, however, is not the case. The results of a study comparing dropout rates of white, African-American, and Hispanic learners in 1975 and 1987 are shown in Figure 8–2. Note that the dropout rates for whites are lower in both years than for either African-Americans or Hispanics. There has been a great deal of improvement in the dropout rates for African-Americans (down from 9.2 to 6.7 percent from 1975 to 1987), but dropout rates for Hispanics have risen (up from 9.2 percent in 1975 to 9.7 percent in 1987).

Admittedly, many students who drop out of high school finish their high school education later. Some do so in the military services; others take courses and work for a

## BOX 8–1
# IS WITHIN-SCHOOL SEGREGATION A "NATURAL" CONDITION?

This is how a teacher described one school's efforts to achieve integration:

I used to think we could really integrate this place, but I'm beginning to have my doubts. I mean, we've done a good job keeping a good racial balance in all of our classes, including the advanced sections. We probably do a better job than most other places when it comes to making sure that we don't assign higher percentages of blacks and Hispanics than whites to our special education programs. In fact, we seem to have done everything we possibly could to make sure that everybody has access to the best academic programs we offer. Yet, we still aren't really integrated.

Take a look in the lunch room. Black kids sit with black kids, Hispanic kids sit with Hispanic kids, white kids sit with white kids. There's even a small bunch of Asian kids who always sit in the far corner. I see the same pattern at football and basketball games. How much integration *really* goes on at this place? These kids are in the same school, but are they really interacting with people from other racial groups?

*What Do You Think?*
1. How realistic is the situation this teacher describes?
2. Do patterns like those described here indicate a failure to integrate the schools?
3. Should educators take any action to change these patterns?

• • • • • • • • • • • • • • • • • • • • • • • • • • • • • • • • • • • • • • • • • • • • • • • • • • • •

high school equivalency certificate of some kind. A 1987 survey of 25- to 29-year-olds revealed important differences among whites, African-Americans, and Hispanics. By the time they fell within this age group, 86.3 percent of the whites had completed high school or a high school equivalency program. The percentage for African-Americans was 83.3 percent; for Hispanics, it was 59.9 percent (Ogle and Alsalam, 1990, p. 22).

These figures suggest a convergence of the high school completion rates for whites and African-Americans. Hispanics continue to lag well behind. Since Hispanics are the nation's most rapidly growing minority group, these figures are of great concern for educators. Unless the schools do a better job of preparing Hispanic learners, an ever-larger percentage of the nation's population is going to be ill-prepared to contribute to a society that increasingly requires an educated work force.

We mentioned earlier the failure of females to score as high as males on the quantitative sections of the Scholastic Aptitude Test. Though more women than men complete baccalaureate degree programs, relatively few elect to pursue advanced work in mathematics and the sciences. The dearth of females in this group is often explained by the inadequate mathematics background that has been the legacy of their experiences in the public schools.

**Figure 8–2**
Dropout rates for learners from different ethnic groups

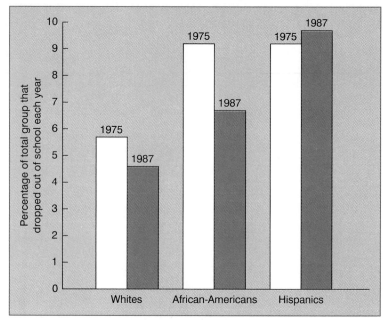

Source: Data from L. T. Ogle, ed., and N. Alsalam, associate ed., *The Condition of Education, 1990,* Vol. 1, *Elementary and Secondary Education* (Washington, DC: National Center for Education Statistics, 1990) p. 20.

Some authorities have hinted that public education has not made a serious effort to develop female learners' abilities in mathematics because of a faulty assumption about their aptitude for the content (Chipman and Thomas, 1987). Some research has demonstrated very minor gender-related differences in males and females in terms of their abilities to deal with spatial abstractions. Chipman and Thomas argue that there has never been any established connection between the kinds of spatial abilities for which there are slight gender differences and the ability to master mathematics; however, a mythology has developed that females are not good at mathematics. Hence, at least in some schools, female students have not been held to the same achievement expectations in mathematics as have been males.

Unless this pattern is broken, females may be disadvantaged in their efforts to break into technical fields. Today, fewer females than males enroll in university programs in mathematics and the sciences (Oakes, 1990). A continuation of this pattern will result in a great underdevelopment of their talents, and it will bar many females from well-paid technical employment. Even though more and more women are entering the work force after they complete their education, there is evidence that they are underrepresented in some technical fields where salaries are high and the demand for trained workers is great (Chipman and Thomas, 1987).

## The Need for Accurate Information

To plan effective school programs, educators must have accurate information about minority-group learners and the capabilities of male and female learners. Superficial

Today, educators strive to ensure that opportunities in all subject areas are available to male and female learners alike. As this photo shows, some subjects, such as woodworking, were in the past considered to be "male"; others, such as sewing and baking, were considered to be "female."

understanding of these issues can lead to school practices that fail because they rest upon faulty assumptions. For example, as noted previously, research has found no basis for the widespread belief that females, as a group, are not good at mathematics. The companion piece of street "wisdom" about males is that they are not as good at reading and writing as are females. Research has also failed to support this myth.

Assumptions about learners from cultural and ethnic minorities also sometimes prompt irresponsible actions on the part of school officials. People sometimes fail to recognize the important differences that exist *within* individual groups. For example, values and perspectives of African-Americans in rural areas may have little in common with those of African-Americans in the nation's inner cities. (Additionally, there is by no means a common world view that characterizes all urban African-Americans, nor a common world view that characterizes all rural African-Americans.)

The nation's Hispanic population is extremely diverse. Some critics charge that there has been a tendency for school authorities to view all Hispanics as linguistically deprived and to treat them as "culturally deficient and linguistically deprived foreign-ers. This treatment helps to explain their high dropout rate, their underrepresentation in advanced courses, and their low rate of college attendance" (Grant, 1990, p. 27). Grant also points out that only 26 percent of Hispanic students have a native language other than English. Clearly, school programs that presume them to be "linguistically deprived foreigners" do them an injustice.

Developing school programs that reflect a genuine appreciation for issues associat-ed with multicultural and gender equity depends on educators who are well-informed. The need for teachers to develop sensitivity to the special perspectives of groups from which their learners come is growing more important as the nation's school population grows more diverse.

## Goals and General Suggestions for Teachers

Many individuals and professional groups have been interested in improving school programs in ways that will better serve the needs of ethnic and cultural minori-ties and females. There is a growing recognition that the nation can ill afford to do any-thing less than fully develop the talents of all of its young people. The high rate at

*"And never let it be said that there is even a hint of sexism or racism in this dis-trict."*
Courtesy of Ford Button.

which minority-group students are dropping out of school is of particular concern. The Quality Education for Minorities Project, in its report *Education That Works: An Action Plan for the Education of Minorities* (Marshall, 1990), notes that between 1985 and 2000 there is anticipated to be a 30 percent increase in the number of jobs open to college graduates and a 35 percent increase in the number of jobs open to nongraduates, but only a 10 percent increase in the number of jobs open to high school graduates. Clearly, young people with less than a high school education are going to find it difficult to secure employment.

In 1990, the Quality Education for Minorities Project issued a number of goals. These goals, targeted for accomplishment by the year 2000, are as follows:

- Ensure that minority students start school prepared to learn.
- Ensure that the academic achievement of minority youth is at a level that will enable them, upon graduation from high school, to enter the work force or college fully prepared to be successful and not in need of remediation.
- Significantly increase the participation of minority students in higher education with a special emphasis on the study of mathematics, science, and engineering.
- Strengthen and increase the numbers of teachers of minority students. (This goal refers to the need to provide for better training of all teachers who work with minorities, to assure that exceptionally able teachers are assigned to work with minority-group learners, and to recruit more teachers who, themselves, are minorities.)
- Strengthen the school-to-work transition so that minority students who do not choose college leave high school prepared with the skills necessary to participate productively in the world of work and with the foundation required to upgrade their skills and advance their careers.
- Provide quality out-of-school experiences and opportunities to supplement the schooling of minority youth and adults (Marshall, 1990, pp. 56–76).

Numerous recommendations have been made regarding what educators should do to respond to multicultural and equity needs (Banks with Clegg, Jr., 1988; Bates, 1990; Marshall, 1990; Savage and Armstrong, 1992).

## Commitment to the Idea That All Can Learn

Unless teachers sincerely believe that young people from ethnic and cultural groups can learn, there is little likelihood of improving these young people's learning performances. Teachers' assumptions about their learners influence their expectations for them. Teachers directing instruction toward individuals from whom not much is expected are not likely to hold those learners to a high standard of excellence. In the long run, students of whom little is expected do not learn a great deal. Such a regimen will not encourage students to stay in school, and it certainly will not produce the self-confident, academically able individuals needed to compete in a workplace that demands increasingly sophisticated skills from even entry-level employees.

## Modifying Grouping Practices

Evidence indicates that grouping practices in many schools have acted to the disadvantage of ethnic and cultural minority students (Bates, 1990; Marshall, 1990).

Individuals who are shunted into a low ability group early in their school years tend to fall farther and farther behind their peers.

Grouping decisions occur at several levels. Sometimes, ability grouping results in the creation of entire classes of learners who are thought to be in a given category. For example, a high school may have a freshman English class specifically designated for low ability students. This kind of grouping can undermine learners' confidence in their own abilities. The content is likely to be much less rigorous than that introduced in so-called regular classes, impairing the students' preparation for more advanced work.

Grouping within classes may also have negative consequences where such grouping is (1) based on the teacher's view that learners' ability level is low and (2) established in such a way that so-called low ability groups include disproportionate numbers of learners from cultural and ethnic minorities. In general, within-class groups function more positively when they are not organized with a view to standardizing ability levels of members within each group, and when learners in each group constitute a representative racial, cultural, and gender sample of the entire class.

## Accommodating Learning Style Differences

Learners vary in terms of the particular instructional styles to which they will positively respond. Research has documented that learners' cultural backgrounds influence their preference for a given instructional style (Grant and Sleeter, 1989). This conclusion suggests a need for teachers to plan lessons that provide for different learners to approach content in different ways. Some young people will profit from opportunities to touch and manipulate objects. Others will do just fine when they are asked to read new information. Still others will respond well to opportunities to work with photographs, charts, or other graphic representations of data.

## Teachers' Awareness of Their Own Perspectives

Because majority-group perspectives are so pervasive, white teachers sometimes fail to recognize the extent to which their own world views have been conditioned by their membership in the majority. The reality is that all ethnic and cultural groups, including the white majority, have certain established assumptions about "how the world is" and about what constitutes "proper" behavior.

If people have not considered their own special assumptions about reality, sometimes they tend to assume that everybody has the same basic views. Teachers who think this way may have problems working with learners from ethnic and cultural minorities whose fundamental perspectives may be quite different from their own. A teacher who has not bothered to learn anything about the traditional culture of Thailand, for example, may be surprised at the negative reaction of a Thai child to a light touch on the head. The teacher's intent may be to convey concern and friendship; but, to a child raised in a Thai home, the gesture may be interpreted as an offensive invasion of privacy. (For one teacher's experiences with cultural and educational views differing from her own, see this chapter's Case Study.)

*Who cares about an African-American German teacher?*

**LaShandra Pierson, who is African-American, teaches German at Milligan High School**. Milligan is located in a suburban school district on the edge of one of the nation's major cities. The school has seen a great change in the makeup of its student body in recent years. Today, about 60 percent of the students are white, 25 percent are African-American, 20 percent are Hispanic, and 5 percent are Asian and Native American.

This is Ms. Pierson's third year at the school. Her interest in German traces to her family background. Her father, a career army officer, was stationed for many years in Germany. She began speaking the language almost as soon as she began speaking English. As she grew up, she learned to love the language, the literature, the music, and other aspects of the culture of Germany. When asked, she also willingly admits that her warm feelings for Germany stem from her recollections of being able to travel about Germany in her teen years without encountering much evidence of racial prejudice.

The impact of her experiences in Germany influenced her choice of German as a major when she entered an east coast university. Her commitment to sharing her enthusiasm for the German language and people led her to pursue a program leading to teacher certification. Her undergraduate years went well, as did her student teaching experience. After graduation, she was offered jobs at several schools and chose Milligan.

At Milligan, her life has not been at all what she expected. First of all, she finds that almost all her students are white. She has no problem with teaching white students, but, as an African-American, she had thought she would have more influence on African-American students. She had hoped they would enroll in her classes and, even if they did not get caught up in her enthusiasm for German, might at least be influenced to complete high school and go on to college.

Ms. Pierson has complained to some of her friends that many of the African-American students in the school have been rude and even hostile to her. One angry young man accosted her at a football game and demanded to know why she was "wasting her time" teaching a "white" subject like German.

At the same time, some of the white faculty members have assumed that, as an African-American, Ms. Pierson is one of the "resident experts" on all matters related to cultural and ethnic minorities. She has been quizzed about her views on Jesse Jackson, Malcolm X, Martin Luther King, Jr., and a host of other present and past African-American luminaries. As well, she has been assigned to countless district-level committees charged with developing programs to serve the needs of African-American and other minority-group learners.

LaShandra Pierson is disillusioned. She feels that no one cares about her hard-won expertise in German. She senses that the very African-American students she wants to help resent her accomplishments. She suspects many of the administrators and faculty think she is just an "intelligent African-American face" to whom they can delegate troublesome duties associated with minority programming. In short, LaShandra Pierson has found the reality of education to be different from her expectations. She is thinking about changing to a different career.

*What has led to LaShandra Pierson's present feelings? What should she do now? Do other teachers bear any responsibility for her situation? What might administrators have done to improve the way she feels? Realistically, is there anything that can be done now, or are the conditions that have led to Ms. Pierson's feelings unalterable features of the "real world" of the school?*

## Less Reliance on Standardized Tests

In recent years, the producers of standardized tests have enjoyed boom times. Legislators throughout the nation have clamored for information about the quality of public school programs, and standardized test results have proved almost irresistibly attractive. They summarize tremendous amounts of information in numerical form, and they allow for easy comparisons among schools. The public also finds numerical ratings easy to understand.

At best, standardized tests provide an extremely limited view of an individual learner's capabilities. Many of these tests probe only very low-level kinds of mental processes; few can assess higher-level thinking skills. Because of the importance of test scores, in some places there are great pressures for teachers to "teach to the test." This has the potential to trivialize what kinds of content are addressed and to encourage teachers to deemphasize higher-level thinking skills.

Standardized tests pose particular problems for learners from ethnic and cultural minorities. Critics contend that standardized tests serve to deny opportunities for minority-group learners to continue their education beyond the high school level (Marshall, 1990). The same critics point out that a system that limits the continued academic development of the fastest-growing component of the total school population makes little sense. We need assessment techniques that will foster the maximum development of minority-group learners' talents. Further, assessment techniques should encourage the development of sophisticated thinking abilities, not simply reinforce the recall-level thinking called for on most of today's standardized tests.

New assessment procedures need to take into account background characteristics that are likely to typify many minority-group learners. The vocabulary of assessment instruments needs to be responsive to the learners' environments. As well, opportunities these learners have had outside of school need to be considered. (For example, how many poor, inner-city children will have computers at home? How many will have traveled extensively? How many of their families subscribe to a large number of periodicals?) We need assessment techniques that look at these young people's potential for future development, not at what they have failed to learn because of conditions beyond their control.

## Avoiding Favoritism in the Classroom

Teachers are human. They have better relationships with some people than with others. They enjoy some of their learners more than others. In the classroom, however, professionalism demands that teachers make an effort to encourage each learner's development. It is particularly important for learners to believe that they will not be singled out in any kind of a negative way because of their ethnicity, race, or gender.

Teachers must strive for equity in their relationships with their learners. Episodes of misbehavior need to be treated similarly, regardless of who was the offender. Encouragement needs to be meted out to all who perform well. The bottom line is that all learners need to feel that they will be treated fairly. The teacher's credibility depends on this perception—when learners believe that the teacher is not being fair, motivation declines, academic performance erodes, and discipline problems increase.

## Providing Good Teachers

In some instances, this concern is related to the issue of grouping. The best teachers may be assigned to high-ability classes that often have small numbers of ethnic and cultural minority-group learners. This means that many learners who greatly need motivating, caring teachers are denied them. We need to encourage outstanding teachers to work with minority-group learners. This step will require a clear break with present trends. One recent study revealed a pattern that typifies the situation in much of the country, showing "that teachers in predominantly minority schools were the least experienced, held the most emergency credentials, and were likely to be teaching out of their fields" (Marshall, 1990, p. 43).

### Promising Initiatives

Problems associated with learners' race, ethnicity, and gender are serious, but they are being addressed successfully in a number of ways. For example, teacher preparation programs are now placing much more emphasis on training people to work with minority-group learners than they used to. In fact, the National Council for Accreditation of Teacher Education (NCATE), the national accrediting body for teacher education programs, insists that such training be included in programs and that future teachers have opportunities for field experiences that bring them into contact with culturally diverse learners (NCATE, 1987).

There is a growing recognition that multicultural perspectives need to be developed across the entire curriculum. Minority-group learners are enrolled in every subject schools offer. It only makes sense for program planning to take their needs into account (see the accompanying What the Experts Say). Schools everywhere are seeking examples of approaches that work well with these young people. Happily, some programs have been able to demonstrate that, given the proper conditions, *all* young people can learn. We will examine two such programs here.

---

WHAT THE EXPERTS SAY

## *Educating minorities and the future of the work force*[*]

Experts associated with the Quality Education for Minorities Project (1990) argue that the future economic health of the nation depends upon school programs that effectively educate learners from ethnic and cultural minorities. Numbers of minorities are growing at a rapid rate, and are expected to account for 60 percent of the total population growth between 1990 and 2000. Looking even further into the future, it is estimated that by the year 2080 (less than a century from now), non-Hispanic whites will be a minority of the total U.S. population. These estimates suggest a clear need to develop school programs that will maximize the talents of learners from cultural and ethnic minorities. To do otherwise will be to accept a decline in the competence of our work force—a condition that is certain to result in a plummeting standard of living.

'For a more detailed treatment of this issue, see R. C. Marshall, chair—Quality Education for Minorities Project, *Education That Works: An Action Plan for the Education of Minorities* (Cambridge, MA: Quality Education for Minorities Project, Massachusetts Institute of Technology, 1990), 11–16.

## The Work of James Comer

Beginning in the late 1960s, James Comer and several of his associates from the Yale Child Study Center developed a program that was adopted in two schools in New Haven, Connecticut. Learners in these schools had the lowest scores on standardized achievement tests and the poorest attendance records of all schools in the district. Populations of the two schools were 99 percent African-American, and the vast majority of learners came from families whose incomes fell below the official poverty line. The Comer team installed a program based on well-researched principles of child development and participatory management. Fifteen years after the program began, though the racial and economic makeup of the schools' population was unchanged, standardized tests scores of learners were above national averages. These scores were close to the top of all New Haven schools' scores, and attendance records of learners were outstanding (Comer, 1989).

The plan initially instituted in the two New Haven schools, known now as the "Comer model," has been widely adopted. Perhaps its most important feature is *shared decision making*. Principals in Comer-model schools invite parents, teachers, and school support staff members (particularly those concerned with learners' mental health) into the decision-making process. These individuals constitute a management team that sets school policies. The Comer Model places an emphasis on developing solutions to problems rather than on assigning blame when young people fail to learn. These solutions have been supported by an undergirding assumption that all pupils and students in the schools *can* learn. The inclusive management structure and the flexibility to take quick action to respond to problems have been credited with much of the success of Comer-model schools.

## Features of Schools That Do a Good Job with Language-Minority Learners

Over five million learners have something other than English as their first language (Borich, 1988). These learners need to know English to succeed in school and to be competitive in the job market. Congress recognized the special needs of these children when it passed the Bilingual Education Act in 1968. This act calls for initial school instruction to be provided in a learner's first language until a level of English proficiency is reached that will allow for success in classrooms where only English is used.

James Comer has found shared decision-making to be an important ingredient in schools that have successfully served large populations of minority-group students. These parents, teachers, administrators, and school support staff members are considering some changes in the school curriculum.

The concern for educating these learners was underscored in the 1974 decision of *Lau v. Nichols*, which required local school districts to develop approaches that would ensure that learners with limited English proficiency were not denied a meaningful education. The court argued that simply providing these learners with the same curriculum and texts as native speakers of English would not suffice.

Many programs have been established to help non-native speakers of English succeed. Lucas, Henze, and Donato (1990) reported on characteristics of some schools with successful responses to this need. Their study focused on secondary schools with huge majorities of students who had Spanish as their native language. Contrary to the national pattern, students in these schools scored high on standardized tests, tended not to drop out of school, and had much higher-than-average high school graduation rates. The researchers identified special features of these schools that seemed to account for their success. Specifically, the team identified the following characteristics:

- Value is placed on students' languages and cultures.
- High expectations of language-minority learners are made concrete.
- School leaders make the education of language-minority learners a priority.
- Staff development is explicitly designed to help teachers and other staff serve language-minority students more effectively.

- A variety of courses and programs for language minority students is offered.

- A counseling program gives special attention to language-minority students.

- Parents of language-minority students are encouraged to become involved in their children's education.

- School staff members share a strong commitment to empower language-minority students through education (Lucas, Henze, and Donato, 1990, pp. 315–40).

These schools pay particular attention to developing learners' levels of proficiency in *both* English and Spanish. For example, advanced literature classes are available that allow students to study the works of Cervantes and other luminaries of Hispanic literature in the original Spanish. The entire program builds learners' pride in their cultural heritage at the same time that it provides them with the tough intellectual tools needed to qualify for both university entrance and decent jobs in the workplace.

## Useful Information Sources

Many sources are available for materials that can help educators become more sensitive to issues associated with cultural, ethnic, and gender equity. Professional periodicals regularly publish useful articles with helpful ideas for classroom practice. Some excellent books are beginning to appear. A particularly good one has been written by Carl A. Grant and Christine E. Sleeter, *Turning on Learning: Five Approaches for Multicultural Teaching—Plans for Race, Class, Gender, and Disability* (Columbus, OH: Merrill, 1989). It contains excellent lesson ideas for teachers.

A useful calendar with references to dates and events of interest to many different ethnic groups is the "Ethnic Cultures of America Calendar." The calendar is published each year and is available from:

Educational Extension Systems
P.O. Box 259
Clarks Summit, PA 18411

The following places are other sources of material that can be used in preparing lessons with a multicultural focus. Write them to ask for materials for classroom teachers and learners. In your letters, suggest grade levels of learners for whom you might be preparing lessons.

The Balch Institute for Ethnic Studies
18 South 7th Street
Philadelphia, PA 19106

Center for Migration Studies
209 Flagg Place
Staten Island, NY 10304

Center for the Study of Ethnic Publications
Kent State University
Kent, OH 44242

Immigration History Research Center
University of Minnesota
Minneapolis, MN 55455

Institute of Texan Cultures
University of Texas
San Antonio, Texas 78294

There are also a number of information sources for materials with a gender equity focus. A long list of sources is available from the Upper Midwest Women's History Center for Teachers. In writing for this list, ask for "Handout 11: Resources and Selected Bibliography." The address is:

The Upper Midwest Women's History Center for Teachers
Central Community Center
6300 Walker Street
St. Louis Park, MN 55416

Other good sources for gender equity information and materials include the following:

Organization for Equal Education of the Sexes, Inc.
P.O. Box 438
Blue Hill, ME 04614

Population Reference Bureau, Inc.
2213 M. Street N.W.
Washington, DC 20037

National Women's History Project
P.O. Box 3716
Santa Rosa, CA 95402

WEAL: Women's Equity Action League
1250 I Street NW
Washington, DC 20005

ISIS—Women's International Information and Communication Services
P.O. Box 25711
Philadelphia, PA 19144

· · · · · · · · · · · · · · · · · · · · · · · · · · · · · · ·

# Key Ideas in Summary

- There is a growing demographic discontinuity between the learner population of the schools and teachers. The learner population is becoming increasingly diverse in terms of its cultural and ethnic makeup. At the same time, the teacher population is becoming increasingly white and female. Because of special perspectives of learners from cultural and ethnic minorities, teachers need to

**Table 8–1**
Summary table: Multicultural and gender equity concerns

| Subject | Key Points |
| --- | --- |
| Ethnic characteristics of teachers and learners | Whereas schools are enrolling ever-higher percentages of nonwhites, the population of teachers is overwhelmingly white and the proportion of teachers who are white is increasing. This means that many teachers will have had little direct contact with the cultural perspectives of their learners. To be effective, they will need to develop a multicultural perspective. |
| Genetic deficit | According to this now-discredited view, minority learners fail to do well in school because they lack the intellectual potential for academic success. |
| Cultural deficit | According to this now-discredited view, failure of minority learners to achieve results from home environments that fail to provide an intellectually stimulating atmosphere. Today, the cultural deficit and the genetic deficit views are generally rejected as scapegoat explanations for poor minority learner performance that have blamed the learner's background and personal characteristics rather than inadequate school programming. |
| *Milliken* v. *Bradley* | In this case, the Supreme Court held that courts could not order busing *between* districts to achieve racial balance. A result has been that many districts have schools with an overwhelming majority of learners from a single ethnic group. Many inner-city schools enroll disproportionate numbers of Hispanics and African-Americans, while many suburban schools enroll disproportionate numbers of whites. |
| Within-school segregation | This refers to patterns of segregation that are found in many schools, even some with integrated student bodies. For example, in some schools researchers have found disproportionate numbers of whites in college preparatory programs and disproportionate numbers of African-Americans in remedial classes. |
| Dropout rates | Dropout rates for African-Americans and Hispanics are higher than for whites. There has been a trend for dropout rates to fall for both whites and African-Americans. African-Americans' dropout rates are beginning to approach those for whites. On the other hand, those for Hispanics are much higher than for either African-Americans or whites, and they still seem to be going up. |

**Table 8–1**
*continued*

| Subject | Key Points |
|---|---|
| Females and mathematics | There is a myth that females are not as good at mathematics as are males. Research does not support this view; however, the myth's widespread acceptance may keep some females out of mathematics courses, keep some from performing at the high levels of which they are capable, and be denying some female graduates access to high-paying technical jobs when they leave school. |
| Differences within groups | There are important differences *within* individual minority groups. When program planners fail to recognize this, lessons presented to learners may be inappropriate for their personal needs. |
| Ideas for helping minority learners | These include:<br>• committing to the idea that all people can learn<br><br>• modifying grouping practices<br><br>• accommodating learning style differences<br><br>• helping teachers become more aware of their own perspectives<br><br>• relying less on standardized tests<br><br>• avoiding favoritism in the classroom<br><br>• providing minority learners with good teachers |
| Comer-model schools | These schools follow procedures suggested by James Comer and his associates to promote the achievement of minority-group learners. These schools place a heavy emphasis on shared decision making. |
| Bilingual education | Mandates school programming for learners with native languages other than English that would provide them with school instruction in their native language until they achieved a satisfactory proficiency level in English. When this occurred, they would move into English-only classrooms. |
| *Lau* v. *Nichols* | As a result of this court case, school districts are required to provide programs specially tailored to the needs of learners with limited proficiency in English. |

develop lessons carefully keyed to respond to needs of the diverse young people in their classrooms.

- An important objective of our educational system is to maximize every child's learning potential. School programs have often failed to serve the best interests of minority-group and female learners. Because the entire society benefits from the contributions of well-educated citizens, our schools can ill afford to not develop the talents of any learner.

- In the early and middle years of the 20th century, many learners from ethnic and cultural minorities were viewed as having a genetic deficit that accounted for their low levels of academic achievement. Later, this explanation gave way to a cultural deficit view, which attributed poor school performance to a failure of the learner's home environment to support school learning. The genetic deficit and cultural deficit positions are now generally rejected. It is recognized that the failure of many minority-group children to learn is due to the failure of schools to provide programs responsive to their needs.

- The case of *Brown* v. *Board of Education* (1954) led to the dismantling of segregated school systems. A subsequent decision, *Milliken* v. *Bradley* (1974), held that courts did not have a right to order busing *across* district lines for the purpose of integrating schools. As a result, schools in many places continue to enroll disproportionately large numbers of learners from certain cultural and ethnic groups because the groups are very heavily represented within the boundaries of their given school district. Many inner-city school districts, for example, have populations that are largely African-American or Hispanic. There are not enough white learners in these districts to supply a high percentage of such learners to any school, even when the district tries to achieve a racial balance.

- There are many concerns today about within-school segregation. Many college preparatory programs in high schools enroll higher percentages of white students than are represented in the overall student body, while learners from ethnic and cultural minorities are overrepresented in special education classes. Segregation by gender has also been observed; for example, the overwhelming majority of learners in high school physical science classes are male.

- Standardized achievement scores of African-American and Hispanic learners have continually lagged behind those of white students. Dropout rates are also higher for African-Americans and Hispanics than for whites. In recent years, the dropout rate for African-American learners has improved; however, the rate for Hispanics has worsened. Since the Hispanic population is the fastest growing of the nation's minorities, the inability of our schools to hold Hispanic learners has become a priority concern of educators.

- In responding to needs of minority-group learners and females, educators must take care to operate on the basis of accurate information. It is particularly important that they do not make some incorrect generalizations on the basis of inaccurate or incomplete information. For example, the idea that females are less capable of learning mathematics than males persists in many places, despite contrary evidence. Generalizations regarding Hispanics sometimes hint at their probable difficulty with English because it is not their native language, while, in fact, English *is* the first language for about three-quarters of all Hispanic learners. Similarly, not all African-Americans live in the inner city or are economically deprived.

- Recommendations for improving the quality of educational services for ethnic and cultural minority learners include (1) a commitment to the idea that all can learn, (2) modification of grouping practices, (3) making certain that teachers are aware of their own perspectives, (4) relying less on standardized tests, (5) ensuring that teachers avoid favoritism in the classroom, and (6) assigning good teachers to work with minority-group learners.

- James Comer and his associates have developed a model for organizing schools to promote greater achievement levels among minority-group learners. Achievement gains by learners in these schools have been impressive. The Comer-model schools feature shared decision making—principals are but part of a management team that also includes parents, teachers, and school support members.

- This nation has a strong commitment to bilingual education, which involves teaching learners in their native language until they become proficient in English. This commitment was evidenced by the passage of the Bilingual Education Act in 1968 and was buttressed by a famous 1974 court case, *Lau* v. *Nichols*, which, in effect, required schools to provide meaningful programs for learners with first languages other than English.

## Review and Discussion Questions

1. In what ways do ethnic and cultural characteristics of learners in the schools differ?
2. How would you assess the adequacy of the genetic deficit and the cultural deficit positions as explanations for the failure of many minority-group learners to do well in school?
3. What are some reasons that certain schools, despite national progress toward desegregation, still enroll learners who overwhelmingly are members of a single ethnic group?
4. Give some examples that illustrate within-school segregation.
5. What are some characteristics of schools that have high percentages of minority-group learners and whose learners score well on tests of academic achievement?

6. What does research say about females' abilities to learn mathematics?

7. What are some problems that have resulted when people have made careless generalizations about *all* members of a particular minority group?

8. Why have people who are concerned about the education of minority-group learners often criticized the schools for relying too much on information from standardized tests?

9. In the case of *Milliken* v. *Bradley* (1974), the Supreme Court held that courts could not order buses to cross school district lines for the purpose of achieving racial balance among a number of school districts in a given area. What were some consequences of this decision?

10. What are some features of Comer-model schools?

......................................

# Ideas for Field Experiences, Projects, and Enrichment

1. If possible, arrange to visit some classes that include a mix of learners from different ethnic and cultural backgrounds. Observe participation patterns. How frequently did learners from minority groups volunteer to answer questions? How often were they called upon? (You may wish to identify other questions that will help you to pinpoint the degree to which minority-group learners were actively involved in lessons.) Share your findings with others in your class, and as a group, respond to these questions:

   • Were minority-group learners as involved in lessons as were majority-group learners?

   • What specific patterns did you note?

   • What might account for these patterns?

2. Some school districts have helped to provide special training for white teachers to sensitize them to perspectives of learners from ethnic and cultural minorities. Interview some local school administrators about programs that may have been implemented in their schools. Alternatively, consult professional journals for descriptions of such programs. Prepare a short paper for your course instructor in which you describe either one or two local programs, or several programs that have been outlined in journal articles.

3. The chapter listed several sources for materials related to multicultural and gender equity issues. Try to add at least five additional sources to those already provided. You might begin by looking for articles in professional journals. The *Education Index* may suggest articles to consult, and your instructor may have other ideas about where to locate such information. Share your five sources

with your instructor. He or she may wish to prepare a composite list of all suggestions that come in from class members.

4. Read about the Comer model and other successful attempts to improve the achievement levels of minority-group learners. Get together with four or five other classmates who have been working on the same task. Organize a symposium to present to your class on the topic "Hope for Learners from Ethnic and Cultural Minorities: Practical Examples from Real Schools."

5. Some have argued that schools, particularly in urban areas and their surrounding suburbs, would benefit if the courts supported busing learners across district lines for the purpose of achieving better racial balance in every school. Others disagree with this approach. Organize a debate on the issue "Resolved: Cross-District Busing to Improve Racial Balance in Schools Will Improve Education."

· · · · · · · · · · · · · · · · · · · · · · · · · · ·

# Supplementary Reading

Banks, J. A., and C. A. Banks, eds. *Multicultural Education: Issues and Perceptions*. Boston: Allyn and Bacon, 1989.

Bates, P. "Desegregation: Can We Get There from Here?" *Phi Delta Kappan* (September 1990): 8–17.

Grant, C. A., and C. E. Sleeter. *Turning on Learning: Five Approaches for Multicultural Teaching—Plans for Race, Class, Gender, and Disability*. Columbus, OH: Merrill, 1989.

Lomotey, K., ed. *Going to School: The African-American Experience*. Albany, NY: State University of New York Press, 1990.

Louis, K. S., and M. B. Miles. *Improving the Urban High School: What Works and Why*. New York: Teachers College Press, 1990.

Taeuber, K. "Desegregation of Public School Districts: Persistence and Change." *Phi Delta Kappan* (September 1990): 18–24.

· · · · · · · · · · · · · · · · · · · · · · · · · · ·

# References

Banks, J. A., with A. Clegg, Jr. *Multiethnic Education: Theory and Practice*. 2d ed. Boston: Allyn and Bacon, 1988.

Bates, P. "Desegregation: Can We Get There from Here?" *Phi Delta Kappan* (September 1990): 8–17.

Borich, G. *Effective Teaching*. Columbus, OH: Merrill, 1988.

*Brown v. Board of Education*, 347 U.S. 483 (1954).

Chipman, S. F., and V. G. Thomas. "The Participation of Women and Minorities in Mathematical, Scientific, and Technical Fields." In E. Z. Rothkopf, ed. *Review of Educational Research*. Vol. 14. Washington, DC: American Educational Research Association, 1987, 387–430.

Comer, J. P. "Educating Poor Minority Children." *Scientific American* (November 1989).

Erickson, F. "Transformation and School Success: The Politics and Culture of Educational Achievement." *Anthropology and Education Quarterly* (December 1987): 335–56.

Grant, C. A. "Desegregation, Racial Attitudes, and Intergroup Contact: A Discussion of Change." *Phi Delta Kappan* (September 1990): 25–32.

Grant, C. A., and W. G. Secada. "Preparing Teachers for Diversity." In R. Houston, ed. *Handbook on Research in Teacher Education*. New York: Macmillan, 1990, 403–22.

Grant, C. A., and C. E. Sleeter. *Turning on Learning: Five Approaches for Multicultural Teaching—Plans for Race, Class, Gender, and Disability*. Columbus, OH: Merrill, 1989.

*Lau* v. *Nichols*, 414 U.S. 563 (1974).

Lucas, T., R. Henze, and R. Donato. "Promoting the Success of Latino Language-Minority Students: An Exploratory Study of Six High Schools." *Harvard Educational Review* (August 1990): 315–40.

Marshall, R. C., chair—Quality Education for Minorities Project. *Education That Works: An Action Plan for the Education of Minorities*. Cambridge, MA: Quality Education for Minorities Project, Massachusetts Institute of Technology, 1990.

*Milliken* v. *Bradley*, 418 U.S. 717 (1974).

NCATE. *Standards, Procedures, and Policies for the Accreditation of Professional Education Units*. Washington, DC: National Council for Accreditation of Teacher Education, 1987.

Oakes, J. *Keeping Track: How Schools Structure Inequality*. New Haven, CT: Yale University Press, 1985.

Oakes, J. "Opportunities, Achievement, and Choice: Women and Minority Students in Science and Mathematics." In C. B. Cazden, ed. *Review of Research in Education* 16. Washington, DC: American Educational Research Association, 1990, 153–222.

Ogle, L. T., ed., and N. Alsalam, associate ed. *The Condition of Education, 1990:* Vol. 1. *Elementary and Secondary Education*. Washington, DC: National Center for Education Statistics, 1990.

Savage, T. V., and D. G. Armstrong. *Effective Teaching in Elementary Social Studies*. 2d ed. New York: Macmillan, 1992.

Simon-McWilliams, E., ed. *Resegregation of Public Schools: The Third Generation*. Portland, OR: Network of Regional Desegregation Assistance Centers and Northwest Regional Educational Laboratory, 1989.

Taeuber, K. "Desegregation of Public School Districts: Persistence and Change." *Phi Delta Kappan* (September 1990): 18–24.

Vergon, C. B. "School Desegregation: The Evolution and Implementation of a National Policy." Paper presented at the annual meeting of the American Educational Research Association, San Francisco, March 1989.

# Chapter 9

# Exceptional Learners

· · · · · · · · · · · · · · · · · · · · · · · · · · · · · · · · · · · · · · ·

## Objectives

This chapter provides information to help the reader to

- recognize that the category of "exceptional learners" includes different kinds of learners, among them learners with disabilities and gifted learners.
- identify different kinds of disabilities.
- describe some concerns new teachers often have about working with learners with disabilities in the classroom.
- suggest implications for teachers of Public Law 94–142.
- point out examples of appropriate teacher responses to different disabilities of learners.
- describe characteristics of gifted learners.
- explain some productive teacher approaches to working with gifted learners.

# Focus Questions

1. What kinds of learners are among those falling under the general heading "exceptional learners?"
2. Why do teachers in regular classrooms today have more daily contact with learners with disabilities than they did 20 years ago?
3. What are some provisions of Public Law 94-142?
4. What are some kinds of disabilities that teachers may find among learners in their classes?
5. What are some ways teachers can respond to special needs of hearing-impaired and deaf learners, visually impaired and blind learners, and orthopedically impaired learners?
6. Why are learners who are emotionally disturbed or otherwise behaviorally disabled among those with whom teachers find it particularly difficult to work, and what are some approaches that have sometimes been successful with these young people?
7. What are some things teachers can do to help educable mentally retarded learners who have been mainstreamed in their classrooms?
8. What kind of information is often considered when identifying individuals to be included in programs for gifted learners?
9. How do enrichment and acceleration programs for gifted learners differ?
10. What can teachers do to stimulate creative thinking among gifted learners?

....................................

# Introduction

The term *exceptional learners* is a general one that is applied to learners who have special or unusual characteristics. Learners with disabilities and gifted learners are among the exceptional learners in our schools today.

Exceptional learners share many of the characteristics of other young people who go to school. Some of them are tall, and some of them are short. Some of them are extremely bright, and some of them find learning difficult. Some of them have positive attitudes about school, and some of them do not enjoy being at school at all. There is much diversity among exceptional learners, just as there is among the total population of school learners.

It is important to keep individual differences among learners in mind; it is also important to understand that there are some common characteristics shared by many individuals within certain groups of exceptional learners. This chapter introduces some of these differences and describes approaches for working with learners who have certain disabilities and learners who are gifted.

## Learners With Disabilities

For many years, most classroom teachers had little contact with learners having disabilities. These young people used to be segregated from nondisabled learners, and were taught in special classrooms. Teachers who worked with these young people took preparation programs leading to certification as teachers of children with disabilities, and generally worked only with groups of such learners.

The isolation of learners with disabilities ceased with the enactment of Public Law 94–142, the Education for All Handicapped Children Act, in 1975. The name was changed in 1990 to the Individuals with Disabilities Education Act. Since 1975, learners with disabilities have increasingly become part of the instructional responsibilities of regular classroom teachers. Today, most young people with disabilities spend at least part of the day in a regular school classroom.

## Public Law 94–142

Public Law 94–142 came about because of a concern that many learners with disabilities were not being served well by existing educational programs. During hearings related to this legislation, members of Congress learned that over half of the approximately eight million children with disabilities in the country had no access to appropriate educational services. Testimony revealed the problem to be a lack of money to serve their needs properly.

Some provisions of the law deserve special mention.

*Federal Money.*    Public Law 94–142 established a formula for providing federal aid to the states to support educational services for children with disabilities between the ages of 3 and 21. A formula based on the percentage of the average amount spent on each child's education in the United States and on the number of children with disabil-

Learners with disabilities can profit from many kinds of instruction. Note this boy's enthusiasm.

ities to be served was developed as a way of determining the amount of money to be spent. Educating children with disabilities is expensive. As Singer (1985) has pointed out, educating a child with special needs costs a school district almost twice as much as educating a nondisabled learner. In some cases, costs are even higher. The federal government initially promised to provide the states with money to cover 40 percent of the cost of educating such learners but, in actuality, has never provided more than 12 percent of this total (Lewis, 1991, p. 573). The states and local communities have had to make up the difference.

*Obligations of the States.* When Public Law 94–142 was enacted, each state was directed to establish specific policies for children with disabilities between the ages of 3 and 18 by 1978. (These policies were later extended to also include individuals between ages 18 and 21.) States were required to have these policies in force before any federal money would arrive to support the education of learners with disabilities. In recent years, some states have found costs of maintaining the policies to qualify for the federal dollars so high that they have considered abandoning the effort, giving up the federal dollars, and supporting such programs exclusively with state funds (Lewis, 1991).

*Individualized Instruction.*    Public Law 94–142 calls for an individualized instructional program to be established for each child with disabilities. Furthermore, the law states that such a program has to be developed and agreed to at a meeting including a representative of the school district, the learner, and a parent of the learner. The individualized instructional plan must include specific information about:

- the learner's present educational attainment level
- goals and short-term objectives
- specific services to be provided to the learner and the time required for each
- the starting date and an estimate of the expected duration of services
- evaluation criteria to be used in determining whether the objectives have been achieved

*Least Restrictive Environment.*    P.L. 94–142 requires states to ensure that, to the maximum extent possible, learners with disabilities are educated in the "least restrictive environment." This means that every effort should be extended to allow them to be taught in regular classes, alongside nondisabled learners. The assignment of learners with disabilities to special classes, special schools, or other alternatives to the regular classroom must be undertaken only when the severity of the disability is so great that education in regular classrooms with the use of supplementary materials and aids cannot be achieved satisfactorily.

The practice of placing learners with disabilities in regular classrooms alongside nondisabled learners is often referred to as *mainstreaming*. Mainstreaming intends to infuse learners with disabilities into the main arteries of the educational system in as many ways as possible, so as to prepare them for the adult world much as nondisabled learners are prepared. Box 9–1 addresses some of the concerns of mainstreaming from a teacher's perspective.

## The Nature of Disabilities

There is some danger in preparing a simple list of disabilities. The general characteristics of individuals who have these conditions are just that—*general*. Great diversity exists among learners in each category. Further, there is a tendency to overlook the point that many school learners fall into several categories simultaneously. The information presented regarding each category should be approached with an appreciation of within-category diversity and multiple-category membership of many individual learners.

*Learners with Physical Disabilities.*    Learners with physical disabilities have a variety of conditions. Among young people in this category are:

- learners who are visually impaired or blind
- learners who are hearing impaired or deaf
- learners who are orthopedically impaired
- learners who have one or more other physical impairments

BOX 9–1
## PREPARING OTHER LEARNERS TO ACCEPT THOSE WITH DISABILITIES

You are a seventh grade teacher. Your principal has told you that, starting about the third week of school, you will have two orthopedically disabled boys in your classroom. One requires the use of a wheelchair; the other walks with crutches and braces. Consider what you might do to prepare members of your class to accept these learners.

*What Do You Think?*
1. What potential problems do you anticipate?
2. How would you respond to these problems?
3. Specifically, what will you do to welcome these students to your class?
4. What ideas do you have for encouraging present class members to make these new learners feel like a part of the group?

*Visually Impaired and Blind Learners.*   Evidence suggests that individuals who are visually impaired or blind can compete well with other learners in regular classrooms provided that their communications skills are well-developed. For blind students, materials must be available in braille. Some states have made braille editions of regular textbooks available to teachers who have several visually impaired or blind learners in their classes.

Many blind learners use typewriters or personal computer wordprocessing programs to communicate in writing with their teachers. It is important that they receive early instruction in using this kind of equipment. Additionally, it is often useful for blind learners to produce braille as well as read it. For example, notes taken in braille can be used by blind learners when they prepare for a test. To acquire expertise in producing braille, blind learners must have access to braillewriters. Tape recorders are also useful to blind and visually impaired learners, as assignments, lectures, and other teacher comments can be recorded. Some teachers find it helpful to assign a sighted learner to serve as a reader for visually impaired and blind learners. The reader serves as an additional source of information for learners who have severe visual impairment. Box 9–2 raises some questions for teachers of such learners to consider.

*Hearing-Impaired and Deaf Learners.*   Hearing-impaired learners' most marked difference from so-called normal learners is their difficulty in producing speech and in acquiring language skills. Amplification of sound through hearing aids provides help for some. In order for a learner to derive the maximum benefit from a hearing aid, it must be in good working order. Teachers need to know how a hearing aid works and what to do when a problem develops.

## BOX 9–2
## VISUALLY IMPAIRED LEARNERS

It is your first year of teaching. Two days before school starts, your principal calls you into the office and informs you that you will have a learner in your class who is legally blind. Money will be available to buy special equipment to help this person learn. Also, a specialist on education of the severely visually impaired will be available in the central district administrative offices to talk to you if problems arise or if you have questions.

**What Do You Think?**
1. What is your first reaction to this news? Describe your general feelings.
2. What kinds of special problems might this learner have?
3. What are some kinds of things you might do to respond to this learner's needs?

Because some learners who are hearing impaired have learned to read lips, teachers should face the class when addressing groups that include learners with severe hearing problems. There should be no exaggeration of speech patterns. Lip readers learn to read lips that produce speech in a normal way.

It is a good idea for teacher directions that are given orally to be supplemented with visual information. For example, the teacher can write assignments on the board, or use an overhead projector. Some teachers write a brief outline of their remarks on a role of acetate mounted on an overhead projector and refer to this outline as they talk to the class.

*Orthopedically Impaired Learners.*    It is difficult to generalize about learners who are orthopedically impaired, as they may suffer from one (or more) of a number of conditions that limit their physical abilities. The classroom teacher must learn the nature of the disability and its implications for the instructional process before specific needs can be identified.

Special equipment may be required in classrooms that include learners with certain kinds of orthopedic impairments. Wheelchairs, special typewriters, and standing tables are examples of items that might be needed. Teachers with orthopedically impaired learners in their classes must think carefully about potential threats to the safety of these young people posed by the general physical environment of the classroom. For example, highly polished floors can be dangerous for individuals who must use crutches. Care must be taken to ensure against accidentally tipping over a wheelchair. Because orthopedically impaired learners who use special equipment usually cannot move as fast as other learners, teachers often arrange for them to leave classes early so they can avoid congested hallways and arrive at their next class on time.

This teacher is working with a learner who is hearing-impaired.

Special aids to learning and retention may help orthopedically impaired young people to succeed on assigned tasks. Those who have difficulty with handwriting sometimes do much better with typewriters. Small, hand-carried tape recorders can serve as notetakers for these individuals. Other aids are also available, depending on a given learner's particular needs.

*Learners with Behavior Disorders.*    Learners with emotional or behavioral disorders deviate from the kinds of behaviors expected for learners in their age group. Their behavior patterns interfere with their development as individuals and their ability to establish and maintain harmonious relationships with others.

Many of these young people find it almost impossible to make independent decisions. They are heavily influenced by their peers. Even though they tend to look to peers for guidance, often their peers do not particularly like them. Many of these unhappy young people sense themselves to be isolated from others of their own age. At the same time, they often have attention disorders that interfere with their progress in the classroom (Bender and Evans, 1989). This results in academic failure. Hence, many of these young people sense themselves to be alienated from the teacher and the school as well as from their peers.

Learners who are emotionally disturbed or who have behavioral disorders are likely to come to a teacher's attention because of either disruptive behavior in class or personality characteristics that mark them as different from their classmates (e.g., extreme withdrawal). Teachers find it extremely difficult to work with some learners with behavioral disorders, particularly those who disrupt classroom activities. These characteristics present teachers with quite different demands than those they face in working with learners with other disabilities (Carri, 1985).

Many teachers report being torn between conflicting goals when working with learners who are disruptive. On the one hand, they have an obligation to meet the special needs of each learner, even a disruptive one. On the other hand, they feel a duty to serve all of the learners in their class, something that is difficult to do when they are faced with one individual who is very disruptive. Teachers in this situation are challenged to strike a balance between meeting the needs of the individual and meeting the needs of the rest of the class.

Because causes of emotional disturbance and problem behaviors are diverse, no list of appropriate responses can claim to be truly comprehensive. There are some general approaches that have been found to be successful with some of these learners. Part of the difficulty many of these learners have is an inability to function well when they are exposed to too many stimuli at one time. When this is true, teachers can respond in a number of ways. For example, these learners can be assigned to do seat work in carrels or partially enclosed booths where extraneous visual stimuli are minimized. When appropriate (and provided that the needed equipment is available), nonessential sounds can be blocked out by providing some instruction to these learners via audiotapes, to which they listen through personal headsets.

Another technique with potential for teaching some learners with behavioral disorders is *relaxation training*. This involves learners in self-monitoring procedures that may focus on such things as muscle-tensing patterns, brain-wave patterns, heart-rate patterns, blood-pressure patterns, and breathing patterns. Self-monitoring has been found to help learners who tend to be hyperactive, impulsive, and frequently out of their seats (Bender and Evans, 1989).

Another technique that sometimes has proved effective in working with learners with behavior disabilities involves the use of classroom meetings. One approach to classroom meetings derives from William Glasser's (1965) *reality therapy* approach. Classroom meetings based on reality therapy are designed to focus on the inappropriate behaviors (rather than on the individuals who are doing the behaving) and on the development of more successful alternatives. This approach has been recommended for use in secondary school classes that include a mixture of learners with behavioral disorders and those without (Bender and Evans, 1989).

Effective class meetings require a teacher who has a good understanding of reality therapy techniques. They also require a situation in which teachers and learners know how to share power and in which all are willing to be involved in frank and open discussions. This presumes a learner maturity level that is not present in all classes.

BOX 9–3
## WORKING IN REGULAR CLASSROOMS WITH LEARNERS WHO ARE DISABLED

You are a sixth grade teacher in a middle school, and have found yourself caught in the middle of two well-organized groups of parents. One group has a high interest in school programs that are heavily weighted toward traditional academics and are designed to prepare learners who will go to high school and, for the most part, on to colleges and universities. A second group of parents includes people with children who suffer from a variety of disabilities. Their children spend a portion of each day in your classroom as part of the mainstreaming requirements of Public Law 94–142. These parents want evidence that you are spending enough time with their children. Many of them feel that their sons and daughters have been shortchanged in the past and that teachers have not given these children the kinds of help they need to succeed.

*What Do You Think?*
1. What incompatibilities are there in the views of the two groups?
2. Is it possible to satisfy both groups of parents?
3. Given this situation, what would you do?

In working with learners with behavior disorders, teachers often seek the help of other professionals. For example, members of the school counseling staff are frequently involved. Sometimes a team of professionals is organized to develop a systematic behavior-management strategy to promote and support more acceptable patterns of behavior.

Box 9–3 deals with one of the problems that teachers of any kind of learners with disabilities may well encounter.

*Learners Who Are Mentally Retarded.*    There are many reasons for mental retardation, and there are many levels of retardation. There are three general categories that have been used to describe learners who are mentally retarded: *educable, trainable,* and *profoundly retarded.* Most learners spending all or part of their school day in regular classrooms, as mandated by Public Law 94–142, are in the *educable* category. This group includes those learners who are mentally retarded who deviate the least from the so-called normal range of mental functioning. These learners often respond well to a number of widely used instructional techniques, including cooperative learning* (Margolis and Schwartz, 1989).

*Cooperative learning embraces several related approaches, most of which feature learners working together in ways that encourage them to help one another and where individual success, to a degree, depends on group success.

Educable learners often have language and speech deficiencies. Because these young people frequently have short attention spans, teachers need to prepare lessons for them that are brief, direct, and to the point. Concrete examples of what is to be done in their lessons can help them to understand what is expected. Directions provided orally as well as in written form are also helpful. Some teachers have found that these learners benefit when another class member is assigned to work with them, particularly to help them understand what they are to do.

There have been some widespread common problems associated with mainstreaming educable learners. One of these is discussed in the accompanying What the Experts Say.

---

WHAT THE EXPERTS SAY

## *What educable mentally retarded learners believe about causes of their academic successes*

Donald L. MacMillan, Barbara K. Keogh, and Reginald L. Jones (1986) surveyed hundreds of studies focusing on education of learners with mild mental retardation. Some of the studies they reviewed explored how educable learners explain both their academic successes and their academic failures. MacMillan, Keogh, and Jones report that many investigators have found a tendency in these learners to blame their own personal inadequacies for their failures. On the other hand, they tend to attribute any academic successes to luck, not to personal competence.

This pattern has important implications for teachers. It suggests that academic successes may not be nearly so personally reinforcing for educable mentally retarded children as they are for learners who are not disabled. This is so because the educable learners' successes are not seen as evidence of personal consequence but instead as capricious, random events that are of little or no long-term importance.

It may be that educable learners develop these attitudes from others. There is evidence that their self-concepts are strongly influenced by how they think parents, teachers, and other learners see them, and also that some parents of educable mentally retarded learners believe any of their children's successes result more from luck than from hard work (MacMillan, Keogh, and Jones, 1986). It may be that learners in this category may be internalizing attitudes of their parents. If this is true, it suggests a need for teachers to think through their own assumptions regarding the abilities of educable retarded learners. Actions that might convey to these young people an expectation that any successes they have will result only from chance factors need to be avoided. The research implies a need for teachers who will convey to educable mentally retarded learners a belief that academic successes will come to them as a result of their own efforts, not because they are occasionally lucky.

---

Source: D. L. MacMillan, B. K. Keogh, and R. L. Jones, "Special Educational Research on Mildly Handicapped Learners," in M. C. Wittrock, ed., *Handbook of Research on Teaching,* 3d ed. (New York: Macmillan, 1986), 686–724.

Public Law 94–142 has been enforced for a long time now. Educators have had years of experience working with learners with disabilities in their classrooms. Today's teachers expect these young people to be in their classes. As one teacher reported to one of the authors, "These children are just some of the kids who come to school."

## Gifted Learners

For over 20 years, the federal government has been interested in programs for gifted learners. As long ago as 1972, Congress established the Office of Gifted and Talented. Public Law 91–230 (*United States Statutes at Large*, 1971, p. 153) defined "gifted learners" as "children who have outstanding intellectual ability or creative talent, the development of which requires special activities or services not ordinarily provided by local education agencies."

## The Issue of Selection

Selection of learners for special programs for the gifted has often prompted controversy. In years past, gifted learners were identified almost exclusively by their scores on standardized tests. Individuals who were selected for these programs had scores markedly higher than those of most other learners. Recently, however, there has been a trend to widen the definition of "giftedness." Often selection criteria consider special psychomotor abilities and creative talents. Efforts have been undertaken to ensure that selection procedures are not biased against learners from ethnic and cultural minorities.

## Image Problems

Educators have long worried about potential self-image problems of gifted learners. There has been a concern that these young people, because they are "different," may not be socially acceptable to their peers. Fortunately, most studies have suggested that gifted learners are well-accepted young people. However, one recent study found that "extremely precocious adolescents" may experience more peer-relations problems than "modestly gifted adolescents" (Dauber and Benbow, 1990). This suggests that teachers may need to be aware of potential problems and resultant feelings of extremely gifted learners. In particular, these extraordinarily bright young people may face pressure from other students to "do less" and, thereby, keep the teacher from setting expectations too high for the class as a whole (Brown and Steinberg, 1990).

Some gifted learners are pressured by parents and teachers to perform flawlessly. This can make them feel that they must be perfect, an attitude that can lead to unrealistic self-expectations and frustration. Teachers need to understand this situation and respond to it by helping gifted learners focus on their strengths and their accomplishments, not their shortcomings (Baum, 1990). They also need to help these learners recognize that everyone has strengths and weaknesses and that it is no sign of personal failure to be less than perfect in some areas.

## Kinds of Programs

Programs for gifted learners fall into two basic categories: *enrichment programs* and *acceleration programs*. Enrichment programs seek to provide learning experiences

*"Your semester project proposals are always interesting, Schuyler. Last fall's light-hearted musical rendering of* The Scarlet Letter *certainly cut new ground. But, I ask you, is the world ready for* Silas Marner Meets Godzilla?*"*
Courtesy of Ford Button.

for gifted young people that are in addition to or go beyond those provided to other learners. In enrichment programs, gifted learners remain members of classes that include a mixture of gifted and nongifted young people who are in the same general age group. They go through the school program at the same rate as all other learners.

Acceleration programs increase the pace at which gifted learners complete their schooling. For example, in an accelerated program, a gifted learner might complete the entire high school program in just two years. There is no attempt to keep gifted learners in classes with nongifted learners in the same age group. This often means that gifted learners are in classes where most of the other students are older.

*Enrichment.*    Enrichment programs try to provide learning experiences that challenge the learners to maximize their use of their considerable abilities. At the same time, enrichment programs seek to maintain continuous contact between gifted and nongifted learners by keeping them together in regular classes and by moving them through the K–12 instructional program at the same rate. This means, for example, that gifted learners will take U.S. history at the same time as their nongifted agemates. But it also means that the specific learning experiences provided for them in the context of the

U.S. history course will be different and more challenging than those to which nongift-ed learners are exposed.

In providing lessons for gifted learners, there is a conscious attempt to ensure that what they are asked to do is truly different from what is expected from other learners. This implies that they will not simply be introduced earlier to material that they would ordinarily encounter further along in the school program. If they are, problems will often result in subsequent years for both gifted learners and their teachers. For exam-ple, if gifted learners have been taught the regular grade 12 English material in grade 10, they may find themselves being retaught what they have already learned two years later when they reach grade 12.

The guarantee that enrichment programs for gifted learners will truly be different is important for another reason as well. Because gifted learners are able to progress through traditional material at a more rapid rate than are nongifted learners, it some-times has been tempting for teachers simply to ask them to do more of the same. For example, while nongifted learners might be asked to do 10 mathematics problems, gift-ed learners might be asked to do 15. This response to giftedness makes special intellec-tual ability a burden rather than a blessing. Gifted learners may sense that they are somehow being punished for their special abilities by being asked to do more than other learners. For this reason, teachers are often cautioned not to simply assign "more of the same" to gifted learners in their classes.

In summary, the enrichment approach is the most popular one for responding to the needs of gifted learners. It enjoys wide support from parents and administrators, and is consistent with a view of the school as a place where all kinds of learners come together. It also conforms to a widely held feeling that there are benefits of keeping learners of approximately the same age together as they progress through the school program. Finally, enrichment programs are relatively easy for school leaders to imple-ment. This chapter's Case Study examines some of the issues associated with enrich-ment programs.

CASE STUDY

## *Dealing with a gifted learner who has a behavior problem*

**Mario is an extremely bright fifth grader**. He ranks in the 99th percentile in every category on the standardized tests used in his school district. He reads novels and other materials that rarely interest young people his age. Yet he is not doing well in school.

He will do assigned work when pressed, but he tends to rush through assignments. His answers are usually technically correct, but the work is sloppy and reflects little serious thought. Mario seems bent on hurrying through his own work to gain time to bother others while they are doing theirs.

The teacher has tried to deal with this situation by asking Mario to do a bit more than others in the class. He complains that this is not fair. He has gone so far as to pub-licly challenge the teacher about both the regular assignments and the proposed extra work. In his words, all of these things are "bogus." He seems to enjoy doing and saying things that make his teacher look bad.

*Do you think Mario is an unusual case, or would you think this sort of behavior might characterize quite a few gifted learners? What would you do if you were Mario's teacher? How secure would you feel if you were asked to work with a group of gifted learners? What special problems might you anticipate, and how would you respond to them?*

*Acceleration.*    Acceleration programs allow gifted learners to progress through school programs more quickly than is normal. Supporters reject the idea that there is something useful or inherently beneficial in keeping learners in a given grade for an entire academic year or in keeping them in classes with learners of approximately the same age. Instead, they believe that giftedness is best developed when bright learners are as intellectually challenged as possible. Often this means moving these learners into classes with older learners, where more advanced content is taught.

There are two types of acceleration: *subject-matter acceleration* and *grade-level acceleration*. Subject-matter acceleration is designed to allow gifted learners to take courses earlier than would be typical. For example, a sixth grader might be enrolled in a ninth grade algebra class. Grade-level acceleration occurs when a learner is allowed to skip an entire grade and enroll as a regular member of a class of older learners. For example, a bright third grader might be accelerated to become a member of a fifth grade class.

Some critics of accelerated programs argue that these programs may interfere with the social adjustment of gifted learners. For example, how is a bright 11-year-old who is accelerated to grade 10 going to deal with the male–female social relationships typical at the high school level? How is a 14-year-old college graduate going to fare in a work environment that may restrict hiring to people who are several years older?

The percentage of gifted learners who are in accelerated programs is small compared to the percentage enrolled in enrichment programs. Enrichment programs have been much easier to sell to education policymakers. Enrichment is simply more consistent with traditional patterns and assumptions than is acceleration.

## Developing the Potential of Gifted Learners

Robert J. Sternberg and Todd I. Lubart (1991), who are recognized authorities in the area of education of the gifted, have identified several things teachers can do to encourage creativity among gifted learners. One important dimension of creativity is a willingness to take risks. Some traditional classroom practices discourage risk taking. For example, a learner may be penalized by a low grade if he or she independently decides to turn in a drawing rather than an essay when asked to present the teacher with something reflecting his or her reactions to a short story. Sometimes, too, unusual responses to teacher questions during discussions are not encouraged because they vary so dramatically from what the teacher expects. Sternberg and Lubart (1991) argue that teachers need to think through carefully their reactions to learner performance, and adjust them so they support, rather than discourage, creativity.

It is also important for teachers to take special steps to help gifted learners understand how the knowledge they will be acquiring can be used. In many traditional classrooms, potential uses of knowledge are not explained. Gifted learners have a need to see why new information is important to them personally and how it can be employed to help them perform innovative and creative tasks (Sternberg and Lubart, 1991).

Gifted learners need help in defining problems of their own and in redefining problems presented by the teacher in ways that make them personally relevant. In some traditional classrooms, the teacher simply defines the problem for learners and tells them how to go about solving it. This practice fails to stimulate the creative powers of gifted learners. When these bright young people play a personal role in identifying the problem or goal, they tend to develop a stronger sense of purpose. This commitment, in turn, often results in the generation of responses that have tapped their considerable intellectual and creative resources.

## Key Ideas in Summary

- The term *exceptional learners* is applied to learners who have special or unusual characteristics. Learners with disabilities and learners who are gifted are among groups of exceptional learners in today's schools. There is much diversity *within* individual types of exceptional learners. It is important for teachers to recognize that differences among exceptional learners are as great as those among the total learner population of the school.

- Before the passage of Public Law 94–142, teachers in traditional classrooms had little daily contact with exceptional learners. When these young people were served by the school, they were assigned to special classrooms and taught by teachers who worked with them exclusively. Public Law 94–142 requires learners with disabilities to be educated in the "least restrictive environment." This means that they are mainstreamed in regular classes as much as possible given their individual conditions.

- Public Law 94–142, the Individuals with Disabilities Education Act, was passed in 1975. Among other things, it provides some federal money to support education of learners with disabilities, requires individualized educational plans to be established for these learners, places obligations on states to establish policies for educating learners with disabilities, and requires learners with disabilities to be educated, to the extent possible, in regular school classrooms.

- In general, visually impaired and blind learners can compete successfully with nonimpaired learners, but this depends on early attention to the development of their communications skills. Often, these students are provided with special equipment such as braillewriters, personal computers, and audiotape recorders that can help them take notes and prepare responses for the teacher.

- Hearing impaired and deaf learners often have difficulty producing speech and acquiring language skills. Teachers need to understand how their hearing aids work and how to make minor repairs on them. Because some of these learners

**TABLE 9–1**
Summary table: Exceptional learners

| Topic | Important Ideas |
|---|---|
| Public Law 94-142 | The Individuals with Disabilities Education Act. This key legislation established guidelines for educational programming for learners with disabilities. Among other things, it requires that these learners be served in the "least restrictive environment," a provision that enables them, to the extent possible, to be in classes with learners who are not disabled. |
| Examples of physical disabilites characterizing some learners in the schools | These include learners who are visually impaired or blind, hearing impaired or deaf, and orthopedically impaired. |
| Learners who are emotionally disturbed or behaviorally disabled | These are learners who deviate from the kinds of behaviors expected of individuals in their age group. These learners are among those with whom teachers find it most difficult to work. They sometimes are very disruptive and make it difficult for teachers to work productively with the class as a whole. |
| Learners who are mentally retarded | Most learners who are mentally retarded and who spend part of the school day in regular school class-rooms are categorized as *educable*. Many of these young people have language and speech deficien-cies. Instructions for these learners need to be brief and to the point. |
| Gifted learners | These are learners who have outstanding intellectual abilities or creative talents that are identified for spe-cial nurturing by the school. Selection of learners for participation in gifted programs is often based on multiple criteria, including test scores, evidence of outstanding creative or psychomotor ability, and rec-ommendations of teachers and counselors. |
| Enrichment program | This is a major category of programs for gifted learn-ers that keeps them with their age- and grademates but provides them with some special instruction tailored to their unique needs. |
| Acceleration program | A less popular approach to serving gifted learners than enrichment programs, acceleration programs attempt to maximize development of gifted learners by allowing them to move through the total school program as quickly as possible. In acceleration pro-grams, gifted learners are often in classes with older students. |

are lip readers, it is important for teachers to face these students directly when speaking. Supplementing oral directions with written versions is an additional helpful practice.

- There are many different kinds of problems faced by orthopedically impaired learners. Many of these young people require special equipment, such as wheelchairs, and teachers must make provisions for such learners to use their equipment. Because some of these students move more slowly than learners who are not impaired, teachers often make arrangements for them to leave class a few minutes early to allow them sufficient time to get to their next class.

- Learners with behavioral disorders represent a group teachers find difficult to handle. Some of these learners have low self-image problems and do not feel they can relate well to either the teacher or other learners. Some of these learners do well when teachers reduce the number of simultaneous stimuli confronting them. Relaxation training has proved beneficial for some hyperactive and impulsive young people. Also, reality therapy approaches have been used successfully in some settings.

- The educable mentally retarded learners who are mainstreamed in many regular school classrooms often have language and speech deficiencies and short attention spans. They often benefit when directions are short and introduced in both oral and written form. Some educable learners profit from having a nondisabled learner assigned to them as a mentor. Some teachers have found various cooperative learning techniques to work well with these young people.

- Gifted learners have outstanding intellectual or creative abilities that need to be nurtured by special school programs that go beyond those provided for nongifted young people. Learners are selected for special school programs by multiple criteria that often include test scores, special creative and psychomotor abilities, and recommendations of teachers and counselors. Some gifted learners experience self-image problems. One common difficulty results when, in response to parental and sometimes teacher pressures, they set impossibly high performance standards for themselves.

- Programs for gifted learners are of two basic types. *Enrichment programs* keep learners in their regular age-group classes and courses, but provide special learning experiences that are designed to develop these learners' special capabilities. *Acceleration programs* are designed to speed gifted students' passage through the school program by allowing them to skip grades and enroll in courses with older learners. Enrichment is by far the more popular of the two approaches.

- It is important that programs for gifted learners do not inadvertently punish these young people by simply requiring them to do more of the same kind of work that nongifted learners are required to do. Rather, programs should be designed to encourage risk taking and creative endeavor. Further, they should help gifted learners to understand how the new knowledge being taught will be particularly useful to them as individuals. Finally, gifted learners ought to participate in identifying the problems they will solve and in redefining problems selected by the teachers so as to make them more relevant to their own needs and interests.

......................................

# Review and Discussion Questions

1. What are some kinds of learners that fall under the general heading "exceptional learners?"

2. What are some important provisions of Public Law 94–142?

3. What are some ways teachers can help learners who are blind or visually impaired?

4. What are some learning difficulties commonly faced by deaf and hearing impaired learners?

5. Why do teachers sometimes allow orthopedically impaired learners to leave classes before the other students are dismissed?

6. Why do many teachers find learners who are emotionally disturbed or who have behavioral disorders difficult to work with, and what are examples of teacher responses that have proved successful with some of these learners?

7. What are some examples of things teachers often do to promote learning among the educable mentally retarded young people who are in their classes?

8. Why do teachers of gifted learners need to be especially sensitive to these learners' potential self-image problems?

9. Why have enrichment approaches generally been favored over acceleration approaches when programs to serve the needs of gifted learners have been established?

10. What kinds of things might a teacher do to promote the development of gifted learners' creativity?

......................................

# Ideas for Field Experiences, Projects, and Enrichment

1. Invite to your class a director of special education or another official from a local school district who is responsible for overseeing programs for learners who are disabled. Ask this person to describe the kinds of federal and state regulations that must be observed, and request information regarding how decisions are made regarding learning experiences to be provided to each

child who is disabled. If possible, ask to see a copy of a typical individualized learning plan.

2. Interview two or more classroom teachers who teach a grade level you intend to teach. Ask them about special things they do to provide instruction for mainstreamed learners. What kind of special training or assistance do they get from the district to help them with these young people? How do they react to working with these learners? Share your findings with the class in the form of a brief oral report.

3. Prepare a collection of professional journal articles that focus on practical things teachers can do to meet the needs of learners with disabilities who have been mainstreamed into their regular classes. Organize a symposium with several others in your class on the topic "Practical Approaches to Helping Mainstreamed Learners." Draw content from your article collection.

4. Make arrangements to visit a class for gifted learners. (Your course instructor may be able to provide some assistance.) What kinds of instructional techniques did you see being used? Were learners asked to do things that were truly different from what goes on in regular classes? Were you able to form impressions of how learners felt about being in the class? Share your findings with your instructor in the form of a brief reaction paper.

5. Some people argue that gifted learners are so bright that they will succeed regardless of what the school provides. Believing this to be true, these critics suggest that it makes little sense for schools to use scarce resources to assist gifted learners. This money, they contend, would be much more wisely spent on average and below-average learners, who need all the help they can get to profit from their school experiences. Organize a debate on this topic: "Resolved: It Is Unwise and Irresponsible to Spend Scarce Educational Dollars on Programs for Gifted Learners." Debate the issue in front of the class, and then organize a follow-up discussion.

• • • • • • • • • • • • • • • • • • • • • • • • • • • •

# Supplementary Reading

Adkins, G. "Educating the Handicapped in the Regular Classroom." *Education Digest* (September 1990): 24–27.

Baum, S. "The Gifted/Learning Disabled: A Paradox for Teachers." *Education Digest* (April 1990): 54–56.

Bender, W. N., and N. Evans. "Mainstream and Special Class Strategies for Managing Behaviorally Disordered Students in Secondary Classes." *The High School Journal* (December–January 1989): 89–96.

Feldhusen, J. F. "Synthesis of Research on Gifted Youth." *Educational Leadership* (March 1989): 6–11.

Johnson, D. W., and R. T. Johnson. *Learning Together and Alone: Cooperative and Individualistic Learning.* 3d ed. Boston: Allyn and Bacon, 1991.

Renzulli, J. S. "The Three-Ring Conception of Giftedness: Developmental Model for Creative Productivity." In R. J. Sternberg and J. E. Davidson, eds. *Conceptions of Giftedness.* New York: Cambridge University Press, 1986, 53–92.

•••••••••••••••••••••••••••••••

# References

Baum, S. "The Gifted/Learning Disabled: A Paradox for Teachers." *Education Digest* (April 1990): 54–56.

Bender, W. N., and N. Evans. "Mainstream and Special Class Strategies for Managing Behaviorally Disordered Students in Secondary Classes." *The High School Journal* (December–January 1989): 89–96.

Brown, B. B., and L. Steinberg. "Academic Achievement and Social Acceptance." *Education Digest* (March 1990): 57–60.

Carri, L. "Inservice Teachers' Assessed Needs in Behavioral Disorders, Mental Retardation, and Learning Disabilities: Are They Similar?" *Exceptional Children* (February 1985): 411–16.

Dauber, S. L., and C. P. Benbow. "Aspects of Personality and Peer Relations of Extremely Talented Adolescents." *Gifted Child Quarterly* (Winter 1990): 10–15.

Glasser, W. *Reality Therapy: A New Approach to Psychiatry.* New York: Harper & Row, 1965.

Lewis, A. "Beefing Up Our Wimpy Words." *Phi Delta Kappan* (April 1991): 572–73.

MacMillan, D. L., B. K. Keogh, and R. L. Jones, "Special Education Research on Mildly Handicapped Learners." In M. C. Wittrock (Ed.), *Handbook of Research on Teaching,* 3d ed. New York: Macmillan, 1986.

Margolis, H., and E. Schwartz. "Facilitating Mainstreaming through Cooperative Learning." *The High School Journal* (December 1988–January 1989): 83–88.

Singer, J. D. "Educating Handicapped Children: 10 Years of PL 94–142." *Education Digest* (December 1985): 47–49.

Sternberg, R. J., and T. I. Lubart. "Creating Creative Minds." *Phi Delta Kappan* (April 1991): 608–14.

*United States Statutes at Large.* 91st Congress, 1970–1971, Vol. 84, Part 1. Washington, DC: U.S. Government Printing Office, 1971.

# Section 4

# Profession and Teaching

## Overview

Can teachers succeed? Though prospective teachers don't always ask this question, it is one they often wonder about. Newspaper accounts of bitter policy debates about education may suggest that the total system is in disarray and nobody has any answers. Reports of occasional violence against teachers and tales of terrible classroom management and discipline difficulties can undermine newcomers' confidence. Alleged learning shortcomings of American young people as compared to their counterparts in foreign lands also fuel concerns about what goes on in today's schools.

We certainly do not want to gloss over problems. On the other hand, we don't want to overplay them. Despite challenges facing educators, many teachers can and do succeed. Learners everywhere benefit from their expertise.

More and more help is becoming available for teachers who wish to improve. For example, professional teachers' organizations are more active than ever. They provide teachers with political and psychological support and are a source of information regarding successful patterns of classroom practice. Much research evidence is now available identifying practices that have been found to work in the classroom. Similarly, much information exists regarding what kinds of classroom management and discipline practices make sense. Finally, new technologies are extending the range of teachers' options as they seek to meet needs of individual learners.

Prospective teachers looking forward to success in the classroom often seek answers to questions such as these:

- What are some of the professional groups for teachers, and what kinds of services do they provide?
- What are some research findings about the practices of successful classroom teachers?
- What must be done to establish effective classroom management and discipline procedures?
- What are some examples of practical classroom applications of new technologies?

Some answers to these questions are provided in the chapters in this section:

# Chapter 10

# Teachers' Professional Groups

## Objectives

This chapter provides information to help the reader to

- identify basic orientations of the National Education Association and the American Federation of Teachers.
- describe some historical patterns in the development of the National Education Association and the American Federation of Teachers.
- point out some arguments both supporting and opposing the idea that teachers are "professionals."
- differentiate between sanctions and strikes.
- recognize how teachers' organizations have enlarged the parts teachers play in formulating educational policy.
- identify some teachers' specialty organizations that seek to improve the teaching of certain subjects and age groups.

## Focus Questions

1. What are the two broad categories of organizations that draw many of their members from the teaching staffs of the nation's schools?
2. What are some changes that have prompted growth of such groups as the National Education Association and the American Federation of Teachers?
3. In what ways has the National Education Association changed since it was founded?
4. What are some differences in how the National Education Association and the American Federation of Teachers view teachers' work?
5. In what kinds of places has the American Federation of Teachers tended to be strongest?
6. What is the relative importance that the National Education Association and the American Federation of Teachers have attached to winning a larger role for teachers in educational governance?
7. What are some of the specialty organizations that serve teachers, and what does each emphasize?
8. What are some of the publications produced by the specialty organizations?
9. In what ways might someone who is preparing to become a teacher benefit from membership in one of the specialty organizations?

• • • • • • • • • • • • • • • • • • • • • • • • • • •

# Introduction

There are two broad types of teachers' professional organizations: general organizations and specialty organizations. The two largest general organizations, the National Education Association and the American Federation of Teachers, seek members from among teachers at all grade levels and across all subjects. The specialty organizations focus their attention on groups of teachers interested in certain subject areas or categories of learners. Both general and specialty organizations actively seek new members. Most of them either have active student affiliates or welcome students as regular members.

## The General Organizations

Probably the biggest change in the teaching profession over the past hundred years has been the emergence of a view of teaching as permanent rather than temporary employment. Throughout most of the nineteenth century, teaching required little formal training, paid poorly, and was regarded by almost no one as an occupation that would provide a fulfilling, lifelong career. Teaching was regarded as a fallback occupation that could tide an individual over until something better came along. Today, teachers regard themselves as being occupationally permanent. This view has led them to support organizations dedicated to improving their long-term career expectations.

In part, interest in large national teachers' associations has been prompted by the increase in the size of school districts that has occurred almost continuously since the early years of this century. Consolidation of districts has doubtless produced some economies of operation; however, at the same time it has tended to distance teachers from many central office administrators. In many larger districts, administrators who make and implement policy affecting conditions of teachers' work in the classroom have little day-to-day contact with teachers in the individual buildings. Teachers' organizations have provided a vehicle for giving a collective voice to teachers who sometimes feel themselves isolated in their classrooms. The organizations function as conduits that can transmit teachers' concerns to central district administrators.

Over the years, several organizations have attempted to attract a nationwide membership of teachers. The following two, however, are much larger than any of the others:

• National Education Association (NEA)
• American Federation of Teachers (AFT)

## The National Education Association (NEA)

The National Education Association, boasting close to two million members, is the largest teachers' organization in the country. It traces its roots to the National Teachers' Association, organized as far back as 1857 (Hessong and Weeks, 1987). In the 1870s, the National Teachers' Association merged with the National Association of School Superintendents and the American Normal School Association, to become the National Educational Association (Donley, 1976). Some years later, the word *educational* was shorted to *education*.

Teachers from all grade levels attend a session at a national convention of the National Education Association.

In its early years, the National Education Association (NEA) was little concerned with teachers' benefits, partly because many of its most active and influential members were administrators, not teachers. (Today, administrators do not belong to the NEA.) This attitude can be attributed to a widespread belief that teaching was a calling in almost a religious sense, and thus it was not proper for teachers to evidence too much concern about financial rewards and working conditions.

The NEA began to become much more attuned to compensation issues after World War II. Low salaries had resulted in large numbers of teachers leaving to take other kinds of work. As a result, for many years the NEA sought to improve teachers' working conditions by lobbying legislators and taking other actions to apprise the public of teachers' plight. Among these other actions were efforts to get school district leaders to sign agreements calling for formal negotiation between teachers' organization representatives and school board representatives on issues pertaining to salaries and working conditions.

During this period after World War II, the NEA leadership was reluctant to use strikes as a policy weapon. To many NEA members, strikes were too closely associated with organized labor. The NEA's view of teachers as "professionals" did not square with the use of strikes as a bargaining tool; instead, the NEA preferred to pressure states and school districts to do right by teachers by threatening to or actually imposing sanctions. (*Sanctions* feature the systematic dissemination of adverse information about a district or group of districts to the entire national community of educators.) The idea was that such negative information would bring pressure on school officials to take action to improve conditions for teachers. Box 10–1 addresses the issue of teachers and strikes.

The limitations of sanctions as a weapon were revealed in the second half of the 1960s, when the NEA placed them on the entire state of Florida. Without going into the details, this effort resulted in only modest improvements for teachers. Some teachers lost their jobs, and a very negative relationship developed between Florida legislators and educators.

Concerns about the effectiveness of sanctions and other circumstances eventually led the NEA to acknowledge the strike as a legitimate bargaining weapon for teachers. By the late 1960s, teachers' strikes had become a predictable early fall event. This pattern continues even today.

The membership of the NEA has continued to grow. In part, this growth has resulted in the organization's successful push for unification. *Unification* means that a

## TEACHERS' STRIKES

Should teachers go on strike? This question has led to heated exchanges between people who support strikes and people who are against them. Individuals opposed to strikes frequently argue that they undermine the image of teachers as professionals. Some fear that teachers' strikes will alienate middle- and upper-class citizens, who have traditionally been extremely supportive of public education. This could well translate into a reduction in their support of funding for the public schools.

Supporters of strikes as an appropriate weapon often argue that most people are indifferent to the many pressures teachers face. As evidence, they point out the conflicting obligations legislatures have placed on teachers. For example, teachers are expected to turn out learners who perform better than ever with little or no increases in funding for the schools. While the public may say improvements in working conditions are needed, there is little evidence that much real action has occurred when teachers have been unwilling to strike.

*What Do You Think?*

1. Is it possible for a person to be a professional and also go on strike? Why or why not?
2. How important is it for teachers to enjoy good relations with middle- and upper-class citizens? Do you believe it is true that teachers' strikes will turn these citizens against public education?
3. Do you think teachers should use strikes as a bargaining weapon?

teacher may not select membership in a local NEA affiliate, a state NEA affiliate, or the NEA itself without simultaneously joining all three groups. All states are now unified. This has resulted in a tremendous gain in the total income of the NEA, and it has turned the group into a very powerful national lobby.

Philosophically, the NEA has taken the position that teachers have much in common with members of the learned professions, such as medicine and law. Like doctors and lawyers, teachers go through a specialized preparation program. The state certifies their competence. Usually they are charged with maintaining their level of competence by participating actively in self-improvement programs and by advanced study. A code of professional ethics guides teachers' behavior.

This view of the nature of teaching has led the NEA to push hard for programs designed to give teachers more control over their professional lives. Many of these efforts have sought to increase teachers' involvement in governance. *Governance* is a broad term, but generally it implies that teachers should have substantive input into profession-related decisions such as training teachers, hiring teachers, determining course content, selecting learning materials, and identifying appropriate instructional methodologies.

Today, the NEA is an organization run by and for classroom teachers. Its publication arm, legal services operation, research division, and other components are all oriented toward serving teachers' interests. For further information about the NEA and its programs, write to:

National Education Association
1201 16th Street, N.W.
Washington, DC 20036

## The American Federation of Teachers (AFT)

The American Federation of Teachers (AFT), a union affiliated with the AFL–CIO, has never enjoyed the numerical strength of the NEA, but it still has had a great impact on teaching. Much of the AFT's influence is explained by the concentration of AFT membership in large cities. Teachers' benefits packages won through AFT action in places such as Chicago and New York have greatly influenced teachers' groups throughout the rest of the country. Because the smaller AFT has always had the potential to chip away at the membership of the much larger NEA, the NEA has become more aggressive in its pursuit of better conditions for teachers. In the absence of a competing AFT, it is doubtful that the NEA would have embraced strikes as a legitimate bargaining weapon as early as it did. Box 10–2 deals with the pros and cons of teachers' affiliation with organized labor.

The AFT has always been strongest where organized labor in general has enjoyed wide support. This accounts for the distinctly urban flavor the group has always had. The organization traces its beginnings to Chicago, where the Chicago Teachers Federation was organized in the late 1890s. A meeting of the Chicago union and others from industrialized parts of the upper midwest resulted in the formation of the American Federation of Teachers in 1916.

From the beginning, the AFT differed from the NEA in two ways. First, the organization sought as its members people who were classroom teachers—it was never domi-

BOX 10–2
# TEACHERS AND ORGANIZED LABOR

Is it desirable for teachers to be affiliated with organized labor? Arguments about this issue have divided teachers for many years. Supporters argue that organized labor represents a good cross-section of Americans, as union members range from unskilled workers to highly trained airline pilots. All are joined together by a common belief in economic equity, and teachers tend to share a commitment to this value. Hence, it makes sense for them to identify with organized labor.

Countering this argument, critics point out that organized labor's influence in our society is declining. They note that the nation's central cities, traditional strong-holds of organized labor, are losing population. Growth is occurring in suburbs and small towns, areas traditionally having little sympathy for organized labor. Teachers' affiliation with organized labor could dismay people in the fastest-growing parts of the country. Further, affiliation with organized labor casts doubts on teachers' profes-sionalism.

*What Do You Think?*

1. Are the objectives of organized labor consistent or inconsistent with the objec-tives of teachers?
2. Can a person be both a professional and a member of organized labor?
3. Would teachers be winners or losers if all had to belong to a group affiliated with organized labor?

nated by university people or administrators. Even very early in the organization's his-tory, teachers played important leadership roles. Second, the AFT had a primary con-cern about teachers' benefits right from the first. While this certainly has also been true of the NEA in recent years, in earlier times the NEA was concerned with educational issues that ranged well beyond teachers' benefits.

The AFT has taken a view of teaching that is quite different from that of the NEA. As the AFT sees it, teachers are more like employees of large corporations than like lawyers and doctors. One reason for this view is that teachers do not go through a lengthy professional preparatory program that extends well beyond the award of the baccalaureate degree. Also, studies reveal that teachers do not have as high a social or economic status as lawyers or doctors. However, the single most important difference that separates teachers from such professionals as lawyers and doctors is that large numbers of lawyers and doctors are self-employed, whereas nearly all teachers work for an institution. In many cases, school systems are large, and teachers have little personal contact with the people responsible for their continued employment. This situation, it is argued, is what makes teachers similar in many respects to employees of large corporations. And thus given this situation, the highest need of teachers is for a strong organization that is able to counterbalance the potential for often-distant administrative authority to be exercised arbitrarily.

The AFT's position regarding the nature of teaching has led the organization to be most concerned with winning improvements in teachers' salaries and working conditions. The AFT has generally been less concerned than the NEA with increasing teachers' educational governance responsibilities. The AFT position has been basically that there are two classes of educators: (1) administrators, who represent management, and (2) teachers, who represent labor. The interests of the two groups are fundamentally different. In a responsible teachers' organization, the primary effort should be to maximize the benefits for teachers and restrict arbitrary administrative power. The right of administrators to manage what has been negotiated is recognized so long as this management remains consistent with the formally adopted agreements. When administrative management is perceived as inconsistent with the agreements, a pattern of teachers' organization–administrator arbitration (based on traditional labor–management practices) is seen as the most productive approach to resolving the problem.

For further information about the AFT and its programs, write to:

American Federation of Teachers
555 New Jersey Avenue, N.W.
Washington, DC 20001

*"He's the best teacher-union negotiator in the business."*
Courtesy of Ford Button.

## The NEA and AFT: Prospects

Chances seem good that the NEA and the AFT will continue to be visible participants in American education. Three types of pressures seem destined to continue to come down on teachers: (1) rising public expectations for public schools, (2) increased demand for cost containment in education, and (3) legally mandated changes directed at school programs. In response to these pressures, teachers will probably want to make their feelings known through major teacher organizations. Each of these areas of concern presents teachers with problems that are difficult to respond to as individuals, but collective action may hold out some promise.

In the area of rising expectations, teachers find themselves confronted by a public alarmed by mediocre learner performances on standardized tests. Many teachers, too, are concerned about this situation, but they point out that learners' performances on these tests are only partly a result of the school program. If parents today watch a great deal of television, then their children are more likely to spend their own leisure time watching television than reading. Teachers are willing to be held accountable for their own actions, but they want the public to understand that children's learning depends on many factors beyond the direct control of the school. It is probable that teachers will increasingly seek the help of their professional groups as they attempt to make the general public aware of this point of view.

Cost-containment efforts also give teachers cause for concern. As taxpayers themselves, of course teachers do not object to efforts to spend scarce tax dollars wisely. But they often feel themselves caught between pressures to improve learners' performance levels and to spend less money to get the job done. They frequently sense an incompatibility between these two expectations. Teachers increasingly seem interested in having their professional groups take action to bring this incompatibility to the public's attention.

Legally mandated changes have placed great strains on some teachers. This is particularly true when legislative action has asked teachers to teach content for which they have not been trained. For example, some years ago elementary school teachers in California found themselves faced with a new requirement to teach Spanish, a language with which few of them were familiar. More recently, some states have passed laws requiring that consumer- or economics-related content be introduced into the existing curriculum. Teachers who lack preparation in these areas have felt their professionalism to be undercut. How, they have wondered, can they properly teach subjects about which they know nothing?

Today, the NEA and the AFT are monitoring a number of evolving situations. For example, there is an effort to establish a national certification board for teachers. The professional organizations are watching this situation carefully, with a particular view to taking action against any move to undercut the validity of the existing state-issued certificates of their members. The move toward site-based management, an innovation that seems destined to involve more teachers in administrative areas of policymaking and management, is also being observed carefully.

The changing nature of the profession has led many teachers to conclude that they need representation by broad-based teachers' organizations, such as the NEA and the AFT (see this chapter's Case Study). In some parts of the country, representatives of teachers' groups have no legal right to negotiate for teachers' benefits. But even where this is the case, these groups *do* exert an influence. For example, they make their views known to those responsible for establishing teachers' salaries and working conditions by appearing at school board meetings, through one-on-one contacts with influential community members, and in numerous other ways.

In other parts of the country, teachers' groups have a legal authority to represent teachers' interests when salaries and working conditions are negotiated. In these areas, the local affiliate of the NEA or AFT (or sometimes a group not connected with either of these national organizations) is designated as the official bargaining agent for teachers. Though teachers in these places are usually free to belong to the organization of their choice, for pragmatic reasons many choose to affiliate with the group that has been designated as the official bargaining agent, as representatives of this group are the only ones authorized to negotiate agreements specifying salaries and other conditions of employment. Thus, many teachers join the bargaining-agent group so that they will have a part in shaping the positions that the teachers' representatives take into the negotiation process.

---

CASE STUDY

## Pressure to join a teachers' organization

**Leonard Stephenson is in his first year of teaching biology at Rutherford Hayes Senior High School, which enrolls about 2,000 students from the West Markley School District.** He is one of 80 teachers in the school.

The West Markley School District has recognized a local teachers' organization as the official bargaining agent for the district's teachers. Its representatives sit down with representatives of the local school board each year to negotiate issues related to salaries and working conditions.

The building representative for the local teachers, Sarana McPartland, has been actively encouraging Leonard to join the group. She has made frequent mention of the point that 78 of the building's 80 teachers are members, and has pointed out that some teachers who pay dues might not feel kindly toward a teacher who enjoys the benefits of negotiated agreements without paying dues and affiliating with the teachers' organization. She has also noted to Leonard that the district allows the annual teachers' organization dues to be paid in installments out of each month's check.

Leonard has no real problem with the costs of the dues, but he does have some philosophical concerns about membership. He knows that some of the local organization leaders have actively talked about the possibility of a teachers' strike if negotiations with the school board do not go well. Also troublesome to Leonard is that some of the organization's publications always seem to paint administrators as villains who are out to exploit teachers.

Leonard feels that the students are being overlooked in the whole process. He is concerned that the teachers' organization needlessly interferes with cooperative efforts of teachers and administrators to meet students' needs. He is afraid that joining the teachers' organization will signal his approval of the breakdown of teacher–administrator cooperation. Sarana has told him that she will be coming by again this afternoon and wants a definite answer to her invitation to join the group.

*What should Leonard do? What problems might result if he decides not to join the organization? What might happen if he does decide to join? How do you think the other teachers might react to each choice? What might be the reaction of the school's administrators to each alternative?*

There has been a tremendous growth in the total membership of general teachers' organizations over the past 50 years. Teachers' interest in influencing decisions related to their professional lives continues to be strong. As a result, the AFT and NEA and their local affiliates probably will continue to enlist the membership of large numbers of the nation's teachers (see the accompanying What the Experts Say for a consideration of how such organizations can ultimately affect learners' achievements).

WHAT THE EXPERTS SAY

## *Is learners' achievement affected when teachers' organizations negotiate wage and working-condition agreements with school officials?*

In some school districts, legal arrangements exist whereby representatives of major teachers' organizations (usually NEA or AFT affiliates) have the legal power to negotiate wage and working-condition agreements with representatives of the school board. These arrangements have much in common with those of industrial labor unions to represent workers' interests when negotiating with management. Researchers have been interested in learning whether teachers working in districts where such agreements are in force produce higher-achieving learners than teachers working in districts where there is no requirement for formal negotiations between a teachers' organization and administrative officials.

Some people who have thought about this situation feel that formal negotiation agreements tend to reduce teachers' effectiveness and, hence, result in diminished levels of learner achievement. These critics argue that negotiated agreements have the potential to shield ineffective teachers from dismissal actions, and that even competent teachers may feel less pressure to produce. Hence, instructional effectiveness may be undermined.

Others have maintained that formal negotiation agreements tend to improve levels of learner achievement. These people suggest that wages for teachers tend to be higher in districts where administrators are forced to negotiate wage and working conditions with representatives of teachers' groups. Because wage rates are high, there are pressures on administrators to derive maximum benefits from the instructional staffs in the school. Hence, these districts may be willing to provide more resources that allow teachers to do their job well. This kind of support has the potential to translate into elevated levels of learner achievement.

Which view is correct? The jury is still out on this question, but some interesting research studies have begun to address this issue. Recently, researchers Paul W. Grimes and Charles A. Register (1990) examined the performance of a national sample of over 1,600 high school economics students on the Test of Economic Literacy. Using an experimental procedure that held other variables constant, Grimes and Register compared scores of students taught by (1) teachers in districts where formal school administration–teachers' organization negotiating agreements were in place and (2) teachers in districts having no such agreements. They found student scores to be significantly higher in districts where there were formal negotiating agreements in place.

In a discussion of their findings, the researchers suggested that higher wages in the districts having formal negotiation agreements may allow these districts to select from a large pool of applicants for each vacancy. This means that exceptionally capable people are likely to be assuming these positions. However, the researchers concluded that much more research remains to be done before more definitive conclusions can be drawn regarding how formal negotiation agreements affect learner performance.

## The Specialty Organizations

Educators are great believers in professional improvement. This interest is reflected in the dozens of specialty organizations that have been formed, at least in part, out of a desire to establish forums where teachers interested in particular kinds of learners or subjects can exchange information and learn about promising new curricular and instructional approaches. Thousands of the nation's teachers belong to these organizations.

Most of these groups have large annual meetings that draw together educators from throughout the country; many also have regional and state meetings. Some of them even have local affiliates that provide opportunities for educators with common interests to more frequently get together to share ideas.

Specialty groups often have arrangements that allow students who are preparing to become teachers to join at reduced rates. Involvement in these organizations affords opportunities for prospective teachers to meet teachers who are already working with kinds of learners and subject areas similar to those with which they will be working when their preparation programs are completed. Many of these specialty organizations also publish excellent professional journals, which are good sources for up-to-date research information and innovative teaching practices.

In the subsections that follow, basic information is provided about some specialty groups that serve teachers. This listing is by no means comprehensive, but it does suggest the wide range of concerns that are addressed by specialty organizations in education. The following specialty groups are discussed:

- American Alliance for Health, Physical Education, Recreation, and Dance (AAHPERD)
- Association for Childhood Education International (ACEI)
- Council on Exceptional Children (CEC)
- International Council for Computers in Education (ICCE)

Teachers often form affiliations with groups sharing interests in certain parts of the overall school program. These teachers are attending a session sponsored by the National Council of Teachers of English.

- International Reading Association (IRA)
- Music Teachers National Association (MTNA)
- National Art Education Association (NAEA)
- National Association for Gifted Children (NAGC)
- National Council for the Social Studies (NCSS)
- National Council of Teachers of English (NCTE)
- National Council of Teachers of Mathematics (NCTM)
- National Science Teachers Association (NSTA)

These specialty groups will each be discussed in detail. For information on some other specialty groups and their publications, see Box 10–3.

## American Alliance for Health, Physical Education, Recreation, and Dance (AAHPERD)

This large national group embraces individuals with interests in health, physical education, recreation, and dance. Membership includes elementary and secondary school teachers, school administrators, college and university professors, and others who share an interest in the group's work. Student memberships are available.

**BOX 10–3**

## OTHER SPECIALTY ORGANIZATIONS AND THEIR PUBLICATIONS

All of the specialty organizations introduced in this section of the chapter publish professional journals, but there are other specialty organizations that also issue periodicals containing articles of interest to classroom teachers. The following are some examples:

*Phi Delta Kappan*
*NASSP Bulletin*
*Educational Leadership*
*Review of Educational Research*
*Educational Forum*

Go to your library and look at one or two issues of each of these journals. Your course instructor may wish to add some additional titles.

*What Do You Think?*
1. What professional organizations produce each of these journals?
2. What kinds of organizations are these (e.g., honorary societies, administrators' groups, curriculum specialists groups, researchers' organizations, etc.)?
3. Cite some examples of articles from each of the magazines you reviewed that might be of interest to classroom teachers.

• • • • • • • • • • • • • • • • • • • • • • • • • • • • • • • • • • • • • • • • • • • • • • • • • • • • • •

AAHPERD sponsors the publication of several journals. The *Journal of Physical Education, Recreation, and Dance* comes out nine times each year. *Health Education* appears six times a year. Members are apprised of ongoing activities through the group's monthly publication, *Update*. Research results are reported in *Research Quarterly for Exercise and Sport*. For information about this group, write to:

American Alliance for Health, Physical Education, Recreation, and Dance
1900 Association Drive
Reston, VA 22091

### Association for Childhood Education International (ACEI)

The Association for Childhood Education International has about 200 chapters scattered throughout the country. Its members are particularly concerned about the development of children from infancy through early adolescence. There are special divisions within the organization that focus, respectively, on (1) infancy, (2) early childhood, and (3) later childhood and early adolescence. Student memberships are encouraged.

ACEI publishes a journal for its general membership entitled *Childhood Education*. It appears five times a year. The group also publishes the *Journal of Research in Childhood Education*, which includes reports of research on child-development topics. For information about this group, write to:

Association for Childhood Education International
11141 Georgia Avenue, Suite 200
Wheaton, MD 20902

## Council on Exceptional Children (CEC)

The Council on Exceptional Children is dedicated to promoting better educational programs for handicapped and gifted learners. Membership includes teachers, administrators, parents, university-based professionals, and others interested in the group's work. Membership is open to students.

CEC publishes two major journals: *Exceptional Children* is issued six times each year, and *Teaching Exceptional Children* is published quarterly. For information about this group, write to:

Council for Exceptional Children
1920 Association Drive
Reston, VA 22091

## International Council for Computers in Education (ICCE)

As its name suggests, the International Council for Computers in Education is a group dedicated to the interests of people committed to making more effective use of computers in schools. It works to promote cooperation among the various groups interested in improving instruction through applications of computer technology. Membership is available to students.

ICCE produces two regular publications: *The Computing Teacher* is issued nine times each year, and *The SIG Bulletin* appears quarterly. For information about this group, write to:

International Council for Computers in Education
University of Oregon
1787 Agate Street
Eugene, OR 97403

## International Reading Association (IRA)

The International Reading Association is one of the nation's largest education specialty groups. It has approximately 90,000 members and about 1,200 local chapters scattered throughout the country. IRA's membership includes regular classroom teachers, reading specialists and consultants, administrators, educational researchers, librarians, and others who are interested in reading. A student membership is available.

IRA publishes several highly regarded journals. The *Reading Teacher*, published nine times a year, contains articles of primary interest to people concerned about improving reading instruction in elementary schools. The *Journal of Reading*, also published nine times a year, focuses on the theory and practice of reading as applied to middle schools, junior and senior high schools, and adult-learning situations. *Reading Research Quarterly*, appearing four times a year, is devoted to disseminating the work of reading researchers. The IRA also publishes a quarterly journal in Spanish, *Lectura Y Vida*. For information about this group, write to :

International Reading Association
800 Bardsdale Road
P.O. Box 8139
Newark, DE 19714

## Music Teachers National Association (MTNA)

The Music Teachers National Association has chapters throughout the country. Members include music teachers in the schools (elementary, secondary, and higher education) and music teachers with private tutoring practices. The group is dedicated to improving music instruction, performance, and understanding. Membership is open to students.

MTNA sponsors several publications: *The American Music Teacher* appears bimonthly, and the *Directory of Nationally Certified Teachers* is an annual volume. For additional information about this group, write to:

Music Teachers National Association
2113 Carew Tower
Cincinnati, OH 45202

## National Art Education Association (NAEA)

The National Art Education Association is the leading national professional group for art teachers. It is dedicated to improving instruction of the visual arts in the schools. Members include teachers, administrators, and others with a direct connection to art education in the schools. Special memberships are available for students who are preparing to be art teachers.

NAEA publishes several journals. *Art Education* and *NAEA News* come out bimonthly. A research-oriented journal, *Studies in Art Education*, is published four times a year. For information about this group, write to:

National Art Education Association
1916 Association Drive
Reston, VA 22091

## National Association for Gifted Children (NAGC)

The National Association for Gifted Children seeks to promote the interest of parents and educators concerned about school programs for gifted learners. The group conducts training sessions for parents and educators and lobbies at the national and state levels for better programs for the gifted. Membership is open to all who support the organization's objectives. Student members are welcome.

NAGC has one major publication, *Gifted Child Quarterly*, which appears four times a year. For information about this group, write to:

National Association for Gifted Children
4175 Lovell Road, Suite 140
Circle Pines, MN 55014

## National Council for the Social Studies (NCSS)

This is the largest national group of educators with interests in history and the social sciences. State and local affiliates are located throughout the nation. Student memberships are encouraged.

NCSS publishes several journals. The group's most widely circulated journal is *Social Education*, which appears seven times each year and contains articles focusing on all aspects of teaching and learning social studies content in grades K through 12. The journal *Social Studies and the Young Learner* appears four times each year. Its articles pay particular attention to classroom activities, curriculum content, and other information related to teaching social studies to elementary school learners. *Theory and Research in Social Education* is a quarterly journal that reports on research related to social studies education. For information about this group, write to:

National Council for the Social Studies
3501 Newark Street, NW
Washington, DC 20016

## National Council of Teachers of English (NCTE)

This national group has chapters in each state, as well as a large number of local affiliates. NCTE is dedicated to improving the quality of instruction in English language and literature. Membership is open to individuals who teach language arts and English at any level. Special membership rates are available for students who wish to join the organization.

NCTE publishes several journals. *Language Arts*, published eight times a year, is a journal for elementary school teachers and administrators. *English Journal*, also published eight times a year, seeks to help middle school, junior high school, and senior high school teachers of literature, language, and composition. A quarterly journal, *Research in the Teaching of English*, covers research into the teaching and learning of English. Several other specialty journals are also published by this group. For information about this organization, write to:

National Council of Teachers of English
1111 Kenyon Road
Urbana, IL 61801

## National Council of Teachers of Mathematics (NCTM)

This large organization has more than 200 state and local chapters throughout the nation. It is dedicated to the improvement of mathematics instruction in the schools. Members include elementary and secondary teachers and others interested in furthering the organization's objectives. Student memberships are available.

NCTM publishes several journals. The *Arithmetic Teacher*, published nine times each year, is directed to individuals interested in the improvement of elementary school mathematics instruction. The *Mathematics Teacher*, also published nine times a year, serves mathematics teachers at the secondary level and in two-year colleges. Research in mathematics education is reported five times each year in the *Journal for Research in Mathematics Education*. For information about this group, write to:

National Council of Teachers of Mathematics
1906 Association Drive
Reston, VA 22091

## National Science Teachers Association (NSTA)

This organization is the largest national group of educators committed to improving science instruction in the schools. Members include elementary and secondary school teachers, administrators, university-based science educators and scientists, and others committed to the group's mission. Student memberships are encouraged. NSTA has active affiliates throughout the nation.

NSTA publishes journals for particular groups of science educators. *Science and Children*, published eight times a year, is targeted at teachers and administrators in elementary schools. *Science Scope*, issued five times a year, provides information about science instructional methodologies and curricula that are particularly relevant for middle school and junior high school learners. *The Science Teacher*, issued nine times each year, serves the interests of junior and senior high school science educators. The *Journal of College Science Teaching* focuses on issues of concern to science instructors in higher-education settings. For information about this group, write to:

National Science Teachers Association
1742 Connecticut Avenue, NW
Washington, DC 20009

All of these organizations are representative of education-related groups that draw much of their membership from among the nation's teachers. There are many other kinds of specialty organizations in education as well. Some of them are directed at school administrators; others serve interests of school boards; and still others are comprised primarily of college and university professors with interests in teacher education.

Affiliation with one or more specialty groups even before certification programs have been completed makes sense for students preparing to teach. Local and regional meetings offer opportunities to meet and learn from teachers who are already in the field. Additionally, these meetings and the professional publications sponsored by most of these organizations are excellent sources of information about innovative approaches to classroom instruction. Finally, affiliation with a specialty group can build a sense of professional community. For example, in a general college Introduction to Education class, there may be only one or two people interested in science teaching, but a local meeting of a National Science Teachers Association (NSTA) affiliate may bring together dozens of people who are enthusiastic about their roles as science educators.

**TABLE 10–1**
Summary table: Teachers' organizations

| General Organizations | Characteristics |
| --- | --- |
| National Education Association (NEA) | • Nation's largest teachers' group<br><br>• Used to oppose use of strikes, but now considers them a legitimate bargaining tool<br><br>• In recent years, concerned about expanding teachers' roles in overall school governance as well as improving salaries and working conditions<br><br>• Has tended to view teachers' work as an activity having much in common with professions such as law and medicine |
| American Federation of Teachers (AFT) | • Affiliated with the AFL–CIO<br><br>• Has long felt that strikes are a legitimate bargaining tool<br><br>• Stronger in large cities than in small towns and rural areas<br><br>• Has tended to view work of teachers as similar to that of employees of large corporations<br><br>• More concerned with improving working conditions and salaries than in gaining more governance authority for teachers |

**TABLE 10–1**
*continued*

| Specialty Organizations | Major Interests |
| --- | --- |
| American Alliance for Health, Physical Education, Recreation, and Dance (AAHPERD) | • Improvement of school programs in health, physical education, recreation, and dance |
| Association for Childhood Education International (ACEI) | • Development of children from infancy through early adolescence |
| Council on Exceptional Children (CEC) | • Promotion of better programs for learners who are disabled and gifted learners |
| International Council for Computers in Education (ICCE) | • More effective use of computers in the schools |
| International Reading Association (IRA) | • Improvement of reading instruction |
| Music Teachers National Association (MTNA) | • Improvement of music instruction, performance, and understanding |
| National Art Education Association (NAEA) | • Encouragement of better visual arts programs in the schools |
| National Association for Gifted Children (NAGC) | • Promotion of better school programs and support of legislation to benefit gifted children |
| National Council for the Social Studies (NCSS) | • Promotion of better social studies programs in the schools |
| National Council of Teachers of English (NCTE) | • Improvement of instruction in the English language and literature |
| National Council of Teachers of Mathematics (NCTM) | • Improvement of mathematics instruction in the schools |
| National Science Teachers Association (NSTA) | • Improvement of science instruction in the schools |

•••••••••••••••••••••••••••••••••

# Key Ideas in Summary

- There are two general categories of organizations that draw many members from the ranks of the nation's teachers: general organizations and specialty organizations. General organizations focus on issues of interest to the profession as a whole. Specialty organizations promote narrower interests—for example, interests of teachers concerned about certain categories of learners or about teaching certain subjects.

- Growth of the large, general professional organizations has been stimulated, in part, by the emergence of the idea that teaching is a career-long rather than a temporary occupation. Growth has also been promoted by the increase in size of the typical school district, something that has created a certain distance between classroom practitioners and the central office administrators who make decisions affecting teachers' working conditions.

- The nation's largest teachers' organization is the National Education Association (NEA), with about two million members. It traces its roots to the middle of the nineteenth century when its forerunner, the National Teachers Association, was formed. In its early days, the NEA included both teachers and administrators; today, it is an organization for teachers only.

- For many years, the leadership of the NEA was reluctant to endorse strikes as a policy weapon. Instead, the organizations favored the use of sanctions—the dissemination of negative information about school districts thought to have poor working conditions for teachers. Because of some problems with sanctions as a tool to gain leverage, since the late 1960s the NEA has changed its earlier stance and now endorses strikes as a legitimate bargaining tool.

- The NEA has tended to view teachers as professionals who have much in common with members of such other professions as law and medicine. This view has led the NEA to push hard to increase teachers' involvement in educational governance—having input into decisions regarding such things as teacher training, teacher hiring, course content, selection of instructional materials, and identification of instructional methodologies.

- The American Federation of Teachers (AFT) has always been smaller than the NEA. This group is affiliated with the AFL–CIO, and its major membership strength has always been in the nation's large urban areas. The AFT grew out of the Chicago Teachers Federation, a group organized in 1890.

- The AFT has tended to view teachers differently than the NEA. In the opinion of the AFT, teachers are more like employees of large corporations than they are like professionals such as doctors or lawyers, and thus teachers' highest need is for an organization that will defend their interest against sometimes-distant administrative authority. This view has led the AFT to be much less interested in the general issue of governance than the NEA, concentrating instead on winning economic benefits and improved working conditions for teachers.

- There are many specialty organizations that serve teachers' interests. These groups tend to focus either on concerns related to certain categories of learners (e.g., gifted learners, handicapped learners, or very young learners) or on concerns related to certain subject-matter areas (e.g., social studies, English, mathematics, music, physical education, etc.).

- The specialty organizations generally publish journals that help bind together their national membership. Among other things, these publications report promising classroom practices, new developments in curriculum, and findings of researchers.

- Most specialty organizations for teachers welcome memberships from students who are preparing to enter teaching. Membership affords an opportunity for prospective teachers to come into direct contact with individuals working in settings similar to those where they aspire to work once they complete their certification programs.

····································

# Review and Discussion Questions

1. What are the two basic types of teachers' professional organizations?

2. What developments over the past hundred years have tended to encourage the growth of such groups as the National Education Association and the American Federation of Teachers?

3. Why was the National Education Association in its early years somewhat less concerned about benefits for teachers than it is today?

4. Why do you think the National Education Association has made a decision to not include school administrators among its members?

5. What are some differences between the National Education Association and the American Federation of Teachers in how they view teachers' work?

6. Are strikes a legitimate weapon for teachers? Why or why not?

7. What impacts are present trends in education likely to have on membership growth of such organizations as the National Education Association and the American Federation of Teachers?

8. What are some examples of professional organizations that are dedicated to serving the special interests of particular groups of learners or of educators strongly committed to teaching certain subjects?

9. What are some periodicals by some education organizations that focus on either special groups of learners or certain school subjects?

10. What are some advantages that membership in a specialty organization can bring to a college or university student who is preparing to enter teaching?

# Ideas for Field Experiences, Projects, and Enrichment

1. Invite a representative from a local unit of either the National Education Association or the American Federation of Teachers to visit your class. (If both organizations are active in your area, consider inviting representatives from each.) Ask the representative(s) to comment on particular services these organizations provide for their members. Inquire about activities at the local level and lobbying at the state and national levels.

2. Invite some representatives from local school districts' central administrative offices to visit your class. Ask them to comment on the nature of their relationships with local affiliates of national teacher groups such as the National Education Association and the American Federation of Teachers.

3. With the assistance of your instructor, find out what prevailing practices are in your state regarding the issue of teachers being obligated to join either the National Education Association or the American Federation of Teachers. (There may well be important place-to-place differences in your state.) Share your findings with others in your class.

4. Organize a group of four or five students in your class to look at some of the publications produced by specialty groups in education. Assign each member of the group to look at issues of a different publication. As a group, make a report to your class in which you address such issues as:

   • general kinds of articles contained in the publication

   • relative emphasis on practical, "how-to-do-it" information and more theoretical and research-oriented pieces

   • your views on the degree to which information in each journal would be helpful to a novice in the profession or field

5. Attend a meeting of a local affiliate of an educational specialty group. Pick one that focuses on areas that are of interest to you. Take some notes on what you observe, and then share your findings with others in your class.

........................................

# Supplementary Reading

Bacharach, S. B. "School Management and Teacher Unions: The Capacity for Cooperation in an Age of Reform." *Teachers College Record* (Fall 1989): 97–105.

Berube, M. R. *Teacher Politics: The Influence of Unions*. New York: Greenwood Press, 1988.

Clamp, P. G. "Professionalism in Education: A State of Mind." *Education Digest* (October 1990): 53–56.

Rist, M. C. "Teacher Empowerment and Teacher Unions." *Education Digest* (February 1990): 7–9.

Shanker, A. "Why a Strong Union Is Essential to Reform." *American Teacher* (May 1989): 5.

Wesley, E. B. *NEA: The First Hundred Years*. New York: Harper Brothers, 1957.

........................................

# References

Donley, M. O., Jr. *Power to the Teacher: How America's Educators Became Militant*. Bloomington, IN: Indiana University Press, 1976.

Grimes, P. W., and C. A. Register. "Teachers' Unions and Student Achievement in High School Economics." *Journal of Economic Education* (Summer 1990): 297–306.

Hessong, R. R., and T. H. Weeks. *Introduction to Education*. New York: Macmillan, 1987.

# Chapter 11

# Effective Teaching Practices

## Objectives

This chapter provides information to help the reader to

- identify the role of research in teaching.
- define the basic features of active teaching.
- explain the importance of teacher clarity.
- identify different time decisions teachers make, and explain how each relates to learner achievement.
- describe how teachers' expectations can influence learners' levels of achievement.
- recognize some elements of effective teacher-questioning techniques.
- describe some procedures that can be used to gather and record data about what goes on in a classroom during an observation session.

## Focus Questions

1. How important is quality of instruction among the variables used to assess teachers' effectiveness?
2. Is there research evidence today that points to the existence of some generally effective teaching behaviors?
3. Why has much interest in teacher effectiveness emphasized behaviors that seem to be associated with enhanced academic performance by learners?
4. What are some of the major roles that a teacher discharges when engaged in active teaching?
5. What are some kinds of things teachers consider as they attempt to match instruction to the needs of individual learners?
6. What are some dimensions of teacher clarity?
7. In what ways are allocated time, engaged time, and academic learning time different?
8. How do differing teacher expectations affect learners' performance levels?
9. What are general characteristics of lower-level questions and higher-level questions?
10. How can narrative approaches, frequency counts, coding systems, and seating-chart systems be used during classroom observations to gather and record information?

••••••••••••••••••••••••••••••

# Introduction

Instruction is what teachers are expected to do. It is true that they manage classrooms, take care of certain administrative responsibilities, and accomplish other tasks. However, instruction more than any other activity defines the role of teaching and clearly sets it apart from other professions.

Teachers have long been judged on their instructional effectiveness. Debates over this issue have sometimes centered on the question of whether there exists a body of research-validated knowledge that adequately defines "effective" teaching. Some people argue that such knowledge does exist and prospective teachers need specific training related to sound instructional methodology. Others maintain that no such specialized training is necessary and that good teaching will automatically follow for teachers who have a good understanding of the subjects they teach. The position of those who argue that teachers can profit from specialized training is being strengthened by a growing body of research, which is beginning to pinpoint certain categories of behaviors that have been found to be associated with effective teaching (Rosenshine and Stevens, 1986).

Most research on effective teaching has focused on teacher behaviors that are associated with increasing learners' academic attainment. Certainly, instruction also has other purposes. For example, learners' psychomotor development, social adjustment, and personal growth are important outcomes of education. Because there is so much present interest in the academic integrity of American schools, the discussion of teacher effectiveness here is generally restricted to those teacher behaviors that have been found to enhance academic achievement.

Research on teacher effectiveness differs from research in such areas as the physical sciences. It focuses on people who may have different personal backgrounds, motivations, and experiences. Because of these differences, findings of teacher effectiveness research do not categorically assert that a specific procedure will work in a predictable way with every learner. Rather, this body of research seeks to identify broad principles that can provide guidance to teachers as they make decisions appropriate for their own instructional settings.

Teaching is a decision-making process. Familiarity with research findings related to teaching effectiveness can assist educators as they diagnose instructional problems and consider alternative courses of action. Note that research findings introduced in this chapter do not represent a comprehensive review of the teacher-effectiveness literature—this information is intended as a brief introduction that can provide a beginning for a career-long interest in how research can influence instructional practice. Findings have been organized under these major headings:

- active teaching
- productive use of class time
- teacher expectations
- teachers' questions

## Active Teaching

A growing body of research suggests that active teaching is associated with enhanced learner achievement (Good and Brophy, 1991). The term *active teaching* refers to situations when the teacher directly leads the class and plays such roles as:

- presenter of new information
- monitor of learner progress
- planner of opportunities for learners to apply content
- reteacher of content (to learners who fail to learn the content when it is initially presented)

The active-teaching role is in contrast to the view of the teacher as a general manager or facilitator of instruction who does not get directly involved in leading the class and personally overseeing learning activities. There are several important dimensions of active teaching.

## Program Planning

*The Problem of Match.*    Active teachers play a leadership role in determining their learners' instructional programs (Good and Brophy, 1991). One problem they face is matching the program to the special characteristics of learners in their classrooms. To accomplish this task, teachers must make two kinds of decisions.

First, they must consider the difficulty level of the new material in light of their understanding of their learners' capabilities. If selected materials are too difficult, frustration is certain to occur and little learning will take place. If the materials are too easy, boredom and motivation problems may result.

Second, teachers need to match the program materials to learners' interests. This is not to suggest that teachers should introduce no content in which learners do not initially display a high level of interest. Rather, the teacher's task is to identify interest levels and, when they are found to be low, think about creative ways to generate greater learner interest and enthusiasm. Ideally, the teacher will develop plans for lessons that will promote in learners a desire or need to acquire the new information. Successful planning of this kind requires that teachers know their learners well.

Planning is closely associated with the concern for motivating learners. To a large degree, individuals' motivation to perform a task is wrapped up in their general interest in the goal and their perception of the likelihood of their completing the assigned work successfully. Planning is geared toward making tasks interesting and convincing learners that they will succeed.

*Task Analysis.*    As they seek to make judgments about the suitability of content for a given group of learners, teachers often engage in task-analysis activities. These require the teacher to look at a proposed body of content that their learners are to master for the purpose of breaking it into several smaller components or subtasks. To determine whether learners have the needed prerequisite information, the teacher identifies what each subtask presumes learners know before they begin work on it. Task analysis helps to establish the appropriateness of proposed content for a given group of learners. Box 11–1 provides a step-by-step breakdown of task analysis.

*Specifying Objectives.*    When the active teacher has determined that the selected content is appropriate, he or she moves on to specifying objectives for learners. These instructional objectives identify what learners should be able to do after they have mastered the new content. Often, separate instructional objectives are written for each of the subtasks identified during the task-analysis phase. Learner attainment of these objectives provides evidence to the teacher that the new material has been mastered.

## Lesson Presentation

Active teachers play important leadership roles during all phases of instructional planning and implementation. This leadership is particularly evident as lessons are being presented in the classroom.

*Stimulating and Maintaining Interest.*    The active teacher considers motivation during the process of identifying and selecting content. The emphasis on motivation is maintained as learners encounter new material in the classroom. During the presen-

---

### BOX 11–1
## COMPONENTS OF TASK ANALYSIS

Task analysis consists of two basic parts: (1) identifying the specific information learners will need in order to master some specific content, and (2) determining a logical beginning point for instruction.

Suppose you were planning to teach a two- to three-week unit in a subject and at a grade level of your choice. Make a list of specific knowledge and skills your learners will need in order to master this content.

Needed knowledge: _____

_____

_____

Needed skills: _____

_____

_____

Now, prepare a brief description of how you would begin instruction. To make this determination, you first need to find out how much of the needed knowledge and skills your learners already know. Then you can identify the appropriate starting point.

_____

_____

_____

tation-of-instruction phase, these three distinct periods of motivation need to be considered:

- motivation at the beginning of the learning sequence

- motivation during the learning sequence

- motivation at the conclusion of the learning sequence

The purpose of initial motivation is to engage learners' interest and to encourage them to want to learn the material. Teachers often attempt to build on learners' general curiosity at this stage. Introducing something novel, unusual, or puzzling often works well. Learners need to understand how the new material connects to their own lives. What will learning it help them to do or understand? Why should they commit themselves to mastering it? Teachers should provide answers to these questions during the first phase of motivation.

As instruction goes forward, teachers sometimes continue to introduce novel or unusual material to help sustain interest levels. Learners are motivated by success. When they accomplish parts of a larger instructional task, active teachers praise them for what they have done. This kind of support helps keep interest levels high. In general, motivation is facilitated when teachers maintain a positive classroom atmosphere that is free from threats and fear. Learners need to know that they have the solid support of their teacher as they struggle with new content.

Motivation at the conclusion of an instructional sequence is important. Active teachers take particular care to point out to learners how much they have accomplished. A sense of achievement functions as an important motivator. Achievement during one instructional sequence makes it easier for learners to be motivated as they begin the next one.

*Sequencing.*    Over the years, many schemes have been proposed regarding sequencing of instruction. Centuries ago, the ancient Spartans developed a four-part sequence, which required the teacher to present instruction according to this pattern of steps:

- introduce material to be learned

- ask learners to think about the material

- repeat the material again and work with learners individually until they have it memorized

- listen to learners as they recite the material from memory (Posner, 1987)

In the nineteenth century, the famous learning theorist Johann Herbart suggested a lesson cycle featuring these steps:

- preparation for learning

- presentation of new information

- association (tying new information to old)

- generalization

- application (Meyer, 1975)

In recent years, many school districts have recommended that teachers follow an instructional sequence suggested by Madeline Hunter and Douglas Russell (1977). The Hunter and Russell scheme includes these steps:

- anticipatory set (focusing learners' attention on the instruction that is about to begin)

- objective and purpose (helping learners understand what they will be able to do as a result of their exposure to the instruction)

- instructional input (conveying information to learners)

- modeling (providing learners with examples or demonstrations of competencies associated with the lesson)

- checking for understanding (evaluating whether learners have the information needed to master the objective)

- guided practice (monitoring learners as they work on tasks calling on them to apply the new information)

- independent practice (assigning learners to work with new content under conditions where they will not have direct teacher assistance available) (Hunter and Russell, 1977, pp. 86–88)

There are other sequencing models that have been developed (e.g., Posner, 1987; Denton, Armstrong, and Savage, 1980), which share many common features. Particularly notable is the emphasis that nearly all of them place on the importance of giving learners opportunities to apply new knowledge. Researchers have consistently

*"Barnes, please tell me this is for 'stimulating learner interest' and not for 'modeling'."*
Courtesy of Ford Button

found improved learning to be associated with instruction that allows learners to engage in application activities (Good and Brophy, 1991).

*Lesson Pacing.*    Good active teaching features a presentation of lessons that moves at a brisk pace and provides for high levels of learner success. The teacher works to maintain a smooth, continuous developmental flow, trying to avoid spending too much time on certain points or matters that are not directly related to the central content. As the lesson develops, the teacher continually asks questions and takes other actions to ensure that members of the class are learning the material.

*Within-Lesson Questioning.*    Active teaching demands the skillful use of questions. Research reveals that questions should be asked at regular intervals and addressed to a large number of class members (Good and Brophy, 1991). Questioning of this type serves two basic purposes. First, it allows the teacher to check on levels of learner understanding. Second, when learners know that the teacher makes a practice of asking many members of the class questions about what they are learning, they stay alert. They come to realize that they need to pay attention because the teacher might call on them at any time.

*Monitoring.*    Monitoring, a key ingredient of active teaching, occurs continuously throughout a lesson. It is particularly important after learners are directed to practice what they have learned by working on their own assignments. Active teachers avoid a retreat to their own desks; instead, they continue to move about the classroom, checking on learners' progress.

Feedback is provided both to learners who are performing the task correctly and to those who are experiencing difficulties. Successful performers need to know they are on the right track (Goodlad, 1984) and to hear supportive comments from the teacher. Those learners who are having problems or who are not doing the work properly also need to be helped. They require specific details regarding (1) what they are doing wrong and (2) how they can change what they are doing so they will experience success.

When a teacher's monitoring activities result in the discovery that many learners are not performing at an acceptable level, it is necessary to halt the independent practice activity. At this point, the teacher engages in reteaching to clear up misunderstandings. Successful reteaching is tightly focused, dealing with only those points that monitoring has revealed to be causing problems for learners.

## Teacher Clarity

Research reveals that instructional practices of effective teachers are characterized by clarity. *Clarity* includes several variables, among which are:

- the teacher's verbal and non-verbal style
- the teacher's lesson-presentation structure
- the teacher's proficiency in providing cogent explanations

Box 11–2 deals with the issue of clarity in textbooks.

A teacher carefully monitors a student's progress.

*Verbal and Nonverbal Style.*    Several issues come into play when defining a given teacher's presentation style. One of these is the teacher's paralanguage. *Paralanguage* includes those things that help shape what is conveyed by words that are spoken but that are not the words themselves. Elements of paralanguage include voice intonation, precision of articulation of words, and rate of speaking. Paralanguage, which also includes many nonverbal behaviors, has a great influence on how listeners hear and interpret what is said.

People acquire paralanguage as a natural overlay on their language skills as they grow to maturity within their families, friendship groups, and communities. There are important regional and cultural differences. When the paralanguage patterns of a speaker and listener differ, the listener may have difficulty understanding all that is being said.

For example, a teacher who was brought up in a part of the country where speech rates and vowel sounds differ dramatically from those in the area where he or she is now teaching may find that the learners sometimes have difficulty understanding what he or she has said. Teachers need to understand that communication problems sometimes result not from the level of difficulty of the words or message, but from the patterns of speech used to deliver them.

Nonverbal behaviors can also impede clear communication. This can happen when a nonverbal message is sent that is not consistent with the teacher's words. For example, suppose a teacher scowled and shook a fist at the class while saying, "I'm really

BOX 11–2
# IDENTIFYING VAGUE TERMINOLOGY IN PROSE MATERIALS

Research evidence suggests that learners have difficulty in understanding teachers when they use vague terminology. Vague terminology is not restricted to oral language—some textbook writers are also guilty of using it. Vague prose usages confuse learners and inhibit learning.

Find a textbook or a supplementary book used at a grade level and in a subject area you might be interested in teaching. Locate five examples of vague usage. Make a copy of each example, and then rewrite each, replacing vague terminology with words that have the potential to communicate more clearly to learners:

1. Original phrasing: _____
   Revision: _____
2. Original phrasing: _____
   Revision: _____
3. Original phrasing: _____
   Revision: _____
4. Original phrasing: _____
   Revision: _____
5. Original phrasing: _____
   Revision: _____

• • • • • • • • • • • • • • • • • • • • • • • • • • • • • • • • • • • • • • • • • • • • • • • • •

proud of the good work you're doing." Signals here are mixed: the nonverbal behaviors are hostile and threatening, but the verbal behavior is warm and supportive. The resulting message is confusing.

It is not unusual for people to be unaware of many of their nonverbal behaviors. Because these behaviors are important, teachers need to develop some awareness of their nonverbal patterns. Class observers sometimes can help by providing feedback to teachers about what they are doing nonverbally to support their verbal instruction.

*Lesson-Presentation Structure.*   Learners profit from an understanding of the general subject matter of new lessons and of how the content is to be organized. One way teachers often help learners grasp the framework of new lessons is through the use of advance organizers. An *advance organizer* is a label that describes a large and important category of content to be covered. It helps learners to sort out fragmented pieces of information and organize them under certain specified category labels. This simplifies their learning task.

Consider the following example. Suppose a secondary school teacher wanted students to study advertising. One purpose of the unit might be to help class members understand that some advertisers make claims that go beyond the evidence available to support them. The teacher might give these instructions to students: "Look through any five magazines of your choice. By Wednesday, bring me three or four ads that you believe make untrue or unfair claims."

This assignment is going to bring students into contact with a huge volume of information. The task, as assigned, provides few guidelines for learners to follow in deciding which ads might be better than others as examples of misleading advertising. The students' task would have been greatly simplified had the teacher provided them with one or two advance organizers.

For example, the teacher might have begun the class with an explanation and a discussion of the term *glittering generality*. The assigned task might then have been stated in this way: "Look through any five magazines of your choice. By Wednesday, bring me three or four ads that contain glittering generalities." This assignment would have provided students with a good sense of direction by clearly communicating to them what needed to be done to complete the task to the teacher's satisfaction.

A widely used type of advance organizer is the *lesson objective*. To assist learners in understanding what the lesson will emphasize, teachers often provide a learning objective that indicates what learners should be able to know or do when they have completed the lesson. Objectives that are conveyed in verbal form need not be complex. For example, a teacher might say something as simple as "When we've finished this lesson, you should be able to identify at least four main parts of a short story."

As lessons are being taught, teachers strive to maintain *connected discourse*. This means that they seek to achieve a smooth, point-by-point development of the content that is being introduced. Once started, the lesson is pursued and carried along to its logical conclusion. There are few digressions that take away from its main flow. The effort is to avoid mid-lesson stoppages that could result in confusion and, ultimately, diminished levels of learner achievement.

Teachers also often take time to provide *internal summaries* as they teach their lessons. These are pause points that allow the teacher and the class to stop, take stock, and reflect upon what has been learned up to that point. Internal summaries allow teachers to clarify any misconceptions. Learners whose teachers use internal summaries pay attention, because they recognize that their teacher may stop from time to time to ask someone in the class to summarize what has been learned.

Clarity is also enhanced when teachers use *marker expressions*, which are used to verbally underline or highlight something that has been said. Marker expressions are employed to communicate the importance of certain kinds of information. Examples include statements such as:

- "Write this down."
- "Pay close attention to this."
- "Listen carefully to this explanation."

The importance of specific content can also be "marked" through changes in vocal intonation or volume.

A certain amount of repetition or redundancy facilitates learning. To be effective, ideas need to be repeated in a slightly different form or context. *Creative repetition* is used by many effective teachers.

A final aspect of structuring is the summary provided at the end of a lesson presentation. The summary includes a recapitulation of major ideas that have been covered, drawing together what has been learned in a way that facilitates retention.

*Providing Explanations.*    At various times during a lesson, the teacher may be called on to explain something. Several things can be done to enhance the clarity of explanations.

It is important that potentially confusing terms be defined. Inexperienced teachers sometimes assume that learners know more than they really do. One of the authors remembers a time when a friend who was a high school teacher developed a marvelous presentation to a class on the topic "Recent Political Trends." At the end of the lecture, a student cautiously raised a hand to ask, "What is a trend?" The teacher had not considered the possibility that the word *trend* would not be in the working vocabularies of all of the students.

Teacher explanations communicate best when they are free from ambiguous, vague, and imprecise terms. Some examples of phrasing to be avoided include terms of approximation such as *kind of, sort of,* and *about.* Ambiguous designations such as *somehow, somewhere*, and *someone* also often fail the clarity test. Additionally, probability statements such as *frequently, generally,* and *often* do not communicate the same thing to all learners.

## Productive Use of Class Time

Researchers have found that learners in classes in which teachers maximize the amount of class time used for instruction perform better than those in classes where less time is spent on instruction (Good and Brophy, 1991). In some classrooms, as much as 50 percent of available time is devoted to nonacademic tasks. This situation deprives learners of much time that they need for working on academic tasks, and can have a strong, negative, long-term influence on achievement.

The time decisions that teachers make involve three basic types of time:

- allocated time
- engaged time
- academic learning time

## Allocated Time

Allocated time decisions are those teachers make concerning how much time is to be devoted to learning specific subjects or materials. Some of these decisions are made in light of state or local regulations. However, on a day-to-day basis these decisions ultimately fall to the teacher, and teachers vary greatly in how much time they allocate to given subjects or skills (Berliner, 1984).

Teachers' decisions about how to allocate time result from several considerations. Among them is a tendency to vary the amount of time allocated based on the difficulty of the material and the level of teacher interest in it. Researchers have found that teachers allocate more time to difficult topics and topics in which they (the teachers) have high levels of personal interest. These findings suggest a need to provide sufficient time for learners to master content that may not be particularly interesting or exciting to the teacher. Time allocation decisions need to be made in consideration of learners' needs, not teachers' preferences.

## Engaged Time

Allocated time is the total amount of time set aside for instruction related to a given subject or topic. Engaged time is that part of allocated time when instructional activities related to the subject or topic are occurring; other activities such as distributing materials, responding to learner questions of various kinds, and dealing with classroom management issues detract from the total of engaged time. Research reveals that teachers whose classrooms are characterized by high percentages of engaged time produce learners who achieve better than teachers whose classrooms are characterized by lower percentages of engaged time. Maintaining a high percentage of engaged time appears to be a particularly important variable in promoting the academic development of low-ability learners.

Engaged time is time spent on work that *clearly* relates to the lesson objective. There is no facilitating effect when learners are kept busy on make-work activities that are unrelated to lesson content.

## Academic Learning Time

Academic learning time is that portion of total engaged time when the learner is experiencing a high degree of academic success while working on the assigned task (Berliner, 1984). This definition goes beyond a concern for learners' working on content-related tasks to a concern for their success rates while they are so engaged. Higher rates of academic learning time are associated with increased levels of achievement (Berliner, 1984).

Teachers whose classes are characterized by high percentages of academic learning time monitor learners carefully to ensure that the learners understand the lesson. These teachers frequently ask learners what they are doing, and circulate through their classrooms as learners work on assigned tasks, providing corrective feedback to those students who are experiencing difficulties.

## Teacher Expectations

Teacher expectations refer to attitudes that teachers have about learners' individual potentials for academic success. They predispose teachers to look for different levels of achievement from different learners. These expectations are rarely verbalized; however, they do exert subtle influences on how teachers interact with different learners. Learners themselves often are affected by their comprehensions of what the teacher expects them to be able to do.

Suppose a learner for whom the teacher has low academic expectations volunteers to answer a question and is recognized. If this learner stumbles at the beginning of the response, the teacher may conclude that his or her difficulty results from a lack of knowledge. In response, the teacher may give the learner part of the answer, call on someone else, or even praise the learner just for being willing to volunteer. Such teacher responses communicate the teacher's lack of confidence in the learner's ability to respond correctly.

Teacher actions may be quite different when the volunteering learner is perceived to be academically talented. If such a student initially experiences difficulty, the teacher may provide cues and continue to work with the person until the correct response, which the teacher "knew" was there, is elicited. This sort of teacher action communicates to bright learners that the teacher will hold them to a high standard of performance and work with them until they meet it.

Good and Brophy (1991, pp. 110–32) point out a number of findings from research studies focusing on teacher expectations. Some of these include:

- Teachers have certain behavioral expectations of learners in their classes.
- Teachers' behaviors toward individual learners vary according to their expectations regarding what the individual learners can do.
- Differences in how they are viewed by teachers result in different learner self-concepts, levels of motivation, and aspirations.
- Teachers who are conscious of the impact of their expectations can monitor and adjust them in ways that can result in enhanced learner performance.

## Teachers' Questions

The view that to teach well is to question well has long had historic standing (DeGarmo, 1903). A large body of research supports the idea that effective teachers ask more questions than less effective teachers. In one study, effective junior high school mathematics teachers were found to ask an average of 24 questions during a class period, while their less effective counterparts asked an average of only 8.6 questions (Rosenshine and Stevens, 1986, p. 383).

Interest in questioning encompasses more than the issue of how many questions teachers ask. For example, many researchers have looked into the character and quality of the questions themselves, and schemes have been developed to categorize types of questions. One very simple approach divides questions into two general groups: (1) lower-level questions and (2) higher-level questions. Lower-level questions call on learners to recall specific items of previously introduced information. They do not demand sophisticated thinking. Higher-level questions, on the other hand, require learners to apply, analyze, integrate, create, or synthesize and use relatively complex thinking processes.

## When to Use Lower-Level and Higher-Level Questions

*Lower-Level Questions.*   Lower-level questions are appropriate when the teacher's purpose is to check learners' understanding of basic information. A productive pattern for this kind of questioning involves a three-part sequence:

- The teacher asks the question.
- The learner responds to it.
- The teacher reacts to the learner's response.

Research suggests that these questions should be delivered at a brisk pace and that learners should be expected to respond quickly (Good and Brophy, 1991). This allows for a large number of recall questions to be asked in a short period of time. It also provides opportunities for many learners in a class to respond. A fairly fast-paced pattern of questioning keeps learners alert, and gives the teacher opportunities to diagnose and respond to any misunderstandings revealed in answers from a wide cross-section of class members.

*Higher-Level Questions.*    If the teacher's aim is to stimulate more sophisticated learner thinking, then higher-level questions are preferred (see this chapter's Case Study). Redfield and Rousseau's (1981) survey of research related to questioning revealed that teachers' use of higher-level questions is associated with better learner achievement.

CASE STUDY

## Effective teaching research vs. standardized tests

**Naomi Belton is in her sixth year of teaching fourth graders at Lomax Elementary School**. During the summers and at night, she has been working on a master's degree in education. At this stage of her career, she is especially interested in improving her classroom instruction. This interest has prompted her to read the teacher-effectiveness literature in great depth, and she has also taken several courses on instructional improvement. From her study, she has become convinced of the importance of using higher-level questions in discussions to prompt more sophisticated levels of thinking from her pupils. She has been quite pleased with the results of her attempts to do so, and she feels that because of these attempts her pupils are becoming much more adept at analyzing sophisticated issues.

For all of her successes, Naomi is facing a problem that has come about from her asking larger numbers of higher-level questions. The problem concerns her social studies lessons. She feels this part of the instructional day lends itself especially well to discussions featuring higher-level questions, but it also happens to be an area that is part of the state's standardized testing program. In late spring, her pupils will spend two hours taking the state's grade four social studies achievement tests. From past experience, Naomi knows that most of the questions on the test are going to demand factual recall, not higher-level thinking skills.

The higher-level questions Naomi has been asking as part of her social studies lessons have brought about lots of good discussion and thinking. But all of this has consumed a great deal of time, and some of the content she used to cover simply has had to be skipped. She is afraid that this will result in her students earning poorer scores on the state achievement test than they would had she stuck to more traditional instruction. Naomi is torn between a desire to continue the lessons with the higher-level questions and a fear that doing so will make her look bad in administrators' eyes because test scores may go down.

*What should Naomi do? Are her concerns real? What are some consequences that might result if she decides to change her teaching style and abandon her commitment to higher-level questions? What are some consequences if she continues to present lessons using higher-level questions? Are there other people she should consult before making a decision? If so, who are they?*

Asking higher-level questions, by itself, will not ensure academic success; learners must have the knowledge base necessary to engage in complex thinking tasks. For a well-prepared high school class, a higher-level question such as "How would you compare and contrast the late nineteenth-century foreign policies of France and the United Kingdom?" might produce some insightful responses from learners. On the other hand, if students who were asked this question lacked basic information about the nineteenth-century foreign policies of the two countries, responses probably would reflect more wild guessing than sophisticated thought.

## Clarity of Questions

One difficulty teachers face is wording questions so that learners clearly perceive the teacher's intent. Many questions that appear deceptively simple on the surface can, upon closer examination, be responded to in many ways. For example, a learner could logically answer the question, "Who was the first President of the United States?" as follows:

- a man
- a Virginian
- a general
- a person named George Washington

To avoid this situation, questions need to be worded in ways that make it unnecessary for learners to guess at the nature of the information the teacher is seeking.

Some research suggests that teachers should avoid beginning a discussion with a series of questions. Cazden (1986) has argued that it is better for the teacher to provide some general background information before beginning to ask questions. This establishes a context for the questions to follow and results in better learner answers.

One practice that greatly interferes with clarity is asking a large question that contains two, three, or even more questions within it. Learners find this practice confusing, and they are often puzzled as to where to start their answers. Some learners deal with this dilemma by refusing to answer the question at all. It is much better for questions to be asked one at a time. Shorter questions are preferred (Good and Brophy, 1991), and the vocabulary used in them should be well within the grasp of the learners to whom they are directed.

## Checking on Learner Responses

Planning for successful questioning requires teachers to do more than prepare good questions—they must also be prepared to listen to what learners say and to respond appropriately. At one level, this amounts to nothing more than listening to responses to ensure that learners have a basic understanding of the content. If they don't, additional information needs to be presented, and low-level questions must then be asked to confirm whether or not they now understand it.

Teachers' responses vary in terms of what is happening in the classroom. For example, teachers often use probing questions to challenge learners' judgments when they jump to premature conclusions about complex issues. When a discussion featuring many questions has gone on for some time, teachers often pause to summarize what has been said. When learners are using vague terminology, teachers step in to ask for clarification. In summary, teachers' reactions should suggest to learners that their answers are being listened to carefully. This plants in learners the idea that responses to questions are important and should be made thoughtfully.

Teachers sometimes rely on homework as a means of checking on what learners have derived from a lesson or series of lessons. Sometimes, too, homework is assigned out of a belief that it facilitates achievement. To see what researchers have discovered about homework and learning, see the accompanying "What the Experts Say."

---

WHAT THE EXPERTS SAY

## The effectiveness of homework

Herman Cooper (1989) reviewed many research studies focusing on the relationship between homework and learner achievement. He found that studies generally reported that although homework had a positive influence on achievement, the magnitude of this effect varied greatly depending on learners' ages. Homework was found to have the most impact on the achievement of high school students. Homework's benefit for junior high school students' achievement was only about half as great as that for senior high school students. For elementary learners, homework was found to affect their levels of achievement only marginally.

For junior high school and senior high school students, length of homework assignments appears to have an impact. Academic achievement for junior high school students tends to go up with length of homework assignments until a limit somewhere between one and two hours a night is reached; longer homework assignments were not found to have a facilitating effect on learning of these students. Senior high school students profit from somewhat longer homework assignments than do junior high school students.

---

### Wait Time

The interval between the time a teacher asks a question and when a learner responds is called *wait time*. Teachers have been found to wait an astonishingly short period before either answering their own questions, rephrasing their questions, or calling on different learners to respond. Rowe (1986) reported that, on average, teachers wait less than one second for learners to respond.

Abundant research exists that supports a connection between the length of time teachers wait for responses after asking questions and learner achievement—achievement levels on tests demanding higher-level thinking have been found to be higher for students in classes where their teachers wait at least three seconds for responses to questions (Tobin, 1987).

Efforts to increase teacher wait time have produced good results. When the average wait time has increased, teachers have tended to ask a smaller number of total questions but to increase the number of higher-level questions among those that they have asked. These teachers have also been observed to make greater use of learners' answers in class discussions. Finally, an addition to their average wait times has changed teachers' attitudes about the capabilities of some learners (Rowe, 1986). This attitude change appears to stem from the fact that when average wait times are longer, some learners who have not previously answered questions become more active participants in discussions, and these increased levels of involvement result in teachers' raising their estimations of these learners' general abilities.

## Observing in the Classroom

Teachers often are interested in knowing whether their patterns of classroom behavior are consistent with those practices that researchers have found to be effective. Prospective teachers frequently have a need for systematic ways to gather information about what they observe in the classroom during observation experiences. Basic tools are available that can help both inservice and preservice teachers.

Basic methods of gathering information about what goes on in the classroom include (1) event sampling and (2) time sampling. Event sampling requires the observer to record information about individual events that are of interest. For example, an observer might be interested in noting what the teacher does to motivate learners. In such a case, the observer would simply write down everything the teacher did related to the general issue of motivation.

In time sampling, the observer records what is happening in the classroom at selected time intervals. For example, an observer could decide to take a sample once every 15 seconds. If the teacher were lecturing at the end of the first 15-second interval, the observer would simply note "1—lecturing." If the lecture were still going on at the end of the next 15-second interval, the observer would write "2—lecturing." If the teacher were asking a question at the end of the third 15-second interval, the observer would write "3—teacher question." This kind of a scheme results in information that will provide a general profile of activity during a lesson. It suggests the general flow of a lesson and provides a great deal of information for analysis.

Many different kinds of observational tools can be developed based on event sampling, time sampling, or a combination of the two approaches. Some examples are introduced in the following subsections.

## Narrative Approaches

Observers using narrative approaches, sometimes referred to as *scripting* approaches, try to capture information about what is going on in the classroom by rapidly writing down everything that is observed. Since much of what happens in a classroom is verbal, narrative approaches often focus heavily on what the teacher and learners say.

A basic problem with an unstructured narrative approach is that so much happens in a classroom so quickly that it is impossible for *everything* to be recorded, and what results is just a partial picture of what happened. To avoid this general limitation of an unstructured narrative approach, some observers prefer to use a more narrowly focused version, called *selective verbatim*.

When using a selective verbatim approach, the observer identifies a particular dimension of classroom verbal interaction in which he or she is interested. Then the

This classroom observer is using an observational tool to gather information that will be shared later with the teacher. The teacher will use this information to make decisions about changes in procedures.

observer records everything said that falls into this targeted category. Targeted categories might include such areas as "teacher questions," "motivational statements," "classroom control statements," and "praise statements." The focus for a selective verbatim approach is limited only by the creativity and interests of the observer.

Suppose an observer were interested in the types of praise statements a teacher made. During the observation period, the observer would write down everything the teacher said each time a learner was praised. (Sometimes observers record the lesson so they can recheck the accuracy of what they wrote down during the live observation.)

Results of a selective verbatim observation can be organized into a selective verbatim record, which can provide data for a useful analysis. For example, had the focus been praise behavior, an observer may want to consider such questions as:

- Did the teacher use a variety of praise statements?
- How adequate was the quantity of praise statements?
- Were praise statements tied more to academic performance or to other kinds of learner behavior?

- Were more praise statements directed toward individuals or to the class as a whole?

An example of a selective verbatim record is provided in Figure 11–1.

## Frequency Counts

Frequency counts focus on the number of occurrences of behaviors of interest. Behavior categories are identified by the observer before the observation begins. Frequency count observations might focus on such categories as:

- the number of teacher praise statements
- the number of high-level teacher questions (demanding sophisticated thinking)
- the number of low-level teacher questions (demanding only simple recall of basic information)
- the number of classroom disruptions
- the number of times individual learners visit learning centers
- the number of times learners made correct (or incorrect) responses to teacher questions
- the number of times learners asked questions

Frequency count systems are easy to use. A simple record is maintained of the number of times each selected focus behavior occurs. Tally marks are often used to indicate each occurrence.

**Figure 11–1**
Example of a selective verbatim record

| **Focus: Teacher praise statements** | |
|---|---|
| **Kind of lesson: Arithmetic—Grade 5** | |
| **Time** | **Teacher Statements** |
| 9:02 | Thank you for sitting down. |
| 9:03 | I appreciate that. |
| 9:05 | You have really been doing a good job on this unit. |
| 9:09 | Good answer. |
| 9:10 | Okay, good. |
| 9:13 | Good, I like that. |
| 9:13 | Right! |
| 9:15 | Good. |
| 9:18 | Juan, you used a good method for finding the answer. |
| 9:20 | I'm glad you all started to work so promptly. |

An example of a frequency count system is provided in Figure 11–2. Look at Figure 11–2. Because frequency count systems do not require much writing, it is possible for tallies to be made related to a fairly large number of behaviors. This particular example yields information that might help an observer to identify some types of teacher behavior that seem to result in greater learner involvement in the lesson. The results of this procedure would not allow for identification of a direct cause-and-effect relationship, but they might hint at behaviors that merit consideration.

**Focus: Teacher statements and their relationship to learner participation in a discussion**

Directions: Tally each teacher behavior that has a positive impact on getting learners involved in the discussion. (These are found under the heading "Teacher Facilitating Moves.") Also tally each teacher behavior that has a negative impact on getting learners involved in the discussion. (These are found under the heading "Teacher Inhibiting Moves.") Tally learner responses that are correct and those that are incorrect. Also provide a tally for each time the teacher asks a question and there is no learner response at all. Finally, tally each time a learner initiates a question or a comment. (These are to be made under the heading "Learner Responses.")

**Teacher Facilitating Moves**

Asks clear question:

Asks for learner response (waits more than three seconds):

Praises learner comment:

Uses learner comment in lesson:

Provides positive nonverbal reinforcement:

**Teacher Inhibiting Moves**

Asks ambiguous question:

Asks multiple questions:

Does not wait for learner response:

Criticizes learner response:

Sends negative nonverbal signals:

**Learner Responses**

Number of correct learner responses:

Number of incorrect learner responses:

Absence of any learner responses to question:

Number of learner-initiated questions or comments:

**Figure 11–2**
Example of a frequency-count system

## Coding Systems

Coding systems require the use of codes or symbols that represent behaviors of interest to the observer. Symbols may vary in their complexity, from a simple system of checks, minuses, and pluses to a complex scheme that assigns numbers to a wide array of individual behaviors. Usually, a record using the codes is made after a preestablished interval of time has passed. For example, the observer might use codes to record behaviors once every 20 seconds.

It is not always necessary for an observer to have the entire coding scheme completely developed before a classroom observation begins. Sometimes new codes can be added during the observation itself as interesting behaviors occur that had not been included in the initial scheme. This ability to add new codes even during the observation gives a great deal of flexibility to observation systems using coding schemes.

For example, suppose an observer began an observation with a very simple coding scheme in mind. It might feature just these two codes:

1—indicates a learner who is working on the assigned task
2—indicates a learner who is not working on the assigned task

During the actual observation, the observer might note that some learners were out of their seat, talking, or working on school work other than the assigned task. The observer may decide to add specific codes to indicate these behaviors. (One way to do this would be to designate code 2a for "out of seat," code 2b for "talking," and code 2c for "other school work." Code "2" would be reserved for all other examples of learners' not working on assigned tasks.)

An example of an observation system using coding is provided in Figure 11–3.

## Seating-Chart Systems

Observation systems involving the use of seating charts often are appropriate when the focus is on learner behaviors. For example, it might be useful to know which learners are contributing to a discussion or which ones are staying on task when the teacher has assigned seat work. Seating chart schemes also work well when there is an interest in pinpointing the location of the teacher during various parts of the instructional period. For example, a system might be devised that would record information about which learners the teacher worked with during a given class period.

In developing a seating-chart system, the observer begins by making a sketch of the classroom that includes the locations of individual learner seats. Once this basic chart has been completed and learners have entered the classroom, often observers note whether individual seats are occupied by males or females. This can be done by writing a small *m* for male or a small *f* for female on each seat represented in the chart.

Next, the observer develops a set of symbols to represent the various aspects of instruction that are to be emphasized. For example, a simple arrow pointing to a seat might indicate a teacher question to a particular learner, and a simple arrow pointing away from the seat might indicate a communication directed from a particular learner to the teacher. Numerals or letters might be designated to stand for different kinds of things individual learners are observed doing at selected time intervals during the lesson. The location of the teacher at specific places in the room at different times

**Focus: Motivational strategies**

Directions: During each five-minute time segment of the lesson, record the letters indicating the motivational strategies used by the teacher. Record letters in the sequence of their occurrence. If new motivational strategies are used that are not on the list, add them and give them a letter.

| Motivational Strategy | Record |
|---|---|
| | 5 min. |
| a.   Uses novelty | _____ |
| b.   Appeals to curiosity | _____ |
| c.   Provides concrete reinforcer | _____ |
| d.   Provides dramatic build-up | _____ |
| e.   Indicates importance of task | _____ |
| | 5 min. |
| f.   Relates to learner needs, interests | _____ |
| g.   Provides encouragement | _____ |
| h.   Predicts success or enjoyment | _____ |
| i.   Warns about testing, grades | _____ |
| j.   Threatens punishment for non-completion | _____ |
| | 5 min. |
| k.   _____ | _____ |
| l.   _____ | _____ |
|      _____ | _____ |
|      _____ | _____ |
|      _____ | _____ |
| | 5 min. |
|      _____ | _____ |
|      _____ | _____ |
|      _____ | _____ |
|      _____ | _____ |

**Figure 11–3**
Example of a coding system observation scheme

might be indicated by a sequence of circled numbers (1 indicating the first location, 2 indicating the second, and so forth). Any symbols that work for the observer are acceptable.

Figure 11–4 provides an example of an observational system that features a seating chart. Many interesting questions can be answered by examining data gathered from a seating chart system. Look at the sample information provided in the chart featured in Figure 11–4. Using this information, an observer might be able to answer questions such as:

- How many learners were involved in the discussion?
- Were more males or females called on?
- Did the teacher have a tendency to call more frequently on learners seated on one side of the room? Seated in the front as opposed to the back of the room?
- How many learners who volunteered were not recognized by the teacher? What might be the long-term impact on a learner's willingness to volunteer if he or she were rarely recognized?

Systematic observation can yield a rich harvest of useful information. These data can pinpoint practices that facilitate learner achievement and contribute to the development of positive concepts. Carefully planned observations undertaken by prospective teachers have the potential to provide them with important insights about the real world of the public school classroom.

........................................

## Key Ideas in Summary

- Arguments have long raged over the issue of whether a body of research evidence exists that can adequately define what is meant by "effective" teaching. Increasingly, though, evidence is indicating that at least some variables associated with effective teaching have been discovered.

- Most research on effective teaching has focused on teacher behaviors associated with increases in learners' levels of achievement. This emphasis has been supported in recent years by public concerns about the issue of subject-matter learning in the schools.

- In active teaching, the teacher plays a central role and leads the class in his/her role as a (1) presenter of new information, (2) monitor of learner progress, (3) planner of opportunities for learners to apply what they have learned, and (4) reteacher of content to learners who are confused.

- Active teachers are much concerned about the issue of matching their instruction to needs of individual learners. In achieving an appropriate match, they consider such things as the difficulty of the material relative to the individual learner's nature and the learner's level of interest in the content to be taught.

**Observation focus: Identifying discussion participants**

**Lesson topic: Review for a test**

Directions: Each space in the chart below represents a learner seat. Sex of learners should be indicated by an *m* for males and an *f* for females. The following symbols are drawn in the box denoting the learner's seat and are used to indicate the first time the particular behavior is noted:

- A learner raises a hand to volunteer (indicated by a vertical line).

- A learner is recognized and makes a contribution (indicated by an arrow pointed away from the learner).

- The teacher calls on a learner (indicated by a down-pointing arrow).

- A learner is called but fails to respond (indicated by a zero drawn immediately below the down-pointing arrow indicating a teacher question).

- Repetitions of the same behavior are indicated by horizontal marks across the vertical ones. Note examples below:

This learner volunteered four times, but was not called on.

This learner was called on and made a contribution twice.

This learner was called on three times.

**Seating Chart with Sample Data**

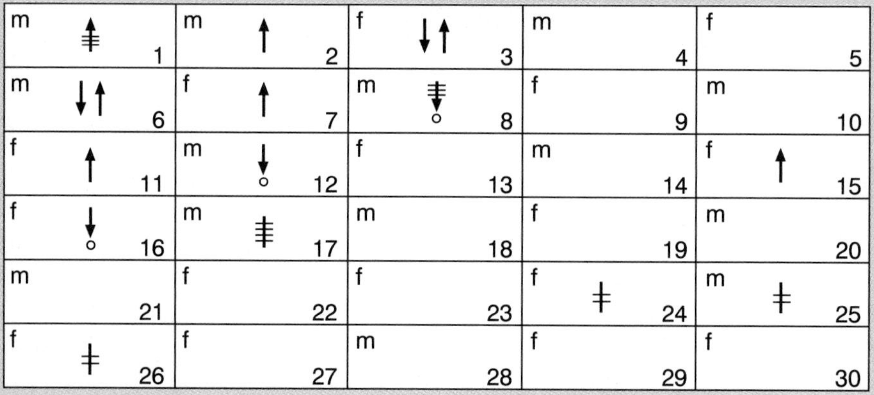

**Figure 11–4**
An example of a seating chart observation scheme (with sample data)

- Active teachers are much concerned about the issue of good lesson presentation. This involves actions designed to (1) stimulate and maintain learner interest, (2) present material systematically, (3) model expected behaviors and expected products of learning, (4) maintain an appropriate lesson pace, (5) ask questions skillfully, (6) provide opportunities for learners to practice what they have learned, and (7) monitor learners' progress.

- Research has established the importance of clarity as a teacher variable associated with learner achievement. Among dimensions of clarity are the teacher's verbal and nonverbal styles, lesson-presentation style, and proficiency in providing cogent explanations.

- Effective teachers use class time productively. They make decisions related to allocated time, engaged time, and academic learning time.

- Teachers' expectations have an influence on how individual learners perform. Researchers have found that (1) teachers have certain behavioral expectations of learners, (2) teachers' behaviors toward learners vary in terms of what they feel that individual learners can do, (3) learners' self-concepts are affected by how they perceive themselves to be viewed by their teachers, and (4) teachers who are conscious of the impact of their expectations can monitor and adjust them in ways that can improve learners' performance.

- Teachers' questioning patterns have been found to influence learning. Teachers tend to ask questions of two basic types: lower-level questions and higher-level questions. Lower-level questions call on learners to recall specific items of previously introduced information. Higher-level questions require learners to use more complex thinking processes.

- Many observation systems are available that can be used to provide specific information to teachers about what goes on in their classrooms. Some of these approaches use time sampling, others use event sampling, and still others employ a combination of the two.

## Review and Discussion Questions

1. Is there research-based knowledge available today that pinpoints behaviors associated with effective teaching?

2. What criteria should be used in determining a teacher's relative effectiveness?

3. What are some general characteristics of active teaching?

4. What goes on during the task analysis phase of instructional planning?

5. What are some differences between motivation that occur (*a*) before a learning sequence begins, (*b*) during a learning sequence, and (*c*) at the end of a learning sequence?

**Table 11–1**
Summary table: Effective teaching practices

| Topic | Key Points |
|---|---|
| Active teaching | Refers to teaching in which the teacher leads instructional activities by personally directing and involving himself or herself in what learners are doing. |
| • Program planning | This dimension of active teaching requires teachers to engage in task analysis and specifying objectives. |
| • Lesson presentation | This component of active teaching gives teachers responsibilities related to stimulating and maintaining interest, presenting information systematically, personal and product modeling, lesson pacing, questioning, establishing an appropriate instructional pace, and monitoring learners' progress. |
| • Teacher clarity | Among variables associated with this are the teacher's verbal and nonverbal styles, lesson-presentation structure, and proficiency in providing cogent explanations. |
| Productive use of class time | Researchers have established that learners in classes taught by teachers who maximize the total amount of class time used for instruction perform better than learners in classes featuring smaller proportions of instructional time. |
| • Allocated time | Refers to time that has been scheduled for a particular instructional purpose. |
| • Engaged time | Refers to that part of allocated time when instructional activities related to a specific topic are actually taking place. |
| • Academic learning time | Refers to that part of total engaged time when learners are experiencing high levels of academic success while working on an assigned task. |

**Table 11–1**
*continued*

| Topic | Key Points |
| --- | --- |
| Teacher expectations | These have been found to exert a strong influence on how learners feel about their own abilities and on their levels of success on academic tasks. |
| Teachers' questions | Teachers tend to ask two basic kinds of questions: lower-level questions and higher-level questions. Research suggests that more-effective teachers ask more questions than do less-effective teachers. |
| • Lower-level questions | These are most appropriate when the teacher's purpose is to check on understanding of basic information. |
| • Higher-level questions | These are recommended when the teacher's purpose is to stimulate more sophisticated thinking. Some research supports the idea that increased use of higher-level questions is associated with better levels of learner achievement. |
| • Clarity of questions | Clarity is enhanced when questions are short, do not have many parts, and are worded in ways that effectively communicate to learners the teacher's intent. |
| • Checking on learners' responses | This requires the teacher to listen carefully and respond appropriately to learners' answers to questions. |
| • Wait time | It takes time for learners to think about what has been asked and develop an answer. Research has found that learner achievement goes up when teachers increase the amount of time they wait for answers to questions. An increase in wait time decreases the number of questions that can be asked, but it increases the number of learners who participate and, often, it changes teachers' preconceptions about the abilities of some learners in their classes. |

**Table 11–1**
*continued*

| Topic | Key Points | |
|---|---|---|
| | **Basic Features** | **Strengths/Weaknesses** |
| Narrative approaches | Observer writes down what he or she sees. Sometimes the focus is narrowed so only certain kinds of behaviors are noted. This is a special feature of the narrative approach referred to as *selective verbatim*. | Very flexible. This approach can gather information both about the teacher and the learners. Too much happens too fast for everything to be recorded. Some important information may be missed. |
| Frequency-count approaches | The observer focuses on a limited number of behaviors and makes a tally each time one of these behaviors occurs. | Frequency-count approaches can be used to focus on many different kinds of behaviors. It must be easy for the observer to see the beginning and ending points of the focus behaviors. Results can be misleading. Tallies may suggest that behavior A occurred 10 times and behavior B only once, but this information says nothing about the duration of these behaviors—the single episode of category B behavior could have lasted longer than the combined total of the 10 episodes of category A behavior. |

**Table 11–1**
*continued*

| Topic | Key Points | |
|-------|------------|---|
| | **Basic Features** | **Strengths/Weaknesses** |
| Coding systems | Coding systems use symbols or codes to denote behaviors that are of interest to an observer. Typically, instruments involving the use of codes ask the observer to use the appropriate code to denote whatever behavior is occurring at preestablished intervals. | Coding systems are very flexible. Codes can be devised to denote many kinds of behaviors. New codes can even be added during an observation. The ease of creating codes can be a limitation. It sometimes is tempting for observers to develop more codes than they can accurately manage during a single observation session. |
| Seating-chart systems | These observation schemes include charts indicating where individual learners are seated. They almost always are used in situations where the observer has some interest in one or more learner behaviors. | Seating-chart systems can generate data that can be used to answer large numbers of questions. They are particularly good when there is an interest in focusing on behaviors of individual learners and on patterns of teacher–learner interaction. Though they can be used in a variety of situations, seating-chart systems do require a setting where the observer can easily view each seat in the classroom. The systems work only when observers have no difficulty observing the behavior of every learner in the class. |

6. What are the steps in the Hunter-Russell model?

7. Why is the issue of clarity so important, and what are some dimensions of teacher clarity?

8. Is a teacher decision to increase the amount of (*a*) allocated time related to a given topic or (*b*) academic learning related to a given topic more likely to increase the overall performance of a class on a test related to the selected topic?

9. In what ways do effective teachers ask classroom questions differently from less effective teachers?

10. What are some features of observation instruments based on (*a*) narrative approaches, (*b*) frequency counts, (*c*) coding systems, and (*d*) seating-chart systems?

......................................

# Ideas for Field Experiences, Projects, and Enrichment

1. Review ideas for gathering observational data. Select one category associated with teacher effectiveness that was introduced in this chapter. Visit a classroom and gather data related to this category using an observation system of your own design. You may wish to consider a scheme based on (*a*) a narrative approach, (*b*) frequency counts, (*c*) a coding system, or (*d*) a seating chart.

2. A thread that runs through much recent teacher-effectiveness research is the idea that effective behaviors are contextual. This means that a pattern that is effective with certain kinds of learners and for teaching certain levels of understanding or skills may not necessarily work well with other learners and for teaching other levels of understanding. With your instructor's guidance, review some research literature associated with the topic of direct instruction. Under what circumstances does this approach seem to work well? Under what circumstances has it been found to be less appropriate? Present your conclusions in the form of a brief oral report.

3. Some of the research on teacher effectiveness has produced results that have surprised some people, particularly when the discovered information has challenged some popularly held beliefs. With your instructor's guidance, look up some research findings associated with teacher praise. Is teacher praise always good? Report your conclusions in the form of a short paper.

4. Today, teachers are increasingly getting involved with research in their own classrooms. Much of this research is directed at improving their own instruction. Review some articles in education journals (look for titles in such sources as the *Education Index*) that focus on the topic of the teacher as researcher. Then share with the rest of the class what you find out about the approaches

teachers are taking to gather research about their own instruction, and some of the things this research is revealing.

5. Prepare a list of source materials related to research data about effective teaching. Ask your instructor for some ideas to get you started. Share your list with those prepared by others in your class. Eliminate common entries, produce a single composite list, and prepare copies for the files of all class members.

••••••••••••••••••••••••••••••

# Supplementary Reading

Berliner, D. C. "Effective Schools: Teachers Make the Difference." *Instructor* (October 1989): 14–15.

Ramsey, I., C. Gabbard, K. Clawson, L. Lee, and K. Henson. "Questioning: An Effective Teaching Method." *The Clearing House* (May 1990): 420–22.

Rowe, M. B. "Wait Time: Slowing Down May Be a Way of Speeding Up." *Journal of Teacher Education* (January–February 1986): 43–50.

Wittrock, M., ed. *Handbook of Research on Teaching*. 3d ed. New York: Macmillan, 1986.

••••••••••••••••••••••••••••••

# References

Berliner, D. C. "The Half-Full Glass: A Review of Research on Teaching." In P. L. Hosford, ed. *Using What We Know about Teaching*. Alexandria, VA: Association for Supervision and Curriculum Development, 1984, 51–77.

Cazden, C. "Classroom Discourse." In M. Wittrock, ed. *Handbook of Research on Teaching*. 3d ed. New York: Macmillan, 1986, 432–63.

Cooper, H. "Synthesis of Research on Homework." *Educational Leadership* (November 1989): 85–91.

DeGarmo, C. *Interest in Education: The Doctrine of Interest and Its Concrete Applications*. New York: Macmillan, 1903.

Denton, J. J., D. G. Armstrong, and T. V. Savage. "Matching Events of Instruction to Objectives." *Theory into Practice* (Winter 1980): 10–14.

Good, T. L., and J. E. Brophy. *Looking in Classrooms*. 5th ed. New York: HarperCollins, 1991.

Goodlad, J. *A Place Called School*. New York: McGraw-Hill, 1984.

Hunter, M., and D. Russell. "How Can I Plan More Effective Lessons?" *Instructor* (September 1977): 74–75; 88.

Meyer, A. E. *Grandmasters of Educational Thought*. New York: McGraw-Hill, 1975.

Posner, R. S. "Pacing and Sequencing." In M. J. Dunken, ed. *The International Encyclopedia of Teaching and Teacher Education*. Oxford, England: Pergamon Press, 1987, 266–72.

Redfield, D., and E. Rousseau. "A Meta-Analysis of Experimental Research on Teacher Questioning Behavior." *Review of Educational Research* (Summer 1981): 237–45.

Rosenshine, B., and R. Stevens. "Teaching Functions." In M. Wittrock, ed., *Handbook of Research on Teaching*. 3d ed. New York: Macmillan, 1986.

Rowe, M. B. "Wait Time: Slowing Down May Be a Way of Speeding Up." *Journal of Teacher Education* (January–February 1986): 43–50.

Tobin, K. "The Role of Wait Time in Higher Cognitive Learning." *Review of Educational Research* (Spring 1987): 69–95.

# Chapter 12

# Classroom Management and Discipline

## Objectives

This chapter provides information to help the reader to

- identify the relationship between instruction and classroom management.
- list aspects of space management that should be considered when thinking about issues related to classroom management and discipline.
- suggest some ways that materials can be organized and managed to facilitate smooth functioning of the instructional process.
- identify routines necessary for a well-ordered instructional environment.
- point out the importance of planning for transitions.
- describe the basic goal of discipline.
- list some characteristics of teachers who effectively respond to inappropriate classroom behavior.
- identify some principles that ought to be considered by teachers when they prepare plans for discipline.
- describe alternative teacher responses to inappropriate learner behavior.

# Focus Questions

1. In what ways are good teaching and good classroom management related?
2. What are some ways that teachers can organize time, space, and materials to facilitate smooth functioning of their classes?
3. How can the class be organized to maximize the specific time that learners spend on productive classroom activities?
4. In what ways can developing procedures for dealing with routine classroom occurrences help teachers when discipline problems arise?
5. What is the major goal of disciplinary procedures in the classroom?
6. What patterns of behavior are characteristic of many teachers who are considered to be effective classroom managers and disciplinarians?
7. What are some alternatives available to teachers when serious misbehaviors occur, and what is the relationship between the nature of the unacceptable behavior and how the teacher reacts?
8. What are some kinds of power available to classroom teachers?
9. What are some reasons that corporal punishment is not recommended as a teacher response to classroom misbehavior?

. . . . . . . . . . . . . . . . . . . . . . . . . . .

# Introduction

Classroom instruction includes two closely related teacher responsibilities: teaching learners and managing the classroom (Savage, 1991). Teaching and managing are closely connected—good teaching deters misbehavior problems, and sound management procedures provide a context within which good teaching can occur.

Teacher-preparation programs devote considerable time to acquainting prospective teachers with how-to-teach information. Sometimes, classroom management issues receive much less attention, and this is a mistake. Fear that they will not be able to control learners is a major cause of stress among prospective teachers.

This potential problem needs to be placed in a proper perspective. The vast majority of difficulties that confront classroom teachers are not serious. They include irritations such as learners' failure to pay attention, talking when they should be doing assigned work, or leaving their desks at inappropriate times. Although more serious problems do occur, they certainly are not present all the time in most classrooms.

In this chapter, two basic aspects of classroom management are addressed. The first focuses on problem prevention through the use of good management techniques. The second introduces procedures that have been found useful as responses to inappropriate learner behaviors.

## Dimensions of Classroom Management

Management decisions relate to organization of time, space, and materials with the ultimate goal of facilitating smooth and efficient classroom operation. Classroom management might be thought of as the prevention dimension of classroom control.

Researchers have identified some characteristics of effective classroom managers. Kounin (1970) found that although successful and unsuccessful classroom managers responded to inappropriate learner behavior in similar ways, there were important differences in how they organized and managed their classrooms.

Subsequent investigations have suggested that smoothly functioning classrooms result when teachers take deliberate actions to plan a management strategy very early in the school year, or even before school starts (Emmer, Evertson, and Anderson, 1980; Evertson, 1989). In making this connection, Carolyn Evertson (1989) commented, " . . . solving managerial and organizational problems at the beginning of the year is essential in laying the groundwork for quality learning opportunities for students" (p. 90). Teachers who follow this practice develop clear ideas about how they expect their classrooms to operate, and then communicate them to their learners. Further, successful managers carefully organize space arrangements and instructional materials to be used in their classrooms in advance of learners' arrival.

## Space Management

Teachers consider several parts of the classroom when they prepare to organize classroom space. Among these are floor space, learner work spaces, wall space, and the space provided for books and materials.

Good classroom managers take action to ensure that learners understand basic rules.

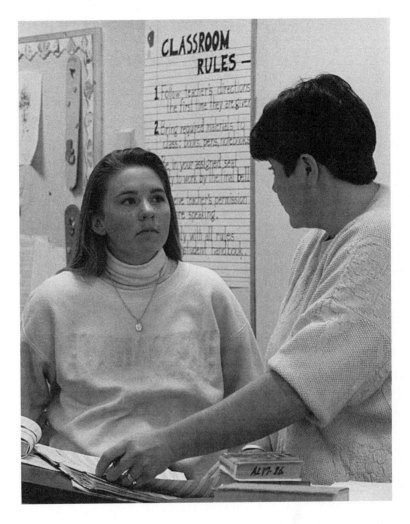

*Floor Space.*    The nature of anticipated instructional activities helps determine the most appropriate organization of classroom floor space. Some types of activities feature whole-group instruction. Others involve the teacher's working with small groups of learners. Still others require learners to be scattered throughout the room at different learning or activity centers.

Whole-group instruction requires a physical arrangement that permits all learners to maintain good eye contact with the teacher. Desks must be arranged to provide for this need. Occasionally, the teacher will want to check on an individual learner's work or understanding during whole-group instruction. To facilitate easy movement throughout the classroom, desks need to be arranged to allow for aisles or spaces that permit the teacher to move quickly to meet personally with learners who might be experiencing problems.

In planning floor arrangements for small-group discussion, learning spaces need to be arranged so the teacher can continue to monitor the whole class while working with one small group. If possible, seating spaces for the small group with whom the teacher is working should be located at some distance from other learners. This diminishes the temptation for small-group members to talk to others in the class. It also helps reduce the general noise level, something that makes it easier for all learners to stay at their assigned tasks.

Learning centers need to be placed in areas of the classroom that are easily accessible to all learners, and yet are not distracting to those individuals who are not working at the centers. When centers feature films, filmstrips, or some other projected media, they should be placed out of the direct sight lines of learners who are not working at the centers, as such media can be very distracting to other learners.

*Traffic Patterns.*    In planning the physical organization of classrooms, traffic patterns must also be considered. As a beginning point, it is necessary to identify those parts of the room that are heavily used. These would include such areas as doorways, places where learners' personal belongings and class materials are stored, book storage areas, and the vicinity of the teacher's desk. Space around these frequently visited parts of the classroom need to be kept obstruction-free. Desks should be arranged so that people going to and from these areas of the classroom can do so without disturbing other learners.

*Teacher's Desk.*    In many classrooms, the teacher's desk is located at the front and center of the room. This may not be the best location. A better choice is an unobtrusive place in the back part of the room. Locating the desk here encourages the teacher to stand up and move around the classroom. This movement, in turn, often leads to more careful monitoring of learners' work. Teachers who circulate through the classroom and avoid sitting behind a desk are perceived by learners as "warmer" (Smith, 1987).

*Wall Space.*    Constructive use of wall space enhances the quality of the instructional environment. Parts of the walls can be devoted to motivational displays to stimulate interests in topics that are being studied. Others can be reserved to display learners' work. (This is particularly important in elementary schools.) Other areas can be used to display schedules, important announcements, and classroom rules.

*Equipment Storage.*    Teachers use a variety of specialized equipment. Many schools have items such as projectors (e.g., 16 mm, slide, opaque, or overhead), video- and audiotape recorders, television monitors, phonographs, and computers. Some of these items are kept in individual classrooms. Storage space for this equipment needs to be both secure and accessible. Maintaining equipment in good operating order is a major headache for school officials. The possibilities for misuse or malicious damage decrease when equipment is stored in a way that permits access only by authorized people. When possible, it is wise to store equipment in cabinets or other areas that can be locked.

Box 12–1 asks you to consider all of these aspects when arranging a classroom of your own.

## Time Management

Effective time management helps to keep learners engaged in academic tasks. Researchers have found that, in many classrooms, a surprisingly high percentage of

BOX 12–1
# ORGANIZING CLASSROOM SPACE

Good instruction and classroom control are facilitated when classroom space is well-organized. Organization will vary depending on such variables as (1) the nature of content being taught, (2) the nature of grouping arrangements to be used, (3) the age and maturity levels of learners to be served, and (4) limitations that have been built into the physical space of the classroom. Suppose you were about to begin your first week of teaching and were working at your school several days before the start of classes. Describe how you would arrange your room. (You might want to draw a sketch of the room that illustrates what you have in mind.)

*What Do You Think?*
1. Where would you locate the teacher's desk?
2. How would learners' desks be arranged?
3. What would be your preferred locations for chalkboards and bulletin boards?
4. If you had movable storage cabinets, where would you want to locate them?
5. Suppose someone challenged you to explain the choices you made in your response to Questions 1–4. What kind of a rationale could you provide to support each of your decisions?

time is spent on noninstructional tasks (Smyth, 1987). They have also determined that learners in classes where teachers spend more time on instruction learn more (Berliner, 1984).

*Transitions.*    Management of transitions is an important dimension of time management. Transitions occur when there is a shift from one activity to another, and they offer the potential for much class time to be lost. To keep this from happening, careful plans need to be made for transition points within lessons.

Materials are often distributed at transition points. If they are organized in advance, new materials can be quickly placed in learners' hands. Sometimes transitions require learners to move from one part of an instructional area to another or from one room to another. Guidelines that explain to learners exactly how these moves are to be made can save valuable time. Time saved through careful planning of transitions can augment the total time available for instruction.

*Beginning Class.*    Classes should start promptly. This means that tasks such as taking attendance, returning learners' work, and other routine administrative duties need to be performed quickly. To cue learners that it is time for instruction to begin, some teachers have developed a system to signal learners that they should be quiet and ready to start the lesson. For example, this sometimes is done by the teacher's moving to a certain place in the front of the class and looking out over the learners. At the beginning of the school year, class members are taught that this action means instruction is about to begin.

A lesson should not be started until all learners are paying attention. Teachers must avoid straining their voices; they are likely to become hoarse if they have to sustain a volume level loud enough to be heard over learners' unauthorized side conversations. Additionally, when teachers insist on quiet before they begin, they signal to learners that what they say is important and worth hearing.

*Lesson Pacing.*    Lessons should move briskly, but not so fast as to confuse learners. A certain amount of repetition is necessary to highlight key points. However, excessive repetition leads to boredom. It is a natural human tendency to seek relief from boredom. In classrooms, this search often results in unacceptable learner behaviors.

To help them decide on an appropriate instructional pace, some teachers select a "reference group" in their class. Members of the reference group include four or five learners who represent a cross-section of class members. The teacher watches the reactions of these learners. Based on how these people are responding, the teacher speeds up, maintains, or slows down the instructional pace.

Part of planning for pacing involves anticipating that some learners will finish assignments sooner than others. Follow-up activities need to be designed for early finishers so that they can immediately make the transition into another productive activity. These follow-up activities need to be carefully chosen—they should not be "more of the same." If this happens, bright learners may conclude that they are being punished for finishing their work quickly. On the other hand, these follow-up experiences cannot be so enticing that learners race through the assigned task just to gain more time for working on them.

*Providing Assistance.*    Often while learners are working on assignments, many of them will seek help from the teacher at the same time. A teacher with 25 to 30 learners can be frustrated when trying to help all of those looking for assistance. Frederic H. Jones (1979) has suggested some guidelines for responding to this problem. In his research, he found that the average teacher spends much more time working with individual learners than is necessary. To decrease the total time spent with each person and, hence, increase the opportunities to help more individuals seeking assistance, the following procedure is recommended for use with each learner seeking the teacher's assistance:

- First, the teacher should build confidence by finding something the learner has done correctly and then praising the good work.
- Second, the teacher should provide a direct suggestion about what the learner should do next. (But the teacher should *not* do the work for the learner.)
- After completing the first two steps, the teacher should move on quickly to the next learner.

Jones (1979) has pointed out that this process will enable the teacher to help a large number of learners in a relatively short time period. He has recommended that, on average, no more than 20 seconds be spent with a single learner. If there is a need to do so, the teacher can check back with learners who are experiencing difficulties after the needs of other learners have been attended to.

### Establishing Routines and Procedures

A basic principle of classroom management is that routines and procedures need to be developed to manage recurring and predictable events (see the accompanying What the Experts Say). During a typical day, a teacher experiences hundreds of personal contacts with learners. Unless systems for managing these contacts are developed, teachers' emotional reserves may be drained by the end of the day.

---

WHAT THE EXPERTS SAY

## *Establishing classroom rules and procedures*

Researchers have found that effective teachers are particularly good at establishing classroom rules and procedures at the beginning of the school year (Doyle, 1986). This is particularly true in elementary and junior high school settings.

Apparently, it is not enough to simply identify and post these guidelines—effective teachers go beyond this and take class time to teach these rules and procedures to their learners in a systematic way. Further, their guidelines tend to be written in language that is clear, explicit, and which makes it easy for learners to know when they are in compliance.

Effective teachers have been found to monitor compliance with established rules and procedures carefully, and are quick to react when learners behave in ways contrary to these guidelines. Finally, these effective teachers periodically take time to remind students about what these rules and procedures specify regarding acceptable patterns of classroom behavior.

---

Routines and procedures are often developed for such things as:

- what learners are to do as soon as they enter the classroom
- what learners should do when they have a personal problem to discuss with the teacher
- what procedures are to be used in passing out and collecting materials
- when and where pencils are to be sharpened
- how daily attendance is to be taken
- what learners are to do when they need to leave the room

Once procedures and routines have been planned, those involving learner behaviors need to be explained to class members. With younger learners, this information sometimes is taught as a formal lesson. With more mature, secondary school students, a

This teacher is helping a learner who is working on an assignment. When teachers develop efficient procedures for helping all learners who experience difficulties with assigned tasks, classroom control problems diminish.

brief explanation of expectations and procedures may suffice. When class members understand operating procedures and learn to follow them, teachers have time to concentrate their attention on dealing calmly and effectively with unexpected events.

## Responding to Learner Misbehavior: Contexts for Effective Practice

Even in classrooms where lessons are exciting and teachers are good managers, learners occasionally misbehave. Dealing with inappropriate behavior involves more than just responding to a specific incident; the teacher should strive to help learners develop internal behavior controls that will prompt them to behave in acceptable ways. The major purpose of teachers' work in the area of discipline is to teach young people to be responsible and self-controlled.

Our society's existence depends on citizens who, by and large, accept responsibility for their behavior. Teaching these values to young people is a legitimate function of schools. Viewed in this light, incidents of inappropriate behavior can be regarded as opportunities to teach learners the importance of self-control and responsibility.

Several elements are involved in this kind of teaching. First, the degree to which people have self-control and a sense of responsibility is related to how they perceive reality. People who believe that their environment is warm, trusting, and positive are more likely to exercise self-control than those who believe their environment is cold, indifferent, and negative. To the extent possible, teachers should create a classroom climate that supports learners' development of self-control.

Learners with positive self-concepts are more likely to develop patterns of self-control and personal responsibility than those with negative self-concepts. Self-concepts derive from interactions with others. Since teachers exercise some control over classroom interactions, they are in a position to influence the nature of the self-concept developed by each learner. A success-oriented classroom in which every effort is made to help each person experience some feelings of achievement encourages the development of positive self-concepts among the learners.

Learners who feel that they "belong" are likely to develop good self-control and a sense of personal responsibility. Pride in group membership is important to many young people. Often, teachers can facilitate efforts of individual learners to affiliate more closely with both the class as a whole and certain groups within the class.

When teachers give young people opportunities to make choices, they are helping them to develop self-control and responsibility. Making decisions from among alternatives and living with the consequences aid learners to mature. Opportunities to choose provide learners with the feeling that they can exercise some personal control over their lives. People who have a sense that their personal actions and decisions count tend to act in more responsible, controlled ways than individuals who lack these feelings.

## Discipline and Teachers' Use of Power

When learners misbehave, teachers must exercise their power to remedy the situation. The nature of teacher power and how it is used can influence general patterns of classroom behavior. Several types of teacher power have been identified:

- expert power
- referent power
- legitimate power
- reward power
- coercive power (French and Raven, 1959)

*Expert Power.*    Expert power is power that comes to a person as a result of possessing specialized knowledge. In general, people who are acknowledged experts in a given area exercise considerable influence over others. Their opinions are respected because they are thought to know a great deal about their specialties.

*Referent Power.*    Referent power is power that results from a warm, positive relationship. People accept advice they receive from those whom they like and respect. For teachers, referent power works only when the teacher enjoys good interpersonal relationships with class members.

*Legitimate Power.*    Legitimate power derives from the particular position a person holds. For example, city mayors can wield certain powers because of the office they

*"Will the pilot of Lakeside Elementary School Airlines report up here to the control tower?"*
Courtesy of Ford Button.

hold. Teachers have some legitimate power because of the authority delegated to them by school administrators and the school board. For example, they have the right to make certain decisions about how to teach and how to deal with behavior of class members. Problems sometimes result because not all learners accept that teachers have this right. Teachers' legitimate power is most effective when they have positive personal relationships with their learners and, therefore, also hold referent power.

*Reward Power.*    Reward power comes to individuals as a result of their ability to provide something that another person sees as desirable. Teachers enjoy some reward power. For example, they can provide benefits in the form of praise and grades. But teachers' reward powers are limited. For instance, they have relatively small numbers of rewards available that they can dispense to learners. Further, what teachers view as rewards are not always seen as desirable by all of their learners. Some learners who do not care what grades they receive (and there *are* such people in the schools) will not be influenced by teachers who offer good grades in exchange for good performance.

*Coercive Power.*    Coercive power is power that people wield because of their authority to administer punishment. Teachers who rely heavily on coercive power often do not have classroom environments that learners perceive as warm, caring, and positive. When coercive power is applied, many learners fail to see compelling reasons to adopt behavior patterns favored by their teachers. In an individual situation, when application of coercive power suppresses one undesirable behavior, another undesirable behavior often springs up to replace the first.

In general, expert power and referent power are the two types teachers find most useful in developing positive working relationships with their learners. Young people are usually willing to accept leadership from teachers whom they perceive to be experts and also warm, caring individuals. This suggests a need for teachers to be well-grounded in the subjects they teach. A solid grasp of these topics gives teachers the credibility needed to establish their expert power. At the same time, they need to establish positive classroom climates. When learners sense that teachers care about them personally and truly support them, these teachers accrue valuable referent power.

## Selected Teacher Characteristics and Effective Discipline

Several characteristics are associated with teachers who are effective in the area of discipline. One is that they tend to be people who try to solve problems without calling for outside assistance. Only when their personal efforts have failed do these people look for help from the school principal or other members of the school's professional staff.

A second characteristic of these teachers is that they take a long-term perspective on learners' behavior problems. Their responses are geared not simply to stopping misbehavior when it occurs, but rather they seek to change conditions so that problem behaviors will not recur. These teachers seek underlying causes of improper behavior and try to remove conditions that reinforce unacceptable patterns (Brophy, 1983).

## Some Basic Principles of Effective Discipline

The following are some key principles associated with effective discipline:

- The dignity of the learner must be preserved.
- Private correction is preferable to public correction.
- The causes of misbehavior must be addressed, not simply the misbehavior itself.
- Distinctions must be made between minor and major misbehavior problems.
- Learners must be helped to understand that they have *chosen* to misbehave and, therefore, have *chosen* to experience the consequences.
- Responses to misbehavior must be consistent and fair.

*Preserving Learners' Dignity.*   When correcting misbehavior, teachers should not subject learners to comments that diminish the learners' self-worth. Such responses have the potential to lead to more discipline problems (Jones and Jones, 1986). Teacher behaviors that assault learners' dignity often lead to power conflicts between teacher and learners. Frustrated learners may feel that their only recourse is to respond with counterassaults on the dignity of the teacher. Older learners report that one of the reasons they misbehave is that they feel themselves to have been "put down" by their teachers.

*Private Correction vs. Public Correction.*   One way to diminish the likelihood of learners' feeling that their self-worth has been attacked is for the teacher to verbally correct a misbehaving learner in a place where the teacher's comments cannot be heard by others. For example, the verbal reprimand might take place outside of the classroom.

Private correction takes pressure off misbehaving young people. On the other hand, public reprimands may make them feel pressed to take action in order to "save face" in front of their peers. Private correction also promotes better, more personal contact between teacher and learners. Learners know that the teacher is committing full and undivided attention to the situation under discussion.

*Addressing the Causes, Not Just the Behavior.*   To change a pattern of unacceptable behavior, the causes supporting it need to be removed. Sometimes an analysis of the cause may suggest inappropriate teacher actions. For example, poorly planned lessons and poorly organized classrooms can stimulate and reinforce unacceptable behavior patterns. On the other hand, the causes of learner misbehavior may lie well beyond the teacher and the school setting.

Sometimes, misbehavior is a learner's way of asking for help. It attracts the teacher's attention, alerts the teacher to a problem, and may prompt the teacher to take immediate action. Given this sequence, learners occasionally will behave in ways they know are unacceptable simply to attract their teacher's attention to a serious problem. Teachers need to recognize that some misbehaving young people are desperately seeking supportive, adult assistance.

*Distinguishing Between Major and Minor Problems.*   Many incidents that happen in schools are a result of learners' immaturity rather than serious attempts to challenge authority. Teachers need to be sensitive to the distinction between these minor behavioral lapses and those that represent more serious challenges to their ability to function as instructional leaders. Care must be exercised to avoid overreacting to minor problems, which can build learner resentment because this resentment, in time, can lead to more serious misbehavior episodes.

*Learners Choose to Misbehave; Hence, They Also Choose the Consequences.*   In teaching young people to be responsible, it is important to convey to them that unpleasant consequences of misbehavior result from their own irresponsible behavioral choices, not from arbitrary and vindictive teacher actions. Teachers must help learners see the relationship between inappropriate behaviors and resultant consequences. To accomplish this, learners need to understand clearly what behaviors are unacceptable and what specific consequences will follow if they engage in these behaviors. The purpose is to help young people recognize that, by choosing irresponsible behaviors, they are also choosing the consequences.

*Consistent and Fair Responses.*   The principle of consistent and fair responses implies that *all* incidents of misbehavior deserve some teacher response. If these episodes are ignored, the teacher signals the learners that there is nothing really wrong with this kind of behavior. When this happens, something that begins as a minor problem often escalates into a major one.

Consistency provides at least two key benefits. First, it communicates to learners that their teacher is serious about discouraging a certain pattern of behavior. Second, it suggests to learners that the teacher is fair. This perception is strengthened when the teacher reacts similarly to a specified type of misbehavior regardless of which person in the class is involved.

This chapter's Case Study examines the problems one teacher is encountering with class management and discipline.

CASE STUDY

## *Nothing works, and they won't behave*

**Conrad Newton teaches seventh grade history at Lowenstein Middle School.** The school is in a suburban area just outside of a major midwestern city. Conrad is beginning his third year of teaching. Recently, he made these comments to a friend:

> I thought things would get better after my first and second years. I knew I had lots to learn, and I think I've changed a lot of things. But these kids are just so hard to work with. I've put together some great lessons—built on some things that really turned me on when I was in school—but the kids say everything is 'too hard.' They want me to spoon-feed them! The least little bit of pressure leads to a noisy rebellion. They can't deal even with minor frustration.
>
> Instead of real teaching, I'm working hard just to keep the lid on. About half of my time is spent trying to quiet the kids down. I get the impression that most of them would rather be anywhere but in my class. Most of them have no interest at all in what I'm trying to teach. One of them even came up to me and said, 'Look, I've got to be here, but I don't have to be happy about it.' I feel that my whole day has become discipline, discipline, discipline. It's not much fun.

*Given what you know about the basic principles of classroom management and discipline, what general suggestions might you pass on to Conrad? In what order should he implement these ideas? Should he seek advice from others? If so, who might these people be? What would you do if you were faced with a similar situation?*

## Planning Responses to Misbehavior

Without a systematic plan, it is difficult for teachers to respond to problems consistently. Responses that are developed at the same time a problem occurs may not be appropriate. Additionally, it is difficult for teachers to maintain a consistent pattern of responding to common misbehavior problems in the absence of planning.

Many teachers find it useful to anticipate potential difficulties and write down brief explanations of how they intend to respond before they begin working with a new group of learners. This procedure allows for some unhurried consideration of alternatives, and helps the teacher to maintain consistent and fair patterns of responses when difficulties arise.

Plans have to be developed to fit individual circumstances. The example illustrated in the subsections that follow lists teacher responses in order of their severity. In this scheme, the teacher has planned to use responses from the first categories when minor problems arise; responses farther down the list are designated for use when more serious problems occur.

## Category One: Responses Supporting Self-Control

Teachers can act in ways that promote responses that support learners' self-control. That is, teachers actions should be designed to help learners reassert personal control over their behavior. It is expected that this personal control will bring about a change from an unacceptable to an acceptable behavior.

*Reinforcing Productive Behavior.* One of the most important things a teacher can do to help learners develop self-control is to reinforce desirable patterns of behavior. This can be done by rewarding individuals and members of an entire class when they have behaved well.

Rewards can take many forms. Verbal praise works well, and there may be special activities that class members particularly enjoy. These function well as rewards. The specific rewards a teacher uses should vary with the interests of his or her learners. To be functional, a reward must be something that learners like—simply because a reward appeals to the teacher does not mean it will necessarily interest class members. Box 12–2 offers some tips for devising such reward systems.

*Using Nonverbal Signals to Indicate Disapproval.* To the extent possible, minor episodes of misbehavior need to be handled so as not to interrupt the flow of the lesson. Nonverbal responses allow a teacher to indicate to a learner that an inappropriate behavior has been noted. Such responses tell learners that they are being given time to

---

BOX 12–2

# REINFORCING ACCEPTABLE PATTERNS OF BEHAVIOR

There is evidence that teachers who reinforce acceptable patterns of learner behavior experience fewer classroom control problems than teachers who do not follow this practice. One difficulty in implementing a reinforcement program is that the teacher must identify and have available options that learners will view as rewarding.

Suppose you have been assigned to your first school as a beginning teacher. You have met your learners and worked with them long enough to identify some of their interests. On a sheet of paper, write a brief description of these learners. Include their age levels, general ability levels, and the subject(s) they will study under your direction. Then provide a list of five specific things you can do with members of this group to reinforce acceptable patterns of behavior.

correct their behavior and, thereby, avoid more serious consequences. Nonverbal signals include direct eye contact, hand signals, and facial expressions. They are useful tools in managing learner behavior in the classroom (Grubaugh, 1989).

*Using Proximity Control.*    A minor behavior problem will often disappear when the teacher moves to the area of the classroom where it is occurring. Many learners find it difficult to misbehave if their teacher is nearby. When a problem arises during a large-group lesson, often it can be eliminated if the teacher simply walks quietly to the part of the room where it is occurring. Many times this can be done without interrupting the flow of the lesson.

*Using a Learner's Name in the Context of a Lesson.*    Using a learner's name during a lesson draws the learner's attention to the fact that his or her inappropriate behavior has been noted. It works something like this: if a teacher noticed that John was allowing his attention to drift during a discussion of explorers, the teacher might say something like, "Now if John were a member of the crew sailing for the New World, he would have to. . . ." The use of a learner's name will often result in a quick cessation of an inappropriate behavior.

*Redirecting Learner Attention.*    Redirecting learner attention is especially useful for teachers who work with very young children, but is sometimes also effective with older learners. The idea is for the teacher to watch class members carefully and take action to redirect misbehaving learners to a more productive pattern of behavior. A few brief words and some teacher guidance to help the learner begin work on an assigned task are often all that is required.

*Encouraging Learners to Take Personal Action When They Are Tempted to Misbehave.*    Encouraging learners to take personal action when they are tempted to misbehave is implemented more frequently in elementary schools than in secondary schools. The children are taught to take some specific action when they feel compelled to act inappropriately. This is designed to give them time to reflect about what they are considering doing, and will provide them with a chance to reestablish their self-control.

Sometimes young learners are taught that when they sense themselves on the verge of misbehaving they should put their heads on the desk, clench their fists, or count to 10. These actions give the learners opportunities to relax and unwind before they do something that they might regret (Brophy, 1983).

In other classrooms, learners are urged to move to another part of the room and talk softly to themselves about the problem they are facing and possible responses they might make. This procedure works best when teachers have taken time to teach learners the process of coping with problems by thinking about them aloud (Camp and Bash, 1981).

## Category Two: Providing Situational Assistance

Responses in this category require more direct teacher intervention than those in category one.

*Taking Time for a Quiet Word.*    To implement taking time out for a quiet word, the teacher moves toward the misbehaving learner. This person is quietly reminded about the kind of appropriate behavior that is expected. Once this message has been delivered, the teacher quickly resumes teaching the lesson.

*Providing a Rule Reminder.*    Providing a rule reminder represents a slight escalation from taking time for a quiet word. When a behavior problem occurs, the teacher stops the lesson and speaks to the misbehaving learner or learners in a voice loud enough for the whole class to hear. This is an example of a rule-reminder statement: "Bill's group, what does our list of class rules say about not talking when someone is asking a question?"

*Removing the Learner from the Situation.*    To implement removal of a misbehaving learner, the teacher arranges for the offending learner to move. This might require having this person go to a different seat nearby or to another part of the room. Instructions related to this movement are brief, direct, and nonconfrontational: "Mary, take your material and go to the empty table. Continue working there."

*Responding with Clarity and Firmness.*    If some of the previous techniques have failed to squelch inappropriate behavior, more intrusive teacher actions are required. Sometimes it is necessary to address a learner by name, using a clear, direct, authoritative, no-nonsense tone of voice. The teacher makes eye contact with the learner he or she is addressing, and the teacher's demeanor takes on an "I mean business" character as the teacher indicates the kind of behavior that must stop and what must replace it.

*Arranging Conferences with Misbehaving Learners.*    A next step often is an individual conference with the offending learner. During the conference, the teacher emphasizes specifically what must be done to correct the behavior problem. Threats are kept to a minimum. Typically, the teacher identifies the problem, shares his or her feelings about it, and asks the learner what might be done to solve it.

Some conferences conclude with the preparation of a "behavior contract" that specifies what the learner will do. Behavior contracts often mention some good things that will result if the contract terms are met. There also frequently are references to consequences that will follow if the unacceptable pattern of behavior continues.

*Asking Parents for Help.*    Beginning teachers sometimes are nervous about talking to parents. They shouldn't be—parents often are the best allies teachers have. Nearly all of them are concerned about the progress and behavior of their children. Parents are often unaware that their child is misbehaving in school. Frequently, a call to a parent to explain what is going on will result in an excellent cooperative plan to solve the problem.

Involving parents does not always lead to the desired result. The success of involving them in situations related to misbehavior in school depends on many variables. The age level of the learner is a factor, as is the kind of relationship the learner has with his or her parents. The nature of the teacher's approach in initiating a contact with a parent is also important. In general, the teacher should emphasize solving the problem rather than assigning blame for inappropriate behaviors.

## Category Three: Implementing Punishment

After responses in categories one and two have been tried with no success, or if the misbehavior is very serious, then punishment may be appropriate. Punishment is most effective when it is used infrequently and is appropriate to the nature of the offense. When overused, punishment can destroy a teacher's credibility, create anxiety among learners, and undermine a classroom's positive learning environment.

*Losing a Privilege.* Loss of a privilege functions as an effective punishment for some young people. The success of this approach rests on learners having some privileges available to them. Depending on age levels, these privileges might vary from a classroom job (such as taking care of erasers) to promises of seats in favored sections at athletic events to opportunities to go on out-of-town field trips. To be effective, learners must really prize the privilege that is taken away. If they do not, then this teacher action is unlikely to influence their patterns of behavior.

Loss of a privilege works better if the privilege is not taken away permanently. The possibility that a valued privilege might be restored in exchange for a modification of behavior sometimes acts as a potent motivator for young people (see Box 12–3).

---

BOX 12–3
# KINDS OF PRIVILEGES LEARNERS SEE AS IMPORTANT

On those occasions when it becomes necessary for a teacher to impose punishment of some kind in response to a serious behavior problem, one option is removal of a learner privilege. The success of this approach depends on (1) learners having certain privileges and (2) these privileges being important to learners.

Think about a grade-level and a subject you might teach. Identify three privileges that you might make available to learners in your class, describe them, and then provide a brief rationale explaining why your learners would be likely to consider these privileges important.

1. Privilege: _____

   Rationale: _____

2. Privilege: _____

   Rationale: _____

3. Privilege: _____

   Rationale: _____

*Providing for In-Class Isolation.*   In some elementary classrooms, teachers designate a certain part of the classroom as an area where misbehaving learners are sent. Often, these areas are located in places where it is hard for offending learners to interact with others and observe what other class members are doing.

Sometimes teachers allow people who have been sent to these isolated areas of the classroom to continue working on assignments. At other times, these learners are asked to write an essay about the nature of their misbehavior and their ideas for change. Occasionally, learners are told to go to these areas and simply sit quietly. Many younger children find the resultant boredom to be a very strong punishment.

*Removing the Learner.*   If serious misbehavior persists, it may be necessary to remove a learner from the classroom. When this happens, the learner is often sent to the principal's or a counselor's office. Initially, the objective is not for the principal or counselor to work with the individual; rather, the idea is to send the learner to an area supervised by another professional. Learners are not sent to unsupervised areas such as hallways. If an accident occurred and a learner were injured in such an unsupervised area, the teacher might be held liable for negligence.

*Making Up Wasted Time.*   When the teacher feels that a learner's misbehavior has resulted in class time not being used effectively, the teacher can require the learner to make up the wasted time. Depending on the grade level, the learner may be kept in the room during recess or may spend extra time in class either before or after school. It is important that this punishment not be converted into a reward. For example, some learners enjoy chatting informally with teachers. If such activity goes on when wasted time is being made up, this approach to changing an inappropriate behavior pattern may fail.

It is not always possible to insist that misbehaving learners make up wasted time. In some schools, many learners ride buses to and from school. If they are kept after school, they have no way to get home. Teachers also are generally reluctant to keep high school students who have part-time jobs after school.

*Corporal Punishment.*   There has been no discussion of corporal punishment in this section. One reason is that corporal punishment of school learners is illegal in some states, and in many others there are extremely strict regulations governing its use. The trend against the use of corporal punishment in schools is international in scope. Among developed nations of the world, it is still condoned only in some of the public schools of Australia, New Zealand, South Africa, and the United States (Jambor, 1988, p. 220).

Even where it is legal, there are negatives associated with the use of corporal punishment. Though administration of corporal punishment sometimes will stop a given undesirable learner behavior, it fails to model an appropriate substitute behavior. There are also important physical, emotional, and legal risks. In summary, corporal punishment is a potentially dangerous response to classroom behavior problems and is of dubious value in ensuring their long-term resolution.

## Category Four: Involving Others

Involving others is a category of last-resort options. When other measures have failed, the teacher actively involves parents or other education professionals, and arranges a conference about the situation. These may include administrators, counselors, and personnel from agencies outside the school system.

*Involving Parents.*    There should be initial contact with parents to apprise them of the problem and seek their help in solving it before a formal conference is scheduled. If a conference proves necessary, the teacher must prepare for it carefully. Often, teachers bring evidence to the conference including anecdotal records that document specific examples of problem behaviors and dates when they occurred. The best conferences feature a sharing of information and a communal effort to work out a proposed solution. Sensitive teachers avoid putting parents in a position of feeling that their own adequacy is being questioned.

*Arranging Conferences with Other Professionals.*    Sometimes it is wise to bring together a group of professionals to discuss a learner's unacceptable behavior patterns. Principals, counselors, psychologists, social workers, and others who might attend need to be introduced to documentation regarding exactly what the learner has been doing. This material is prepared by the teacher in advance of the meeting.

Meetings of this kind often result in the development of a specific action plan. For example, such a group might decide to place the learner in another class, temporarily suspend the learner from school, or assign the learner to a special counselor. Typically, the plan is put in place under the authority of the school principal. Usually, there are provisions requiring periodic reporting of results to either the school principal or someone whom he or she has designated to watch over the situation.

...................................

# Key Ideas in Summary

- Conveying information and managing learners are among teachers' most important responsibilities. Teaching and managing are closely connected. Good teaching can prevent control problems, and good management establishes an environment for productive teaching.

- Classroom management is concerned with decisions teachers make regarding the organization of time, space, and materials. This organization is designed to facilitate smooth and efficient instruction. Good management produces an environment that reduces the likelihood of discipline problems, and results from careful teacher planning.

- Effective classroom teachers make good use of time. They strive to reduce periods when no productive learning activities are occurring. They plan carefully for

**Table 12–1**
Summary table: Classroom management and discipline

| Topic | Important Ideas |
| --- | --- |
| Relationship between teaching and management | Good teaching reduces the number of classroom control problems. Good management, in turn, enables good teaching to continue. |
| Space management | Organization of instructional space involves decisions regarding use of floor space, traffic patterns, location of the teacher's desk, use of wall space, and equipment storage. |
| Time management | Effective time management helps to maximize the time that learners spend on their school work. Management of time requires decisions at transition points, at the beginning of the class, about lesson pacing, and about helping learners in time-efficient ways. |
| Establishing routines | Effective teachers establish regular procedures for handling routine tasks. These are communicated systematically to learners. When they are understood, these routines facilitate smooth and efficient operation of the classroom. |
| Kinds of teacher power | Kinds of teacher power include expert power, referent power, legitimate power, reward power, and coercive power. There are certain characteristics associated with each type. For example, learners perceive teachers who rely on referent power as more warm and caring than teachers who rely on coercive power. |

**Table 12–1**
*continued*

| Topic | Important Ideas |
|---|---|
| Basic principles of effective discipline | These include preserving learners' dignity, private correction versus public correction, addressing the causes instead of the behavior, distinguishing between major and minor problems, helping learners realize that when they choose misbehavior they also choose the consequences of misbehavior, and consistent and fair responses. |
| Responses to help learners reassert their self-control | These include reinforcing productive behavior, using nonverbal signals to indicate disapproval, using proximity control, using a learner's name in the context of a lesson, redirecting learner attention, and encouraging learners to take personal action when they are tempted to misbehave. |
| Providing situational assistance | Responses include taking time for a quiet word, providing a rule reminder, removing a learner from the situation, responding with clarity and firmness, holding conferences with misbehaving learners, and asking parents for help. |
| Implementing punishment | Responses include losing a privilege, providing for in-class isolation, removing the learner, and making up wasted time. |
| Corporal punishment | Not recommended. Its use may suppress an undesired behavior, but it fails to model and reinforce an acceptable alternative. It also poses other ethical and legal problems for teachers. |
| Involving others | Responses include involving parents and arranging for conferences with other professionals. |

how to use their time efficiently when beginning each class period, arranging for learners to make a smooth transition from one activity to another, and working individually with particular learners who need special assistance.

- It is important for teachers to develop routines for handling recurring events. Teachers who have mastered procedures for dealing with regular occurrences are better able to handle unexpected behavioral problems in ways that respond to the problems and are minimally disruptive to the instructional program.

- The goal of disciplinary procedures in the classroom is to teach learners responsibility and self-control. Methods used should be consistent with this aim.

- Effective classroom managers solve most discipline problems themselves. Only occasionally do they require assistance from principals and other school officials. They seek long-term solutions to behavioral problems, and they look for remedies directed at the underlying causes of unacceptable patterns of behavior.

- Several principles are related to appropriate teacher responses to misbehavior in the classroom. Teachers need to respect learners, deal with problems quietly and unobtrusively, distinguish between minor and major problems, and help learners grasp the connection between unacceptable behaviors and unpleasant consequences that come their way as a result.

- Several basic types of teacher power have been identified. These include expert power, referent power, legitimate power, reward power, and coercive power.

- Corporal punishment is illegal in many nations of the world and in several states. Even in states where corporal punishment is legal, many guidelines govern its use. Corporal punishment is not recommended. Its use may eliminate a given undesirable behavior, but it fails to reinforce an acceptable alternative. Consequently, an even more undesirable behavior may appear in place of the one that initially got the learner into difficulty.

- Teacher responses to misbehaviors range across a number of alternatives. These vary from actions designed to allow the teachers to reassert their self-control to those requiring recommendations of groups of professionals with specialized skills.

## Review and Discussion Questions

1. What is the relationship between good classroom management and effective teaching?

2. What are some things teachers can do to organize space efficiently?

3. Why is time management important as a management tool, and what are some things teachers do to make better use of class time?

4. What are some examples of recurring classroom events for which teachers can establish regular routines and procedures?

5. Are there legitimate educational purposes associated with what teachers do related to classroom management? If so, what are they?

6. What kinds of power do teachers exercise in the classroom, and what are the relative merits of each?

7. What are some basic principles of effective discipline, and how would you rate the importance of each?

8. What are some categories of teacher responses to learner misbehavior?

9. How do you view corporal punishment as a response to learner misbehavior in the classroom?

10. What role or roles must parents play in situations concerning their children's classroom misbehavior?

........................................

# Ideas for Field Experiences, Projects, and Enrichment

1. Chapter 11 introduced a classroom observation technique called *selective verbatim*. Visit a classroom and use this procedure to record what the teacher says to control episodes of misbehavior. Share your findings with others in your class.

2. Invite a principal or other school district official who has responsibilities related to helping teachers manage learners. Ask this person to describe special approaches to classroom management and discipline. Some school districts have districtwide programs that all teachers are to follow, while others allow a great deal of latitude from building to building and from teacher to teacher. Ask the visitor about his or her district's policies.

3. Interview several local principals regarding state and local policies concerning corporal punishment. If it is permissible for teachers to use it, find out what guidelines must be followed. Present your findings to others in your class.

4. Prepare an annotated bibliography of professional journal articles that focus on classroom management and discipline procedures. You may wish to make copies of several articles that you feel might be of use to you given the grade and subject you intend to teach. Gather together all of the annotated bibliographies prepared by all class members. With a group of several others, eliminate duplicate entries and prepare a master annotated bibliography that can be distributed to each class member. Encourage people to retain these materials for their files and read those articles that seem to be particularly worthwhile.

5. Invite a panel of first- and second-year teachers to visit your class. Ask them to talk about classroom management and discipline problems they have encountered, and encourage them to share the kinds of responses they have found to be effective.

## Supplementary Reading

Charles, C. W. *Building Classroom Discipline: From Models to Practice*. 3d ed. New York: Longman, 1989.

Doyle, W. "Classroom Organization and Management." In M. C. Wittrock, ed. *Handbook of Research on Teaching*. 3d ed. New York: Macmillan, 1986, 392–431.

Emmer, E., C. Evertson, J. Sanford, B. Clements, and M. Worsham. *Classroom Management for Secondary Teachers*. 2d ed. Englewood Cliffs, NJ: Prentice Hall, 1989.

Rosen, L. A., S. A. Taylor, S. G. O'Leary, and W. Sanderson. "A Survey of Classroom Management Practices." *Journal of School Psychology* (Fall 1990): 257–69.

Savage, T. V. *Discipline for Self-Control*. Englewood Cliffs, NJ: Prentice Hall, 1991.

## References

Berliner, D. C. "The Half-Full Glass: A Review of Research on Teaching." In P. L. Hosford, ed. *Using What We Know about Teaching*. Alexandria, VA: Association for Supervision and Curriculum Development, 1984, 51–77.

Brophy, J. "Classroom Organization and Management." *The Elementary School Journal* (March 1983): 265–85.

Camp, B., and M. Bash. *Think Aloud: Increasing Social and Cognitive Skills: A Problem-Solving Program for Children (Small Group Program)*. Champaign, IL: Research Press, 1981.

Doyle, W. "Classroom Organization and Management." In M. C. Wittrock, ed. *Handbook of Research on Teaching*. 3d ed. New York: Macmillan, 1986, 392–431.

Emmer, E. T., C. M. Evertson, and L. Anderson. "Effective Classroom Management at the Beginning of the School Year." *Elementary School Journal* (May 1980): 219–31.

Evertson, C. M. "Improving Elementary Classroom Management: A School-Based Training Program for Beginning the Year." *Journal of Educational Research* (November–December 1989): 82–90.

French, J. R. P., and B. H. Raven. "The Bases of Social Power." In D. Cartwright, ed. *Studies in Social Power*. Ann Arbor, MI: University of Michigan Press, 1959, 118–49.

Grubaugh, S. "Nonverbal Language Techniques for Better Classroom Management and Discipline." *High School Journal* (October–November 1989): 34–40.

Jambor, T. "Classroom Management and Discipline Alternatives to Corporal Punishment: The Norwegian Example." *Education* (Winter 1988): 220–25.

Jones, F. H. "The Gentle Art of Classroom Discipline." *National Elementary Principal* (June 1979): 26–32.

Jones, V. F., and L. S. Jones. *Comprehensive Classroom Management: Creating Positive Learning Environments.* 2d ed. Boston: Allyn and Bacon, 1986.

Kounin, J. *Discipline and Good Management in the Classroom.* New York: Holt, Rinehart and Winston, 1970.

Savage, T. V. *Discipline for Self-Control.* Englewood Cliffs, NJ: Prentice Hall, 1991.

Smith, H. A. "Nonverbal Communication." In M. J. Dunkin, ed. *The International Encyclopedia of Teaching and Teacher Education.* New York: Pergamon Press, 1987, 466–76.

Smyth, W. J. "Time." In M. M. Dunkin, ed. *The International Encyclopedia of Teaching and Teacher Education.* New York: Pergamon Press, 1987, 372–80.

# Chapter 13

# Technology and Schools

## Objectives

This chapter provides information to help the reader to

- point out some forces that are encouraging schools to make increasing use of technology in their programs.
- explain why some past introductions of technology have not changed school practices as much as had been expected.
- compare the use of modern technologies in the school with their levels of use in the larger society.
- describe some alleged advantages of increasing use of state-of-the-art technology in school programs.
- cite some examples of how teachers are using new technologies in planning and delivering instructional programs.
- point out some educational changes that may come about as a result of technological innovations.

# Focus Questions

1. What changes have occurred that are putting pressures on schools to turn out graduates who are not just technologically literate, but also technologically competent?
2. How do electronic innovations vary from innovations of the past?
3. How does the amount of use of newer electronic technologies in the schools compare with their use in the larger society?
4. Why do some critics claim that piecemeal introduction of electronic innovations won't work and that massive efforts to install them are necessary to maximize learners' benefits?
5. What are the barriers to school adoption of innovations, and how might they be overcome?
6. What are a few of the things today's school software allows teachers and administrators to do?
7. How can computers tied to phone lines increase teachers' options as they plan instruction?
8. What are some instructional uses of interactive videodisc and CD-ROM technology?
9. What future changes may result from large-scale use of new electronic technologies in the schools?

# Introduction

Technology is rapidly changing our world. In recognition of this reality, in the past decade schools began to develop programs designed to produce young people who would be technologically literate by the time they entered the work force. Technological literacy implies an ability to accept technological innovations and use them with a modest level of proficiency.

Today, technological literacy is no longer enough. Our society is increasingly insisting that employees be technologically *competent*. This refers to a level of understanding that goes well beyond technological literacy—competence suggests the presence of a confident ability to use and extend present technologies and adapt quickly to new technologies as they emerge.

Schools are under great pressure to become active participants in the technological revolution. Educators are being asked to develop learners' expertise so that they will be capable users of technology when they enter the workplace. Additionally, schools are being encouraged to utilize modern technologies to help learners master important content of the prescribed curriculum.

Pressures on schools to incorporate state-of-the-art technology pose problems. For one thing, these technologies and the associated equipment are expensive. The rapidity

More and more computers are being used in classrooms as educators strive to produce technologically competent young citizens.

of technological change also requires schools to be prepared to replace equipment frequently. Additionally, the "fit" of programs delivered through the use of advanced technology with the prescribed curriculum is an issue. For example, available computer software may not relate well to what is taught in a given course. Finally, many experienced teachers have had little experience utilizing new technologies and are not always eager to embrace them.

Younger teachers often are more familiar with the newer electronic innovations than teachers who are longtime veterans in the profession. Often, this means that technologically competent beginners are called on to assist older, more experienced colleagues who are just beginning to learn about technologies that did not exist when they entered teaching. Many school districts look to their younger, less experienced teachers for leadership as technological changes are implemented. For this reason, it makes particularly good sense for individuals preparing to enter the profession to develop a solid grounding in the technologies that are gaining wide use in the schools. Box 13–1 addresses some of the concerns related to the technological revolution and the schools.

### Basic Features of Today's Technological Innovations

Personal computers, on-line data systems, cable television, electronic bulletin board systems, and videodiscs are examples of technological innovations that are having an impact on school programs. In a sense, these innovations represent recent manifestations of a long-standing tradition of incorporating new technologies into instruc-

---

BOX 13–1
## WILL AN EMPHASIS ON TECHNOLOGY UNBALANCE SCHOOL CURRICULA?

These comments were made recently to school board members:

I am willing to accept a future in which many people will need to have sound technical backgrounds, but this certainly doesn't mean *everybody* will. I am concerned that we are spending so much time teaching learners how to become proficient in the use of computers, videodiscs, and so forth that the 'meat' of important academic subjects such as history, mathematics, and English is not getting its full due. In the long run, this traditional kind of content will do young people more good than learning how to run today's high-tech equipment, which, five years from now, will be totally out of date.

*What Do You Think?*
1. Do you think there *is* a possibility that efforts to make learners technologically competent are stealing time from important school subjects?
2. How do you react to the argument that not everyone in the future will need to be proficient in the use of technology?
3. If you were to respond to this person's concerns, what would you say?

tional programs. There is, however, an important common feature of the newer electronic innovations that make them quite different from older technologies.

Many earlier innovations featured improvements of a mechanical rather than an electronic nature. Such innovations as high-speed book presses and self-threading film projectors, for example, featured dozens (even hundreds) of moving parts. Though it is possible to design such mechanical parts to move at high speeds, there are practical limits on how fast they can operate. Friction caused by moving parts results in wear, and thus in mechanical devices there is a tendency for functional problems to increase as the speed of operation increases.

The newer electronic innovations, however, have fewer upper-limit restrictions on speeds, because they depend much less on moving mechanical parts than did their predecessors (Hawkridge, 1983). Mechanical technology has been succeeded by electronic technology, in which potential speeds of operation are incredibly high. Electronic innovations depend on devices that manage the flow of electrons through elaborate circuits. Although problems do occur, in general new electronic technology offers the possibility of designing equipment that is less subject to breakdown than is the equipment based on older, mechanical technology.

Electronic innovations have been made possible because of new developments in microelectronics. Microelectronics is concerned with the production of extremely small electronic devices, particularly switches and circuits. Thousands of circuits can be embedded on small chips about the size of the smallest fingernail on an adult's hand. These chips, called *microprocessors*, are now manufactured by the millions. Once a production line is started, it is relatively inexpensive to produce many additional copies of a similar circuit. As a result, many of today's electronic devices are small and inexpensive.

## The Need for Technological Competence

One important force behind efforts to expand the role of technology in schools is economic. There are fears that our education system is not producing young people who will have the technological know-how required by employers. In particular, areas where technological competence is a must are considered to be the fields where, in the future, jobs will be most plentiful.

Some critics have suggested that the technological sophistication of schools has fallen far behind that of the society as a whole (Mecklenburger, 1990). Whereas businesses and governmental agencies have been quick to take advantage of the speed and efficiencies of the new technologies, schools have been slow to follow. James A. Mecklenburger (1990), who directs the National School Boards Association Institute for the Transfer of Technology to Education, has commented that ". . . schools today reflect their 19th century technological roots more than do most other institutions" (p. 106).

Mecklenburger goes on to argue that if the schools fail to embrace electronic technology, many of education's functions will be co-opted by the private sector. The advantages of using modern technology to teach learners is so great that our society will not allow the opportunity to be missed. As evidence of private-sector responses to educational opportunities made possible by electronic innovations, Mecklenburger cites the development of Channel One and CNN Newsroom, which are cable news programs specifically designed for use by learners in their classrooms during the school day.

## What Must Happen If Schools Are to Take Advantage of Today's Technologies?

In the past, innovations have been introduced to the schools relatively slowly. In part, this has resulted from budgetary constraints. It has often been simply too expensive to provide every teacher or every classroom with a given innovation at the same time. For example, for many years it was the practice of some schools to purchase two or three overhead projectors each year. Over a number of years, the goal of providing one for each classroom in each school was reached.

Critics who want schools to move faster to take advantage of the capabilities of new electronic innovations say this approach is inappropriate (Levinson, 1990; Mecklenburger, 1990). They argue that these innovations should not be regarded as ways to deliver traditional education more effectively, but rather should be seen both as opportunities to challenge some basic organizational features of today's schools and as catalysts to basic educational change. Supporters of increased use of technology in the schools contend that a mindless commitment to the maintenance of traditional norms of school practice stands as a barrier to widespread adoption of electronic innovations. Box 13–2 presents two opposing views of computers in the classroom.

It has been noted that in its time the classroom itself was an innovation (Mecklenburger, 1990). This proved to be an efficient way to gather together groups of children and expose them to the special expertise of an educated adult. Establishment of the classroom freed parents to develop their expertise in other areas and allowed a specialist, the classroom teacher, to devote full attention to becoming truly proficient at the task of organizing and transmitting information to children.

Invention of the school classroom was an innovation that saved time and resources. Its advantages over the traditional scheme of parent-to-individual-child instruction were clear. Today, it may be that functions long discharged by the classroom can be better accomplished in another way. Modern technology allows for information to be widely disseminated through telephone lines. It may no longer be necessary to gather learners together in individual classrooms that feature the teacher as the primary information source. Perhaps school districts should invest money in computer terminals and information networks that would give learners access to much more information than could ever be expected to be provided (or even known) by an individual classroom teacher. It might be that the teacher should become a specialist skilled in guiding learners' work with data bases and other information sources, such as videodiscs (Levinson, 1990).

As critics see the situation, relatively few school learners have as yet benefited from the new electronic technologies. But this is not a negative comment on the educational potential of these innovations; rather, it reflects an inadequate supply of equipment in the schools. One survey revealed that learners outnumber computers in the schools by 20, 30, or even 40 to 1 (Mecklenburger, 1990). Further, large numbers of

BOX 13–2
## TECHNOLOGICAL ILLITERACY: ARE TEACHERS TO BLAME?

Mr. Jones: It is shameful that computers are so little used in our schools. Teachers should be forced to incorporate their use into day-to-day lessons. There is evidence that young people learn more, learn faster, and retain more when they are taught with computers. I can't understand why teachers seem to be standing in the way of this kind of progress.

Ms. Smith: Teachers should not be forced to use computers. It may be true that good computer programs can help some learners improve their comprehension. But how will they feel about this experience? Will they be more interested or less interested in academic content than when it is taught by traditional methods? The job of the teacher is to engender positive attitudes toward learning. This is what the emphasis should be. If a teacher needs a computer to do this, that's fine. If not, that is fine too.

*What Do You Think?*

1. What does Mr. Jones see as teachers' most important responsibility?
2. What is of greatest concern to Ms. Smith?
3. If you were to get involved in a discussion with both Mr. Jones and Ms. Smith, what would you say?

• • • • • • • • • • • • • • • • • • • • • • • • • • • • • • • • • • • • • • • • • • • • • • • • • •

these computers are outdated models. James Mecklenburger (1990) has estimated that "students might outnumber the truly capable computers by even 400 or 1,000 to one" (p. 106). More sophisticated electronic technology is even less abundant in the schools. (See the accompanying What the Experts Say for more on this issue.)

WHAT THE EXPERTS SAY

## *Actions necessary to encourage more use of technology in the schools*

The International Society for Technology in Education (ISTE), headquartered at the University of Oregon, is a strong proponent of increased application of electronic technology in the schools. ISTE has issued a report entitled *Vision Test: Three New Rs for Education* (1990) that makes a number of recommendations designed to encourage more effective use of technology in education.

The report proposes as a 1995 goal to increase the number of computers in schools so that there is one for every five learners. This will require at least four times the number of computers than are in schools at the present time (Mecklenburger, 1990). Extensive inservice technology training for both preservice and inservice teachers is also recommended.

The ISTE report recognizes that achievement of these recommendations will be expensive. In response to this situation, it proposes the creation of a National Technology Trust Fund. The fund would receive money from proposed new sales taxes to be levied against high-tech hardware and software, and from contributions made by major corporations. To underscore the important connection between education and technology, the report suggests that the president declare the 1990s to be the Decade of Technology in Education.

Source: *Vision Test: Three New Rs for Education* (Eugene, OR: International Society for Technology in Education, 1990).

Some critics of present practices contend that schools cannot expect to produce technologically literate learners without a massive infusion of money to purchase large quantities of state-of-the-art equipment. Advantages that can accrue from this technology require that all of the necessary pieces be in place. For example, while learners can do a few things with personal computers and good software, the range of potential learning increases dramatically when these computers are tied through telephone lines to national data bases and electronic bulletin boards. Monetary costs of large-scale implementation are high, but, argue the critics, so are the social costs of turning out learners who are ill-prepared to work in a world that expects them to be technologically competent.

## Barriers to the Adoption of Technological Innovations

The relatively slow pace of school adoption of electronic innovations is not a matter of ill will on the part of school authorities. For many years, educators have been asked to embrace changes that have been promoted as cures for persistent problems. Larry Cuban (1986) has identified some persistent patterns that have occurred when innovations have been proposed.

When a change is initially proposed, often there is an "exhilaration phase." This phase is characterized by announcements regarding the dramatic improvements that will result once the innovation is in place. Often, these claims have been made by people who are not educators and may have little understanding of the public schools.

Next, there has been a tendency for innovations to go through a "scientific-credibility phase." This often comes in response to needs of school officials to establish a research base supporting the effectiveness of the innovation. At this point, published reports often appear indicating that the innovation either improves learner performance as compared to traditional methods or achieves comparable performance more efficiently or less expensively.

Usually, research reports cited during the scientific-credibility phase have been used to build a rationale for adopting the innovation. After it has been implemented, evidence often mounts that there has been less extensive use of the innovation than had been anticipated and less overall effectiveness than had been predicted. Cuban (1986) refers to this part in the life cycle of an innovation as the "disappointment phase."

This disappointment often has been felt most keenly by people who were strong supporters of the innovation. Sometimes they begin to search for reasons to explain what went wrong. In such investigations, teachers have often been blamed for the innovation's lack of effectiveness. This part of the innovation adoption cycle has been called the "teacher-bashing phase," and in it teachers may be depicted as people who have stubbornly stood in the way of a change that, had it been properly and enthusiastically implemented, would have done wonderful things for learners.

Cuban (1986) suggests that it is inappropriate to charge teachers for the failure of innovations to take root. Implementation problems, he notes, often reflect problems with the innovations themselves and the working conditions teachers face in schools. When innovations that have worked well in nonschool settings are adopted for school programs, the decision has often been made by administrators who have been pressured by influential people outside of education. Frequently, teachers have had little involvement in the decision and have felt little emotional commitment to the innovation imposed on them.

Sometimes, too, the problem has been the supply and availability of equipment. Supplies of even such old innovations as film projectors tend to be very thin as compared to such traditional technologies as textbooks and chalkboards. Lessons based on equipment that is not readily available are not dependable. Hence, many teachers prefer to plan instruction on the support tools they know they will have as opposed to those that they might have. Cuban's finding regarding the importance of providing a large and dependable supply of the innovation is clearly consistent with the concerns of many advocates of electronic innovations, who make a strong case for schools investing a large-scale financial commitment to ensure wide availability of the innovation (Levinson, 1990; Mecklenburger, 1990).

Increasingly, proponents of electronic innovations are recognizing the importance of involving teachers in their selection. It is also widely understood that teachers must be trained to use the innovations before they can be expected to develop a strong emotional commitment to them.

## Electronic Technology in the Schools: Selected Examples

Educational programs everywhere are being influenced by electronic technology. Some applications of technology that are described in this section are currently available in many schools; others are candidates for increased use by the middle or late 1990s. This section introduces information about the following:

- instructional and managerial software
- on-line data systems
- bulletin board systems
- interactive videodiscs
- CD-ROM
- interactive distance learning systems

Courtesy of Ford Button

## Instructional and Managerial Software

Personal computers have become common in many schools. Because of this, software vendors have dramatically increased the quantity and quality of programs designed to be used in schools. This situation represents a great improvement over circumstances prevailing even five years ago, when many educational programs represented little more than conversions of dull workbook activities to a computer-based format. Vendors have also recognized that computers in many schools are not up-to-date models, and thus much software is available that will work even on somewhat dated computer hardware.

Much early school-related software was directed at teaching learners computer programming skills. Today, this is a minor emphasis. Instructional software increasingly is oriented to teaching academic content associated with the individual school subjects. For example, software is available that focuses on developing learners' writing skills, increasing their sophisticated analytical thinking processes through exposure to data associated with simulation activities, and helping them develop mechanical drawing proficiency. The best of the new instructional programs require students to confront content and work actively with it to develop a "product" (a chart, written response, formal presentation, or something else that will indicate that higher-level thinking processes have been engaged). Box 13–3 discusses a newly emerged problem associated with learners' acquisition of computer skills.

BOX 13–3
## DOES AN EMPHASIS ON COMPUTERS PLACE LEARNERS FROM ECONOMICALLY DEPRIVED FAMILIES AT A DISADVANTAGE?

Results from the First National Assessment of Computer Competence revealed that learners who had computers in their homes scored higher than those who did not. The impact of school classes dedicated to helping learners become proficient computer users did not compensate for the lack of computers at home. Even learners who had never studied computers in school but had access to them at home scored higher than learners who were enrolled in computer classes at school but had no computers at home (Baker and Ogle, 1989, p. 89).

School emphases on computer use seem to be widening the learning gap between our society's "haves" and "have nots." To ensure fairness, schools may need to buy computers that can be checked out for long-term home use by learners from economically deprived families.

*What Do You Think?*

1. Are you surprised about reported differences in achievement levels between learners who have computers at home and those who do not?
2. How do you react to the idea of the schools supplying computers for home use to learners whose parents lack the resources to buy them?
3. Do you have some other ideas about what could be done to narrow the computer-learning gap between "haves" and "have nots?"

Excellent software is now available to assist teachers and administrators with many of their managerial tasks. For example, there are programs that teachers can use to record attendance, create and print individual lesson plans, and record and average grades. School administrators often use software to generate master schedules, keep track of budgets, maintain addresses of learners and parents, and produce memoranda and informal notices for faculty and staff members. Counselors, school nurses, and other school personnel also are finding software that allows them to perform some aspects of their duties more effectively.

Many firms are now publishing good education-related software. Some of the following companies are among the leaders in this growing field:

Aquarius
P.O. Box 128
Indian Rocks, FL 33535

Broderbund Software
345 Fourth Street
San Francisco, CA 94107

Educational Activities
1937 Grand Avenue
Baldwin, NY 11510

Grolier Electronic Publishing
Sherman Turnpike
Danbury, CT 06816

Learning Arts
P.O. Box 179
Wichita, KS 67201

MicroEd
P.O. Box 24750
Edina, MN 55424

Milliken
1100 Research Boulevard
St. Louis, MO 63132

Scholastic Incorporated
P.O. Box 7502
Jefferson City, MO 65102

SVE
1345 Diversey Parkway
Chicago, IL 60614

Tom Snyder Productions
90 Sherman Street
Cambridge, MA 02140

Unicorn Software
2950 E. Flamingo Road
Las Vegas, NV 89121

## On-Line Data Systems

More and more educators are linking personal computers to data sources via phone lines. This greatly expands the range of computer-based instructional technology, as lessons are no longer dependent on information contained in available software.

A number of information sources that can be electronically tapped by computers are now available. This technology has been on the market for several years, but until recently access costs discouraged widespread use (Grunwald, 1990). However, several new entries into this market have now greatly reduced the costs of these services. They offer information options that can greatly expand the instructional resources available to the classroom teacher.

The PRODIGY Service is an on-line information service that is jointly sponsored by IBM and Sears. Unlike many earlier services that billed users for minutes and seconds of connected computer time, PRODIGY charges a flat monthly fee regardless of the actual time subscribers are tapped into the system. This feature makes monthly costs much more predictable, and it has attracted some schools as subscribers. Monthly subscription rates are kept fairly low, in part because there is some advertising included among the information choices. Information options are extensive, numbering well over 700. Among the categories of information relevant for educators are the electronic version of *Grolier's Encyclopedia* (users can look up information), a program produced by the National Geographic Society that features a different world area each week, and material from public television's "NOVA" series.

Other on-line data are available from a number of Quantum Computer Services' offerings. These include America OnLine (for owners of Apple computers) and PC-Link (for owners of IBM-compatible computers) (Grunwald, 1990). These services also include the *Grolier Encyclopedia*, as well as a number of other useful references.

These services represent the beginnings of what may be a tremendous expansion of inexpensive electronic information services. Peter Grunwald (1990), an executive for a telecommunications marketing firm, points out that soon there will be a great expansion of information transmitted to personal computers using part of a cable television signal or optical fiber networks. These services, in time, will allow learners to access a tremendous volume of information in their own homes. Such changes may greatly increase teachers' options as they plan learning activities for their pupils and students.

## Electronic Bulletin Board Systems

Electronic bulletin board systems allow for exchanges of messages among personal computer users. The computers are tied to the "bulletin boards" via telephone lines. More and more schools are providing teachers with modems and phone lines, which permits them to access electronic bulletin board systems with their computers. These systems allow for school-to-school communications as well as for exchanges of personal information, sharing of lesson plans and units, and communications about tests. In some places, these systems can be used by teachers to order instructional materials. Learners can use them to search data bases for information needed to complete assignments (Watson, 1990).

There is a trend for individual electronic bulletin boards to join together to form elaborate electronic bulletin board networks. Seventeen states have gathered together local school district bulletin boards into statewide networks that can be accessed by educators throughout the state (Watson, 1990).

Instructional applications of electronic bulletin boards are just beginning to be widely appreciated. Some teachers of foreign languages are encouraging their students to write letters in the target foreign language to learners in a country where the language is spoken. For example, Spanish teachers may have their learners post letters on an electronic bulletin board that is accessible to young people in Mexico or elsewhere in Spanish-speaking Latin America.

At the elementary school level, pupils in many schools regularly use classroom computers to tap into the National Geographic Society's Kids' Net to share information about classroom science experiments. This system allows for a nationwide sharing of data gathered about a common problem, such as acid rain (Watson, 1990).

Learners in one West Virginia school have used their computers to develop pen-pal friendships with students in a Moscow school. Another group in Massachusetts has been writing descriptions of New England for the benefit of a Saskatchewan class in western Canada (Watson, 1990). Possibilities for educational uses of bulletin board systems are just beginning to be explored. What has been done to date suggests that they have excellent potential for linking learners with information and people located at great distances from the school.

## Interactive Videodiscs

Videodiscs store both sight and sound information on plastic discs. Though some disks employ other storage systems, most today rely on laser beams. Information is read by a laser beam and converted to visual and sound signals that are played back through a monitoring system.

Interactive videodisc systems allow users to customize what is played back. For example, individual sequences can be arranged and specific parts of the information coded on the videodisc can either be included or excluded. To accomplish this kind of flexibility, interactive videodisc systems couple videodisc and computer technologies. Systems typically use a 12-inch videodisc that can store as many as 54,000 still frames of video or 30 minutes of full-motion video (Seal-Warner, 1988). In the future, storage capacity of individual videodiscs is expected to increase.

Interactive videodisc systems allow teachers to prepare instruction that is designed in response to specific learner interests and needs. Learners, too, can be involved in the preparation of their own programs.

An example of a promising interactive videodisc program is GTV. This interactive American history program is designed for use in grades 5 through 12. There are two full hours of available video that are divided into 40 short segments that last between three to five minutes each. Users are able to identify which segments they want, and then can sequence them. Learners can be involved in sequencing decisions. The program allows them to pursue a common theme across a number of segments they select, develop short programs to support content in the text, and otherwise get directly involved in decisions involving selection and organization of information. A word-processing feature allows either the teacher or learners to write scripts to accompany the visual stories.

For information about GTV, write to:

National Geographic Society
Department GTV
Washington, DC 20077-9966

## CD-ROM

Compact disc, read-only memory—or CD-ROM—is a technology that is beginning to revolutionize management of computer, audio, and visual information. This technology entered the education market in the second half of the 1980s (Phillipo,

1989). In CD-ROM, information is stored in digital form on a small disc (4.75 inches in diameter). Information is recorded on the disc by a light beam that burns tiny pits on the surface. Information is read by a device connected to a computer that reads reflections of a laser light that bounce off the disc. Information is converted into computer language.

For educators, there are two important advantages of CD-ROM technology. First, information can take many forms, including audio, graphics, printed text, and video. Second, each disc has an enormous storage capacity. John Phillipo (1989), an authority on educational applications of electronic technology, points out that a single CD-ROM "disc is capable of storing the equivalent of 1,200 floppy discs, 250 large reference books, 2,400 full screen photos, or 550 MB [megabytes] of storage" (p. 40).

Learners can access information contained on a CD-ROM disc in many ways. They can browse through pages of an electronic encyclopedia in much the same way they would use a printed version in the school library. They can use key words or phrases to locate specific information. They can easily transfer prose and graphics from the CD-ROM disc to a floppy disc or a computer's hard disk. Using word-processing and desk-top publishing programs, this information can easily be incorporated into term papers and other learner-produced materials.

CD-ROM technology affords many opportunities for teachers to prepare customized instructional materials. Conceivably, an entire series of textbooks could be produced in CD-ROM format. Assuming that copyright releases were obtained, teachers would have little difficulty in preparing different configurations of this material for different learners in their classrooms.

Some firms that market CD-ROMs designed for use by teachers and schools are listed here:

This student is working with data from the 1990 census that is stored on a CD-ROM disc.

Broderbund Software, Inc.
17 Paul Drive
San Rafael, CA 94903

Encyclopedia Britannica Educational Corp.
Britannica Centre, 310 S. Michigan Avenue
Chicago, IL 60604

Grolier Electronic Encyclopedia
Sherman Turnpike
Danbury, CT 06816

Microsoft Corp.
Box 97017
Redmond, WA 98073

PC SIG Inc.
1030 Duane Avenue, Suite D
Sunnyvale, CA 94086

Tri-Star Publishing Company
475 Virginia Drive
Ft. Washington, PA 19034

### Interactive Distance Learning System

*Distance learning* has been around for years. The term refers to a system of instruction whereby learners are located at a considerable distance from the place where the instruction is delivered. Correspondence courses are an example of distance learning. For many years, educators in Australia have used the radio to broadcast lessons to learners in that country's remote outback. Televised instruction is another example of distance learning.

Throughout much of its history, distance learning has been a noninteractive, one-way phenomenon. That is, the teacher presented information to learners at remote sites, but there was no way for the teacher and the learners to interact as the lesson was being taught. Modern electronic technology has made this kind of interactive communication possible. See this chapter's Case Study for one such example.

---

CASE STUDY

## *On the road with educational technology*

**On September 7, 1989, most school-age children in the Denver, Colorado suburb of Englewood were in their traditional four-walled classrooms.** Eleven-year-old Jeff Heim and his 15-year-old brother J. J. were not. They were with their mother, former schoolteacher Jane Heim, in the family van heading east, at the beginning of a four-and-a-half month distance learning project.

The van was equipped with two Zenith laptop computers, a modem, printer, VCR, videocamera, boom box, camping supplies, and a semester's worth of assignments for each of the boys. The idea was for Jeff and J.J. to travel to places their classmates would only read about, experience firsthand the government in Washington, D.C. and the landmarks of the American Revolution in New England, and practice their Spanish in Mexico. While on the road, the students would electronically communicate with their teachers and classmates back home in Englewood.

The Heim family traveled by day, with the boys doing homework while Jane drove. For the first half of the trip, the family camped out. Electronic communication with the two schools took place about once a week. Homework assignments and tests were sent by regular mail, and teachers sent corrections and updated assignments via the computer and modem. Occasionally the Heims put down roots, albeit temporarily, in cities such as Washington, D.C. and Boston. "That's when the kids knew they were no longer in a traditional classroom situation," says Jane Heim. "We did a lot of sightseeing and exploring in the cities and the boys were too tired to do homework at night. Saturdays and Sundays soon became regular class days for them."

The high point of the trip for all involved was a joint audiovisual presentation set up by AT&T. The Heims went to San Francisco and the teachers went to an AT&T facility in Denver. Each location had televisions to allow the parties to see each other, and computers to transmit lessons. The teachers gave the traveling students a quick lesson and discussed any questions or problems with assignments.

*How do you react to what the Heim family did? What kinds of attitude differences toward learning might young people taught in this way have compared to those of learners in traditional classrooms? What do you see as limitations of this approach to learning? Would you expect to see more "learning on the road" in the future?*

Source: Condensed from Bill Morgan, "Distance Learning: The Van as a Classroom," *Electronic Learning* (April 1990): 20. Copyright © 1990 by Scholastic Incorporated. Reprinted with permission.

Keene, New Hampshire is surrounded by a number of small communities that, individually, are not able to offer some of the courses taught in Keene. An innovative interactive distance learning program now links Keene Junior High School with classrooms in the outlying communities of Westmoreland, Marlborough, and Chesterfield (Washor and Couture, 1990). A microwave transmission system now allows a teacher in Keene to use video monitors to see learners in these outlying schools. It is possible for students in these schools to ask questions and participate actively in class much as the students who are physically present in the Keene Junior High School classroom can ask questions and participate. There are telephone lines and fax machines in all of the classrooms. Thus, when written communication is necessary, it can be accomplished almost instantaneously.

Results of Keene's interactive distance learning program have been very positive. Learners at the remote sites have performed equally as well as those at Keene Junior High School. Plans are afoot to expand the number of schools served by Keene's program (Washor and Couture, 1990).

The isolation of learners at remote sites was for a long time a barrier to the growth of distance learning programs. Now, though these learners still are physically separate from their teachers, interactive systems can remove the learners' sense of psychological separateness. The technology now exists for young people even in the most remote areas of the country to feel that they can participate as active, contributing members of a class (even though other members may be hundreds of miles away).

## Electronic Innovations: Some Implications

Predicting the future is always hazardous. Unforeseen circumstances often shape events in unanticipated ways. Yet the temptation remains to look carefully at emerging patterns and suggest what kinds of futures they may portend. These changes may be among those resulting from an increased use of electronic technologies by professional educators (Grunwald, 1990):

- Teachers will increasingly serve as information guides for their learners, accessing them to information sources outside of the school.
- More learning will occur outside of the classroom.
- Schools will communicate more effectively with the communities they serve.

### Teachers as Information Guides

Information sources that are becoming available to teachers through computers linked to data sources via telephone lines are almost limitless in their scope. Future teachers may need to spend a good deal of their time becoming familiar with the contents of various sources and with procedures for accessing information. An important part of their instructional role will be to direct learners quickly to electronic information sources containing material needed to complete assignments.

### Learning Outside the Classroom

The traditional classroom made sense as an educational innovation when learning resources had to be physically located at the same place as the learners. The classroom was an efficient way to serve a large number of learners by gathering them together at one place that featured expensive learning materials and a trained teacher.

Today, computers and phone lines allow individuals to tap into information sources that may be hundreds or even thousands of miles away. Potentially, learning can take place wherever access to a computer and a phone line is available. Hence, it may be that learners in the future will do much more of their academic work in their own computer-equipped homes than is presently the case. When students and pupils work with information in the comfort of their own homes, they may develop important lifelong learning habits.

### Communicating with the Community

In the future, schools may be able to maintain almost continuous lines of open communication with parents and other school constituents. Information about upcoming events, scheduling of classes, absences, and other matters can easily be sent to home computers over phone lines, even using today's technology. In the future, electronic systems may allow reactions to proposed school policies to be transmitted back to the school. This kind of electronic dialogue has the potential to generate considerable interest in problems facing schools and to develop a broad base of support for their programs.

## Key Ideas in Summary

- Our society is becoming increasingly dependent on a work force that is conversant with technology. This implies that today's schools must go beyond the objective of producing individuals who are technologically literate to those who are technologically competent.

- In school settings, younger teachers often assume roles as technological mentors to older teachers who have had little training in the use of sophisticated electronic technologies. This situation suggests that individuals preparing to teach should develop a solid grounding in technologies that are increasingly appearing in the schools.

- Many newer technological innovations depend on electronic rather than mechanical features. This characteristic allows for tremendous speed of operation. Additionally, since many of these innovations have few moving pieces, they tend to require less maintenance than many earlier innovations that featured extensive movement of complex parts.

- There is some evidence that schools have been less quick to adopt new technologies than has our society as a whole. Some critics allege that much of education continues to reflect practices that are more consistent with nineteenth-century than with late twentieth-century technologies.

- Proponents of educational uses of technology are calling for large expenditures to equip schools with the electronic infrastructure that will allow educators to derive a maximum benefit from technological innovations. These people argue that piecemeal introduction of technology will not produce desired results in learners.

- Significant barriers to the adoption of educational innovations have always existed. Often, innovations have been introduced in a "top-down" fashion and have not recognized practical constraints faced by teachers in the classroom. There is a need for teachers to play a substantive role in the decision to adopt technological innovations. Further, once an innovation has been adopted, sufficient supplies of needed equipment must be purchased if there is to be a real expectation that the innovation will be implemented as intended.

- Increasing quantities of instructional and managerial software are available for teachers to use. In the last few years, the quality of education-related software has improved tremendously.

**Table 13–1**
Summary table: Technology and schools

| Technology | Characteristics |
|---|---|
| Instructional and managerial software | • Requires personal computer.<br><br>• Early examples for learners emphasized basic-skills instruction.<br><br>• Today's software for learners often focuses on sophisticated academic content and demands higher-level thinking.<br><br>• Much new software helps teachers and administrators with grading, general recordkeeping, and budgeting. |
| On-line data systems | • Require a computer and a telephone line.<br><br>• Subscription services provide data in many categories.<br><br>• Subscribers can access systems from any location with a computer hooked to a phone line. |
| Electronic bulletin boards | • Require a computer and a telephone line.<br><br>• Permit interconnections among many computers.<br><br>• Allow for a broad range of information exchange.<br><br>• Useful to learners, teachers, and administrators. |
| Interactive videodiscs | • Require a videodisc player coupled to a computer.<br><br>• Allow users to prepare customized sequences of the audio and video information contained on the videodiscs. |
| CD-ROM | • Digitally stores information on a small disc.<br><br>• Information can take many forms: audio, graphics, printed text, and video.<br><br>• Storage capacity of individual disks is enormous.<br><br>• Maximizes teachers' opportunities to customize instructional materials to meet individual learners' needs. |
| Interactive distance learning | • Instruction occurs in a situation where the teacher and learner are in separate locations but can maintain more or less continuous communication with one another.<br><br>• Has important implications for delivering excellent instruction to learners in remote areas. |

- Phone-line connections to computers in schools are greatly increasing computers' potential for supporting instructional programs. For example, on-line services such as PRODIGY and PC-Link make tremendous quantities of data available to learners in individual schools. Electronic bulletin boards allow for exchanges of messages among computer users in the schools. Some electronic bulletin boards include unit and lesson plan information for teachers, and others facilitate exchanges among learners in different schools.

- Interactive videodiscs allow teachers and learners to organize graphic and visual information to meet their own needs. This technology involves a coupling of a videodisc and a computer. CD-ROM features discs capable of storing enormous quantities of computer, audio, and visual information. This technology allows for easy transferring of information to a computer floppy disc or hard disk. Data contained on CD-ROM discs are particularly useful for learners working on research projects.

- Distance learning involves an instructional situation in which the teacher is at a different location than the learners. Classes taught over public television stations are an example. Traditionally, distance learning broadcasts have allowed learners either to hear or both hear and see the teacher, but they have not been able to communicate with the teacher while the class is being taught. New technologies using microwave transmission and other means now allow learners and teachers to both see one another and converse as lessons are being presented. This interactive distance learning is thought to have great promise as a means of providing much better instruction to learners in remote areas.

- If school use of new electronic technologies increases, several important changes may occur. Teachers may increasingly serve as guides to electronic information sources. Learners may spend more of their time learning outside of school. Information will be available to them wherever a computer can be connected to a phone line. Schools may find it easier to communicate with parents and other school patrons. Finally, there may be two-way communication, via computers, with community members when policy changes are being considered.

# Review and Discussion Questions

1. What are some examples of technological innovations that are having an impact on today's school programs?
2. Why is it possible for many of today's innovations to achieve much faster operating rates than innovations that appeared in years past?
3. What evidence is there to support the idea that graduates of our schools need to be technically competent?

4. Why do some experts suggest that a gradual introduction of technological innovations will not be effective?

5. What are some typical stages an innovation goes through when it is adopted in a school setting?

6. What are some of the ways today's computer software assists teachers and administrators?

7. How can on-line data systems aid instructional programs?

8. In what ways can experiences requiring learners to use electronic bulletin board systems enrich their learning?

9. Why have schools tended to lag behind the larger society in the use of electronic technology?

10. How can electronic innovations be introduced in ways that will encourage more teachers to take advantage of their capabilities?

......................................

# Ideas for Field Experiences, Projects, and Enrichment

1. Conduct a survey in a local school to determine the extent to which the following electronic technologies are being used:

   - computer software

   - on-line data systems

   - electronic bulletin boards

   - videodiscs

   - CD-ROM

   Share your findings with those of classmates who have completed similar surveys of different schools. Study all information that has been collected. As a class, respond to these questions: Are some of these technologies being more widely used than others? Are there important school-to-school differences?

2. Read five or six articles in periodicals such as *Electronic Learning, T.H.E. Journal*, and *Educational Technology* that focus on imaginative uses of electronic technology. Share your findings with your class, and comment on costs and other information related to the likelihood that these uses could be spread to other schools.

3. Invite a school administrator in charge of curriculum and instruction to visit your class. Ask this person to comment on the kinds of problems that arise

when teachers are asked to work with technologies that are unfamiliar to them.

4. Contact 10 teachers and 10 businesspeople from your local area. Ask each person to respond to this question: "Is the amount of up-to-date electronic technology used in our schools inadequate, about right, or more than is really necessary?" Compare responses of teachers and businesspeople. If there are differences, explain why this might be. Present your findings to class members in the form of a brief oral report.

5. Join with a few other class members to form a team. As a group, review professional journals for information about new technologies and how they may affect education. (You may wish to consult the *Education Index* for article and journal titles.) Present your findings to the class in a form of a symposium on this topic: "A School with State-of-the-Art Technology—What It Might Be Like."

•••••••••••••••••••••••••••

# Supplementary Reading

Garrison, D. R. *Understanding Distance Education*. London: Routledge, 1989.

Levinson, E. "Will Technology Transform Education or Will the Schools Co-Opt Technology?" *Phi Delta Kappan* (October 1990): 121–26.

McClintock, R. O., ed. *Computing and Education: The Second Frontier*. New York: Teachers College Press, 1988.

Mecklenburger, J. A. "Educational Technology Is Not Enough." *Phi Delta Kappan* (October 1990): 105–08.

Watson, B. "The Wired Classroom: American Education Goes On-Line." *Phi Delta Kappan* (October 1990): 109–12.

•••••••••••••••••••••••••••

# References

Baker, C. O., ed., and L. T. Ogle, associate ed. *The Condition of Education, 1989*: Vol. 1. *Elementary and Secondary Education*. Washington, DC: National Center for Education Statistics, 1989.

Cuban, L. *Teachers and Machines: The Classroom Use of Technology since 1920*. New York: Teachers College Press, 1986.

Grunwald, P. "The New Generation of Information Systems." *Phi Delta Kappan* (October 1990): 113–14.

Hawkridge, D. *New Information Technology in Education*. Baltimore, MD: Johns Hopkins University Press, 1983.

Levinson, E. "Will Technology Transform Education or Will the Schools Co-Opt Technology?" *Phi Delta Kappan* (October 1990): 121–26.

Mecklenburger, J. A. "Educational Technology Is Not Enough." *Phi Delta Kappan* (October 1990): 105–08.

Morgan, W. "Distance Learning: The Van as a Classroom." *Electronic Learning* (April 1990): 20.

Phillipo, J. "CD-ROM: A New Research and Study Skills Tool for the Classroom." *Electronic Learning* (June 1989): 40–41.

Seal-Warner, C. "Interactive Video Systems: Their Promise and Educational Potential." In R. O. McClintock, ed. *Computing and Education: The Second Frontier*. New York: Teachers College Press, 1988, 22–32.

*Vision Test: Three New Rs for Education*. Eugene, OR: International Society for the Study of Technology in Education, 1990.

Washor, E., and D. Couture. "A Distance Learning System That Pays All Its Own Costs." *T.H.E. Journal* (December 1990): 62–64.

Watson, B. "The Wired Classroom: American Education Goes On-Line." *Phi Delta Kappan* (October 1990): 109–12.

# Section 5

# Schools

## Overview

We have found that beginning teachers often are surprised by the organizational complexity of schools and school districts. As students in the schools and even as student teachers, they had little contact with people other than teachers, administrators, and counselors, all in a single building. Few beginners initially are aware of the many professional roles that may be discharged within a school district and the tremendous number of support staff people needed to keep the schools in operation.

As school districts and individual schools grow in size, there is an accompanying increase in the numbers of specialized roles people play. Though teachers are by far the most numerous employees of school districts, they represent only one of several categories of professional employees. Districts almost universally have a superintendent and other central office administrators, building principals and subordinate administrators, counselors, and nurses. Large numbers of districts will also have specialists such as psychometrists, psychologists, and curriculum supervisors. Nonprofessional employees such as food-service personnel, transportation workers, custodial engineers, clerks, and secretaries are also numerous.

Over the years, a system of governance has developed for managing complex school district bureaucracies. In most places, school boards make policies in areas where local officials have the authority to make decisions (as opposed to those policy areas governed by the state). School boards make their decisions after receiving advice from many constituencies, including district administrators, teachers, and various community groups.

Though certain state (and occasionally federal) guidelines must be followed, some local school board decisions affect what is taught in schools. The adopted curriculum

gives individual schools their special flavor. As important as the curriculum is, researchers have found that the quality of the academic program alone is an insufficient indicator of a school's overall excellence—a sound curriculum is but one of a number of features that characterize effective schools.

In thinking about organizational features of districts and schools, the nature of the school curriculum, and characteristics of schools that have been found to be doing exceptionally good jobs, answering these questions may be helpful:

- How are school districts organized?
- What types of organizational features characterize elementary schools and secondary schools?
- What are some categories of professional and nonprofessional personnel who work in school districts, and what do they do?
- What are some general curricular orientations found in the schools today?
- What are some basic curriculum patterns in elementary and secondary schools?
- What characteristics have researchers found that characterize effective schools?

Chapters in this section provide answers to these questions. These chapters are:

Chapter 14: Organization and Personnel
Chapter 15: The Curriculum
Chapter 16: Effective Schools

349

# Organization and Personnel

## Objectives

This chapter provides information to help the reader to

- point out basic patterns of school district organization.
- recognize that the organizational patterns of school districts vary with the size of the learner enrollment.
- identify some of the kinds of professionals who work in school districts.
- describe some basic organizational patterns of individual schools.
- identify responsibilities of different categories of employees who work in individual school buildings.
- suggest several categories of nonteaching professionals who work in individual school buildings.

## Focus Questions

1. What contributes to the complexity of the administrative organization of a given school district?
2. What is the relationship between (*a*) the size of a school district or an individual and (*b*) the kinds of professionals with whom a typical teacher will interact during a typical day?
3. Why does the school board play such an important role in the operation of a school district?
4. Who are some of the people that may work in a district's central administrative offices, and what do they do?
5. What are some of the responsibilities of a school superintendent?
6. What do elementary principals do?
7. What professionals other than regular classroom teachers often work in individual schools?
8. How are general administrative schemes in elementary and secondary schools similar and different?
9. What are some responsibilities of grade-level leaders and department heads?
10. What functions are performed by some of the support personnel who work in individual schools?

· · · · · · · · · · · · · · · · · · · · · · · · · · ·

# Introduction

Public education is big business. In 1990, total annual expenditures to support it were about $200 billion. A recent survey determined that there were 4.4 million school employees (Ogle and Alsalam, 1990, p. 174). In the year of the survey, nearly 2 percent of the entire population of the United States were full-time employees of the schools.

School employees comprise many categories. Classroom teachers make up only slightly more than half of the total number—53 percent in 1989 (Ogle and Alsalam, 1990, p. 88). Support staff, including personnel attached to administrative offices, transportation people, food-service personnel, plant-and-maintenance employees, health professionals, and assorted other categories, account for nearly 32 percent of all school employees. Instructional staff other than teachers (classroom aides, librarians, guidance counselors, and psychological personnel) represent about 11 percent of the total school employment force. The final category, principals and district administrators, account for between 4 and 5 percent of the total (Ogle and Alsalam, 1990, p. 88).

Leaders of school districts have had to develop sophisticated organizational plans to manage the educational enterprise. Larger school districts have more complex organizational schemes than smaller ones. Similarly, individual schools with many learners also have more intricate organizations than those enrolling fewer learners.

The kinds of contacts teachers have with individuals who play various roles within school districts and buildings vary with district and school enrollment size. For example, teachers in a small elementary school are apt to have frequent (often daily) conversations with the school principal, whereas in a large high school, weeks may go by without a teacher having occasion to speak to the principal. Indeed, in the latter situation the principal may never step into the teacher's classroom during an entire school year. In large schools, the principal's administrative subordinates often are responsible for handling routine matters with teachers.

There are many employees of school districts with whom individual teachers have infrequent personal contact. For example, in some districts much of the custodial work is done at night, after teachers have left for the day. Individual teachers and school nurses (especially in large buildings) rarely have occasion to meet during the working day. Central administrative office support personnel (for example, people assigned to manage the district's transportation system) spend little time in the district's schools. Hence, teachers are not apt to meet many of these individuals.

## How School Districts Are Organized

There are thousands of school districts in the United States. These vary from small operations in isolated rural areas to districts encompassing the densely populated core areas of the nation's major cities. The kind of management scheme needed to oversee the operation of a given district depends, in large measure, on the number of learners enrolled in the district's schools.

Even districts that enroll roughly equivalent numbers of learners reflect some differences in their administrative organization schemes. These variations result from

*"And now we will consider district policies related to role differentiation, appropriate patterns of leadership influence, warm and symbiotic ties between those in line and staff positions, and a host of ways to optimize productive decision-making within the framework of a sensitive, hierarchical management structure. In other words, we are going to find out who gets to tell whom to do what."*

Courtesy of Ford Button

unique local conditions, special requirements imposed by state education authorities, and long-standing traditions. An example of an organization scheme for a school district is provided in Figure 14–1.

## The School Board

The school board is the basic policymaking body of a school district. It may be known by other names such as board of education, board of trustees, or school council. School boards represent a link between the local school district and the state department of education. Because the state department of education implements mandates of the state legislature, local school boards are also indirectly linked to the legislature. The state legislature, in fact, exercises ultimate control over local school districts. In most states, the legislature has the right to create, modify, eliminate, and otherwise affect the operation of local school districts.

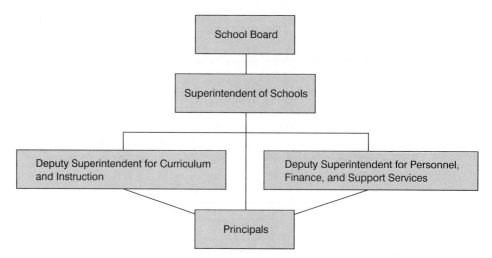

**Figure 14–1**
Example of the basic administrative organization of a school district

School boards vary in size, usually containing from five to nine members. In most places members are elected; in a few they are appointed. Members of elected school boards are supposed to reflect general community sentiment regarding the schools. In reality, though, school board members are often well-established community members who reflect mainstream and somewhat conservative thinking. People who agree to serve on school boards often do so as a matter of public service. In many parts of the country school board members receive no compensation, but in some places they are paid for their work.

The school board's primary responsibility is to establish basic policy for the district. Part of its role is to oversee implementation of state requirements. The school board adopts the budget and reacts to recommendations regarding personnel and curriculum that it receives from the district superintendent and his/her staff.

School board members are among the unheralded heroes of American education. They put in long hours on school-related work. They receive telephone calls late into the night from school patrons who have grievances to air. Their decisions are watched closely by the local media, and sometimes their actions draw negative comments on the editorial pages of local newspapers—letters to the editor and editorials often question the motives of school board members (and sometimes even their basic integrity). Angry taxpayers freely let school board members know their displeasure when tax rates have to be hiked to fund school budgets. In short, school board members find themselves torn between the competing perspectives of dozens of contending interest groups, each of which is certain that it holds the key to a policy decision that will improve the schools.

Given the pressures they face, it is a wonder that people want to fill vacancies on school boards. But they do, and in many communities school board service confers an important status on board members. Schools everywhere are beneficiaries of the willingness of these good people to serve.

These school board members are reviewing the agenda before their meeting begins.

Many citizens in local communities believe that school board members are intimately involved in the day-to-day operations of the school, but this generally is not the case. The board directs the superintendent to oversee the running of the school, while its own task is to frame policy and hold the superintendent responsible for implementing it. In some districts, board members do try to involve themselves in operational decisions (see this chapter's Case Study). This invariably leads to conflict between the board and the superintendent, which sometimes results in a change of superintendents. Neither the school board nor the superintendent can discharge responsibilities appropriate to each function unless there is trust and confidence on both sides.

CASE STUDY

## A visit from the school board

**Woong Kim teaches second grade in a suburban district outside of a major west coast city.** He is in his second year of teaching. Woong is particularly interested in teaching reading. As an undergraduate, he was influenced by several of his professors who believed in a whole-language approach to reading instruction. This method builds on learners' natural patterns of oral language, and Woong has found it to be effective in working with his own pupils. Members of his class are a diverse group, representing many ethnic groups. Some of them do not speak English at home. Large numbers of families in the area have incomes below the official poverty level.

Loretta Robinson, a newly elected member of the local school board, recently sent a letter to all of the district's elementary school teachers. In the letter, she pointed to some research studies that strongly support the use of a phonics approach to reading. Ms. Robinson went on to note that standardized reading test scores of children in the district are well below national averages, and recommended that teachers adopt the phonics approach to teaching reading. Ms. Robinson indicated that she would be contacting selected teachers in the district later in the year regarding what they were doing to improve their reading programs.

Woong recalled that the university professors who favored the whole-language approach had not had many good things to say about phonics-based reading instruction. Many of them had cited research supporting whole-language instruction that seemed to say quite different things from those studies contained in Ms. Robinson's letter.

To get another point of view, Woong checked with his grade-level leader and principal. Both of them said that district policy prescribes no specific method of reading instruction. Teachers are assumed to be professionals who are expected to make instructional decisions that are appropriate for the children in their own classrooms. The principal also pointed out that the superintendent has an excellent working relationship with most members of the school board and that it is very unusual for a school board member to make a direct appeal to teachers regarding a specific instructional approach.

After thinking about the situation, Woong initially decided to keep using the whole-language approach. But yesterday something happened that has made him uneasy—he received a letter from the president of the school board announcing that the entire board will spend a day visiting his school. Though it is not clear which board members will visit which classrooms, Woong is worried that Ms. Robinson may visit his. He is afraid she might notice that he is not using a phonics approach, and is wondering whether she might make negative comments about his teaching that could hurt his career.

*What should Woong do? Is there someone specific he should talk to? What might happen if Ms. Robinson asks him about his commitment to phonics-based instruction and he gives her an honest response? Will honesty hurt his career? Is Ms. Robinson justified in questioning a teacher's instructional approach? How might other school board members react to her actions? Does the superintendent have a role to play in this situation?*

Most school board meetings are open to the public. State laws vary from place to place regarding the kinds of circumstances that allow boards to meet in private (usually called *executive*) sessions. Often, boards have the right to do so when they are considering sensitive personnel matters.

At one time, many school boards scheduled their meetings during the day, but this practice is dying out. Increasingly, school boards meet at night to allow members of the community with daytime jobs to attend. It is common practice for school boards to set aside some time after the formal agenda has been completed for members of the public to speak briefly about issues of concern to them. When the board is considering a controversial policy issue (e.g., whether to implement a busing program to establish a racial balance in the district's schools), board meetings are very well-attended.

In summary, the school board acts as the district's major policymaking body. It functions as a political entity that allows members of the public to make their influence on school policy decisions felt. At the same time, it represents the broader interests of the state legislature and the state department of education.

## The Superintendent of Schools

The superintendent is the chief executive officer (CEO) of a school district. A school district superintendency is a challenging position, particularly in a large school district. In such a setting, executive responsibilities of the superintendent parallel those of top corporate administrators.

Often the superintendent is hired by the school board, but in a few places superintendents are chosen in other ways (e.g., some superintendents are publicly elected officials). The superintendent usually attends all school board sessions except for those where his/her own performance is being evaluated. The superintendent, who may argue against a certain course of action when it is being considered by the school board, is obligated to support and implement all school board policies once they have been adopted.

The superintendent exercises some control over the school district's work force because, in most places, it is the superintendent who officially recommends candidates for employment to the school board. All other employees of the school district are directly or indirectly accountable to the superintendent. Though specific responsibilities may be delegated to others, ultimately the superintendent is held accountable for their performance.

The superintendent is responsible for all aspects of the school program. For example, he or she monitors all academic programs and arranges for periodic status reports to the school board. The superintendent oversees the maintenance of all school buildings and equipment, and approves expenditures of funds within the general guidelines authorized by the school board.

The superintendent works closely with administrative subordinates to ensure smooth functioning of the entire district operation. One of the superintendent's most important jobs is overseeing the preparation of the annual budget, which must be submitted to the school board for review and approval. Budget proposals always attract a great deal of scrutiny from board members and from the public at large.

The superintendent, as the chief public relations officer of the school district, must defend school policies in many public forums. Superintendents are often called upon to speak before civic groups and other citizens' organizations. They tend to be individuals who are comfortable with many different kinds of people. Because public relations is such an important part of the job, many superintendents have exemplary writing and speaking skills.

## The Deputy Superintendents

In medium- and large-sized school districts, the superintendent has several subordinate administrators to whom responsibilities for specific managerial tasks are delegated. These people have titles such as deputy superintendent, associate superintendent, or assistant superintendent. The administrative scheme illustrated in Figure 14–1 provides for two deputy superintendents: the deputy superintendent for curriculum and instruction, and the deputy superintendent for personnel, finance, and support services.

Each of these deputies is responsible for a major component of the district's operation. As the title suggests, the deputy superintendent for curriculum and instruction has responsibility for managing the district's academic programs. This person oversees a number of other administrators. Three key subordinates include the executive director of elementary education (responsible for programs in grades pre-kindergarten through 6), the executive director of secondary education (responsible for programs in grades 7 through 12), and the executive director of student support services.

The executive director of elementary education and the executive director of secondary education supervise a number of people who have specialized responsibilities for maintaining and enhancing the quality of the instructional program. Many of these people are specialists in teaching specific academic subjects. The executive director of student support services oversees leaders of the district's psychological services, counseling, and guidance programs; its special education programs; its health service operations; its school-attendance monitoring function; and its federal programs. Figure 14–2 illustrates an example of an organizational plan for that part of a district's operation falling under the jurisdiction of the deputy superintendent for curriculum and instruction.

Note that Figure 14–2 does not provide a separate leadership structure for junior high schools or middle schools. These schools are administered either by personnel charged with responsibilities for elementary education or secondary education.

Even the terms *elementary education* and *secondary education* are not interpreted in the same ways in all places. For example, in some areas "elementary education" is often thought of as embracing grades K through 6, while in other places grades K through 8 comprise the elementary program. Similarly, in some districts "secondary education" is often interpreted to mean grades 7 through 12, but other districts consider it to be grades 6 through 12, 9 through 12, or some other set of grades. (Grades 10, 11, and 12 are almost always included within the designation "secondary education.")

The pattern becomes even more confusing in districts that identify separate organizational structures for junior high schools and middle schools. The term *middle school* has been particularly difficult to pin down in terms of the grade levels it embraces. Where middle schools exist, they ordinarily include grades 6 and 7 (Lounsbury and Vars, 1978; Armstrong and Savage, 1990). Beyond these two grades, middle school grade configurations vary tremendously from place to place. For example, some middle schools have grades 5, 6, and 7; some have grades 5, 6, 7, and 8; some have grades 6, 7, 8; some have grades 6, 7, 8, and 9; and some have still other arrangements.

The deputy superintendent for personnel, finance, and support services has a wide range of responsibilities. This person may be assisted by subordinate administrators, each of whom has responsibilities for one of these areas: personnel, finance, and support services. An example of an organization plan for the part of a district's operations that is the responsibility of the deputy superintendent for personnel, finance, and support services is provided in Figure 14–3 (p. 360).

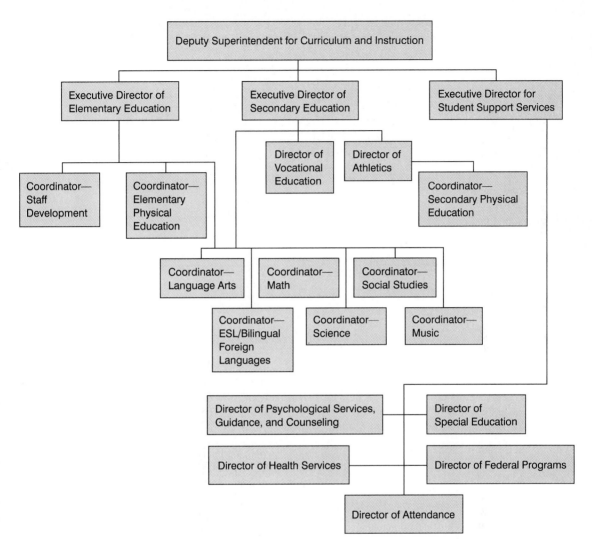

**Figure 14–2**
Example of the administrative jurisdiction of a deputy superintendent for curriculum and instruction

The executive director for personnel is responsible for screening candidates and making hiring recommendations. These decisions often involve cooperation with other district administrators. For example, it may be necessary to get the concurrence of the principal in the building to which a prospective new employee is to be assigned. The executive director of personnel's office also often monitors all records of existing faculty and staff members, keeps track of where each person is on the salary scale, monitors employee benefits programs, and takes charge of many other duties having to do with employee relations.

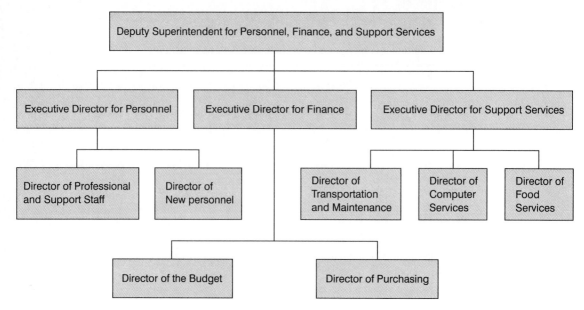

**Figure 14–3**
Example of the administrative jurisdiction of a deputy superintendent for personnel, finance, and support services

The executive director for finance, as the title implies, has broad authority in areas related to budgeting and purchasing. Often, this office is responsible for drafting initial versions of the proposed annual budget. This administrator is responsible for overseeing expenditures to ensure that they are in line with what has been authorized. School purchases of all kinds are often executed and monitored by personnel attached to the executive director for finance.

The executive director for support services oversees a variety of important functions. For example, this office will often manage all transportation and maintenance operations. Additionally, food services provided by the schools frequently come under the jurisdiction of this executive director. Other support services, including printing and computer services, may also be managed by the executive director for support services and this person's subordinates.

## Other Central Office Professional Personnel

Some school districts, particularly large ones, have many professionals with specialized skills who are headquartered in the district's central administrative offices. (A number of these people are referenced on the charts in Figures 14–2 and 14–3.) Typically, they have responsibilities that are either districtwide in scope or that serve at least some of the district's schools.

Figure 14–2 identifies a number of "coordinators." These are individuals responsible for instruction in the area under their jurisdiction. Some districts use different terms to describe these individuals. For example, they may called consultants, directors, or district program chairs. Often, these positions are held by former teachers who proved to be exemplary performers in the classroom and have gone on to do advanced study in their specializations and in curriculum. Some states and districts require coordinators to hold special kinds of certificates.

Many school districts have several people attached to an office who are responsible for overseeing guidance and counseling activities throughout the district. For example, there may be one or more professional psychologists attached to this office, as well as other people with advanced training in specialized areas related to the counseling and guidance function.

Many districts employ psychometrists. *Psychometrists* are people who have had advanced training in the construction and administration of sophisticated tests that are designed to measure mental abilities of various kinds. These individuals frequently have advanced degrees and, in many places, must qualify for a special certificate.

There may also be some special kinds of teachers attached to the central administrative offices. These include specialists in such areas as reading who work with teachers and learners in several of the district's schools. Additionally, there may be homebound teachers who are assigned to work with learners in the district who are unable to attend regular school classes. Many teachers in these specialty areas have advanced academic training in their fields.

Some districts have research and evaluation specialists who are charged with monitoring innovations and overseeing the administration of standardized testing programs. Many of these people tend to hold advanced degrees, and some districts require them to hold special certificates as well.

These are just some examples of the kinds of professionals who often work out of a district's central administrative offices. Today's school districts employ large numbers of people besides school principals and regular classroom teachers.

## How Individual Schools Are Organized

Administrative organization schemes for schools are varied, though some features are quite common. Most school-to-school differences result because of variations in enrollment. Elementary schools tend to have organizational patterns that distinguish them from secondary schools, which draw learners from several "feeder" elementary schools. This means that, typically, an elementary school enrolls fewer learners than a secondary school. Hence, in most cases, administrative organizational schemes in elementary schools are somewhat less complex than those in secondary schools.

### Organization of Elementary Schools

*Building Administrators.*    The school principal is the chief executive officer of an elementary school, responsible for all aspects of the school's operation. The principal oversees the academic program and ensures that it is in compliance with state and local regulations. Welfare of individual pupils comprises another important responsibility of the principal. Except in the very largest of elementary schools, principals often know the names of large numbers of pupils in every grade.

Parents of elementary school children take an active interest in the operation of the school. The principal is charged with winning parental support for school programs and encouraging active parental participation in parent-teacher groups and other school activities.

Principals are also responsible for the performance of each teacher in their building. Teachers look to the principal for guidance and support. The principal is expected to provide leadership in assisting teachers who may be experiencing difficulty in the classroom. Some common attitudes that teachers have toward principals are listed in the accompanying What the Experts Say.

WHAT THE EXPERTS SAY

## Relationships between teachers and principals

Sharon Feiman-Nemser and Robert E. Floden (1986) have summarized findings of a number of researchers who studied teachers' feelings about principals. They found the following attitudes to be common:

1. Teachers do not want the principal to interfere with the daily decisions they make about their instructional programs.
2. Teachers expect the principal to act as a kind of buffer between themselves and potential critics in the local community.
3. Teachers want the principal to take the lead in establishing and maintaining a disciplined learning environment in the school.
4. Teachers will cooperate with the principal when they believe that he or she is properly discharging the responsibilities associated with the role of principal.
5. The most important lever a principal has in getting teachers to comply with a request to maintain high academic standards is the good will that has been established between the principal and the teachers.

Principals also oversee the work of other professional and staff employees. Depending on the size of the school, other employees might include assistant principals, counselors, individual subject specialists (e.g., in reading), special education teachers, nurses, and custodians.

Because of their broad-ranging responsibilities, most principals are issued contracts that call for them to be at the school for many more days than classroom teachers need to be present. Often, principals are expected to be in their buildings for at least 11 months of the year.

Larger elementary schools have one or more assistant principals. These individuals oversee certain aspects of the school program, as directed by the principal. Assistant principals' employment contracts also typically require them to work a longer school year than do classroom teachers.

An example of an administrative organization plan for a medium-sized elementary school (approximately 450 pupils) is provided in Figure 14–4.

**Figure 14–4**
Example of the administrative
organization of a medium-sized
elementary school

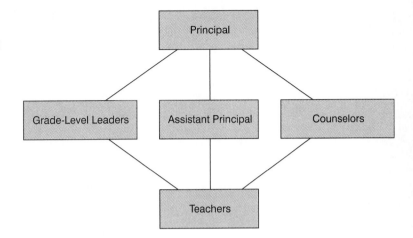

*Grade-Level Leaders.*    Larger elementary schools often have teachers who are assigned to play special leadership roles as grade-level leaders. Grade-level leaders are found in schools where two (and often three or more) classes exist at each grade level. Teachers who fill these positions represent the concerns of all teachers at their grade level in meetings with the principal. They work with all teachers at their grade level to plan and coordinate learning experiences for children. They sometimes take the lead in introducing new techniques and in modeling their use in the classrooms. Often, they are responsible for ordering materials for all teachers at their grade level. These people usually are selected on the basis of their years of successful teaching, interpersonal-relations skills, and advanced academic training.

*Specialty Teachers.*    Elementary schools often include a few teachers who have received specialized training. Among these individuals are teachers who are specialists in working with learners having emotional or physical handicaps. There may be one or more reading specialists assigned to a single building, and/or there may be several teachers with training in working with gifted and talented learners. Some schools have teachers who have been hired to work with categories of learners for whom special educational support money is available (e.g., children of migrant workers).

*Other Professional Employees.*    Elementary schools often employ several categories of nonteaching professional employees.* For example, a school nurse may be in attendance for at least part of the school day. This person's responsibility is to deal with minor health problems and to oversee the management of learners' health records.

The school may have one or more counselors. Counselors typically are professionals who have taught for several years and have completed advanced course work leading to special counseling certification. Their role is to help learners work through personal and academic problems, and they also frequently have responsibil-

---

*It should be noted that some principals teach classes. Other nonteaching employees also may have some teaching responsibilities. In general, the term *nonteaching employee* is meant to suggest that the major responsibility of the individual involves something other than classroom teaching.

ity for managing and administering standardized tests. Counselors often are issued contracts that call for them to work two or three weeks longer each school year than do teachers.

A title such as "learning resource specialist" is increasingly being used to describe professionals who, formerly, were known as librarians. The adjustment in title reflects the broadening range of these employees' responsibilities. In addition to managing all aspects of the school library (including teaching classes in library skills), these people are often responsible for managing instructional support equipment such as VCRs, film projectors, tape recorders, audiocassette players, computers, and television sets. Many of them have special training in instructional technology as well as in library science. Because of the need to process books, inventory equipment, and take care of other job-related matters, some learning resource specialists work a longer school year than do classroom teachers.

Reading specialists often are part of the professional staff serving learners in the school. This reading specialist works in an elementary school.

*Other Employees.*    Elementary schools have employees who perform many other important functions. One or more secretaries may work in the principal's office. In larger schools, there may also be secretaries assigned to work with the assistant principals and counselors. There may be a supply room clerk who takes charge of ordering and distributing materials. Sometimes this person also is in charge of managing and maintaining duplicating equipment.

Paraprofessionals are people who, although lacking formal professional training as teachers, are hired to assist teachers in various ways. They may work with individual learners who experience problems, help teachers prepare instructional materials, monitor learners when they take tests, and do other things to support the work of classroom teachers.

Many elementary schools prepare lunches for pupils. A kitchen staff headed by a chief cook is responsible for this activity. Additionally, virtually every school has a custodial staff that is responsible for cleaning the building and taking care of routine maintenance tasks. In small schools, there may be only one custodian; larger schools will employ several.

Box 14–1 addresses the problem of lack of public recognition of the large numbers of nonteaching staff whom the schools employ.

## Organization of Secondary Schools

*Building Administrators.*    Secondary schools vary greatly in size. The complexity of the administrative arrangement tends to increase as school enrollment increases. An example of an administrative arrangement for a high school enrolling between 1,500 and 2,000 students is provided in Figure 14–5.

The principal of a large high school has a demanding job, supervising a huge teaching and support staff. For example, in a school with 2,000 students, there may be more than 75 teachers. As well, the principal must manage a large budget. This administrator also has a challenging public relations role—a principal of a large high school must deal effectively with parents and other citizens who have differing views about what a "good" school should provide. This requires the principal to be visible in the local community— which means attendance at all major school events as well as participation in service and other community organizations. Finally, the principal must exercise leadership over the school program and ensure that all federal, state, and local requirements are met.

In most secondary schools, the principal has one or more assistants. In the example provided in Figure 14–5, the principal has four assistant principals, one to work with each class (grade 9, grade 10, grade 11, and grade 12). Individual assistant principals are responsible for instruction, guidance, scheduling, and other functions as they relate to students at their assigned grade level. This arrangement is only one of several that are commonly found in secondary schools.

An alternate scheme followed in many high schools assigns responsibilities for one or more functions to each assistant principal. Each assistant works with students and teachers in all grades, but only in a limited number of areas of responsibility. For example, there may be an assistant principal for scheduling and discipline; an assistant principal for curriculum; an assistant principal for budget, computing, maintenance, and food services; and an assistant principal for guidance and student services. Whatever

## ARE THERE TOO MANY SCHOOL ADMINISTRATORS?

Schools are often accused of being top-heavy with administrators. This point of view is reflected in the following comments from a recent editorial in a local newspaper.

> Only slightly over half of our school employees are teachers. These teachers complain that they are overburdened with paperwork requests from building administrators. Is it possible that we have too many administrators and that they are generating paperwork requests to justify their own existence? Wouldn't it be better to halve the number of administrators, hire more teachers, and decrease class size? We think so.

***What Do You Think?***

1. Why do you think that people often suppose there to be too many administrators in the schools?
2. Based on what you know, is this an accurate perception?
3. If you were to write a letter to the editor in response to this editorial, what would you say?

the administrative arrangement, however, the principal and the assistant principals typically work a much longer school year than do teachers.

In addition to the principal and the assistant principals, a large high school may have other administrators. For example, there may be a head counselor. This person is responsible for assigning responsibilities to members of the counseling staff.

There may also be an athletic director. As the title implies, this person oversees budgets and personnel associated with interschool and intramural athletics. Another sort of director found in many secondary schools is the finance director, who oversees a small staff of people who monitor the school budget and manage accounts for student organizations.

There may be a vocational programs director, who monitors mandated federal and state programs designed to prepare high school graduates for specific kinds of jobs. This individual manages the required paperwork and often makes contacts with employers in the local community, who cooperate in school-based training programs of various kinds.

The head custodian is an important administrator in large secondary schools. This person supervises a considerable staff of people who clean the building and take care of routine maintenance. Classroom teachers may never encounter some members of the head custodian's staff because, in many large buildings, there is a night shift that comes on duty after teachers and students leave for the day.

There often is a head dietitian, who is responsible for planning lunch menus and overseeing a large kitchen and cafeteria staff. The school lunch program is a large and

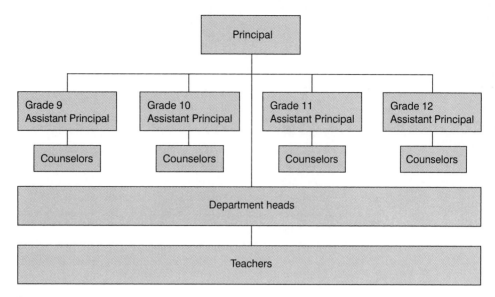

**Figure 14–5**
Example of an administrative organization plan for a high school

complex activity, and the head dietitian must handle a great deal of paperwork as well as direct the activities of food-service employees.

In large schools, there may also be a head resource specialist. This person oversees the work of school library personnel as well as the staff responsible for maintaining media equipment. Identifying learning resource needs, ordering, and processing new material and equipment also fall under this person's jurisdiction.

*Department Heads.*    Department heads are teachers who lead the individual academic departments in a secondary school. They report either directly to the school principal or indirectly to the school principal through one of the assistant principals. Department heads often are relieved of one instructional period a day to allow them time to take care of department business. Their employment contracts often require them to work two or more weeks longer than do other teachers.

Department heads are experienced, respected teachers. Their duties include such activities as informing members of their departments about important administrative policies, working with teachers new to their staffs, passing on concerns of department members to the principal, making recommendations for assigning department members to individual courses, allocating the materials' budget among department members, arranging for textbook distribution, and representing the department at district-level curriculum meetings.

*Specialty Teachers.*    As is the case with elementary schools, secondary schools also include some teachers who have received specialized training. Because the average secondary school is larger than the average elementary school, frequently a secondary school will employ more specialty teachers than will an elementary school. Groups served by these individuals are emotionally disturbed learners and learners with physical disabilities, gifted and talented students, learners with reading problems, and learners in a variety of other special programs.

*Other Professionals.* Most secondary schools have several counselors who have had advanced course work in guidance and counseling. Many of them have advanced academic degrees. In most places they hold special counseling certificates, though this pattern varies somewhat from state to state and from place to place within some states. Many counselors handle both academic and personal counseling. In very large schools, some counselors may have specific responsibilities. For example, there may be a counselor who works only with college and university placement issues. Another may be concerned only with vocational counseling and aptitude testing. Another may work exclusively with managing the standardized testing program.

There may also be several school nurses in a large secondary school. These individuals are responsible for maintaining health records and dealing with minor health-related situations that arise during the school day.

There likely are a number of learning resource specialists within a large secondary school. Some of them work full time in the library; others may be assigned to work exclusively with specialized instructional support equipment.

*Other Staff Members.* Secondary schools often have large secretarial staffs. There may even be a head secretary, who is charged with overseeing the work of all other secretaries in the building. Individual secretaries may be assigned to the principal, the assistant principals, the counselors, the finance office, and the main-office reception area. There may be one secretary who is assigned to do nothing but handle incoming telephone calls—telephones ring constantly at larger secondary schools, and answering them and finding the appropriate party is a time-consuming activity.

Custodial staffs in large high schools are extensive. This also tends to be true for kitchen staffs. However, not all kitchen-staff employees work a full eight-hour day—some come in for only a few hours during the middle of the day.

There may be one or two supply room clerks. These people are responsible for maintaining an inventory of paper, pens, pencils, and other items. Teachers contact these clerks when they need supplies. Because of the nature of their responsibilities, supply room clerks are individuals with whom teachers come into frequent contact.

Paraprofessionals are less common in secondary schools than in elementary schools. In the secondary schools that employ them, they function much as they do in elementary schools; that is, they are assigned to help individual teachers and, in discharging this responsibility, they do many different kinds of things.

# Key Ideas in Summary

- School districts have developed sophisticated organizational plans for managing their activities. In general, administrative schemes are more complex in larger school districts than in smaller ones. Similarly, school buildings enrolling larger

**Table 14–1**
Summary table: Organization and personnel

| Topic | Key Points |
| --- | --- |
| School board | This is the primary policymaking body of a school district. Members represent local citizens. The school board is an important link between the local district and state education officials. |
| Superintendent | The superintendent is the chief executive officer (CEO) of a school district. He or she has general responsibility for all aspects of the school district's operations. |
| Deputy superintendents | These people, sometimes known by other titles, are delegated by the superintendent to monitor specific components of the overall operation of the school district. For example, a deputy superintendent for curriculum would have responsibility for all instructional programming in the district. |
| Principals | These are the top administrators in individual school buildings. Each building has one. This person may be assisted by one or more assistant principals. |
| Grade-level leader | In an elementary school with two or more teachers per grade, this person represents the concerns of other teachers working at his or her grade level, often representing the grade-level group in meetings with the school principal. |
| Department head | This person chairs an academic department in a secondary school. He or she coordinates workloads and acts on behalf of the department in meetings with the school principal. |
| Psychometrist | This is a specialist with advanced training in evaluation, particularly in measuring mental abilities of various kinds. Psychometrists often have offices in a school district's central administrative headquarters. |
| Subject-area coordinator, consultant, or director | This person, often a former teacher, is a specialist in one of the subject areas taught in the schools. Often he or she will have an office in the central administrative headquarters of the school district. This person is in charge of overseeing curricula in the area of specialization, and will often plan some of the inservice programs for teachers in his or her subject area. |

numbers of learners tend to feature administrative organizations that are more complex than those serving smaller numbers of learners.

- The specific categories of school personnel with whom teachers are likely to have frequent daily contact vary from place to place. In part, these variations are related to the numbers of learners attending the school. For example, a teacher in a small elementary school may well interact with the principal every day, while in a large high school several days may pass without the teacher even seeing the principal.

- The school board (sometimes known by names such as *board of education, board of trustees,* or *school council*) is the basic policymaking body of a school district. It represents a link between the local district and the state department of education. In most places, school board members are elected. The school board hires and monitors the work of the district's superintendent.

- The superintendent is the chief executive officer of a school district, responsible for all aspects of the district's day-to-day operations. Among other responsibilities, the superintendent is the ultimate supervisor of all employees, responsible for ensuring that academic programs are in compliance with federal and state regulations, charged with preparing budget proposals for the school board, and the top professional public-relations spokesperson for the district. Depending on the size of the district, the superintendent may be assisted by one or more deputies, associates, or assistants.

- Principals are the chief executive officers of individual schools, responsible for all aspects of their school's operation. Among other things, they oversee the academic program, monitor learners' progress, check on teachers' performances, manage budgets, and work to maintain good public relations with parents and other citizens. In larger buildings, they are aided by assistant principals.

- In some elementary schools, the principal and assistant principals may be assisted by grade-level leaders. These teachers represent the interests of other teachers at the grade level they teach in interactions with the principals and, sometimes, in meetings with central office personnel. Other professionals in larger elementary schools include school nurses, counselors, and learning resource specialists. There often are other support personnel, including secretaries, food-service workers, and paraprofessionals.

- Administrative arrangements in secondary schools vary somewhat from those in elementary schools. Secondary schools typically enroll more students and, in general, have more elaborate administrative management schemes than do elementary schools. In addition to the principal and assistant principals, administrators in a medium-to-large-sized high school might include a head counselor, an athletic director, a finance director, a vocational programs director, a head custodian, a head dietitian, and a head learning resource specialist.

- Department heads in secondary schools lead the departments with which they are affiliated. They inform department members of important policy decisions. Also, they meet frequently with the principal or an assistant principal and, hence, function as an important conduit between the school administrative office and teachers in the departments they represent. Often, department heads represent the school in districtwide meetings of subject-area specialists. They typically work a slightly longer academic year than do other teachers, and they often have one nonteaching period a day reserved for their departmental administrative responsibilities.

- There are many support personnel in secondary schools. Among these are food-service workers, custodians, secretaries, clerks, and paraprofessionals.

# Review and Discussion Questions

1. In general, secondary schools have more complex administrative organizations than do elementary schools. Why is this true?

2. What are the functions of school boards?

3. What are some of the basic responsibilities of the superintendent?

4. Describe some of the duties of grade-level leaders in an elementary school.

5. In addition to the principal and his or her assistants, a number of other administrators are often found in larger secondary schools. Who are these people, and what do they do?

6. Who are some of the professionals who might be assigned to a specific school building for purposes other than teaching regular classes?

7. Should the superintendent try to sell the local community on innovative new programs, or should he or she attempt to read the local community and provide programs that do not need to be sold? Why or why not?

8. Individuals who have studied school board members agree that serving on the school board is a taxing, demanding responsibility. Yet few districts have any difficulty finding candidates to run for vacancies. How can this be explained?

9. Many elementary schools have grade-level leaders, and many secondary schools have department heads. Do you think that a grade-level leader is likely to have more influence on a beginning elementary teacher than a department head is likely to have on a beginning secondary-school teacher? Why do you think so?

10. Some critics argue that principals in large high schools are so consumed by basic management issues that they cannot adequately monitor the quality of

instruction being delivered in their classrooms. Do you agree or disagree with this position? Why?

• • • • • • • • • • • • • • • • • • • • • • • • • • • •

# Ideas for Field Experiences, Projects, and Enrichment

1. Set up an interview with a principal of a school at the level you would like to teach. During your interview, ask the principal to identify all of the categories of nonteaching personnel who work in the school. Ask what these people's specific responsibilities are. Take notes. When you return to class, share your findings with others. As a class, identify some common patterns observed by individuals who visited elementary schools and those who visited secondary schools.

2. Attend a local school board meeting. What kinds of topics were on the agenda? How was time allocated among topics to be covered? What kinds of people were invited to speak at the meeting? What sorts of controversial issues were discussed? What role did the superintendent play in the meeting? Were citizens invited to speak on any topics of interest (including those not on the agenda)? If possible, ask a school official how a given issue gets added to a meeting's agenda. Prepare a short written report that summarizes your findings.

3. Invite a superintendent to visit your class. Ask this person to describe a typical week on the job. Specifically, ask about what percentage of time is devoted to (*a*) curriculum and instructional matters, (*b*) personnel matters, (*c*) budgetary matters, and (*d*) public-relations matters. What does the superintendent do to ensure that policies are being carried out in the individual buildings? How do administrators in the buildings communicate their concerns to the superintendent? What kinds of contact, if any, does the superintendent have with beginning teachers? (Devise other questions designed to provide class members with insights about the superintendent's role.)

4. If you are planning to teach elementary school, interview one or more grade-level leaders. If you are planning to teach secondary school, interview one or more department heads. Ask these people what their general responsibilities are, whether they are released from any teaching obligations as a result of their appointment to the position of grade-level leader or department head, and to whom they report. If you are a future elementary teacher, get together with three or four others in the class who also interviewed grade-level leaders. If you are a future secondary teacher, get together with three or four others from the class who also interviewed department heads. In your groups, try to

write a formal job description for either a grade-level leader or a department head. Share your work with the course instructor, and ask for comments.

5. Select a school district either where you might like to teach or is convenient to your college or university. Call the district's central administrative offices and ask whether any charts or descriptive materials are available that show the district's basic administrative organizational material. (Many districts have this kind of information on hand.) Look at the organizational scheme of the district you select. How is it similar and how does it differ from the examples of organization plans displayed in this chapter? How do you explain any differences?

......................................

# Supplementary Reading

Cuban, L. *The Managerial Imperative and the Practice of Leadership in Schools*. Albany, NY: State University of New York Press, 1988.

Holmes, M. *Making the School An Effective Community: Belief, Practice, and Theory in School Administration*. New York: Falmer Press, 1989.

Nelson, A. "Teacher, Principal, Superintendent: The Link." *T.H.E. Journal* (April 1989): 73–76.

Rosenholtz, S. J. *Workplace: The Social Organization of Schools*. New York: Longman, 1989.

Sergiovani, T. J., ed. *Directing Reforms to Issues That Count*. Boston: Allyn and Bacon, 1989.

Swanson, A. D. "Restructuring Educational Governance: A Challenge of the 1990s." *Educational Administration Quarterly* (August 1989): 268–93.

Walberg, H. J., and J. J. Lane, eds. *Organizing for Learning: Toward the 21st Century*. Reston, VA: National Association of Secondary School Principals, 1989.

......................................

# References

Armstrong, D. G., and T. V. Savage. *Secondary Education: An Introduction*. 2d ed. New York: Macmillan, 1990.

Feiman-Nemser, D., and R. E. Floden. "The Cultures of Teaching." In M. C. Wittrock, ed. *Handbook of Research on Teaching*. 3d ed. New York: Macmillan, 1986, 505–26.

Lounsbury, J. H., and G. E. Vars. *Curriculum for the Middle Years*. New York: Harper and Row, 1978.

Ogle, L. T., ed., and N. Alsalam, associate ed. *The Condition of Education 1990*: Vol. 1: *Elementary and Secondary Education*. Washington, DC: National Center for Education Statistics, 1990.

# Chapter 15

# The Curriculum

· · · · · · · · · · · · · · · · · · · · · · · · · · · · · · · · · ·

## Objectives

This chapter provides information to help the reader to

- point out some basic characteristics of curricula that reflect a needs-of-learners orientation.
- summarize several advantages and disadvantages of planning curricula that are consistent with a needs-of-learners orientation.
- describe characteristics of an academic-subject-matter orientation to curriculum planning.
- point out some advantages and disadvantages of academic-subject-centered curricula.
- explain features of curricula that are organized according to a broad-fields approach.
- describe characteristics of a needs-of-society orientation to curriculum planning.
- point out some advantages and disadvantages of using a needs-of-society orientation as a basis for curriculum planning.
- describe content patterns in elementary and secondary schools.

# Focus Questions

1. What is the function of the school curriculum, and why do issues associated with it frequently lead to arguments?
2. What are some points that have been made for and against the needs-of-learners orientation to curriculum planning?
3. What stages did Rousseau believe children passed through, and how did he think educators should respond to each of them?
4. What are some strengths and weaknesses that have been reported for the academic-subject-matter approach to curriculum development?
5. What is meant by the term *structure of the disciplines,* and what is its relevance for organizing school programs?
6. How do broad-fields curricula attempt to respond to some criticisms of those school programs that have been organized around traditional academic disciplines?
7. What are some features, advantages, and disadvantages of curricula developed according to a needs-of-society orientation?
8. What curricular patterns are common to many of the nation's schools?

# Introduction

The term *curriculum* comes from a Latin word that refers to a track for running. Over the years, the term has come to mean a running sequence of learning experiences. In a modern school setting, the curriculum reflects decisions that have been made relating to the selection and organization of content and learning experiences. The nature of these decisions varies from place to place. Even within individual buildings, not all teachers agree about the characteristics of a "good" school program.

A school's curriculum acts as a kind of screen or filter. Because possible information that might be taught far exceeds the time available to teach it, there is a need for a mechanism to establish priorities. That is what a curriculum does—it reflects decisions about the goals of education and the kinds of content and learning experiences that should be provided to help learners achieve them. Because different people have different values, their educational priorities differ. Consequently, debates about what should be included in curricula are common.

For example, some teachers are strongly committed to a learner-centered approach that emphasizes learners' individual needs more than subject-matter content. People who subscribe to this position see personal development as the most important obligation of the school.

This teacher examines a curriculum guide supplied by a commercial publisher of textbooks.

Other teachers are convinced that schools should be devoted to helping young people move smoothly into the workplace. They believe that educators should carefully analyze the needs of society and develop instructional programs that will prepare young people to meet them. Many supporters of this view are concerned that learner-centered programs may not provide young people with useful employment skills.

Still other teachers reject both learner-centered and needs-of-society approaches. They fear that learner-centered programs lack intellectual rigor, and note that the needs of society change frequently and hence do not provide dependable guidelines for planning and organizing school learning experiences. Often, teachers rejecting these two approaches contend that school programs should be built around the traditional academic disciplines (English, history, mathematics, etc.).

These three basic views are widely represented in the schools today. Partisans of each position are sincere in thinking their view to be the best or the most responsible. Differences in priorities reflected in these positions underscore the difficulties that policymakers face when they make decisions about what must be taught. Whatever approaches they take are likely to be applauded by some people and attacked by others. Box 15–1 asks you to review some of your own academic experiences in light of these orientations.

## The Needs-of-Learners Orientation

An early proponent of focusing on the needs of individual learners was eighteenth-century philosopher Jean Jacques Rousseau. As he studied the world, Rousseau concluded that human civilization was corrupt and rejected the idea that learners should be educated to meet the needs of society. In his view, this would result in an irresponsible transmission of corrupt social values from generation to generation.

Rousseau believed that children were born good, and whatever evil might come to characterize them later in life was imposed by society's negative influences. To remedy this situation, Rousseau believed that the school should protect children from society and furthermore should let the children's naturally good instincts unfold with a minimum of disruption.

Rousseau was convinced that people pass through four distinct growth phases on the way to maturity. From birth to age 5, perceptual skills and muscle coordination developed. At this stage, Rousseau recommended that educators protect children from social restraints and allow them to experience directly the consequences of their own actions.

During the next stage, from ages 8 through 12, Rousseau recommended that there be no formal education—the child should simply be allowed to do what comes naturally. Rousseau felt that personal experience alone was a sufficient teacher for young people in this age group.

Rousseau believed that education should become a formal enterprise during the next chronological stage. During the years from ages 12 to 15, children should be exposed to teachers who would make learning opportunities available to them. Instruction should not be heavy-handed or prescriptive. Teachers should function primarily as motivators, and their roles should be to stimulate learners' curiosity to the extent that they would want to study such subjects as astronomy, geography, and agriculture.

BOX 15-1
## SCHOOL SUBJECTS AND THEIR ORIENTATIONS

List some subjects you studied in elementary school, middle school, junior high school, or senior high school. In the three right columns, indicate whether you think each subject reflected more of a needs-of-learners orientation, an academic-subject-matter orientation, or a needs-of-society orientation.

| Subjects | Needs of Learners | Academic Subject Matter | Needs of Society |
|---|---|---|---|
| _____ | _____ | _____ | _____ |
| _____ | _____ | _____ | _____ |
| _____ | _____ | _____ | _____ |
| _____ | _____ | _____ | _____ |
| _____ | _____ | _____ | _____ |
| _____ | _____ | _____ | _____ |
| _____ | _____ | _____ | _____ |
| _____ | _____ | _____ | _____ |

*What Do You Think?*
1. Were your school subjects more geared to one of these orientations than to the other two? If so, how do you explain this pattern?
2. Did a number of your school subjects reflect a blend of these orientations?
3. If you identified some subjects you studied in elementary school and some others you studied in high school, did you find a difference in basic orientation based on the school level at which the subjects were offered?

Rousseau saw the final stage of development occurring between the ages of 15 and 20. During this time, he believed that individuals developed refined human-relations skills, an appreciation of beauty, and a sense of personal and religious values. Young people in this age group should be encouraged, but certainly not forced, to study such subjects as religion and ethics.

The needs-of-learners orientation has influenced the development of educational programs for many years. For example, many curricular innovations directed at "humanizing" school programs are clear linear descendants of the beliefs of Rousseau. Perhaps the best-known American to be associated with learner-centered education was the eminent American educational philosopher John Dewey. Dewey believed that the curriculum should be constructed out of the actual experience and curiosity of the child. However, Dewey did not reject inclusion of traditional subject matter; he believed this academic content, when included, should be organized in such a way that it related to learners' life experiences.

## Advantages of Curricula Based on Learners' Needs

Probably the most important strength of programs associated with the needs-of-learners orientation is that they place concern for individual pupils and students at the heart of the planning process. Such programs remind educators of their responsibilities to serve young people and provide experiences that will help them to live rich and fulfilling lives.

Learning experiences associated with this orientation have the potential to break down artificial barriers among subject areas. When the interests of young people become the basis for planning and organizing courses, then specific information can be drawn from a wide selection of academic specialties. This approach frees knowledge from its artificial compartmentalization into the traditional disciplines. It also has the potential to support the development of a highly motivating learning environment.

## Disadvantages of Curricula Based on Learners' Needs

Critics of curricula based on learners' needs often focus on its alleged inefficiency. They point out that efforts to diagnose and respond to special needs of each individual are not cost effective; nor is it practical to create unique programs designed to meet the special needs of each learner. Some specific kinds of content, these people argue, should be mastered by all learners, regardless of their levels of initial interest.

There is some concern, too, that learners may be poor judges of their own real needs and will opt for academic experiences that are shallow. The net result of such programs may be graduates who are ill-equipped for the demands of living in a complex, technological society.

## The Academic-Subject-Matter Orientation

Throughout history, one of the most common ways to organize the curriculum has been to divide it along the lines of academic subjects. Even in Roman times, educational programs were separated into subjects based on the assumption that there were disciplines (or bodies of knowledge) that were related in some natural way. Learning was thought to be easier when young people were introduced to knowledge that had been organized into academic subjects such as mathematics or music.

Many people who organize school curricula around academic subjects believe that scholars in individual disciplines have developed reliable, responsible, and precise ways of knowing about the world. These supporters of the academic-subject-matter orientation contend that there is merit in having learners master certain kinds of information, and are convinced that learning this content enables young people to gain control of their own destinies. Indeed, some bodies of knowledge are considered so important that they are absolutely essential for everyone. Subjects that have frequently been denoted as essential for all learners in American schools include English, history, science, and mathematics. Usually, courses dealing with these major subject areas are mandated by state law.

Exactly *which* subjects are "musts" for learners has been the subject of considerable debate. Perhaps not surprisingly, scholars in each subject have found compelling reasons for placing a very heavy emphasis on their own specializations. Conflicts among supporters of different academic subjects have become familiar events in state capitals throughout the nation, as legislators have called on expert witnesses to help them define the essential elements of a "basic education."

Some people linked with the academic-subject-matter orientation have maintained that the emphasis should not be on having learners master factual content associated with each subject, but instead on introducing learners to the organizational features of each discipline. Initial interest in the "structure of the disciplines" (the organization of the individual academic subjects and how professionals in these disciplines ask and answer questions) developed after the Soviet launch of *Sputnik* in 1957.

Supporters of the structure-of-the-disciplines emphasis believed that many school practices featured too much attention on isolated facts. They favored instead new programs that would help students to recognize basic principles associated with each major subject area. The idea was to develop learners' thinking abilities and engage them in learning activities that, to the extent possible, paralleled problem-solving procedures used by professional academic scholars in each subject area. There was great interest in this approach through the 1960s and into the early 1970s. An underlying theme was that learners who became thoroughly familiar with the structures of the academic disciplines during their school years would enter college ready to do more advanced work.

Beginning in the 1970s and continuing through the decade of the 1980s and on into the early 1990s, concerns about the Vietnam War, treatment of minorities at home, and other social issues eroded support for a strong structure-of-the-disciplines emphasis. Mandates for academic programs emphasizing equity and fairness dominated much of the educational debate in the 1970s.

In the 1980s, there was renewed interest in programs with a traditional academic subject focus, but the reform reports of the 1980s tended to promote school programs that sought to familiarize learners with the *findings* of academic specialists, not with the structures of their disciplines. Concerns about the nation's relative intellectual and economic competitiveness prompted critics to call for school programs that would produce students who were well-grounded in academics, particularly in content associated with mathematics and the sciences.

During the middle and late 1980s and the early 1990s, some critics of school practices expressed increasing concern about whether teachers had adequate preparation in the academic subjects they were teaching. In response to these concerns, over the past decade many teacher preparation programs have extended the length of their programs. Others, while continuing to offer traditional four-year teacher certification schedules, have increased content requirements in the fields students have been preparing to teach.

## Advantages of the Academic-Subject-Matter Orientation

Individual subjects tend to organize content that contains many common elements. For example, mathematics courses of all kinds have much more common content than would be found in a course that contained content blended from English and French. The common focus of each academic discipline is thought to make learning easier, as exposure to information in a single discipline introduces learners to content that is limited in scope and logically related.

As the most traditional form of organizing school programs, this pattern enjoys a certain respectability because of its long familiarity to parents and other patrons of the school. School programs organized in this way provide an aura of stability and continuity that many people find attractive. Teachers, for example, may appreciate the security of knowing that they will be teaching familiar subjects. Administrators generally feel confident in explaining this kind of organizational pattern to parents.

The vast majority of school textbooks are organized on the assumption that they will be used in programs based on traditional academic subjects. For example, there are separate books for classes in mathematics, English, and biology. Textbooks that represent a fusion of content from several academic disciplines are rare. Since the textbook continues to be a very widely used instructional resource, it acts as an influence to support an academic-subject-matter orientation throughout the school program.

## Disadvantages of the Academic-Subject-Matter Orientation

While individual academic subjects have a certain internal consistency, it is by no means clear that the world is organized into "history," "mathematics," "English," "biology," and other separate subjects. Learners do not encounter a reality that is neatly sliced and filed into individual disciplines. Since the world is not divided into individual subject areas, critics of the academic-subject-matter orientation often suggest that the school curriculum should be more interdisciplinary in character. That is, individual courses should be organized in a way that allows content to be drawn from many sources.

Critics also argue that dividing school programs into packages associated with academic disciplines inhibits transfer and integration of knowledge. For instance, some learners may produce flawless prose in their English classes but in other classes turn in papers with many mistakes, assuming the attitude: "This is history. We aren't *supposed* to write perfect papers here. That's for English. Here we learn names and dates."

Some learners complain that the learning experiences they encounter in the traditional academic subjects are irrelevant. For example, a student studying algebra might ask: "Why should I study this stuff? What good is it?" Though content from algebra certainly does have some important links to real life, many learners fail to make the connection between the content of the course and the demands of life beyond the school. The accompanying What the Experts Say discusses a similar problem of mixed messages in our schools.

## The power of the hidden curriculum

Schools teach learners more than the topics introduced in the formal, written curriculum—learners are also greatly influenced by their exposure to what experts have variously described as the "implicit" or "hidden" curriculum. The hidden curriculum includes all of those things in the school setting that send learners messages regarding what they ought to be doing and even how they should be thinking. Gail McCutcheon notes that "the hidden curriculum can be thought of as having two characteristics: (1) it is not intended, and (2) it is transmitted through the everyday, normal goings-on in schools" (1988, p. 191).

Curriculum researcher Decker Walker (1990) points out that features of the hidden curriculum include teachers' general expectations about how learners should control their emotions in class, what learners should do when there is a need to move from one area of the classroom to another, and how learners should act when they wish to participate in a discussion.

Teachers' own actions help shape the hidden curriculum in a classroom, sending signals to students about what the teachers consider important. If teachers are unconscious of their hidden-curriculum actions, they may not realize that they are sending unintended messages to learners. For example, a social studies teacher may make a point of emphasizing the importance of reading articles on the front page of the newspaper every day. But if learners observe this teacher in the morning, at lunch, or during a planning period reading only the sports section, they may well conclude: "People who are interested in social studies are insincere; they say hard news on the front page is important, but they really only pay attention to sports. Because these people aren't credible, I don't need to pay attention to what they say."

Some authorities who have studied the hidden curriculum fear that it sometimes sends messages to learners that are inconsistent with the values of their own cultural or social group. For example, curriculum experts Michael Apple and Landon Beyer (1988) note that the hidden curriculum in many schools emphasizes deference to authority and an attitude that competence in school subjects will result in high status and lucrative jobs for graduates. Many learners find these perspectives inconsistent with the attitudes of their parents, families, and friends, and hence they may reject the entire school program as irrelevant.

Nearly all authorities agree that the hidden curriculum influences learners' attitudes toward the school program. There is a consensus that teachers should develop a sensitivity to any messages that learners may be getting from the school program and environment. What students have learned from this hidden curriculum has been found to have an important influence on young people's attitudes toward schools and teachers.

## Broad-Fields Curriculum

One interesting approach that seeks to respond to certain criticisms of the academic-subjects orientation is the broad-fields curriculum. In this scheme, two or more traditional subjects are combined into a broad area. These broad areas sometimes center on large themes such as "industrialism" or "evolution." Using these basic themes, instructional planners prepare lessons that draw on knowledge from several subject areas. This approach has been promoted as a means of breaking down barriers that separate knowledge into individual academic disciplines. It is assumed that learners who are exposed to broad-fields programs will develop the ability to transfer what they have learned to challenging new situations.

The approach is not without its problems. One major difficulty is that few teachers possess a breadth of knowledge in more than one or two academic disciplines. Hence, many of them find it difficult to identify and utilize relevant content from a wide variety of sources. With few exceptions, the college and university courses that teachers have taken were not organized according to a broad-fields approach. Consequently, many teachers do not feel adequately prepared to teach in broad-fields programs (See Box 15–2).

## The Needs-of-Society Orientation

The needs-of-society orientation represents another point of departure for curriculum organization. According to W. H. Schubert, "Part of the reason for the existence of schools is that they fulfill social needs. Societies ostensibly establish schools to help further their goals and promote their values in successive generations" (1986, p. 217). Curricula developed from this perspective may be one of several basic types. Among them are curricula organized according to a problems approach and those designed to promote citizenship development.

The problems approach has been favored by educators who believe that schools should provide experiences designed to help learners develop skills and insights relevant to solving pressing social problems. Supporters contend that the schools are institutions charged with ensuring social survival. These people maintain that to accomplish this objective, young people should be introduced during their school years to problems that challenge our social order. Such exposure, it is believed, will produce future citizens who will be willing to confront problems and work for their solution.

Proponents of citizenship development point out that adult members of society need certain basic skills in order to make a contribution. Programs consistent with this emphasis place a high priority on teaching those things that will be useful to learners in their adult years. Vocational education of all kinds is assigned a high priority. Some partisans of this view are suspicious of school experiences that do not seem to have a clear relationship to what young people will be encountering as working adults.

The citizenship-development approach has appealed to many pragmatically oriented Americans. Frequently, attacks on so-called "frills" in school programs are reflections of the concerns of people who want the schools to concentrate more heavily on providing learning experiences more clearly relevant to the future career and vocational needs of young people.

## Advantages of the Needs-of-Society Orientation

Content for school programs associated with this perspective is drawn from a variety of academic subjects. This process helps break down the idea that knowledge must

BOX 15–2
# RELATIVE ATTRACTIVENESS OF DIFFERENT TEACHING ASSIGNMENTS

Assume you are a certified teacher who has just graduated from a college or university. Suppose you are offered teaching positions by two different districts. Salaries and general working conditions are about the same in each place, and in both positions you will be expected to teach five classes a day at the high school level. Your assignments for each district would be as follows:

| *School District One* | *School District Two* |
|---|---|
| American history | Technology and society |
| American history | Technology and society |
| World history | (Planning period) |
| (Planning Period) | Militarism |
| World history | Militarism |
| World geography | Dynamics of leadership |

How would you feel about accepting a position in either of these districts given these prospective teaching assignments?

### What Do You Think?

1. In general, would you prefer district one or district two?
2. For which teaching assignments do you have the better college or university preparation? Why do you think so?
3. In which situation do you think you would experience the most difficulty in locating appropriate instructional materials? Why?
4. How do you think learners would react to the courses in the two districts? Why do you think so?

be compartmentalized into artificial categories labeled "history," "English," "mathematics," "physics," or something else. Needs-of-society curricula help young people to integrate knowledge from a variety of sources as they use it to make sense of the world as it really is.

Proponents of this orientation point to the motivational advantages of organizing programs around reality. For example, if a class is oriented toward a career in which a young person is interested, he or she is likely to have a personal desire to learn the material. A learner might find it much easier to master mathematics in the context of studying to become a pilot than by plodding through a traditional mathematics textbook page by page.

There is also an important motivational appeal that often accompanies a focus on important social problems. Young people more easily see the relevance of a topic such

The belief that students should develop leadership skills as part of the school experience is consistent with the needs-of-society orientation.

as consumer rights than one such as decision making in Ancient Sparta. Social problems quite often will have been the focus of discussion in learners' homes. Many learners prefer to study issues of concern to their parents, friends, and others in the community beyond the school.

## Disadvantages of the Needs-of-Society Orientation

A major problem of the needs-of-society emphasis is the difficulty educators face in identifying just which needs to address in school programs. There is a danger that such needs will be identified in haste and the resulting programs will be excessively narrow in scope and nonsubstantive in content.

The rapidity with which needs change also poses difficulties. Given problems pass away; new problems emerge. Over time, technical changes alter job requirements tremendously. When needs are viewed too narrowly, there is a danger that the school curriculum will provide learners with information that will be obsolete by the time they leave school, and they will lack the flexibility needed to adapt easily to changing conditions.

Some critics of needs-of-society programs contend that they often encourage learners to make career choices too early in their school years. Learners who express a personal interest based on a whim or enthusiasm of the moment may find themselves "tracked" into a set of courses relevant for only a limited number of career options. It may prove difficult for these learners to move into another track should their interests change.

Needs-of-society programs that focus heavily on social problems have often drawn criticism from parents and other community members. There have been fears that such instruction has the potential to impose values or perspectives that are at odds with those held by parents, certain religious organizations, and other groups of citizens. These concerns have made school authorities in some places hesitant to organize school programs around a social-problems emphasis.

## Basic Patterns in Elementary and Secondary Schools

Though there are some place-to-place differences, much uniformity can be found among the basic programs offered in most of the nation's elementary, middle, junior high, and senior high schools. Guidelines governing general categories of information to be taught are often included in state regulations governing education (See box 15–3).

Elementary school programs nearly always include instruction in these areas: reading and language arts, mathematics, social studies, science, health, physical education, and fine arts. It is very common in elementary schools for reading instruction to occur at the beginning of the day. Reading is considered to be a critically important subject, and many educators believe that pupils should be exposed to its instruction when they are well-rested and ready to learn.

The amounts of time devoted to each subject area in elementary schools vary from place to place. In some parts of the country, there are strict state regulations mandating that minimum amounts of time be devoted each day to certain "high-priority" areas of the curriculum. In other areas, no such guidelines exist, and time-allocation decisions are left to local districts, principals, and individual teachers. Because proficiency in reading is a key to academic success in so many other areas, nearly all elementary school teachers devote a great deal of time to reading instruction. Recent unfavorable comparisons of U.S. learners' proficiency in mathematics and science as compared to learners in other countries (Ogle and Alsalam, 1990, pp. 32–33) have tended to prompt increased emphases on these subjects in elementary school programs. Increasingly, too, elementary schools are providing basic instruction in computers.

Middle school and junior high school programs tend to feature many of the same subjects taught in elementary schools. Particularly in grades 7 and 8, options for students with different interests and abilities are available. For example, several mathematics options may be available: some students may take algebra, others may take a less rigorous course, and still others may enroll in a more challenging class. Unlike the situation that prevails in most elementary schools, at the junior high school level, students are allowed to take some elective courses. (However, teachers cannot always elect how to teach these courses, as shown in this chapter's Case Study.)

**BOX 15-3**

# ONE STATE'S REQUIREMENTS FOR GRADES 1 THROUGH 3

At times, the state of Texas has exercised strong central control over the curricula of its elementary and secondary schools. The following requirements, adopted in 1984, comprise part of the requirements for grades 1 through 3.*

- No fewer than 120 minutes a day shall be devoted to teaching English language arts.
- No fewer than 60 minutes a day shall be devoted to teaching mathematics.
- Within each semester, the equivalent of at least 100 minutes per week shall be devoted to teaching science.
- Within each semester, the equivalent of at least 100 minutes per week shall be devoted to teaching social studies.
- The daily schedule shall include instruction in physical education.
- The weekly schedule shall include instruction in fine arts and health.
- Each school district is encouraged to offer other languages to the extent possible.

*What Do You Think?*

1. What differences in the relative importance of various school subjects are implied by these guidelines?
2. How does this scheme compare with regulations in your state? With practices in elementary schools with which you are familiar?
3. Should there be state curriculum guidelines of this type, or should control over content priorities be left to individual districts, school administrators, or teachers?

• • • • • • • • • • • • • • • • • • • • • • • • • • • • • • • • • • • • • • • • • • • • • • • • • • • • • • • • • • • • • • • • • •

*\*(State Board of Education Rules for Curriculum* (Austin, TX: Texas Education Agency, 1984), p. 229.

The programs at the senior high school level are largely driven by state and local high school graduation requirements. These requirements vary somewhat from place to place, but patterns tend to converge around a set that prescribes a minimum number of years or semesters of high school instruction in English/language arts, mathematics, science, and physical education. In many places, there are now also requirements that students achieve certain levels of computer literacy. However, large numbers of electives are also available to high school students.

Many reform reports that were issued in the 1980s called for more work to be required for high school graduation in certain so-called "basic" subjects, including English, mathematics, social studies, and science. For example, the National Commission on Excellence in Education, in its report *A Nation at Risk: The Imperative*

## *Is relevance irrelevant?*

**Sondra McPhee put down the report from the National Center for Educational Statistics**. She nodded her head in agreement with its finding that eighth graders believed their social studies classes to have much less relevance for their future lives than their classes in English, mathematics, and science. As a second-year grade 8 U. S. history teacher, Sondra's own observations squared perfectly with this conclusion. She had frequently told anyone who would listen that "My kids just don't seem to care. I think I'm simply boring them to death."

The national report convinced Sondra that her problem wasn't something unique and something needed to be done. She spent several weeks reading everything she could find relating to motivation, eighth graders, junior high school social studies, and, most particularly, ideas for inspiring the Hispanic and African-American young people who accounted for about 70 percent of her learners. Late one Saturday after-noon, after several nonproductive hours in the library, she stumbled onto some mate-rial on oral history lessons. It was as if a light had been turned on. "This is *it*," she said to herself.

A few weeks later, she went to visit her principal, Viola Gutierrez. She told Dr. Gutierrez that she had some ideas for changing the grade 8 social studies program, explaining that she wanted to orient the course around the use of oral history tech-niques. Specifically, she wanted to have her Hispanic students interview their parents and relatives about experiences that they and their forebears had had during the bloody Mexican revolution of the early decades of the twentieth century. As well, she wanted her African-American students to gather information on such issues as patterns of living in the days before the civil rights movement. She pointed out to Dr. Gutierrez that her students would see the topics as relevant, and researchers had found oral history lessons to be highly motivating.

Dr. Gutierrez, a cautious administrator, was noncommittal, but told Sondra that she would think about her ideas. Three weeks later, Sondra found a note in her box from Dr. Gutierrez, asking her to come in during her planning period to talk about the oral history proposal.

Dr. Gutierrez expressed appreciation to Sondra for her willingness to innovate and for her professionalism in searching out pertinent research literature to support her case, but went on to say that she was going to deny permission for the oral history approach. She proceeded to explain her reasons.

First of all, Dr. Gutierrez pointed out, the course text didn't emphasize the Mexican Revolution, nor did it deal much with the lives of African-Americans in the years before 1960.

Dr. Gutierrez further noted that the state tested all eighth graders at the end of the school year, and test items tended to be drawn from content covered in the adopted textbook. She also emphasized that very few parents ever experienced an oral history approach when they were in school, and many of them might be skeptical of the tech-nique. Dr. Gutierrez suggested that as most parents seemed to prefer textbook-based reading assignments accompanied by traditional homework, some influential parents might view the oral history project as an attempt to "water down" the history program.

Finally, Dr. Gutierrez pointed out that the administrators at the district's high school continued to be concerned about the lack of subject-matter preparation junior high school graduates had when they entered grade 9. She indicated that the school simply couldn't take a chance that an oral history program would make students appear to be even less prepared for high school than they currently were.

*How should Sondra have reacted to Dr. Gutierrez's decision? To what extent do the contents of textbooks shape curricula? Are textbook contents always appropriate for the learners who study them? Should concerns about standardized test scores play a role in shaping the curriculum? Is high school preparation the driving force that shapes junior high schools' curricula? If so, should this be the case?*

*for Educational Reform* (1983), called for changes in high school graduation requirements that would call on schools to require all students to complete a minimum of four years of English, three years of science, three years of social studies, and three years of mathematics. By the late 1980s, there was evidence that these recommendations were having an influence. Whereas in 1982, only 13.4 percent of all high school graduates

*"It's Ms. Clark, our new first grade teacher. She says she's been working on Item A-I of the Handwriting Curriculum Guide for three days now, and she wants to know when the kids can stop positioning their papers and begin writing."*

Courtesy of Ford Button.

had taken the number of courses in English, science, social studies, and mathematics recommended by the Commission on Excellence in Education, by 1987, this figure had increased to 28.6 percent (Baker and Ogle, 1989, pp. 22–23).

These figures suggest that more students are taking more of the designated "basic" courses. What they do not reveal is the nature of the content that these learners are encountering in the courses. At best, displays of curricular programs provide a sketchy outline of what goes on in schools. The real school program continues to be shaped by the actions of teachers as they work with learners in individual classrooms.

••••••••••••••••••••••••••••••

# Key Ideas in Summary

- The term *curriculum* refers to the selection and organization of content and learning experiences. Because different people use different criteria in making decisions about selection and organization of content, there are important place-to-place variations in elementary and secondary school curricula.

- Curricula that reflect a needs-of-learners orientation are developed as a result of program planners' perceptions of learners' needs and interests. Jean Jacques Rousseau was an early proponent of this perspective. In this approach, learners are placed at the center of the planning process. These curricula are alleged to motivate learners and avoid unnecessary fragmentation of content. Critics argue that it is impractical to prepare separate academic experiences for each learner's needs and interests, and are also concerned about whether learners are the best judges of their own and society's needs.

- The academic-subject-matter approach to curriculum development divides content into individual disciplines such as mathematics, history, and English. This approach is based on the assumption that contents contained within an individual discipline share certain similarities. These commonalities, it is alleged, make it easier for learners to master the material. Critics of the approach point out that the real world is not divided into separate academic disciplines, and they also note that division of content into packages associated with separate subjects fragments learning and makes it difficult for young people to transfer information to situations beyond the setting in which it was learned.

- There have been two general approaches to preparing programs using an academic-subject-matter orientation. The most common of these has featured the development of learning experiences designed to familiarize learners with the findings of subject matter specialists. A second approach has favored familiarizing learners with the "structure of the disciplines"—programs designed in this way seek to introduce young people to the processes that professionals in the disciplines use as they study data and arrive at conclusions.

- Broad-fields curricula attempt to respond to some criticisms that have been made of programs organized around traditional academic disciplines. Broad-

**Table 15-1**
Summary table: The curriculum

| Topic | Key Points |
|-------|------------|
| Curriculum | The curriculum is a screen for content and learning experiences provided to learners in the school. Curriculum decisions reflect priorities; priorities depend on values; and, hence, decisions about the curriculum often engender debates. |
| Needs-of-learners orientation | This orientation to curriculum development places individual learners at the center of the planning process. It is an orientation long associated with the beliefs of Jean Jacques Rousseau. Arguments for include: (1) individuals to be taught are carefully studied, and hence programs tend to respond to their needs, and (2) learning experiences are not constrained by artificial boundaries of the traditional academic subjects. Arguments against include: (1) because of the need to spend time assessing unique qualities of each individual, the approach is not cost effective, and (2) learners may be poor judges of their own real needs. |
| Academic-subject-matter orientation | School programs tend to be organized around traditional subjects such as mathematics, music, and history. One variant of this orientation is the structure-of-the-disciplines view, which suggests learners should be taught the processes scholars use in arriving at conclusions, not just their findings. Arguments for include: (1) the clustering together of related content in one discipline may make learning it easier, and (2) this approach has a long history. As a result, parents, administrators, and producers of learning materials know it well, which may provide much external support for learners exposed to it. Arguments against include: (1) the world does not divide naturally into traditional disciplines; rather, people experience it as a seamless whole, and thus curricula organized around the disciplines give learners a distorted view of reality, and (2) packaging learning in the individual disciplines may inhibit transfer of learning to other settings. |

**Table 15-1**
*continued*

| Topic | Key Points |
|---|---|
| Broad-fields curriculum | This approach combines two or more traditional subjects into a general or broad theme that becomes the basis for planning educational experiences. Arguments for include: (1) it is said to break down barriers that separate traditional academic disciplines, and (2) the approach is supposed to make transfer of content to other settings easier. Arguments against include: (1) few teachers are well-enough grounded in diverse disciplines to make the approach work, and (2) colleges and universities, for the most part, are not organized this way, and thus the approach is not familiar to many people. |
| Needs-of-society orientation | A fundamental assumption of this orientation is that school programs should produce learners who are prepared to solve pressing social problems and meet other social needs. Arguments for include: (1) it helps break down barriers separating academic disciplines, doing so by focusing on issues and drawing content from many sources, as needed, and (2) because programs are organized around reality, they are alleged to be motivating for many learners. Arguments against include: (1) it is difficult to identify just what society's "needs" are. If the wrong ones are selected, learners may receive instruction that bears little relevance to the "real world" they encounter as adults, (2) some critics argue that needs-of-society-based programs encourage learners to make career choices at too young an age. A temporary enthusiasm may prompt them to take courses that will have little bearing on interests that may evolve in other directions as they mature, and (3) any choice regarding "society's needs" reflects a decision based on values. Some parents may not agree that the "needs" identified by program developers are important. If this happens, conflicts may develop between parents and those who teach their children. |

fields approaches combine two or more traditional subjects into a single broad area or theme. This broad area or theme is used as a basis for planning, and programs are developed that draw content from several disciplines. Broad-fields curricula are promoted on the basis of their capacity for helping learners break down boundaries between and among individual subjects. Problems with the approach include (1) a lack of instructional materials of an interdisciplinary nature and (2) a difficulty in finding individual teachers who have sufficient enough depth in a variety of disciplines that they can draw materials responsibly from a wide selection of content areas.

• Curricula developed according to a needs-of-society orientation are designed to produce learners capable of maintaining and extending broad social goals. These curricula sort into two basic types: some programs focus on content designed to help learners recognize and respond to important problems, and others center on citizenship development. Many of the latter emphasize providing young people with the kinds of skills they will need to make a living. Supporters of these programs suggest that they promote learners' levels of interest because the content is highly relevant to their own lives. Critics suggest that identification of so-called "problems" may bring teachers into unproductive conflicts with parents and other community members who have different perspectives on these issues. These critics also maintain that vocationally oriented programs may not be responsive to rapid changes in the job market, and school programs may be providing learners with training experiences that will not match up well with the real needs of the employment market they will enter when they leave school.

• Though there are important place-to-place differences, certain common patterns are found in many elementary and secondary schools. Large numbers of elementary schools require learners to be exposed to instruction focusing on reading and language arts, mathematics, social studies, science, health, and physical education. Increasingly, elementary pupils are also being introduced to the use of computers. In secondary schools (particularly in senior high schools), learners have a number of electives from which they may choose. However, they are usually still obligated to take certain numbers of courses in such areas as English, social studies, mathematics, science, and physical education. At the secondary level, too, there is an increasing tendency to expose students to computers.

• • • • • • • • • • • • • • • • • • • • • • • • • • • •

# Review and Discussion Questions

1. To what does the term *curriculum* refer?
2. What are some characteristics of the needs-of-learners orientation?
3. What are some characteristics of the academic-subject-matter orientation?

4. What are some features of a broad-fields curriculum?

5. What are some characteristics of a needs-of-society orientation?

6. Think about some characteristics of the school programs you experienced during your elementary and secondary school years. Can you identify some aspects of these programs that reflected a needs-of-learners orientation?

7. Some people argue that the entire school program should reflect an academic-subject-matter orientation. What are some strengths and weaknesses of this idea? Today's learners represent a very diverse group. Are there some learners who would profit more than others from such a program? Are there some learners who would be hurt? What is your own position regarding this suggestion?

8. Certain critics argue that our schools are doing a poor job of preparing young people for work in an increasingly technologically complex society. How do you react to this view? If you accept the validity of this contention, what specific changes would you make in the present grades K through 12 school program?

9. Supporters of the needs-of-learners orientation point out that learners tend to be motivated by school programs based on this point of view. By implication, are they suggesting that programs developed from the perspectives of the academic-subject-matter orientation and needs-of-society orientation are less motivating? If you agree with these people, what do you think might be done to make school programs based on these orientations more interesting to learners?

10. Some of the reform proposals of the 1980s recommended that students be required to take more courses in English, mathematics, science, and social studies as requirements for graduation. Does requiring students to take more courses ensure that they will necessarily know more about these subject areas? Why or why not?

. . . . . . . . . . . . . . . . . . . . . . . . . . . . . . .

# Ideas for Field Experiences, Projects, and Enrichment

1. With the assistance of a school principal or of your course instructor, locate in your library a list of subjects taught at two or more grade levels within a given school. From titles and descriptions of these subjects, decide whether they are based on a needs-of-learners orientation, an academic-subject-matter orientation, a needs-of-society orientation, or whether they reflect a combination of two or even all three of these perspectives. Prepare a written report that summarizes your findings.

2. Write a position paper focusing on one of these topics:

   a. School programs need to reflect more of a needs-of-learners orientation.

   b. School programs need to reflect more of an academic-subject-matter orientation.

   c. School programs need to reflect more of a needs-of-society orientation.

3. Examine two or more reform proposals that appeared during the 1980s. (Ask your instructor for suggestions.) Note at least three recommendations for changes in school curricula made in each proposal. Then interview a school principal or a school district curriculum director about changes in local programs made in the last decade. Determine whether any of these changes were in correlation with those suggested in the national reform proposals. Share your findings with members of the class.

4. Interview several teachers within a single building who teach a subject or grade level that interests you. Ask them about state, district, or school requirements for learners who take this subject or who are enrolled at this grade level. Also ask whether these requirements are well-suited to learners' needs. Finally, ask these teachers what specific changes in requirements for students they would recommend. Prepare an oral report of your findings to share with members of your class.

5. Join together with three or four others in your class to prepare a report on one of these topics:

   a. What should a "good" elementary school program look like today?

   b. What should a "good" middle school or junior high school program look like today?

   c. What should a "good" senior high school program look like today?

   Present your conclusions in the form of a symposium, and then write them up into an article. Consider sending it to the features editor of the local newspaper.

## Supplementary Reading

Brandt, R. S., ed. *Content of the Curriculum: 1988 Yearbook of the Association for Supervision and Curriculum Development.* Alexandria, VA: Association for Supervision and Curriculum Development, 1988.

Goodlad, J. *A Place Called School.* New York: McGraw-Hill, 1984.

Hass, G. *Curriculum Planning: A New Approach.* 5th ed. Boston: Allyn and Bacon, 1987.

Miller, J. P. *The Educational Spectrum: Orientations to Curriculum.* New York: Longman, 1983.

Tanner, D., and L. Tanner. *History of the School Curriculum.* New York: Macmillan, 1990.

Walker, D. *Fundamentals of Curriculum.* Orlando, FL: Harcourt Brace Jovanovich, 1990.

•••••••••••••••••••••••••••••••

# References

Apple, M. W., and L. E. Beyer. "Social Evaluation." In L. E. Beyer and M. W. Apple, eds. *The Curriculum: Problems, Politics, and Possibilities.* Albany, NY: State University of New York Press, 1988, 334–49.

Baker, C. O., ed., and L. T. Ogle, associate ed. *The Condition of Education, 1989.* Vol. 1: *Elementary and Secondary Education.* Washington, DC: National Center for Education Statistics, 1989.

McCutcheon, G. "Curriculum and the Work of Teachers." In L. E. Beyer and M. W. Apple, eds. *The Curriculum: Problems, Politics, and Possibilities.* Albany, NY: State University of New York Press, 1988, 191–203.

*A Nation at Risk: The Imperative for Educational Reform.* Washington, DC: National Commission on Excellence in Education, U.S. Department of Education, 1983.

Ogle, L. T., ed., and N. Alsalam, associate ed. *The Condition of Education, 1990.* Vol. 1: *Elementary and Secondary Education.* Washington, DC: National Center for Education Statistics, 1990.

Schubert, W. H. *Curriculum: Perspective, Paradigm, and Possibility.* New York: Macmillan, 1986.

*State Board of Education Rules for Curriculum.* Austin, TX: Texas Education Agency, 1984.

Walker, D. F. *Fundamentals of Curriculum.* Orlando, FL: Harcourt Brace Jovanovich, 1990.

# Chapter 16

# Effective Schools

· · · · · · · · · · · · · · · · · · · · · · · · · · · · · · · · · · · ·

## Objectives

This chapter provides information to help the reader to

- describe what is meant by the term *effective schools*.
- suggest some general criticisms that have been made of research directed at identifying features of effective schools.
- point out characteristics of effective schools delineated in the early 1980s by Ronald Edmonds.
- describe characteristics of "effective schools" as determined by investigators working in the late 1980s and early 1990s.
- identify some places in the country where school districts have attempted to make changes consistent with findings of effective-schools research, and comment on the success of these efforts to improve learners' performance levels.

1. What belief(s) divide(s) those who believe it possible to identify general characteristics of effective schools and those who do not?
2. What characteristics of effective schools were identified by Ronald Edmonds?
3. In what ways have more recent studies of effective schools modified Edmonds's list of characteristics?
4. What kinds of actions have schools with diverse learner populations taken to improve the quality of educational experience they provide?
5. What benefits can result to schools that actively involve parents?
6. What are some things done in effective schools to help new teachers adjust?
7. In what ways can schools help learners develop a sense of ownership toward the school and its programs?
8. What are some features of schools that have warm and supporting environments?
9. How successful have attempts been to implement what research has specified about effective schools?

. . . . . . . . . . . . . . . . . . . . . . . . . . . . .

# Introduction

Do individual schools have so many unique features that administrative practices and instructional programs that work well in one place are likely to fail in another? Or are enough features common among schools to allow certain successful school practices to be exported from one school to another?

These questions have been widely debated by people concerned about improving the quality of our schools. Ralph Tyler, one of the leading educational thinkers of this century, has come down squarely in support of the argument that schools' diversity makes it difficult for reformers to improve education by developing prescriptions that can be applied universally. Tyler has written that "because of variations among schools, they rarely share in common any single, serious problem" (1987, p. 278).

Others, including Ronald Edmonds (1982), Lawrence Stedman (1987), and Tamara Lucas, Rosemary Henze, and Ruben Donato (1990), disagree. They suggest that while school-to-school differences are important, certain school practices can be productively transferred from one school to another with a view to making programs more effective.

Box 16–1 presents two varying views of this issue.

The term *effective school* suggests "a belief and argument that school process, environment, and structure can make a difference in student achievement" (Witte and Walsh, 1990, p. 188). Despite pre-existing differences among students and teachers, paying attention to the general school environment alone is seen as having potential to improve learners' performance levels.

This chapter introduces ideas generated by effective-schools researchers. It reviews what certain critics have said, identifies some school practices that are consistent with findings of effective-schools researchers, and cites examples of efforts to introduce practices consistent with this research into the nation's schools.

## Determining Characteristics of Effective Schools

Each school has its own culture. This culture includes patterns that govern relationships among teachers, learners, and parents (Feiman-Nemser and Floden, 1986). Variations in school cultures can affect teachers in important ways. For example, if one school has a tradition of viewing teachers as independent, autonomous professionals, teachers may be little inclined to talk to one another about what they are doing in the classroom. In another setting where the school culture has long been characterized by cooperative planning, teachers might routinely visit one another's classrooms.

An important premise of effective-schools researchers is that some school cultures are more likely to support learner success than others. Further, it is assumed that it is possible to change the culture of a given school in a way that will make the school more effective. Much early work of these effective-schools researchers was directed at identifying variables that go together to shape the culture of an effective school. One of the best-known of these researchers was the late Ronald Edmonds, whose research led him to identify the following characteristics of effective schools (Edmonds, 1982, p. 4):

BOX 16–1
# CAN WE IDENTIFY THOSE CHARACTERISTICS OF EFFECTIVE SCHOOLS THAT CAN BE SUCCESSFULLY TRANSFERRED TO OTHER SCHOOLS?

*Speaker A:*     Learners in American elementary and high schools share a common national culture. While there are important place-to-place differences, similarities are more important. Textbooks and other materials tend to be published by national firms. Patterns of teacher training vary little from one section of the country to another. Common standardized tests are taken by learners everywhere. Hence, research findings that identify characteristics of schools can be applied to good effect to nearly any school in the country.

*Speaker B:*     Differences among individual schools are profound. Physical facilities are dilapidated in some places, while other schools are situated in buildings sitting on beautifully landscaped campuses and equipped with the most up-to-date equipment possible. Working conditions of teachers vary enormously from place to place. Administrators and parents are much more supportive of the teachers' efforts in some places than in others. Differences among schools are so profound that it is foolish to expect that general findings of effective-schools researchers can be widely applied to improve the nation's schools.

### What Do You Think?
1. What do you view as strengths and weaknesses of speaker A's arguments?
2. What do you view as strengths and weaknesses of speaker B's arguments?
3. If you were to participate in this discussion, what would you say?

- strong instructional leadership by the principal
- high academic expectations of learners by teachers
- strong emphasis on basic skills instruction
- an orderly environment
- frequent, systematic evaluation of learners

Edmonds's work developed a huge following in the early and middle 1980s. His list of effective schools' characteristics, sometimes extended by the addition of a sixth item (increased instructional time), was adopted by many school systems as a model for their school improvement projects (Stedman, 1987).

In the late 1980s, however, researchers began to raise doubts about the adequacy of Edmonds's list (Stedman, 1987; Zirkel and Greenwood, 1987). One of the components of Edmonds's list that came under particular attack was his suggestion that effective schools focused heavily on basic skills instruction. Some critics charged that this prescription had led schools to depress their academic expectations by reorienting their curricula to emphasize lower-level thinking skills (Stedman, 1987). This resulted in (1) too much emphasis on standardized tests and (2) highly prescriptive suggestions for teaching that took away much of the teacher's discretionary authority (Berry and Ginsberg, 1990).

Some critics, for example Lawrence Stedman (1987), argued that the call for basic skills instruction was having a particularly bad effect on schools in inner cities. Because achievement levels of learners in the nation's central cities have long lagged behind national averages, many urban school districts were quick to embrace Edmonds's ideas as a means of improving their programs. Stedman (1987) pointed out that a move by inner-city schools to emphasize basic skills had the potential to create "a widening of the social class achievement gap, as many suburban schools move rapidly into high-tech, problem-solving curricula, while urban schools remain focused on lower-order test items" (p. 217).

Edmonds's idea that the school principal should play a key role as an instructional leader has also been questioned. Critics point out that principals have so many other responsibilities that they are unlikely to have sufficient time to give instructional leadership the attention it deserves. Increasingly, researchers have recognized that teachers may possess more instructional expertise than do principals (Berry and Ginsberg, 1990).

The issue of what criteria should be applied in determining the relative effectiveness of a given school has been the focus of much attention. Some authorities support the idea that effectiveness should relate to the ability of a given school to better serve those learners who, traditionally, have not done well. Lawrence Stedman (1987), for example, has argued that an effective school program should be one that produces improved achievement on the part of learners from low-income families over a period of several years. Researchers Tamara Lucas, Rosemary Henze, and Ruben Donato (1990) imply that an effective school should also have a good record of promoting learning among cultural and linguistic minorities.

A number of research-based lists of characteristics of effective schools have been published. One that reflects a desire to measure effectiveness by looking at achievement of learners who come from groups that often have not done well in school was developed by Lawrence Stedman (1987, p. 218). It identifies the following characteristics of effective schools:

- ethnic and racial pluralism
- participation of parents
- shared governance with teachers and parents
- academically rich programs
- skilled use and training of teachers
- personal attention to learners

This teacher has high expectations of his learners, and he carefully monitors their progress. Such teacher behaviors are often found in classrooms in effective schools.

- learner responsibility for school affairs
- an accepting and supporting environment
- teaching aimed at preventing learning problems

## Ethnic and Racial Pluralism

Effective-schools projects of the early 1980s that developed around Edmonds's (1982) ideas featured strong emphases on teaching basic skills and establishing good classroom management and discipline routines. By the late 1980s and on into the early 1990s, some critics were beginning to suggest that not all learners would fare well in schools with these emphases. Particularly, critics concerned about achievement levels of learners from impoverished families and minority groups suggested that these young people might do better in a different kind of a school environment (Stedman, 1987; Lucas, Henze, and Donato, 1990).

Schools that do a good job of serving economically deprived and cultural-minority learners are quick to adjust their programs in response to special perspectives that these young people might possess. The curriculum takes into account special contributions of individuals from different ethnic groups. Often, these schools recognize holidays important to learners from some of the school's cultural groups. Additionally, there may be advanced instruction in sophisticated subjects—calculus, for example—conducted in Spanish or other languages spoken by large numbers of learners in the school (Lucas, Henze, and Donato, 1990). This approach underscores the point that complex thinking is not the exclusive property of the English-speaking majority. As well, there may be efforts to communicate to parents and other patrons of the school in a language other than English—school announcements, for example, may be sent to parents of some students in both English and Spanish (Stedman, 1987).

Programs at effective schools that are directed toward racial- and language-minority learners are designed to promote in young people and their parents a sense of ownership of the school program. These schools work hard to promote the view that there is nothing derogatory about being a member of a group whose members may not be white, middle class, or native speakers of English.

## Participation of Parents

When learners' parents have a compelling interest in school programs, their children do better academically and have more positive feelings about their school (Henderson, 1981). Effective schools attempt to develop parental interest by actively soliciting their involvement. This involvement breaks down perceptions parents may have that schools are run by the authorities and that the parents themselves are expected to remain passive outsiders.

Parental participation in effective schools occurs on two basic levels. First, these schools work hard to maintain open lines of communication between the school and learners' parents. Second, they adopt procedures that engage parents directly in the school's administrative and instructional processes. To accomplish this purpose, parents are invited to come to the school building to assist in the decision-making process and get actively involved in some classroom activities.

Effective schools have adopted imaginative ways of opening up the school–parent communication process. For example, because many parents work during the regular school day, some effective schools regularly schedule evening group meetings of administrators, teachers, and parents to enable these parents to attend.

Many approaches have been taken to involve parents more directly in the activities that support instruction. One program teaches learners' grandparents, parents, and older siblings how to work with learners at home to improve their verbal skills (Stedman, 1987). Other schools have developed successful parental aide programs, in which parental aides are brought directly into the classrooms and encouraged to help individual learners who are having difficulty. This activity helps parents develop more sensitivity to problems learners (including their own children) face as they struggle to master new content. Involved parents tend to work more carefully at home with their own children and be more supportive of the work of teachers.

Effective schools are particularly careful to communicate with parents when their children have done something good. Traditionally, except for the distribution of report cards, school personnel have not made serious efforts to communicate with parents about their children except when there has been bad news to deliver. ("Your child is ill and needs to be picked up," ". . . has been misbehaving in class," ". . . has been truant.") Over the years, many parents have learned that a call or letter from the school is likely to be a negative experience. When a principal or teacher reports to parents that their child has done something especially good, the parents experience an unexpected sensation of self-satisfaction and pleasure. Such calls often transform parents into strong supporters of the school.

## Shared Governance with Teachers and Parents

Some early research on characteristics of effective schools seemed to suggest that the principal should be the school's undisputed instructional leader. More recent scholarship, however, has pointed out that although the principal's general leadership is important, a collaborative relationship including teachers and others may result in a more effective instructional program (Berry and Ginsberg, 1990). Governance that is shared yields instructional programs that are well understood and strongly backed by administrators, teachers, and parents.

Researchers have found that in good schools, teachers are satisfied with their jobs and turnover rates are low (Purkey and Smith, 1983). Teachers' satisfaction is heavily dependent on the degree to which they sense themselves having control over decisions

*"This is an intriguing approach to gaining more attention for faculty views at meetings of our Administrator-Teacher-Parent Policy Council, but . . ."*
Courtesy of Ford Button.

relating to how they discharge their responsibilities. When teachers feel that they are being buffeted by irresponsible decisions made by impersonal bureaucrats, they become dissatisfied with their work (Feiman-Nemser and Floden, 1986). To ensure that teachers are committed to the instructional program they are required to teach, administrators in effective schools directly involve the teachers in the process of making those decisions affecting what they will be expected to do in the classroom (although, as this chapter's Case Study shows, mere inclusion on decision-making teams is not always effective).

CASE STUDY

*Do parents really work for the kids when they participate in making decisions about school programs?*

**My name is Irma Ruiz.** I am in my fifth year of teaching third graders at Chester A. Arthur Elementary School. I took a job at this school because of its reputation. When I was looking for my first position, I read a nice article in the local paper about the school's forward-looking principal, Corrine Chu, and her efforts to take advantage of what research defined as the characteristics of an effective school. When Ms. Chu interviewed me, I was pleased to learn that three teachers from the school, six parents, and three administrators (including Ms. Chu) shared responsibility for establishing and overseeing school programs. This shared governance idea was something new to me, and I thought it made a lot of sense.

This fall, I was thrilled to become appointed as one of the teacher representatives on the school's management team. I have learned a lot during the past few months. For one thing, I am not nearly so starry eyed in my appreciation of the idea of parent representation. The idea still appeals to me, but I must say I have been disappointed in how it seems to be working out at our school.

Our group of parents is a racially and ethnically diverse group. There are two African-Americans, two Hispanics, one Asian, and one white. My concern is that some of these people seem to have more interest in power politics and policies designed to benefit only certain groups than in the welfare of *all* our kids. Let me give you a few examples of what I mean.

At one of our early meetings, the two Hispanic parents made a big push for a policy that would have required all students to receive some instruction in the Spanish language and to read some books and stories, either in translation or in Spanish, written by Hispanic authors. At the same meeting, the two African-American parents called for a policy that would ensure that all African-American pupils would have an African-American teacher for at least three of the six years they were enrolled in the school.

The white parent put forward a proposal to upgrade the quality of our teaching staff by hiring more teachers from Upsilon University, an expensive private institution with an excellent academic reputation. Interestingly, Upsilon enrolls a few students of Asian heritage, but virtually no African-Americans or Hispanics. The Asian parent on our team enthusiastically embraced this proposal.

Meeting after meeting has been characterized with this kind of polarization along racial and ethnic lines. It seems that nobody can just look at kids as kids anymore—they are just a sideshow in a main event that is really a competition for power among ethnic and racial groups in the area served by our school. It is very hard to make *any* kind of a decision with this kind of division among our parental representatives. I am becoming more and more frustrated, and I am thinking seriously about tendering my resignation from the management team.

*What should Irma Ruiz do? Are there some actions she personally could initiate? Should the principal take some specific actions? If so, what might they be? Would resignation be a good move? What sorts of things might be done to refocus parents' attention on the general needs of children in the school as opposed to the perceived needs of children from specific groups? Is it possible to have parental representation without it degenerating into a turf battle among representatives of different groups?*

Parents also are often involved in the decision-making process. They may serve on committees looking at proposed changes in the curriculum, suggested changes in rules for learners, and proposed testing programs. Many benefits flow from this kind of parental involvement: first, they come to sense that their views really do count, and second, they often learn for the first time that school personnel are sincerely interested in improving their children's education (Lucas, Henze, and Donato, 1990). Involved parents frequently become unofficial school ambassadors to the community.

There is an important benefit for administrators and teachers of parental participation in decision making. When principals and teachers realize that parents will play an active role in making policy, they pay more attention to views of the larger community that, in part, are reflected in parents' attitudes. And because they are more tuned in to the perspectives of the community, principals and teachers often find it easier to develop programmatic responses that are closely aligned to community thinking. Over time, this can bring about a widened base of citizen support for the school.

## Academically Rich Programs

Some initial research on effective schools suggested that they were characterized by an emphasis on basic skills, but more recent research has disputed this. In a review of schools that had developed programs that served the needs of economically deprived learners exceptionally well, Lawrence Stedman (1987) found the schools to be providing a rich array of course offerings. His research reported an absence of a narrow focus on basic skills.

What seems to be happening is that a rich and diverse academic program motivates learners. In such a setting, the students appear to work harder and learn more. On the other hand, attempts to narrow the variety in a school program by focusing heavily on basic skills can have undesirable side effects, among them that learners may become bored. When this occurs, achievement scores are likely to fall because unmotivated learners rarely do well on tests.

### Skilled Use and Training of Teachers

Administrators of effective schools place their best teachers in high-need areas. For example, if a school has a large number of learners needing remedial instruction, some of the most outstanding teachers in the building are assigned to provide it (Stedman, 1987). Improvements in learning result from this convergence of teaching talent and high-priority learning needs.

Some effective schools feature teams of roving expert teachers. These outstanding professionals help other teachers by serving as consultants and troubleshooters. All teachers in effective schools tend to receive inservice training that is highly specific to their own needs and relevant to their unique instructional situations. Teachers often participate in identifying areas in which they would like help, and inservice assistance is provided in response to these requests (Stedman, 1987).

First-year teachers often receive especially strong support from building administrators and their more experienced peers. Teaching assignments are made in such a

This experienced teacher is providing some suggestions to a colleague who is a first-year teacher.

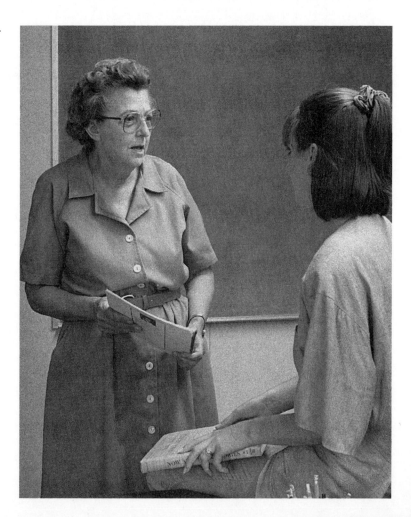

way that their prospects for achieving success are high. Members of the building staff work hard to help new teachers develop more confidence in their abilities. In some places, these teachers are provided with extra preparation time (Urbanski, 1988). There may be arrangements that allow first-year teachers to visit other classrooms and profit from their observations of more experienced teachers.

Beginning teachers who have a positive first-year experience are likely to develop a long-term commitment to the profession, and effective schools produce teachers who see themselves as career professionals. In such buildings, staff turnover is low and it is easier for administrators, parents, and teachers to engage in serious long-term planning.

Some schools now are beginning to formalize programs for beginners into what is sometimes called an "induction year" (see Box 16–2). Induction programs are designed to ease the entry of newcomers into the profession. Often these programs assign a men-

---

BOX 16-2
## SHOULD THERE BE A RIGOROUS EVALUATION OF TEACHERS DURING THEIR INDUCTION YEAR?

The idea that a teacher's first year on the job should be considered an "induction year" has been gaining in popularity. The induction year is supposed to provide a careful transition from the world of the university to the real world of professional teaching.

Authorities are at odds over the issue of special assessment of induction-year teaching. Some argue that the induction year should be regarded exclusively as a nurturing, supportive experience for newcomers. They contend that it should be a time when experienced teachers provide all possible assistance to help the beginner to succeed. A rigorous evaluation program for induction-year teachers, they say, would undermine the nature of this supportive, nurturing relationship.

Others argue that without a strong evaluation component, little will happen during the induction year. By adding evaluation to the experience, there is incentive for mentor teachers to actually deliver the support services envisioned by designers of the induction-year program, as they will have an interest in ensuring the success of the new teacher. A poor evaluation will reflect as negatively on them as on the inductee.

*What Do You Think?*
1. How strong is the case made here for not including an evaluation component in the induction-year program?
2. How strong is the case made here for including an evaluation component in the induction-year program?
3. What are your own feelings about including a rigorous evaluation scheme as part of the induction year?

tor to each new teacher. The mentor is a highly qualified, experienced teacher who works closely with the beginner during his or her first year of teaching. In some places, professors from teacher preparation institutions continue to work with teachers during their first year on the job.

### Personal Attention to Learners

Effective schools establish high academic expectations for learners (Purkey and Smith, 1983), and these expectations are well-understood by learners as well as teachers (Rutherford, 1985). To accomplish this kind of understanding, many effective schools have "designed their programs so that they could provide close, personal attention to students" (Stedman, 1987, p. 221). This assistance is provided in many ways. Often, programs seek to increase the numbers of contacts individual learners have with adults who are in a position to help them. Some schools bring in adult volunteers to assist teachers, others use older and brighter learners to assist pupils who need help.

When teachers have volunteers to assist them, they have more time to devote to pupils who are in special need of assistance and can develop instructional responses that are especially well-suited to these learners. As a result, performance levels of these young people often increase.

Use of volunteers and other teaching assistants also allows time for teachers to better monitor the progress of individual learners. A growing body of research suggests that consistent monitoring of learners is associated with enhanced scholastic performance (Good and Brophy, 1986). Good monitoring provides feedback to learners regarding their errors. Learners then have opportunities to correct their mistakes and master assigned content. This mastery, in turn, leads to greater self-confidence and, often, improved performance on subsequent learning tasks.

### Learner Responsibility for School Affairs

Effective schools assign important responsibilities to learners. These may consist of academic tasks, nonacademic tasks, or a mixture of the two. In some schools, student-tutors work with other learners who need assistance with certain aspects of content they are studying (Stedman, 1987). Another approach that some effective schools use involves appointing learner representatives to work with parents, teachers, and community representatives on advisory councils to develop recommendations for improving the school program.

Nonacademic responsibilities assigned to learners in effective schools vary widely from place to place. For example, some learners may be assigned to organize groups to remove debris from the area surrounding the school building. Others may have responsibilities for keeping halls and public areas attractive. Still others may be assigned to help in maintaining good order in the cafeteria and at athletic events.

When learners are assigned specific responsibilities related to the operation of the school, they often develop positive attitudes toward the school and its programs. This is particularly true when learners are given opportunities to actively participate in making important decisions. When this happens, their academic achievement levels frequently go up (Good and Brophy, 1986).

## An Accepting and Supporting Environment

A positive school environment has often been associated with effective schools (Levine and Ornstein, 1989). Teachers in an accepting and supporting environment have been described as having a "sense of efficacy" (Ashton and Webb, 1986), which means that they have confidence in themselves as professionals and, particularly, in their ability to transmit information to their learners.

In schools with accepting and supporting environments, teachers sense that they exercise significant personal control over the nature of their work. Their rate of turnover is low because they generally are pleased with their jobs (Purkey and Smith, 1983). They feel that they have the authority to make modifications in their instructional programs in order to meet learners' needs.

Teachers and administrators in effective schools work hard to take note of all kinds of learner achievements. This recognition goes beyond traditional awards for athletic prowess; for example, some schools prominently display names of learners who have done excellent academic work, performed well in a one-act play competition, been recognized by local civic organizations, won awards in scouting organizations, been recognized for musical talents, or achieved some other kind of special recognition. The idea behind this practice is to build schoolwide support for the notion that success in all areas merits commendation.

Schools with warm, supportive, and positive atmospheres often have pleasant physical surroundings. This does not necessarily imply new, well-landscaped, or spacious buildings; in fact, some effective schools occupy very old buildings in neighborhoods with few trees. What makes the atmosphere pleasant is the attention given to repair and maintenance of the building. Needed repairs are done quickly. Any disfigurations are removed immediately. Hallways and rooms are pleasantly decorated. There is an absence of clutter. The idea is to maintain a physical appearance that reflects a sense of pride and engenders a feeling that the educational experiences provided in the school are important (see Box 16–3).

## Teaching Aimed at Preventing Learning Problems

Teachers in effective schools try to deal with learners' potential learning difficulties before they become serious. Different approaches have been taken to accomplish this objective. One idea has been to establish a "parent-alert" system in which teachers communicate immediately with a learner's parent when there is a preliminary indication of a learning problem (Stedman, 1987).

For example, an elementary school teacher might call a parent of a child who appears to be having difficulty mastering multiplication tables. The parent (or another relative) is encouraged to work with the learner at home to reinforce what is being taught at school. This underscores in the mind of the learner the importance of the task and also develops a sense of community in which both teachers and parents consider themselves to have a collective interest in helping the learner. Early intervention that involves both a parent and the teacher often assists learners to overcome initial difficulties. When this happens, their confidence grows, and often they do better on subsequent learning tasks.

To be successful, programs designed to spot learning difficulties early require teachers to know individuals in their classes well. The teachers must be able to spot ini-

BOX 16-3
## WHAT WERE THE ENVIRONMENTS LIKE IN SCHOOLS YOU ATTENDED?

School-effectiveness researchers have found that better schools are places learners view as warm and caring. A positive atmosphere tends to be associated with buildings and rooms that are well-maintained and pleasant, where teachers get along well with one another, and where there are pleasant and cordial relationships between teachers and learners. Reflect for a moment about the elementary and secondary schools you attended.

*What Do You Think?*

1. What were some characteristics of these schools that contributed to their either having or not having warm and caring atmospheres?
2. Were there some specific things that could have been done to improve the environments of these schools? If so, what were they?
3. Did you find much difference in the environments of the elementary and secondary schools you attended? If so, how might these differences be explained?

tial difficulties quickly and develop appropriate responses before minor problems become serious barriers to additional learning. These responses often take the form of highly individualized instruction for learners who are experiencing difficulty. This kind of personalized instruction is commonly found among teachers in effective schools.

## Effective Schools Research: Present Status

For over 10 years, researchers have been publishing results of investigations designed to highlight special features of effective schools. Many lists of these characteristics have been published, and although a number of these lists include some common elements, researchers are far from arriving at a consensus of defining features that, if present at a given school, could be taken as incontrovertible evidence that the school was "effective." Indeed, some authorities question whether any such list of characteristics can ever be identified (or, indeed, implemented—see the accompanying What the Experts Say).

WHAT THE EXPERTS SAY

*Conflicts regarding what effective-schools research says teachers should do and what recent reform legislation requires*

Barnett Berry and Rick Ginsberg (1990) have surveyed research focusing on what teachers do in effective schools and the constraints imposed on teachers by much recent educational reform legislation. They have identified a number of noteworthy conflicts.

Effective-schools research suggests that teachers should be individuals who are flexible, adaptable, and creative. According to this view, teachers should function as authoritative professionals who draw on their own expert professional knowledge to develop instructional programs that are suitable for the particular learners they are assigned to teach.

This view of the teacher's role, however, is contrary to what has been mandated in much recent educational reform legislation, which has frequently reflected a suspicion of teachers' intellectual attainments. Teachers often have been portrayed as semi-skilled laborers whose responsibilities are limited to transmitting content mandated by the state—in other words, the teacher is little more than a factory worker.

A common feature of educational reform legislation is an emphasis on standardized testing of learners. The increasing importance of standardized test scores has encouraged teachers to emphasize low-level knowledge and skills content related to categories of information that the tests assess. This trend has been a force working against attempts to support teachers in their efforts to act as independent professionals who can design site-specific, challenging instructional programs for their learners.

Berry and Ginsberg argue that unless greater attention is paid to the actual contexts within which teachers work, findings of the effective-schools research are not likely to influence teachers' behaviors. In particular, state governments need to take action to "loosen the organizational, curricular, and pedagogical reins that inhibit talented teachers and principals."*

*B. Berry and R. Ginsberg, "Teachers, Principals, and Educational Leadership," in B. Mitchell and L. L. Cunninghnam, eds., *Educational Leadership and Changing Contexts of Families, Communities, and Schools,* 89th Yearbook of the National Society for the Study of Education, Part II (Chicago: The University of Chicago Press, 1990), 155–183.

Among other things, these critics of effective-schools research suggest that instructional contexts vary greatly from school to school. Hence, it is unlikely that imposing a set of conditions associated with "effectiveness" in one setting necessarily results in "effectiveness" in others. For example, some authorities have pointed out that much of the effective-schools research implies that teachers should design instructional programs that are uniquely responsive to the needs of the learners they serve. Yet, in some places, state control of curricula places severe restraints on what teachers are allowed to do (Berry and Ginsberg, 1990). In these states, even teachers who are willing to make the necessary adjustments to meet particular needs of their pupils and students may not legally be able to do so.

Despite such concerns, effective-schools research findings have been used by some school districts as bases for planning school improvement projects. Results have been mixed: heartening gains in learner achievement have been attributed to implementation of such projects in places such as Milwaukee, Kansas City, Washington, D.C., and San Diego, but projects in many other places have failed to demonstrate significant improvement in learner achievement (Levine and Ornstein, 1989). In spite of their exposure to programs based on school-effectiveness research, many learners, particularly those in inner-city school districts, continue to reflect disappointingly low levels of achievement.

**Table 16-1**
Summary table: Effective schools

| Characteristics | Contributions |
| --- | --- |
| Ethnic and racial pluralism | Builds learners' confidence and develops in learners a sense of ownership of the school. |
| Participation of parents | Breaks down idea that parents are outsiders and makes parents advocates of the school and its programs. |
| Shared governance with teachers and parents | Yields programs that are understood and supported by teachers and parents and improves teachers' and parents' morale. |
| Academically rich programs | Motivates learners and improves their achievement levels. |
| Skilled use and training of teachers | Builds an environment that allows teachers to succeed and brings maximum talent to where it is most needed. |
| Personal attention to learners | Increases learners' performance levels and builds their confidence. |
| Learner responsibility for school affairs | Develops positive learner attitudes toward the school and improves achievement levels. |
| An accepting and supporting environment | Improves teachers' professional self-confidence and encourages learners to value success. |
| Teaching aimed at preventing problems | Remediates problems before they become serious and builds learners' confidence in their abilities to achieve. |

· · · · · · · · · · · · · · · · · · · · · · · · · ·

# Key Ideas in Summary

- One issue that has been much debated is whether common features of schools are sufficient in number to allow for identification of some general characteristics of effective schools. Individuals who perceive schools to have many individual differences doubt whether this can be done, but others, who emphasize important place-to-place commonalities, are more convinced that general effectiveness principles can be applied to schools in diverse settings.

- An early proponent of the idea that certain characteristics of effective schools could be identified was Ronald Edmonds. Edmonds suggested that these schools featured strong instructional leadership by the principal, high academic expectations of learners by teachers, strong emphasis on basic skills instruction, an orderly environment, and frequent and systematic evaluation of learners.

- In recent years, a number of researchers have produced lists of characteristics of effective schools. Lawrence Stedman identified features of schools that had programs that helped economically deprived learners to improve their achievement levels, including ethnic and racial pluralism, participation of parents, shared governance with teachers and parents, academically-rich programs, skilled use and training of teachers, personal attention to learners, learner responsibility for school affairs, an accepting and supportive environment, and teaching aimed at preventing academic problems.

- Schools with diverse populations of learners have been found to make special efforts to recognize and build on contributions made by people from different groups. For example, holidays of different cultural groups may get special recognition in school programs, or instruction in advanced subjects may be provided in students' native languages. (Where the latter has been done, Spanish has been the most frequent language of instruction used.)

- Leaders of effective schools seek to give parents a sense of ownership in the school and its programs. Often, parental help is solicited to augment and reinforce instruction provided by teachers. As well, parents are often invited to participate (along with teachers) in groups charged with framing school policy. This participation gives parents a substantive role in determining characteristics of the school program.

- Some of the more recent effective-schools research suggests that these schools offer a rich array of courses that go well beyond basic skills instruction, and learners have been found to be motivated by this diversity. Additionally, teachers in these schools tend to play active personal roles in identifying their own professional development needs. Further, special efforts are made to mentor the development of new teachers—experienced teachers often work with them in systematic programs designed to smooth their entry into the profession.

- In effective schools, teachers respond quickly to particular needs of individual learners. Many of these schools provide parent volunteers and other teacher assistants, whose presence in the classroom allows teachers to spend more time monitoring individual learners and tailoring their instruction to meet special needs. These schools also tend to give learners important responsibilities. Every effort is made to instill in them a sense of pride and ownership in the school.

- The general environment of effective schools tends to be warm and supporting. For learners, this means that special steps are taken to recognize all kinds of achievement; for teachers, it means that administrators provide them with a great deal of autonomy. Teachers are encouraged to use their best professional insights to develop instructional programs that will allow learners to succeed. This freedom is coupled with teaching that is oriented toward prevention of learning problems. To deal with potential problems early, these teachers often engage the assistance of learners' parents.

- Results of efforts to build programs based on the results of school-effectiveness research have been mixed. In some places, such programs have resulted in dramatic achievement gains, but in other places there has been less success. One persistent problem seems to be an inconsistency between what research says about the need for teachers to be flexible and the legislation in some states that prescribes what teachers are to do and limits their authority to exercise their own professional judgments about how instruction should be organized and delivered.

...........................

# Review and Discussion Questions

1. What is meant by the term *effective school*?
2. What are some features of effective schools that were identified by Ronald Edmonds?
3. What is meant by the statement, "Each school has its own culture"?
4. In what ways do the views of Lawrence Stedman differ from those of Ronald Edmonds regarding characteristics of effective schools?
5. What are some characteristics that Lawrence Stedman found in schools that were doing a good job of helping economically deprived learners to achieve?
6. Some experts seem to place a great deal of emphasis on the importance of parental involvement. Why do they think involving parents is a necessary characteristic of an effective school? Do you agree?
7. How is it possible for educators to take advantage of a school's diverse racial, ethnic, and language characteristics to develop programs that will encourage young people to learn?
8. Some experts recommend sharing powers of school governance with parents. Is this a good idea? Do parents have the necessary expertise to make good decisions? On what do you base your answers?
9. Lawrence Stedman reports that effective schools tend to allow teachers to identify their own inservice needs. Are teachers likely to have an accurate picture of their own needs? Is it a good idea to allow them to decide what kind of additional information and training they should receive to improve their levels of performance? Why do you think so?
10. In many parts of the country, state authorities place limitations on what teachers can do in their classrooms. For example, there may be requirements related to what content can be covered. Financial limitations also tend to restrict what teachers can do, particularly in impoverished school districts. Given the

nature of these place-to-place differences, is it realistic to expect that implementation of characteristics that researchers have found to be associated with effective schools will have a positive effect regardless of where they are implemented? Why or why not?

# Ideas for Field Experiences, Projects, and Enrichment

1. Form a team with several others from your class, and conduct a survey of a local school district. Try to determine the extent to which the characteristics identified by Lawrence Stedman are reflected in the district's schools. Prepare a report to share with the class.

2. Invite several school principals to your class. Ask them to share their reactions to Stedman's list of school-effectiveness characteristics. In particular, solicit comments about potential problems local school authorities might face in implementing particular recommendations (e.g., shared governance with teachers and parents).

3. Organize a debate on this topic: "Resolved That School-to-School Differences Are So Profound That It Makes Little Sense to Implement a General Set of School-Effectiveness Characteristics With Any Expectations That Improved Learning Will Result."

4. Interview a president or other active member of a local teachers' professional organization. Ask for comments regarding the degree to which the kind of roles for teachers envisioned in the school-effectiveness research mirrors teachers' actual roles in the local schools. Also, solicit some reactions from this person regarding the desirability and feasibility of teachers behaving in ways consistent with what Stedman determined to be going on in effective schools. Report your findings to your course instructor.

5. Review articles in professional journals (ask your instructor about possible sources) that have focused on school-effectiveness research. Prepare a paper in which you compare and contrast findings.

# Supplementary Reading

Berry, B., and R. Ginsberg. "Teachers, Principals, and Educational Leadership." In B. Mitchell and L. L. Cunninghnam, eds. *Educational Leadership and Changing Contexts* of *Families, Communities, and Schools. 89th Yearbook of the National Society for the Study of Education.* Part II. Chicago: The University of Chicago Press, 1990, 155–83.

Edmonds, R. R. "Programs of School Improvement: An Overview." *Educational Leadership* (December 1982): 4–11.

Feiman-Nemser, S., and R. E. Floden. "The Cultures of Teaching." In M. C. Wittrock, ed. *Handbook of Research on Teaching.* 3d ed. New York: Macmillan, 1986, 505–26.

Goodlad, J. *A Place Called School.* New York: McGraw-Hill, 1984.

Levine, D. U., and A. C. Ornstein. "Research on Classroom and School Effectiveness and Its Implications for Improving Big City Schools." *The Urban Review* (June 1989): 81–94.

Lucas, T., R. Henze, and R. Donato. "Promoting the Success of Latino Language-Minority Students: An Exploratory Study of Six High Schools." *Harvard Educational Review* (August 1990): 315–40.

Stedman, L. C. "It's Time We Changed the Effective Schools Formula." *Phi Delta Kappan* (November 1987): 215–224.

Tyler, R. W. "Education Reforms." *Educational Leadership* (December 1987): 227–80.

Witte, J. F., and D. J. Walsh. "A Systematic Test of the Effective Schools Model." *Educational Evaluation and Policy Analysis* (Summer 1990): 188–212.

# References

Ashton, P. T., and R.B. Webb. *Making a Difference: Teachers' Sense of Efficacy and Student Achievement.* New York: Longman, 1986.

Berry, B., and R. Ginsberg. "Teachers, Principals, and Educational Leadership." In B. Mitchell and L. L. Cunninghnam, eds. *Educational Leadership and Changing Contexts of Families, Communities, and Schools. 89th Yearbook of the National Society for the Study of Education.* Part II. Chicago: The University of Chicago Press, 1990, 155–83.

Edmonds, R.R. "Programs of School Improvement: An Overview." *Educational Leadership* (December 1982): 4–11.

Feiman-Nemser, S., and R. E. Floden. "The Cultures of Teaching." In M. C. Wittrock, ed. *Handbook of Research on Teaching.* 3rd ed. New York: Macmillan, 1986, 505–26.

Good, T. L., and J. E. Brophy. "School Effects." In M. C. Wittrock, ed. *Handbook of Research on Teaching.* 3d ed. New York: Macmillan, 1986.

Henderson, A., ed. *Parent Participation—Student Achievement: The Evidence Grows.* Columbia, MD: National Committee for Citizens in Education, 1981.

Levine, D. U., and A. C. Ornstein. "Research on Classroom and School Effectiveness and Its Implications for Improving Big City Schools." *The Urban Review* (June 1989): 81–94.

Lucas, T., R. Henze, and R. Donato. "Promoting the Success of Latino Language-Minority Students: An Exploratory Study of Six High Schools." *Harvard Educational Review* (August 1990): 315–40.

Purkey, S. C., and M. S. Smith. "Effective Schools: A Review." *Elementary School Journal* (March 1983): 427–52.

Rutherford, W. L. "School Principals as Effective Leaders." *Phi Delta Kappan* (September 1985): 31–34.

Stedman, L. C. "It's Time We Changed the Effective Schools Formula." *Phi Delta Kappan* (November 1987): 215–24.

Tyler, R. W. "Education Reforms." *Educational Leadership* (December 1987): 227–80.

Urbanski, A. "Rochester Plan: A Collaborative Model." Address given at the Second Annual South Central Holmes Group Spring Faculty Conference: Houston, TX: April 23, 1988.

Witte, J. F., and D. J. Walsh. "A Systematic Test of the Effective Schools Model." *Educational Evaluation and Policy Analysis* (Summer 1990): 188–212.

Zirkel, P. A., and S. C. Greenwood. "Effective Schools and Effective Principals: Effective Research?" *Teachers College Record* (Winter 1987): 255–67.

# Section 6

# Legal Relationships

## Overview

Think about these two views:

*Person A:* "All education is local. What young people learn occurs in individual classrooms, not in state legislatures or in Washington, D.C. Real improvement in education will come only when people in local districts and, most especially, teachers and principals in individual schools are given real power. They understand what their learners need, and they should be given the power to shape curricula to best help the young people they serve. The best thing we could do for education would be to get federal and state bureaucrats off the backs of local educators."

*Person B:* "Proposals to give local districts, principals, and teachers more power are a sham. Vesting decision-making authority at local district and school levels is certain to be followed by attempts to place responsibility for funding schools at the local level as well. The blathering about local control and local expertise is just a cover for an irresponsible attempt by the federal government and the states to abdicate their responsibilities for education and dump an impossibly large financial burden on local communities."

These contrasting views represent two that are being hotly debated in education today. Resolutions of conflicts such as these affect how power is shared among federal, state, and local authorities. Controversy regarding legal relationships is a defining fea-

ture of our society. The United States has 70 percent of the world's lawyers, and in a recent year 18 million new lawsuits were filed (Carelli, 1991, p. 4A).

Schools and educators have not escaped our national interest in legal relationships. Many court cases have helped establish the boundaries of "appropriate" conduct for both teachers and learners. It is in the self-interest of prospective teachers to know something about legal guidelines affecting those who work and study in the schools. Answers to questions such as these may provide useful information:

- What is the proper alignment of educational responsibilities among federal, state, and local authorities?

- What kinds of constraints are put on individuals' personal behaviors when they accept employment as a teacher?

- What have been some patterns of court decisions in areas related to academic freedom?

- What are some legal rights and responsibilities of learners as defined by the courts?

Chapters in this section provide answers to these questions. The chapters are:

Chapter 17: Who Controls?
Chapter 18: Legal Concerns of Teachers
Chapter 19: Learners' Rights and Responsibilities

# Chapter 17

# Who Controls?

· · · · · · · · · · · · · · · · · · · · · · · · · · · · · · · · · · ·

## Objectives

This chapter provides information to help the reader to

- recognize changes over time in relative influences of local, state, and federal authorities over education.
- suggest arguments supporting and opposing local control of education.
- point out how the issue of educational equity has acted to move control of education away from local school districts.
- suggest some factors associated with the expansion of federal involvement in education.
- describe views of individuals favoring and opposing an increased role for state authorities in education.

# Focus Questions

1. How has the pattern of influence of local, state, and federal authorities over education evolved?
2. Why, traditionally, was local control of education considered to be so important?
3. Is local authority over education increasing or decreasing, as compared to state authority?
4. What are some examples of controls over education exercised by local authorities?
5. In what ways have state authorities traditionally controlled education?
6. What arguments have been made for and against local influences over education?
7. What arguments have been made for and against state influences over education?
8. What arguments have been made for and against federal influences over education?
9. What is the present status of local influence over education? Of state influence? Of federal influence?
10. In what ways may court decisions in the area of funding equity change the relative influence that state and local authorities have over education?

...............................

# Introduction

The pattern of control of American education is a result of conflicts and compromises among local, state, and national forces. These forces include legislative, administrative, and judicial actions of federal, state, and local authorities. The relative importance of federal, state, and local influences has fluctuated over time.

Traditionally, state governments have exercised much control over education. This arrangement is rooted in the U.S. Constitution. The Constitution, as initially drafted and approved, made no reference to education. However, the Tenth Amendment provides some general guidance in the section that points out that "the powers not delegated to the United States nor prohibited by it to the States, are reserved to the States respectively, or to the people." These words imply that, since the Constitution makes no mention of specific federal responsibility for education, this responsibility falls to state authorities.

Based on this constitutional situation, states have adopted bodies of laws relating to the operation of their schools. These laws have established centralized procedures for financing and managing school systems. Typically, state educational programs and policies are overseen by a central state department of education. (Specific names of this unit of government vary from state to state.) State legislation generally allows local authorities to implement the general school law and policy decisions that are made at the state level.

State legislation usually provides for the establishment of local school boards, which determine policies for individual school districts. School boards establish general operational guidelines for their districts. They are often charged with raising local revenues as needed to supplement state support for instructional programs and the construction of facilities. Additionally, they oversee the hiring of key administrative and teaching personnel. Consistent with individual state guidelines, school board members may also have some discretion over the instructional programs offered in local schools.

The federal government, operating under its constitutional authority to look after the "general welfare" of the population, plays a more direct role in education than was true even a quarter of a century ago. Similarly, there has been a trend for state governments to enlarge the roles they have played in the educational enterprise.

At each level of government, political decisions result when specific political constituencies win majorities in support of their points of view. Sometimes, groups have been unsuccessful in gaining support for their views at the local and state levels, and then have tended to concentrate their attempts at the federal level. The effort to secure better educational services for handicapped learners, something that came about largely because of federal legislation, is an example of a successful national lobbying effort by people who felt that local and state authorities were not responding to their concerns.

In recent years, there has been a trend for educational decision-making power to shift away from local authorities to state and federal authorities. Some explanations for this pattern are introduced in the following sections, which focus on:

- local influences
- state influences

- federal influences
- equity issues associated with funding

## Local Influences

Sentiment for local control of schools represents a value that runs deep and has long historical roots. Education was a frequent topic of debate in early town meetings in colonial New England. Regardless of their geographic location, when communities were small and somewhat isolated from one another, few challenged the right of local leaders to exercise control over what went on in the schools. Local control ensured local citizens that appropriate values were being transmitted to their young people. Further, the system built a sense of community that cut across class and age lines. This approach worked well when communities and problems were small and manageable, but as towns and cities grew larger, local decision making that involved personal participation by the entire community was no longer possible. With growth came a pattern of growing separation between the people making decisions about the schools and the people affected by those decisions.

Despite changes in the size and complexity of many American communities, local control of education is still a value that many prize. However, it is also fair to say that today the idea of local control has many critics. See Box 17–1 for a consideration of these views as they relate to your own educational experiences.

---

BOX 17–1
# WHAT MIGHT A SCHOOL PROGRAM EMPHASIZING LOCAL VALUES LOOK LIKE?

One of the arguments that has sometimes been made by people who strongly support local control of education is that differences among communities are profound. They believe that individual communities have unique sets of values and, properly, educational programs should be designed to respond to these local values. Consider the nature of the community where you spent most of your school years, and then think about the nature of its school program.

### What Do You Think?

1. If the school program was totally consistent with the nature of the community, would it be different from the one you actually experienced? If so, what would the differences be? If not, how do you think school officials were able to keep their program so consistent with community values?
2. What advantages do you see in having a school program that is as consistent as possible with local values? What disadvantages?
3. Some people argue that there are important differences among American communities. Others admit that although there are differences, they are relatively unimportant. What are your views?

## The Case *for* Local Influences

Although Americans in different parts of the country share many common values, differences do exist. The special characteristics of people in individual communities are best understood by those people themselves. Subtle characteristics of individual places cannot be fully appreciated by officials living in state capitals or in Washington, D.C. Local people know what their young people need, and they are capable of developing sound programs.

Local schools unify local communities. They provide athletic programs, plays, evening classes for adults, voting sites for elections, and other services that are of great interest to the adult population of the community. Although all of these things contribute to developing a positive community spirit, athletic competitions do an especially good job of helping people in a community pull together. A sense of community "belonging" results from supporting local teams, and a fear of losing this has often led people to oppose moves to consolidate school districts. (Consolidations sometimes result in school closures and an accompanying elimination of school athletic teams.)

Although in recent years there has been a trend for higher percentages of school funds to come from state rather than local sources, substantial amounts are still raised

Parents and members of other community groups often organize to press for educational change. This group is using a picketing technique to emphasize their opposition to proposed budget cuts.

locally. Local control of education has meant that school board officials, in response to community wishes, have set tax rates to generate sufficient revenue to provide the desired level of educational services. It should be pointed out that, almost always, state authorities have decreed that certain minimum standards be met. But districts often have had the option of providing more than these minimums. Given this situation, many school districts have prided themselves on developing school systems superior to those that have chosen to do little beyond what the state requires.

The right to hire teachers is a privilege that local educational leaders have defended strongly against state and federal encroachment. People often believe that teachers represent adult role models for young people, and therefore only those people whose basic values are compatible with those of the local community should serve as teachers. It is argued that when local officials hire individuals who mirror local values, young people in the schools encounter adults similar to those they meet in nonschool community settings, which helps to enhance teachers' credibility in the eyes of learners.

Local control of education has also been defended because of its consistency with American political tradition. A core American value is the prizing of individualism, and individualism is thought to be less threatened by decisions of local authorities than by decisions of more distant state and federal authorities. Further, efforts to expand state and federal control have sometimes been seen as unwelcome attacks on the competence of local leaders.

*"He says he wants to discuss the school district's tax increase."*
Courtesy of Ford Button

## The Case *Against* Local Influences

Local schools may *think* they know their own needs best, but do they really? The local community is part of both a larger state community and a still larger national community. While there may be a few characteristics unique to a given community, it makes little sense to give local people authority to shape school programs that are designed to respond to a small number of special circumstances. American society is mobile. Students must leave school capable of fitting into communities anywhere in the state and nation. (Indeed, given the interconnectedness of the whole world, it is desirable to look beyond our own borders when thinking about where graduates of our schools will ultimately reside.) Too much "localism" in school management can result in programs that do not adequately prepare learners for life beyond the local community.

The alleged unifying function of school in the local community has been exaggerated. True, small towns continue to be dependent for much of their organized social life on programs associated with schools, but in urban and suburban America (where most of us now live), school programs represent only a fraction of the opportunities people have to come together.

Absolute local control over teacher selection can result in a body of teachers who mirror all the prejudices of the local community. If, for example, a community has few African-American residents, all teachers hired may be white. If there is a strong local prejudice against Roman Catholics, subtle means may be used to ensure that only Protestants are hired as teachers. Such practices fail to take into account that learners should be prepared for the world, not just the local community. State and federal actions designed to ensure that local hiring practices are free from unacceptable biases are a reasonable and appropriate response to a potentially dangerous problem.

In reply to the argument that local control reflects a traditional national commitment to individualism, it should be pointed out that, in America, individualism has always gone forward within a social context. That is, the value has not been that "anything goes" in response to individual whims; rather, individualism has been defined and limited by our society. There has been a strong tradition of collective help in support of individual development. Frontier farmers called in neighbors when they roofed barns. Lewis and Clark did not go alone to the Northwest frontier. Even the most outrageous individual behavior is so described because people, collectively, have defined more generally accepted patterns. Looked at in this way, there is no necessary conflict between the individual and the larger society. The relationship is properly viewed as one of mutual interdependence.

## Local Influences: Status Report

In this century, there has been an erosion of the control that local authorities exercise over education. But this general pattern by no means indicates that local authorities do not continue to have a very significant influence over school programs in their districts—many of the decisions they make impart special favors to local programs.

Efforts to professionalize education have often sought to involve state-level education officials. When policies are adopted and implemented at the state level, a certain efficiency results because they can be imposed by the state on all of its school districts. Change that requires individual school district leaders to debate and approve policies is very time consuming. For this reason, many school reform efforts have preferred to modify educational practices by working with state legislatures and putting the enforcement apparatus of state departments of education behind mandated policy changes.

At the federal level, organized interest groups have been able to secure passage of much legislation that has an impact on local school districts. For example, many programs relating to bilingual education, the treatment of minorities, vocational education, and the education of handicapped learners have been sponsored by federal authorities. Requirements that are placed on local school districts regarding implementation of these programs takes away some decision-making power from local education officials. Today, even very small school districts frequently employ people who work part or full time in coordinating various federal education programs.

In summary, many people remain strongly committed to the idea of local control of education (see this chapter's Case Study for one example). However, over time, actions of state and federal authorities have tended to diminish the real power of local education authorities.

---

CASE STUDY

## *Local influences go beyond official political power*

**The influence that local communities have over their schools is not just a matter of official political power**—it also is expressed in how citizens in general feel about their schools. Positive feelings often result when people feel that something they personally do can affect the school program. Paulette O'Connell recently was involved in a situation that typifies what local educators can do to build a sense of community ownership of the schools.

Paulette is in her first year of teaching at Coral Reef Elementary School. Her principal, Dr. Manuel Salinas, is widely known for his forward-looking leadership. He is an administrator who recognizes that effective schools result from a commitment of the local community as well as of professional educators. Dr. Salinas frequently challenges his faculty to come up with ideas to involve the local community in improving the school program. Two weeks ago, Paulette O'Connell overcame some of her nervousness as a beginning teacher and approached him with an idea for improving the playground.

Paulette has always been especially interested in physical education. From her professional reading, she has come to understand that more than just an open-field playground is necessary for a quality program. In her meeting with Dr. Salinas, she outlined some things that could be done to improve the area outside of the school to make it a better environment for physical education classes. Dr. Salinas expressed immediate appreciation for her suggestions and got on the phone to the president of the school's "Parents for Excellence" committee. This prompted a sequence of events that resulted in an amazing flurry of activity on the school grounds over the past two weekends.

Parent volunteers, teachers, and administrators arrived early each Saturday morning armed with shovels, saws, hammers, and other tools. Gradually, huge stacks of raw lumber and other materials were transformed into a new physical education area. Huge timbers were cut and fitted into the ground to secure some of the climbing structures. A tunnel was built out of dozens of used tires. Other tires were laid out flat in patterns that learners would use in developing dexterity and coordination skills. Bars were set up for older learners to hang from for chin-ups and other exercises. Everyone worked very hard. Photographers from the local paper and the central school district publicity office came by to take photos.

A special dedication ceremony was held this afternoon. It drew newspaper reporters, school administrators from the central office, and, most important, many of the parents and other adults who had worked on the project. The ceremony concluded with a teacher directing a class of learners in the use of some of the new equipment. Adults in the crowd congratulated themselves on having done "something good for our kids."

*What kind of long-term benefits might a project of this kind have for teachers in this building? Is it fair to say that people in this part of the community really did exercise some control over at least part of the school program? Were there some things that the local community did when you were in school that influenced what went on at the school? As you think about your future role in education, do you have some ideas that might help local people feel that they have some real control over what takes place in the schools?*

## State Influences

Traditionally, states have enjoyed a great deal of influence over public schools. Though state guidelines have affected the school curriculum tremendously, sometimes this influence has not been as visible to citizens at the local level as has that of local school officials. For example, local press coverage of specific issues being weighed by local school officials may convey the impression that few constraints on educational programs are exercised at the state level.

State control is reflected in many ways. State authorities typically control the certification of teachers, administrators, curriculum supervisors, and many other professionals who work in the schools. Often college and university preparation programs for teachers, counselors, and administrators are subject to a measure of state control. Through the state's various control mechanisms, state education officials strive to establish quality standards that must be met by the professionals hired to work in all of the state's schools.

In some parts of the country, states have established regional units that represent an intermediate authority between state and local education officials. These units are known by such names as "regional service centers" or "intermediate school districts." In states that have them, these regional units ordinarily serve the needs of school districts within a particular geographic area. They may sponsor inservice activities for teachers, interpret state guidelines for local school districts in their areas, and provide curriculum development help.

State legislatures often require that certain subjects and even specific topics be taught in all state school districts. In some parts of the country, state officials even

This state legislative hearing provides opportunities for interested parties to comment on proposed changes in state high school graduation requirements.

decide which textbooks may be used in the schools. The pattern of state practices in this area varies greatly from place to place—some states play an active role in textbook selection; others play no role at all.

The legal basis for state control of schools is a nineteenth-century judicial decision that gave us what has come to be called *Dillon's Rule*. In essence, Dillon's Rule holds that the "state can create and destroy all local units and it can grant or withhold authority for them to act" (Wirt, 1977, p. 164). This judicial precedent has provided a legal ground for state educational authorities to hold local school districts accountable for their decisions and actions, and is an authority that state agencies have not been reluctant to use. As is pointed out in the following subsections, debate continues regarding whether giving significant authority over education to state officials is a good idea.

### The Case *for* State Influences

Expertise in curriculum development and management is vested in relatively small numbers of people who have undergone special training. It is unrealistic to suppose that extremely large numbers of people will succeed in achieving the sort of professional depth in these areas that is needed for first-class curriculum development and program management. Thus it makes good sense to concentrate the limited supply of expert talent at the state level. This allows a competent group of state-level professionals to develop curricula and program-planning guidelines that can be disseminated to local school districts. This practice relieves local school districts of an obligation to perform tasks that lie beyond the real expertise of local-level school-district employees, but it properly leaves implementation decisions to local authorities. Enough expertise exists in local districts to manage programs professionally, and it is to this task that local district resources should be committed. Further, when local officials are freed from curriculum and program development tasks, they gain time that can be productively spent in fitting state guidelines to unique characteristics of local schools and learners.

State control of education promotes accountability. State legislatures often mandate certain program minimums. It is only logical that the responsibility for overseeing the implementation of these guidelines should fall to state rather than local officials. Further, purely from the standpoint of efficient management, it makes sense to implement tested innovations at the state level rather than on a district-by-district basis. For example, should a fine new reading program be developed, state action can ensure its rapid adoption by every school district in the state, but were local school districts individually allowed to consider the change, squabbling could delay statewide implementation for years.

State control ensures that competent people will be hired to work in the schools. Though most local districts are managed by competent people, a possibility for abuse exists given the local district's power to hire teachers and administrators. Inevitably, some people will be hired because of their personal ties to influential community members. Through its control of certification requirements, the state insists that all people hired must meet certain minimum criteria before they can be authorized for employment as school teachers or administrators.

In all areas, state control acts to professionalize education. State agencies act as conduits that communicate information to local school districts. New research results, opportunities to participate in statewide assessment efforts, and other chances to link with state and national education-improvement efforts become available to even remote school districts because of the existence of strong, centralized state-education agencies. A diminished level of state influence on education would have a negative effect on the quality of programs in many school districts.

## The Case *Against* State Influences

At one time, there were few people with advanced training in curriculum development and program management. Today, this is no longer the case—many people working in local school districts have had extensive preparation in both curriculum development and program management. For example, it is quite common now for superintendents of even quite small school districts to have a doctoral degree. Many others who have doctoral degrees or at least extensive graduate-level training head important curriculum and administrative departments in local school districts. These talented local people are capable of doing much more than managing programs designed and sent down by state officials.

State control of education often overlooks differences among individual school systems in a state. This diversity underscores the need to tailor school programs to the particular learners being served. Further, there are issues of community values involved. Some communities wish an emphasis on area A, others on area B, and still others on areas C through Z. Too often, state officials fail to take into account these important local differences and, consequently, some programs promoted at the state level simply are not appropriate for certain communities. It would make better sense to increase the power of local officials to make substantial modifications in the school program to better serve unique local needs. In too many instances, state control keeps local education professionals from acting as they know they responsibly should be acting.

No one argues against the idea of accountability, but assessment of school programs should be undertaken at the local level, not at the state level. State evaluators, because they must deal with information from all districts in a state, often assess programs in terms of state averages. These averages may be totally inappropriate yardsticks for some communities. For example, a school district in a small community populated by a disproportionately large number of professors, who have always encouraged their children to read and have supported their children's efforts to learn in other ways as well, might report test scores that look absolutely outstanding in terms of state averages. But these scores are likely to result as much from the home backgrounds of these learners as from any inherent excellence in the local school program. It such situations, it would make much more sense for local school officials to make year-by-year comparisons of learners *within* the district. This would reveal a good deal more about how well the program was working than any comparison against a state average.

State control does not professionalize education; rather, it bureaucratizes it. Attempts of the state to establish quality control often result in paperwork overload for local administrators. Further, the state's effort to ensure that all people holding professional positions in the schools have the proper credentials is credible only if there is a pool of appropriately trained individuals available for hire. Often this is not the case. Nearly every state has an "emergency certificate" of some kind that can be issued at the request of a local school district to a person having a deficiency in his or her formal training. The legal availability of these exceptions makes a sham of state pretensions to function as guarantors of "quality" personnel.

### State Influences: Status Report

Evidence suggests that state control over education is increasing. Beginning in the early and middle 1980s and continuing into the 1990s, a trend developed for the federal government to give states more control over how federal money for education was spent. This represented something of a gain for state authority at the expense of federal authority.

State control seems to be increasing at the expense of local control as well. This latter trend is partially explained by taxpayers' growing unwillingness to support education through a system of locally collected taxes on real estate. The effect of this reluctance has been to shift a greater portion of school costs to state instead of local revenue sources (see Figure 17–1). As states become the major bill payers, they have more and more wanted to look after their expenditures.

**Figure 17–1**
Changing patterns in sources of public school revenues

| School Year Ending | Percentage from Each Source | |
|---|---|---|
| 1920 | Federal | 0.3% |
| | State | 16.5 |
| | Local | 83.2 |
| 1960 | Federal | 4.4 |
| | State | 39.1 |
| | Local | 56.5 |
| 1988 | Federal | 6.3 |
| | State | 49.5 |
| | Local | 44.1 |

Source: L. T. Ogle, ed., and N. Alsalam, associate ed., *The Condition of Education, 1990:* Vol. 1—*Elementary and Secondary Education* (Washington, D.C.: National Center for Education Statistics, 1990), 80.

State legislatures throughout the nation have increasingly demanded that schools be held accountable for their performance and that learners be expected to achieve certain minimum levels of competence. Legislation associated with both accountability and minimum levels of competence has concentrated more control in the hands of state-level education authorities. These officials are responsible for pressuring school districts to perform and for gathering necessary data to convince skeptical legislators that progress is being made.

Educational trends are difficult to project into the future. Nevertheless, little evidence is available today that suggests an imminent reduction in the level of state control of education. The tendency for power over schools and educational programs to be increasingly concentrated at the state level may persist for some time.

## Federal Influences

Though the federal government has played some role in education for many years, this involvement has greatly increased over the past four decades. In the late 1950s (when the first Russian space orbiter, *Sputnik I*, was launched), questions were raised almost immediately about the quality of technical training provided in American schools. In response to this concern, the National Defense Education Act was passed in 1958. This law allocated money for sending teachers to special training programs to upgrade their skills. At the same time a number of national curriculum development projects were started, bringing top talents together to prepare new school programs. Many of these projects were underwritten, at least in part, by the federal government. Most of the early projects focused on the sciences; later projects were aimed at developing new foreign language and social science curricula as well. As a result of these efforts, programs that were sponsored entirely or in part by the federal government began to greatly influence curricula in the nation's schools through the 1960s and on into the 1970s.

During the late 1960s and throughout the 1970s, federal programs directed toward improving educational programs for specific groups were developed. For example, the Education for All Handicapped Children Act was passed in 1975. It required schools to provide better school programs for handicapped learners. (For a more complete discussion of this legislation, which was renamed in 1990 to be the Individuals with Disabilities Education Act, see Chapter 9.) Other federal programs required schools to establish programs to help other groups of learners, including those who were not native speakers of English. Much federal education legislation passed during this period not only identified problems, but also ordered schools to implement specific procedures in responding to them.

Since the early 1980s and continuing to the present time, federal legislation involving education has been somewhat less interventionist. There has been a trend for the federal government to identify general problem areas and to allocate funds for solving them to the states in the form of block grants. What this means is that the federal government basically says, "Here is the problem. Here is some money. You spend the money in ways that will fix the problem—it is up to you to identify the ways." The idea has been that conditions vary from place to place across the country, and it makes sense for state and local officials to decide on the specifics of programs that are funded with federal education dollars (Hinchliffe, 1989).

## The Case *for* Federal Influences

The federal government speaks for our entire society. Because leaders in Washington receive signals from the entire population, they are in a position to take actions representing the real national interest. For example, federal authorities can take action when national data reveal a deficiency in mathematics programs in the schools that might have long-term negative influences on our economic vitality and defense capability. Although states and local authorities might be willing to do something, they are unlikely to have in hand the kind of information that is readily available to federal authorities. Hence, the federal government should be empowered to take decisive action when there are indications of serious problems in the schools.

Interests of some groups have not been served well by programs implemented by state and local authorities. For example, in some places few resources have been dedicated to meet special needs of minority-group learners. In other instances, children with learning handicaps have been inadequately served. Since education properly addresses the special needs of every segment of the population, there must be an authority to ensure that these needs are met. Because federal decisions have an impact on all states and school districts, federal actions to assist groups whose educational needs have not been well met are appropriate. Federal educational programs ensure that learners will have access to programs that meet their needs regardless of where they live, which results in an upgrading of the educational competence of the entire population.

Increasingly, we are becoming a nation of Americans, not a loose association of Texans, Kentuckians, Californians, New Yorkers, Georgians, Montanans, Minnesotans, and so forth. Because our similarities today are more profound than our differences, our educational system should be standardized. This will ensure that a learner who moves to a different state will be able to make an easy adjustment to the new educational setting.

Today there is a regrettable lack of uniformity in school programs, which may be hurting achievement levels in some areas. For example, Joe Crosswhite (1986), a former president of the National Council of Teachers of Mathematics, has attributed American learners' poor performance on international tests of mathematical competence to the absence of a standard, national mathematics curriculum. Box 17–2 presents some opinions and questions related to the issue of federal control of our schools.

## The Case *Against* Federal Influences

It is a failure of logic to argue that the federal government speaks for the entire society. At best, the government represents only a majority opinion; at worst, it adopts the view that those in power believe ought to represent majority opinion, whether or not it actually does so.

Anyone who has worked with federal programs will attest to the frustration involved in dealing with the associated paperwork. It certainly is not surprising that the federal government wants to hold those who receive federal money accountable, but this laudable desire often poses real problems for local and state officials. The real problem results from the distance of federal authorities from individual local schools—

---

BOX 17–2
## NEEDED: MORE FEDERAL CONTROL

Americans have little reluctance to move from one part of the country to another. In addition, we have a superb communications system that allows for almost instantaneous communication between even widely separated parts of the country, and the national television media reaches us all. The point is that Americans in one part of the country tend to be growing more like Americans in all other parts.

For this reason, we need a national system of education. The federal government should step in and manage all of our schools as a nationwide enterprise. This would ensure high levels of educational services for learners everywhere.

### What Do You Think?

1. What advantages and disadvantages do you see for an education system controlled exclusively by the federal government?
2. What is your reaction to the contention that similarities of American towns and cities are more important than any differences? What evidence supports your view?
3. What do you think might happen to teachers' salaries if all education were controlled by the national government and, hence, teachers were federal employees?

documents must flow through a host of intermediate agencies. Often, each intermediate agency adds some documentation of its own to what the federal funding agency requires. When all this paperwork lands on the desk of local school administrators, its bulk is sometimes overwhelming. This situation is reflected in the tendency of even tiny school districts to hire full-time administrators to do little other than manage federal programs documents.

The lack of place-to-place differences in this country has been exaggerated. It is true that technological changes have brought us closer together, but strong local differences remain. Preservation of regional differences is very important to many Americans. (Consider the pride that New Englanders, Virginians, Texans, and other regional Americans take in their parts of the country.) Further, the ability to move from place to place remains, for many, a choice not taken. Significant numbers of people continue to be born, live, and die close to their birthplaces. The sense of place should be supported by an education system that reflects regional differences by vesting much more authority in local and state officials than in federal officials.

Implementation of some federal programs has proved very disruptive to the overall operation of school programs. The federal government has often mandated that something be done, but has left the "how" to individual schools. This has resulted in haphazard introduction of new programs and has played havoc with careful and systematic curriculum development.

## Federal Influences: Status Report

As noted, there has been a trend since the early 1980s for the federal government to assign more decision-making authority about how federal money is to be spent to state and (to some extent) local officials. This pattern seems likely to persist through at least the mid-1990s.

Some state and local officials have complained that older federal programs (those developed before the early 1980s) came about because of congressional responses to groups outside of education. For example, national organizations of Spanish-speaking Americans strongly supported the effort to require bilingual education programs, and parents of children with disabilities lobbied for passage of the Education for All Handicapped Children Act of 1975. While lauding the beneficial purposes of such legislation, some state and local officials felt that, by responding to pressures of organized interest groups, federal money was being targeted toward only a few of the numerous important educational needs.

Since the early 1980s, the federal government has been generally sympathetic to these concerns. For the present, there seems to be a tendency to view the federal government as an authority that is well-positioned to recognize potential educational problems and provide some financial resources for dealing with them. Increasingly, however, specific decisions about how to shape and deliver individual programs paid for with federal dollars are being left to state and local officials.

## The Equity Issue and Control of Education

In part, discussions about how much influence over education should be exercised by local, state, and federal authorities relate to the issue of money and who controls it.

In the realm of school finance, the federal government has, overall, been a relatively minor player. For example, in the last years of the 1980s, federal expenditures totaled just under 6.5 percent of the total spent on education in this country. Nearly half of the cost of education was borne by state governments, and something over 44 percent was paid out of locally generated funds (Ogle and Alsalam, 1990, p. 80).

Local school districts have traditionally raised most of their revenue from taxes on real estate. This has meant that districts with large amounts of valuable property have been able to raise a great deal of local money to support school programs but, in school districts where the total value of commercial and personal real estate is low, even high tax rates fail to generate large amounts of money for the local schools. The disparity in wealth among local school districts within individual states has resulted in some school districts having a great deal of money to support educational programs and others having relatively little. As a result, quality of educational services provided from district to district within a state often varies tremendously (see the accompanying What the Experts Say).

---

WHAT THE EXPERTS SAY

## Are school districts that spend more money better?

Some critics of education assert that throwing money at problems won't solve them. The general question of whether increased funding does make a difference in a school's quality has attracted the interest of several educational researchers and policymakers.

A particularly thorough study of this matter was made by researcher William T. Hartman (1988), who investigated differences among "high-spending," "middle-spending," and "low-spending" school districts in Pennsylvania. Hartman found important differences favoring high-spending districts. For example, the average learner–teacher ratio* in high-spending districts was 15.7 to 1; in middle-spending districts, 19.2 to 1; and in low-spending districts, 21.0 to 1. In high-spending districts, teachers had an average of 5.8 years of college training and 17.3 years of experience (p. 450). This contrasted with figures of 5.5 years of college training and 15.5 years of experience in middle-spending districts, and 5.4 years of college training and 5.4 years of experience in low-spending districts (p. 450). There was also a consistent pattern of higher administrative salaries, more average education per administrator, and more average years of administrative experience that were associated with higher levels of spending.

Arthur E. Wise and Tamar Gendler (1989) reviewed the work of Hartman and others who have studied this issue. They concluded that "districts that spend more money can build nicer buildings, supply more staff, pay their teachers more, and thereby attract better teachers" (p. 17).

---

*The learner–teacher ratio is a measure of the number of learners that must be served, on average, by a single teacher. A learner–teacher ratio of 20 to 1 indicates that, for every 20 learners, there is one teacher. A district having a lower learner–teacher ratio (e.g., 15 to 1) means that the district has the resources to hire enough teachers to keep class sizes relatively small, as compared to a district with a higher learner–teacher ratio (e.g., 25 to 1).

Sources: W. T. Hartman, "District Spending Disparities: What Do the Dollars Buy?" *Journal of Education Finance* (Spring 1988): 436–59; and A. E. Wise and T. Gendler, "Rich Schools, Poor Schools: The Persistence of Unequal Education," *The College Board Review* (Spring 1989): 12–17, 36–37.

In recent years, some critics have charged that allowing local school districts to raise revenues and spend them to the exclusive benefit of their own residents' children is unfair. Learners, they argue, have no control over their places of residence. Why is it, then, that some learners are "punished" by being forced to attend school in districts that have little valuable property to tax while other learners are the "beneficiaries" of excellent programs funded out of revenues generated by the high property values in their school districts?

Many residents of school districts with little valuable taxable property are not financially well-off. On the other hand, many residents of school districts with higher taxable property values are relatively affluent. In the minds of some educators, this has created a system that provides the fewest educational benefits to needy children. Speaking to this issue, Arthur Wise and Tamar Gendler (1989) have commented that "when the advantaged have the better-financed schools, and the disadvantaged the poorly financed schools, America continues to provide unequal education to those who most need what school has to offer" (p. 12).

The last 10 years have witnessed a number of court cases challenging state funding schemes that allowed local school districts to control money raised within their boundaries. The idea behind these cases is to force changes in educational funding that will allow more money to be diverted from relatively wealthy areas to relatively poor ones. As already stated, there are tremendous differences in the amount of money spent on education in different communities. For example, the 150,000 learners in the poorest school districts in Texas have less than one-half as much spent on their schooling as the 150,000 learners living in the most affluent school districts (Wise and Gendler, 1989).

Though judicial decisions have varied somewhat depending on the circumstances in each case filed, there is an emerging trend for courts to support the idea of reducing the disparity in funds expended for education among various school districts. This pattern suggests that forces are at work that will somewhat diminish influences of local officials (particularly in the area of funding) and increase those of state officials. The final outcome of the effort to diminish funding differences among districts is by no means clear. What does seem certain, though, is that sometimes-acrimonious debates will continue between (1) supporters of affluent school districts that have historically developed strong school programs funded by local revenues and (2) supporters of less affluent districts who would like to attract to their own programs some of the tax money that has traditionally been reserved for the exclusive use of wealthier school districts.

## Key Ideas in Summary

- The pattern of control in American education is the result of conflicts and compromises among local, state, and federal influences. Traditionally, most control has been exercised by state and local governments. The federal government has been a relatively minor player particularly in the realm of school finance.

- The idea of local control over the schools has lengthy historical roots. It is still a widely prized value. Proponents often point out that local people know the

**Table 17–1**
Summary table: Who controls?

| Issue | Findings |
|---|---|
| Local influences | Arguments for: <br>• Long tradition of support. <br><br>• Local communities know their own needs. <br><br>• Local schools unify local communities. <br><br>• Programs are more credible when they reflect local values. <br><br>Arguments against: <br>• Communities today are characterized more by their similarities than by their differences. <br><br>• Too much local control can produce programs dysfunctional for learners who might move to other places. <br><br>• Local communities are very much tied to the state, national, and world communities. <br><br>Present status: <br>• Local control is eroding; the shift is mainly in the direction of increasing state authority. |
| State influences | Arguments for: <br>• Real expertise in curriculum development and program management is not widespread; more benefits will accrue to education when this small pool of talented people exercise their authority at the state level. <br><br>• State authority gives state-level officials the power to hold local education officials accountable for their decisions and actions. <br><br>• State control ensures that trained people will be hired for professional positions in schools. |

**Table 17–1**
*continued*

| Issue | Findings |
|-------|----------|
| State influences (cont.) | Arguments against:<br>• The pool of talented curriculum and administrative personnel is large; many of these people now work at the local level.<br><br>• State authorities frequently overlook important local differences in their policy mandates, which causes hardships.<br><br>• More meaningful accountability will occur when a school's progress is measured against local conditions rather than against standardized state averages.<br><br>• State control introduces an unnecessary layer of bureaucracy that inhibits efficient school operation.<br><br>Present status:<br>• State influence over education is increasing; much of the gain is coming at the expense of local control. |
| Federal influences | Arguments for:<br>• Federal authorities are in a position to pinpoint and respond to educational problems affecting the nation as a whole.<br><br>• Federal authorities have better information-gathering capabilities than do individual state and local officials.<br><br>• A lack of uniformity in curricula hurts the overall performance of American learners.<br><br>Arguments against:<br>• The federal government does not truly speak for the entire country; it speaks only for those in power. |

**Table 17–1**
*continued*

| Issue | Findings |
|---|---|
| Federal influences (cont.) | Arguments against (cont.)<br>• Heavy paperwork is associated with many federal programs; this exacts a significant administrative cost.<br><br>• Place-to-place differences may be ignored in federal programs that must be implemented uniformly throughout the nation.<br><br>Present status:<br>• In terms of total school funding, the federal government remains a relatively minor player as compared to local and state authorities.<br><br>• There is a trend for federal help increasingly to take the form of general block grants. These provide funds directed at resolution of a general problem area, but they leave much of the detailed planning to state and local authorities. |
| Equity in funding | Basic issues:<br>• School districts with much valuable property can raise more money for their schools through taxes than can those with little valuable property; learners living in wealthier districts tend to have better programs available than do learners from poorer ones; critics have declared this disparity to be unfair.<br><br>• Court decisions seem to be trending in the direction of forcing some wealth sharing between wealthier and poorer districts.<br><br>• Efforts to achieve more funding equity among state school districts may result in shifting more power away from local school authorities and toward state school authorities. |

needs of the community's learners better than do state or national officials. Critics of local control point out that young people today are very mobile and, hence, programs that might make good sense to the local community could yield an education that is dysfunctional for a young person who moves and attends school elsewhere.

- Today, local influences on schools are less profound than they once were. Efforts to professionalize education have been more frequently driven by actions of state rather than local authorities. Federal legislation has also mandated programs in ways that have, in some cases, overridden desires of local leaders.

- State control over education is manifested in many ways. One of them has to do with state curriculum requirements. For example, in many parts of the country basic graduation requirements are established at the state level. Certification of professional school personnel is also usually a state function. Supporters of state control often point out that relatively few people have the expertise needed to provide first-class leadership in program development and management and, hence, it makes sense to concentrate them at the state level, where their decisions will benefit all. Others argue that today there is plenty of expertise around and much of it is concentrated in local school districts. Further, there are fears that broad state policies will fail to consider important differences among individual local school districts.

- There is evidence that state control over education is on the upswing. Increasingly, federal money is being funneled through state authorities who have the responsibility to oversee its dissemination to local school districts. Courts are becoming increasingly concerned about the traditional authority of local school districts to spend locally generated tax money exclusively within the districts where it is raised. This may have the effect of strengthening the power of state officials in attempts to provide more equity in educational funding throughout an entire state. Legislatures, in their attempts to hold schools accountable, seem to be vesting more authority in state officials to oversee testing and other programs designed to provide evidence about the quality of school programs.

- The federal government has always had a much smaller influence on public education than either state or local authorities have. Federal involvement is often defended with the argument that federal authorities are best positioned to recognize educational needs that are countrywide in scope. A frequent criticism of federal programs is the overabundance of recordkeeping and paperwork that goes along with many federally sponsored efforts. Some people, too, argue that federal programs are not sensitive enough to important regional differences.

- In recent years, involvement of the federal government in education has neither grown nor shrunk appreciably. There has, however, been a trend for federal involvement to be less focused on meeting needs of specific neglected groups; instead, the federal government has tended to act as an authority that recognizes important educational problems, alerts the country to their existence, and provides some financial support for the states to respond to them.

- The issue of equity has important implications for how control over education is exercised. In recent years, there have been concerns that affluent school districts, using money collected from taxes on local property, have been providing higher-quality educational services than have poorer school districts. This has placed learners in poor school districts at an educational disadvantage. A number of court cases filed have been designed to force affluent school districts to share some of their tax revenues with less affluent school districts. Though patterns vary somewhat from case to case, in general there seems to be a trend for courts to support efforts to achieve funding equity.

## Review and Discussion Questions

1. What does the U.S. Constitution say about the control of education?
2. What are some traditional responsibilities of local school boards?
3. What are some historical reasons for the development of the idea that local control of education is good?
4. Why have local school districts jealously guarded the right to hire the teachers who work in the local schools?
5. What are some traditional ways that state authorities have exercised control over public education?
6. How do you explain the general growth of state authorities' influence over education in recent years?
7. Should local officials or state officials have more authority concerning what goes on in the schools? Why do you think so?
8. How do you rate the relative merits of arguments made by people favoring state control of education? By people against it?
9. Should the federal government play a larger role in controlling the nation's schools? Why or why not?
10. Why have people from some poorer school districts claimed that existing funding arrangements are unfair?

## Ideas for Field Experiences, Projects, and Enrichment

1. Invite a school district administrator in charge of managing federal programs to speak to your class. Ask this person to speak about the kinds of programs

funded by the federal government and about the sorts and amounts of paperwork the district and its personnel must complete as part of their participation in these programs.

2. Organize a class debate among several members of your class on the topic, "Resolved: American Education Would Be More Likely to Improve if Greater Power Were Vested in State as Opposed to Local Education Officials."

3. With the assistance of your instructor, locate information related to changes in regulations affecting education in your state over the past five years. Have these changes altered the relationship between state and local authorities? If so, what is the nature of this altered relationship? Present your findings to the class in the form of a brief oral report.

4. Individual states vary in terms of the kinds of regulations they have regarding state control of schools and school programs. For example, most states have some basic regulations regarding graduation requirements. With the assistance of your instructor, find out what basic requirements for school programs (both elementary and secondary) are required by your state. Prepare a short paper explaining your findings.

5. In recent years, the question of equitable funding of school programs has come in for a great deal of attention. Prepare a symposium with four or five others in your class that focuses on this topic: "Equalizing Funding for Educational Programs to Ensure Equity: What the Courts Are Saying." Present your findings to the class and lead a follow-up discussion focusing on the funding-equity issue.

# Supplementary Reading

Cardenas, J. A. "Political Limits to an Education of Value: The Role of the State." In J. I. Goodlad and P. Keating, eds. *Access to Knowledge: An Agenda for Our Nation's Schools.* New York: The College Board, 1990.

Finn, C. E. "Why We Need a National Education Policy." *Education Digest* (April 1990): 8–10.

Frymier, J. "Legislating Centralization." *Phi Delta Kappan* (May 1986): 646–48.

Hill, P. R. "The Federal Role in Education: A Strategy for the 1990s." *Phi Delta Kappan* (January 1990): 398–402.

Wise, A. E., and T. Gendler. "Rich Schools, Poor Schools: The Persistence of Unequal Education." *The College Board Review* (Spring 1989): 12–17, 36–37.

# References

Carelli, R. "Quayle Pushes for Limits on Personal Injury Suits." *Bryan-College Station Eagle* (August 14, 1991): 4A.

Crosswhite, J. "The Findings of the Third International Study of the Teaching of Mathematics." Address delivered at the University of Alabama, Tuscaloosa, January 10, 1986.

Hartman, W. T. "District Spending Disparities: What Do the Dollars Buy?" *Journal of Education Finance* (Spring 1988): 436–59.

Hinchliffe, K. "Focus on Federal–State Relations in Educational Finance." *Comparative Education Review* (November 1989): 437–39.

Ogle, L. T., ed., and N. Alsalam, associate ed. *The Condition of Education, 1990.* Vol. 1. *Elementary and Secondary Education.* Washington, DC: National Center for Education Statistics, 1990.

Wirt, F. M. "School Policy, Culture, and State De-Centralization." In J. D. Scribner, ed. *The Politics of Education. The 76th Yearbook of the National Society for the Study of Education.* Part II. Chicago: National Society for the Study of Education, 1977, 164–77.

Wise, A. E., and T. Gendler. "Rich Schools, Poor Schools: The Persistence of Unequal Education." *The College Board Review* (Spring 1989): 12–17, 36–37.

# Chapter 18

# Legal Concerns of Teachers

## Objectives

This chapter provides information to help the reader to

- recognize some legal issues associated with conditions of employment.
- identify some rights of teachers associated with their personal lives, appearances, and lifestyles.
- point out some legal considerations related to the delivery of instruction.
- describe what is meant by "professional negligence."
- identify some legal issues that may be involved in teachers' excessive use of force in discipline.

1. What are the benefits conferred by a teaching certificate, and under whose authority is one issued?
2. What kind of information is typically included in a teaching contract?
3. What criteria are used in determining the appropriateness of questions asked during a job interview?
4. What types of oaths can a person be required to take as a condition for employment as a teacher?
5. What standard is usually considered when the courts consider lifestyle issues involving teachers?
6. What are some examples of immorality that have led to teacher dismissal?
7. Is it ever legal for a school district to dismiss a teacher who has been charged with and subsequently acquitted of a felony?
8. On what grounds can a school board prohibit certain material from being used in the classroom?
9. What limitations can be placed on teachers concerning the use of a particular instructional method?
10. What constitutes a violation of the "fair use" standard of the copyright law?
11. What are the three types of negligence?
12. Must teachers report suspected cases of child abuse?

• • • • • • • • • • • • • • • • • • • • • • • • • • • •

# Introduction

What would you do if

- You were asked questions of a highly personal nature during your interview for a teaching position?

- You were told by your principal not to teach a particular social studies topic because it was too controversial?

- You suspected that a youngster in your class was a victim of child abuse?

- A pregnant student came to you and asked for information about getting an abortion?

- During an emotional school board meeting, a parent accused you of being an incompetent teacher?

All of these questions involve legal issues, and are examples of those that teachers confront. Today's teachers need some familiarity with the law. Actions they take that are defended on the ground of ignorance will not stand up in court. In fact, certain actions could even result in the loss of a teaching credential, a document that is almost universally required of public school teachers as a condition of their employment. This chapter sketches some of the kinds of legal issues that commonly affect teachers today.

## Conditions of Employment

### Teachers' Certification

Today, possession of a valid teaching certificate is a basic requirement for employment in public education. Teaching certificates were not always required of individuals interested in teaching in the schools, but they were eventually established out of a belief in the importance of setting minimum standards for teachers. Mandatory teaching certificates were viewed as a means of improving the quality of the teaching force. But even today, not all people accept this view—consider some of the arguments posed in Box 18–1.

Certification is a function of state government—each state legislature establishes standards for certification in its state. Though each state has a unique set of certification requirements, this does not mean that a person has to start all over again should he or she want to teach in a state other than the one from which the teacher obtained his or her initial teaching certificate. Most states have reciprocal certification agreements. This means that when someone has received an initial teaching certificate in one state and wishes to teach in another, the second state ordinarily will grant a certificate authorizing the holder to teach in that state's schools. The second state may require the person to take some specified courses within a given period of time to maintain the new certificate but, typically, these course requirements are not oppressive. Often, little is required beyond taking one course in the history or government of the new state.

A teaching certificate is essentially a license to practice, and it confers a number of benefits. Teachers with certificates receive either the state-mandated minimum salary

BOX 18–1
# DOES TEACHER CERTIFICATION ENSURE QUALITY?

The following editorial recently appeared in a local newspaper:

> Teacher certification stands as the greatest barrier to improvement of instruction in our schools. It is defended as a guarantor of quality. In fact, certification protects mediocrity.
>
> Certification is rigidly controlled by educational bureaucrats. It keeps enrollments in education courses high. The dull, unnecessary courses required for certification discourage the best of our young people from entering teaching. This is especially true of those who have majored in solid academic disciplines such as mathematics and physics. The exclusionary bias that certification exercises against talented college and university students must stop. Legislators, are you listening?

### What Do You Think?
1. What evidence is there that certification requirements discourage talented people from going into teaching?
2. What advantages would you see resulting from a state decision to scrap certification requirements? What disadvantages?
3. What are your personal reactions to the position taken by the writer of this editorial?

or that salary plus any supplements provided for in the locally adopted teachers' salary schedule. A certificate provides the holder with an "assumption of competence," meaning that any charge of incompetence made against a certified teacher will receive serious consideration only if it is backed up with evidence compelling enough to demonstrate the error of the competence assumption.

## The Hiring Process

Prospective teachers need to know something about the legal aspects of interviewing and hiring. Today, state and federal laws exist that govern the process of screening applicants for positions. Many of these laws address the issue of discrimination in employment. For example, the Washington State Law Against Discrimination (RCW 49.60) makes it an unfair practice for an employer of eight or more employees to use any form of application for employment or to make any inquiry in connection with prospective employment that expresses any limitation, specification, or discrimination as to age; sex; marital status; race; creed; national origin; color; the presence of sensory, mental, or physical handicap; or any intent to make any such limitation, specification, or discrimination, unless based upon a bona fide occupational qualification. In plain English, this statute means that questions asked of applicants must have a demonstrated relationship to the job. For example, a question regarding a physical disability would not be legal unless such a disability would prevent the accomplishment of tasks associated with the position being sought.

Most states have laws similar to the Washington statute. Such legislation restricts what school personnel people can ask during interviews with candidates for teaching positions. Though practices vary from place to place, questions regarding marital status, pregnancy, age, and religious preferences generally cannot be asked.

Some laws, such as Title VII of the Civil Rights Act of 1964, apply to public as well as private educational institutions. Others relate only to public institutions. This area of the law is complex; for example, if a particular condition can be demonstrated to hinder the ability of a person to teach or to interfere with the mission of the school, it may legally be included as condition for employment. In other words, a private religious school can legally give preference to individuals with a particular religious affiliation if such affiliation is required for the school to fulfill its mission. Box 18–2 addresses the issue of appropriate and legal interview questions.

---

BOX 18–2
## WHAT CAN TEACHER CANDIDATES LEGALLY BE ASKED DURING HIRING INTERVIEWS?

Ms. Lupe Alvarado Donato was being interviewed for a position as a third-grade teacher in a small rural community. These are among the questions she was asked:

- What approach do you use when you teach reading?
- How do you feel about corporal punishment?
- What are some ideas you have about discipline?
- Would you ever buy wine or beer in a local store?
- If you were assigned to manage the playground, what would you do?
- What are some things you would do to maintain good relationships with parents?
- Do you have plans to marry soon?
- How long do you expect to be a teacher?
- Would you be willing to participate in setting up a science laboratory program with all of our third-, fourth-, and fifth-grade teachers?
- Would you be likely to spend weekends in our community?

*What Do You Think?*
1. Are all of these questions appropriate? Are all of them likely to be legal?
2. Which questions are most legitimate? Least legitimate? Why do you think so?
3. How would you respond to an interviewer who asked questions you believed to be inappropriate?

## Teachers' Contracts

The contract is one of the most important documents that prospective teachers encounter. Contracts spell out salary levels and other conditions of employment. They need to be read carefully before they are signed.

Contracts are legally binding documents. They set forth the teacher's responsibility and the school district's responsibilities, and place obligations on both parties.

In some places, a teacher who fails to report to work after having signed a contract can be stripped of his or her teaching certificate. Hence, it is not advisable for a person who has signed one contract to later sign a second contract with another district that might offer a higher salary. Such a practice puts the individual in the position of being obligated to perform duties simultaneously in two places. In such a case, the proper procedure is for the individual to call the first district and ask to be released from the first contract "without prejudice." Though there is no guarantee a district will agree to such a request, very frequently it will be honored. (Most districts do not want to employ a teacher who would really prefer to be working elsewhere.) A release from the first district's contract dissolves the individual's legal relationship with this district and makes it acceptable for the teacher to enter into a contractual arrangement with the second district.

Sometimes the issue of oral contracts arises; that is, a person who has applied for a teaching position may believe that a spoken offer from a personnel official representing a school district constitutes a binding contract. It does not. The binding contract is the written document that has been approved by the school board. Since this is the case, it is important that individuals who are offered a teaching position read the written contract carefully to ensure that all provisions cited during their oral discussion with the district's personnel office representative have been included in the written document. For example, if the interviewer stated that the regular salary would be increased by an additional $700 to compensate the teacher for bus supervision, this proviso must be included in the written contract. Otherwise, the school district is under no legal obligation to pay the extra money.

## Testing for AIDS and Substance Abuse

Recent concerns about substance abuse and the spread of AIDS have led to proposals for universal drug and AIDS testing for teachers. Court decisions in this area suggest that tests of this type qualify as a form of search. To be legal, these searches must be consistent with guarantees outlined in the Fourth Amendment to the U.S. Constitution. A school district must demonstrate a "compelling interest" in the results of any tests that have the potential to infringe on individuals' rights. A compelling interest would be evident if it could be demonstrated that a teacher who was under the influence of a controlled substance or who had AIDS presented a threat to a group of learners. At present, there is no evidence that AIDS is transmitted through the kinds of regular contacts that characterize teacher–learner interactions. Therefore, a school district might well find it difficult to justify AIDS testing for all employees.

One district decided to require urinalysis as a part of its mandatory physical examinations for teachers seeking tenure. Before implementing this policy, the district's administrators had found no evidence that any of the teachers were users of illegal substances. Teachers challenged the policy, and took the issue to court. In its decision, the court ruled that although identification of teachers who were using illegal substances was important, it did not outweigh teachers' expectation of privacy. The absence of any reasonable suspicion of drug abuse and the lack of indication that this problem presented a grave threat to learners led to a ruling against the practice of requiring urinalysis tests [*Patchogue-Medford Congress of Teachers* v. *Board of Education*, S05, N.Y.S. 2d 888 (N.Y. App. Div. 1986)].

## Loyalty Oaths

Some school districts ask prospective employees to sign an oath affirming their loyalty to the American form of government. These oaths have been the subject of much debate and the focus of considerable legal action. In some cases, the oaths that individuals have been required to sign have been declared unconstitutional; in other cases, the oaths have been found to be acceptable. What seem to be the critical variables in these decisions are (1) the actual content of the oath and (2) the specificity of the language.

For example, some courts have ruled that it is permissible for school districts to require teachers to swear that they will uphold the federal and state constitutions. In these cases, the judges have generally decided that such an oath does not constitute an undue invasion of a teacher's freedom of expression, nor is it a mandate for blind subservience. Rather, the oath has been viewed as calling on the teacher simply to acknowledge a general belief in our system of constitutional law (Fischer, Schimmel, and Kelly, 1987, p. 174). A similar line of reasoning has been used in cases upholding school district policies calling on teachers to acknowledge their opposition to overthrowing the government by illegal or unconstitutional means.

Oaths requiring teachers to swear that they will faithfully perform their duties have also generally been found to be acceptable. The courts have concluded that these oaths are basically asking teachers to promise professional competence. This is acceptable because there is no right to be unfaithful in the performance of professional duties (Fischer, Schimmel, and Kelly, 1987, p. 174).

On the other hand, oaths that include statements such as "undivided allegiance" to the government or "a reverence for law and order," or oaths requiring teachers to swear that they are not subversive, have been found to be unconstitutional. In these cases the courts have felt that the oaths potentially threatened First Amendment guarantees. Typically, oaths in question have failed to define meanings of such key terms as "subversive activities."

## Teachers' Rights
## Personal Lives

"What is done away from school is my business and should not have any bearing on my status as a teacher." This is the argument many teachers voice when the issue of their private conduct is raised; not everyone agrees with this position, however.

For example, school administrators and other community members often maintain that teachers serve as role models for impressionable learners and, as such, have a responsibility to behave in a suitable way that goes beyond what is expected of typical citizens. Hence, teachers' behavior both in and out of the classroom is a proper concern of school officials. In an important court decision that supported this view [*Board of Trustees of Compton Junior College District* v. *Stubblefield*, 94 Cal. Rptr. 318, 321 (1971)], the court declared that certain professions, such as teaching, impose limitations on personal actions that are not imposed by other occupations.

In the not-too-distant past, numerous restrictions on teachers' personal lives were common, and teachers generally accepted them. Teachers who violated community standards of propriety were dismissed—only rarely did they challenge school officials' right to take this action. This is no longer the case. Teachers have become increasingly willing to challenge restrictions on their personal behavior. School districts must be able to support dismissal actions based on teachers' personal lives with evidence that courts will find convincing. Box 19–3 presents one view of this issue.

## Freedom of Association

Teachers have occasionally been dismissed for belonging to radical organizations or even for being active in partisan politics. Other teachers have found that they were dismissed or put into a do-not-hire category because they were related to a school board member or married to a school administrator. These actions have been challenged on the grounds that they violate an individual's right to freedom of association.

The courts have generally ruled that teachers cannot be dismissed simply because they belong to controversial groups such as the communist party or a revolutionary organization unless there has been evidence that the individual supported illegal activities. A basic test that is generally applied in these cases is whether participation impairs teaching effectiveness (Fischer, Schimmel, and Kelly, 1987, p. 189).

The courts have also ruled that teachers cannot be dismissed because of their political support of candidates for school boards or other elected offices, or for participating

---

BOX 18–3
## PERSONAL STANDARDS OF TEACHERS

"Teachers are special. They work with our children. Hence, we don't want just anybody for a teacher. The teacher cannot be just Mr. or Ms. Average—he or she must be better. Teachers are beacons for children. They should be upstanding and inspirational models. Individuals who are not willing to bear this moral burden have no business in the profession."

*What Do You Think?*
1. How do you react to the position taken?
2. Would fewer people be attracted to teaching if more rigid moral and ethical standards were set for teachers?
3. To what extent do you think learners acquire their moral and ethical standards from teachers?

personally in partisan political activities (including wearing political buttons to school). The line is drawn, however, if the teacher attempts to indoctrinate learners. As with other issues of a similar nature, the courts typically consider whether a teacher's partisan political activities have caused substantial disruption or otherwise seriously impaired the instructional process (Fischer, Schimmel, and Kelly, 1987, pp. 177–79).

Interestingly, some courts have sustained actions of school districts to dismiss a teacher who has married a school administrator. These courts have argued that school policies prohibiting the marriage of a teacher and administrator do not violate the right to marry but only prohibit a conflict of interest that might occur in areas such as teacher assignments, teacher evaluations, or school resource allocations (Fischer, Schimmel, and Kelly, 1987, pp. 178–79).

## Personal Appearance

Another controversial area relating to conditions of employment concerns dress and grooming standards for teachers. The courts have generally ruled that it is acceptable for a school district to establish such standards, arguing that such restrictions are relatively minor and are not matters of constitutional importance. Hence, courts generally have overturned grooming and dress standards only (1) if teachers have been able to prove that the regulations were unreasonable or (2) if teachers have been able to establish that grooming standards affected matters of racial pride or academic freedom (Fischer, Schimmel, and Kelly, 1987, pp. 346–47).

## Lifestyle Issues

A wide range of concerns related to teachers' rights to choose their own lifestyles have resulted in litigation involving school districts and teachers. Among other issues, courts have heard cases related to homosexuality, unmarried cohabitation, and rights of teachers to breastfeed their own infants in school. For the most part, the courts have maintained that teachers have a right to privacy and school officials cannot take actions that infringe on this right. However, the decisions in privacy-right cases have varied depending on the issues associated with the specific situation being litigated. Typically, courts have been very much concerned about whether the lifestyle of the teacher has had a negative impact on his or her ability to discharge instructional responsibilities effectively. A few examples will illustrate some issues with which courts have had to grapple.

In the area of homosexual behavior, the California Supreme Court rejected the notion that an individual could be dismissed solely because of homosexual behavior [*Morrison* v. *State Board of Education*, 461 P. 2d 375 (1969)]. In this case, two teachers engaged in a brief homosexual affair. About a year later, one teacher reported the incident to the superintendent of the district where the second teacher was employed. In response to information supplied by the superintendent, the school board took action to strip the second teacher of his teaching credential. In its decision, the court noted that there was no evidence that this conduct had affected the instructional performance of the teacher, and the dismissal action was overturned. In this case, the court suggested that a teacher cannot be dismissed simply on the ground that school authorities disapprove of his or her personal conduct—there must also be evidence that this conduct has impaired the teacher's ability to function in his or her professional role. Other court cases have followed this general line of thinking. For example, a federal court in Oregon ruled that a teacher could not be dismissed simply because he or she openly admitted to being homosexual [*Burton v. Cascade School District Union High School No. 5*, 353 F.Supp. 254 (D.Ore. 1973)].

In another case involving the issue of homosexuality, a secondary school teacher was arrested for making a homosexual advance to an undercover officer on a public beach. The teacher's school district took action to revoke the teacher's certificate, and the teacher filed a court action to challenge this decision. In this case the court upheld the action of the school district, pointing out that the teacher's conduct was clearly contrary to social and moral standards of the people in the community. The guideline followed here was that the public nature of the incident and its incompatibility with community standards had destroyed the ability of the teacher to be a credible instructional leader in this community [*Sarac v. State Board of Education*, 57 Cal. Rptr. 69 (1967)]. This same general theme was reflected in a 1984 Oregon court decision, in which the court upheld the dismissal of a teacher who was observed engaging in homosexual conduct in an adult bookstore [*Ross v. Springfield School District No. 19*, 691 P2d 509 (Ore. App. 1984)].

Courts have also been concerned about the issues of publicity and potential instructional impairment in cases involving unmarried cohabitation. In one case, a teacher moved in with her boyfriend. Two months later, the school administration informed her that she could either resign or be fired. Ten days later, she married her boyfriend. Nevertheless, the district took action to suspend her on grounds of immorality. She challenged this decision in court. In its decision, the court upheld the rights of the teacher, noting that prior to the dismissal action most people in the community had been unaware that the teacher was cohabitating with her boyfriend. Furthermore, there was insufficient evidence to sustain the contention that the teacher's behavior had in any way interfered with her effectiveness in the classroom [*Thompson v. Southwest School District*, 483 F. Supp. 1170 (W.D.M.O. 1980)].

On the other hand, a court upheld the discharge of an unmarried teacher in a small rural community who was let go after a large number of parents asked the school board to dismiss her because she was living with her boyfriend. In this case, the court ruled that it had to balance the privacy right of the teacher against the interests of the school board in promoting the education of its students [*Sullivan v. Meade Independent School District, No. 101*, 530 F2d 799 (8th Cir. 1976)].

A Florida case centered on the right of a teacher, who was a nursing mother, to breastfeed her infant at school. Her principal refused to allow her to do so, and the teacher challenged this decision by arranging for the child to be brought to school during her lunch period and then nursing the child in a private room. This situation ultimately resulted in a court case. In its decision, the court supported the teacher, ruling that the Constitution protects individuals from undue state interference in their freedom of personal choice in some areas of their family life, and that breastfeeding is the most elemental form of parental care [*Dike v. School Board of Orange County, Florida*, 650 F2d 783 (5th Cir. 1981)]. It should be noted that this ruling did not imply that school districts cannot adopt rules that restrict these freedoms in order to prevent disruption of the educational environment or to ensure that teachers perform their duties. In the case in question, there was no convincing evidence presented to suggest that the teacher's instructional effectiveness had been impaired.

## Immoral and Unprofessional Conduct

A number of cases have been brought before the courts involving the issue of immoral or unprofessional behavior. Most states include immorality as one of the acceptable causes for teacher dismissal. Typically, the courts have dealt severely with teachers who have been found to have acted immorally. The difficulty in these cases has been in defining what constitutes immoral behavior. As indicated earlier, unmarried cohabitation or homosexuality might be considered immoral in some places and not in others.

In dealing with issues of moral behavior, the courts have tended to look at how the behavior influenced both the credibility of the teacher in the community and his or her ability to teach. When the behavior has been viewed as violating prevailing moral standards and when it has resulted in widespread public outrage, the courts have tended to support teacher dismissal. However, the outcome has been less certain when the teacher's behavior has not had a clear and obvious impact on the school and community.

In general, the courts have been less tolerant of teachers who have been accused of immoral behavior involving learners than with immoral behavior involving adults. This has been particularly true in cases involving sexual misconduct.

In one case, a police officer came upon a California junior college teacher who was having sex with a student in a car. When this happened, the teacher knocked the officer down and drove away at a high speed in an attempt to flee. The teacher was caught and, because of this incident, dismissed from his teaching position. The teacher challenged this decision in court, arguing that what had occurred was an example of out-of-school behavior and therefore was not grounds for dismissal. In its decision, the court ruled that the teacher's assault on the police officer, the teacher's misconduct with the student, and the notoriety of his behavior were sufficient evidence that he was unfit to teach. The court also stated that because of the power and authority that teachers have concerning grading and the granting of diplomas, the integrity of the school system can be threatened when teachers become involved with students [*Board of Trustees of Compton Junior College District* v. *Stubblefield*, 94 Cal Rptr. 318 (1971)].

In another case involving teacher–learner immorality, a high school teacher was dismissed after he was discovered, partially undressed, playing a game of strip poker with a female student. The teacher challenged the dismissal action in court, but the court supported the action of the school authorities [*Yang* v. *Special Charter School District No. 150*, Peoria County, 296 N.E. 2d 74 (Ill. 1973)]. Another dismissal was upheld after a court considered a situation involving a female teacher who had ignored warnings to avoid the "appearance of impropriety" with a male student and had visited his apartment on several occasions, once spending the night [*Clark* v. *Ann Arbor School District*, 344 N.W.2d 48 (Mich. App. 1983)].

Sexual activities that have not included teacher–learner relationships have also often resulted in dismissal actions. In one case, a woman who had taught successfully in a school district for years became involved in a group that promoted deviant sexual behavior. She was arrested by an undercover police officer at a swingers' club party after publicly engaging in sexual activity with three different men. The court upheld her dismissal on the grounds that her behavior displayed a notable lack of concern for the preservation of her dignity or reputation and indicated "a serious defect of moral character, normal prudence and good common sense" [*Petit* v. *State Board of Education*, 513 P.2d 889 (Cal. 1973)].

Other behaviors relating to the unprofessional conduct of teachers that have led to successful dismissal charges include such irresponsible actions as calling learners "dumb niggers," drinking to excess, serving alcohol to learners in the teacher's home, and telling learners to lie about their weights at a wrestling tournament.

## Criminal Conduct

Conviction or even indictment on a criminal charge can be the basis for teacher dismissal or suspension. In several states, prospective teachers are required to reveal when applying for a teaching certificate whether they have been convicted of a felony. Admission of a conviction or a failure to answer the question truthfully may be sufficient grounds for denial of a certificate to teach.

However, not all felony convictions are considered as justification for dismissal or removal of a teaching certificate. The courts have occasionally weighed the seriousness of the offense and whether the crime involved immoral behavior. This is a fuzzy distinction because some courts have indicated that most convictions are an indication of immoral behavior. A few cases illustrate the difficulty of describing general guidelines related to the area of criminal conduct.

In a case in Pennsylvania, a teacher convicted of shoplifting was dismissed on the ground that this action constituted an immoral act. The court agreed, maintaining that shoplifting was clearly within the definition of immoral behavior [*Lesley* v. *Oxford Area School District*, 420 A2d 764 (Pa. 1980)].

In another case a school district dismissed a teacher who took a teapot, $20.00 from baseball gate receipts, and a set of books from the school over an eight-year period. Even though the property was returned and the value of the items was quite small, the courts upheld this dismissal, ruling that such behavior was unacceptable for teachers who were in daily contact with impressionable youth [*Kimble* v. *Worth County R-111 Board of Education*, 669 S.W.2d 949 (Mo. App. 1984)].

Even conviction on a misdemeanor charge has been used as grounds for dismissal. A teacher in Alaska was fired after being convicted of illegally diverting electricity to his home. The court upheld the dismissal on the grounds that the act was a form of theft and involved moral turpitude. Therefore, the teacher was not seen as fit to continue as a teacher [*Kenai Peninsula Borough of Education* v. *Brown*, 691 P2d 1034 (Alaska 1984)].

On the other hand, the Supreme Court of the state of Washington held that the conviction of a teacher for grand larceny after he purchased a stolen motorcycle was insufficient grounds for dismissal. In this case, the court ruled that the district had failed to prove that the conviction "materially and substantially" interfered with the individual's ability to teach [*Hoagland* v. *Mount Vernon School District No. 320*, 623 P.2d 1156 (Wash. 1981)]. Similarly, the dismissal of a school counselor convicted of shoplifting at a local mall was overturned on the basis that the conviction was not a sufficient indication that the person was unfit to be a counselor [*Golden* v. *Board of Education of the County of Harrison*, 285 S.E. 2d 665 (W.Va. 1981)].

Because of varied judicial reactions to criminal convictions and indictments of teachers, few clear patterns can be identified. It is generally true, though, that the continued employment of teachers who run afoul of the law is at risk (see the accompanying What the Experts Say).

---

WHAT THE EXPERTS SAY

## *Can a teacher lose a job for being indicted on a criminal charge?*

In our country, citizens are generally considered innocent until they have been proven guilty. Indictment on a criminal charge does not ordinarily carry with it either the assumption of guilt or any sanctions; penalties come only when a person has been convicted of a crime.

Experts who have studied legal actions against school district officials point out that standards of evidence required for conviction of a crime and dismissal of a teacher are different. If charges are brought against teachers for crimes such as child abuse or selling illegal substances, which are thought to have some connection to their professional roles and might impair their credibility and effectiveness as teachers, they may well lose their jobs. Over the years, courts have established the principle that for a person to be convicted of a crime he or she must be proven guilty "beyond a reasonable doubt." However, dismissal requires only "a preponderance of evidence" that the individual engaged in immoral or criminal activity of a nature likely to interfere with his or her teaching effectiveness (Fischer, Schimmel, and Kelly, 1987, p. 234). Hence, it is possible that a teacher who is not proven guilty of a crime in a court of law may, under certain circumstances, legally be dismissed from a teaching position.

---

### Instructional Concerns

There are categories of teacher behavior related to instruction that sometimes have resulted in court cases. Among them are instructional actions related to:

- grading and uses of learner records
- academic freedom (what is taught and how it is taught)
- reproduction of copyrighted materials
- expression of the teacher's personal religious and moral convictions
- excessive use of force in discipline

### Grades and Statements about Students

The courts have generally considered school officials to be uniquely qualified to judge the academic achievement of learners, and thus have been reluctant to overturn teachers' grading decisions unless it could be demonstrated that the grades were arbitrary, capricious, or otherwise given in bad faith. To avoid a possible charge of "arbitrary grading," teachers should have clear grading standards, keep accurate records, and not lower grades as a punishment for nonacademic misbehavior.

In addition to the issue of grading, courts sometimes have heard cases related to the issue of the records that schools keep on individual learners. The Family Rights and Privacy Act of 1974 established standards for what can be contained in learner records. It is legal, for example, for teachers to make notes about learners for their own personal use as long as these notes are not shown to another person. However, if teachers place defamatory comments in learners' permanent records, they may be sued for libel. Similar actions may result if defamatory comments are included in letters of recommendation. It is particularly important that any statements a teacher makes on permanent records and in letters of recommendation describe relevant and observable behaviors.

A teacher who knowingly spreads gossip that harms a learner's reputation faces the possibility of being successfully sued for slander. It is in teachers' own self-interest to be professional in the statements they make about learners in all public places, including faculty lounges in their own school.

## Academic Freedom

One aspect of teaching that has generated considerable discussion over the years is what is termed *academic freedom,* which refers to the idea that, in the classroom, teachers and learners should be able to inquire into any issue, even one that might be controversial and unpopular. The courts have held that academic freedom is a fundamental component of our democratic society that derives from the First Amendment. There are, however, limits to academic freedom—problems arise when there is a conflict between the right of the teacher to conduct the classroom according to his or her best professional judgment and the responsibility of the school district to ensure that the prescribed curriculum is being taught. This area has been one of considerable interest in recent years as some groups have sought to censor materials that are used in the classroom.

In cases involving academic freedom, courts generally have supported teachers' rights to introduce material that is relevant to the subject that is being taught, appropriate to the age and maturity level of the learners, and unlikely to interfere with the educational process. School boards do, however, have the right to prohibit certain texts and materials from inclusion in the classroom, but the reasons for prohibiting material must be justifiable and constitutionally reasonable, not based on a desire to avoid controversial issues or to promote particular religious or political viewpoints. In other words, a school board must establish specific, clear, and defensible criteria for determining whether material is to be excluded.

Academic freedom does not allow a teacher to disregard the approved course syllabus and the assigned text, nor does it sanction discussions or materials that are not relevant to the subject being taught. Neither can the teacher preach his or her own religious beliefs. A few cases will illustrate the nature of teachers' academic freedom rights.

In one case, an American history teacher used a simulation exercise that evoked strong student feelings on racial issues. Acting on the complaints of a number of parents, the school board advised the teacher to stop discussing the controversial material. When she continued to use the material, the board made a decision not to renew her contract. She took the issue to court. In its decision, the court ruled that the district had violated the teacher's First Amendment rights [*Kingsville Independent School District* v. *Cooper*, 611 F. 2d 1109 (5th cir. 1980)].

In another case, an eleventh-grade English teacher assigned a story to her class. Her principal and associate superintendent described the story as "literary garbage" and advised her not to teach it again. However, the teacher felt it was a good piece of literature and refused to take the administrators' advice. She was subsequently dismissed, and then took legal action against the district, claiming that the dismissal action was a violation of her right to academic freedom. A federal court found that the school board failed to show that the assignment was inappropriate for the eleventh-grade students or that it created a significant disruption in the educational process. Therefore, the case was decided in favor of the teacher [*Parducci* v. *Rutland*, 316 F.Supp. 352 (N.D. Ala. 1970)].

Three cases that were ruled against dismissed teachers involved (1) a teacher who continued to teach sex-related issues in a health class because he believed the topic was of great interest to learners, (2) an art teacher who taught her religious beliefs in class and actively encouraged youngsters to attend meetings of her religious group, and (3) a mathematics teacher who encouraged learners to protest the presence of army recruiters on the school campus. In each of these cases, the courts saw these teachers' actions as going beyond the limits of academic freedom and hence upheld their dismissals.

In summary, decisions in the area of academic freedom related to what can be taught are very situation-specific. Teachers do have a right to deal with controversial topics that are relevant to the subject they are teaching. However, they must exercise caution and common sense because the courts have clearly indicated that academic freedom does not imply an open license for teachers to do anything they desire in the classroom. This chapter's Case Study provides an example of a teacher encountering conflict over the issue of academic freedom.

CASE STUDY

## *Can the teacher's method be defended?*

**Mr. Allenby teaches 9th-grade English.** One of his classes is difficult to handle, and most of the students are unmotivated and low-achieving. His experience in giving them writing assignments has been disheartening: often, many papers have come in with nothing written on them at all, and most others have contained only a few hastily scrawled sentences.

Last week, in an effort to "get them to do something," Mr. Allenby announced that members of the class could write stories on any topic at all. He went on to say that copies would be made of all of the stories and distributed to everyone in the class.

To Mr. Allenby's surprise, most of the class began work on this project with real enthusiasm. His excitement, however, turned to dismay when the papers came in and he began to read them. Many of the stories were liberally sprinkled with profanity, and some of them had very explicit sexual references. The students reminded him of his pledge to copy and distribute all of the stories. After thinking about his commitment, Mr. Allenby decided to make good on his promise.

Yesterday, he was summoned to the office of Ms. Michaelson, the school principal. Copies of several of the more lurid stories had found their way to her desk. After a discussion in which Mr. Allenby admitted that students had been encouraged to write the material and that he had arranged for copying and distributing the stories, Ms. Michaelson informed him that she was going to initiate a dismissal action. She pointed out that his teaching method was totally inappropriate and the school district would not continue to employ a teacher who not only failed to censor student-produced work but actually went on to distribute profane and sexually explicit materials to students.

*What are your thoughts about Mr. Allenby's assignment? Did he make an error? What would you have done had you been in his place? How do you react to the principal's decision to seek his dismissal? If Mr. Allenby were dismissed and then challenged this action in court, what criteria might the court apply in considering this case? In general, how much freedom do you think teachers should have in deciding what instructional approach to use?*

## Copyright Law

Copy machines, VCRs, and computers are common items in most schools and homes. It is very easy for a teacher to make multiple copies of printed material to use with class, videotape a television program to use as an instructional tool, or copy computer software programs. These practices are all governed by strict legal guidelines, and an increasing number of teachers have discovered that ignoring these strictures can lead to severe legal consequences.

Under a doctrine known as *fair use,* the courts have ruled that it is in the public interest to allow certain uses of copyrighted materials. Fair use provides for some limited use of copyrighted material in a reasonable manner without obtaining permission. Federal copyright legislation as delineated in the Copyright Act of 1976 (Public Law 94-553) and the Berne Convention Implementation Act of 1988 recognizes these four criteria in determining fair use:

- the purpose and character of the use, including whether such use is commercial or for nonprofit educational purposes
- the nature of the copyrighted material
- the amount of the material used in relation to the length of the copyrighted work as a whole
- the effect of the use upon the potential market for or the value of the copyrighted work (*West Educational Law Reporter,* 1977, and Supplement, 1985).

Although specific standards for educational fair use were not adopted in the copyright law, the guidelines of the Ad Hoc Committee of Educational Institutions and

Organizations on Copyright Law Revision; the Author's League of America, Inc.; and the Association of American Publishers, Inc. were endorsed (Committee on the Judiciary, 1976). This means that specific guidelines for fair use of material in educational settings have been established. The guidelines state that a teacher can make a single copy of the following for his or her own use in scholarly research or classroom preparation:

- a chapter from a book
- an article from a periodical or newspaper
- a short story, short essay, or short poem
- a chart, graph, diagram, drawing, cartoon, or picture from a book, newspaper, or periodical

Multiple copies can be made for use in the classroom provided that no more than one copy per student is made and that the copying meets the standards of brevity, spontaneity, and cumulative effect. The "standard of brevity" is defined as a completed poem or excerpt of a longer poem of no more than 250 words; a completed story, article, or essay of no more than 2,500 words; and an excerpt of no more that 1,000 words or 10 percent of a prose work. The "standard of spontaneity" refers to the idea that the copying was the inspiration of the teacher and the decision to use the material was so close in time to the need to use it that a timely reply from a formal request for permission could not reasonably be expected. The "standard of cumulative effect" requires that copying of material be for only one course and that not more than one short poem, article, story, essay, or two excerpts may be copied from the same author or more than three from the same book or periodical during any one class term.

Specific guidelines have also been established governing the use of videotapes. Generally, the guidelines state that a videotape of a television program may be kept for only 45 days, and only during the first 10 days after the taping may teachers use the tape for instructional purposes. The teacher may repeat the use of the tape only once for reinforcement. At the end of 45 days, the tape is to be erased.

These guidelines call into question the practice of making multiple copies of material and using them over and over in classrooms. Similarly, the practice of making videotapes of television programs or movies and replaying them to numerous classes over a long period of time is clearly prohibited. Teachers who have material that they wish to use repeatedly should get written permission from the copyright owner. Permission requests should contain information relating to the exact material to be copied, the proposed use of the material, and the number of copies to be made.

Computer software is copyrighted material that does not fall under the fair use doctrine. Therefore, it is illegal to copy computer software except when the copy is for archival purposes or is an essential step in the utilization of the program. Teachers need to be aware that copying of computer programs for classroom use is a violation of copyright law, and should therefore consider not only the legal consequences but also the message they may be sending to students when they are seen to be violating the law.

## Freedom of Conscience

The separation of church and state and the role of religion in the schools continue to be controversial. Although most issues relating to religion in the schools have focused on curriculum and students, teachers also have religious convictions and these may conflict with views of parents and other community members. Learners have little choice about where they go to school and who will teach them. Hence, our society has generally frowned on teachers who, instead of dealing with the prescribed curriculum, attempt to impose their own religious views on young people who have no legitimate alternatives as to where they can go to school.

Some cases involving teachers' religious views have been tied to subjects the teachers have been expected to teach. In one case, a teacher who belonged to a religious group that opposed references to patriotism and national symbols informed the principal that she would not teach her learners any content promoting love of country, and would refuse to acknowledge such national holidays as Lincoln's Birthday. The principal, backed by the central school district administration, informed the teacher that she would be required to follow the prescribed curriculum. The teacher challenged this decision, and the case ultimately went to the Supreme Court. In its decision, the court upheld the school district and stated that the First Amendment does not provide license for a teacher to teach a curriculum that is at variance with the one prescribed by the state. The court further noted that, while the teacher had a right to her own religious beliefs, she had no right to require others to submit to her views and, thereby, to be deprived of a portion of their educational experience [*Palmer* v. *Board of Education of City of Chicago*, 603 F.2d 1271 (7th Cir. 1979), cert. denied 44 U.S. 1026 (1980)].

Cases have also come to court concerning whether teachers need to lead learners in saluting the flag. Some states and school districts have policies requiring teachers, particularly elementary teachers, to lead their class in a flag salute on a regular basis. When one New York teacher refused to participate in the required flag salute, she was fired. She contested the decision in a court suit. In its decision, the court upheld the teacher's right not to participate in this activity [*Russo* v. *Central School District No. 1*, 469 F.2d 623 (2d Cir. 1972), cert. denied, 411 U.S. 832 (1973)].

Another controversial issue relates to teachers' rights to be absent from school to observe religious holidays. For the most part, the courts have ruled that teachers do have a right to take a leave for a religious holiday as long as the leave does not cause undue hardship on the school district. This indicates that the leaves must not be excessive. While allowing for leaves for religious holidays, however, the courts have ruled that the school district is under no obligation to pay for such leaves unless the contract specifically states that such leaves will be paid.

### Excessive Use of Force in Discipline

A number of court cases have focused on the issue of the rights of teachers to use force when disciplining learners. Physical punishment, such as paddling, has been the special concern of many of these cases. In the case of *Ingraham* v. *Wright* [*Ingraham* v. *Wright*, 430 U.S. 651 (1977)], the Supreme Court ruled that teachers could use reasonable, but not excessive, force in disciplining a learner. Furthermore, the court declared that corporal punishment in the classroom did not constitute "cruel and unusual punishment" and, hence, was not a violation of a learner's constitutional rights.

The *Ingraham* v. *Wright* case suggests a need to define the term *reasonable force*. In general, the courts have considered several factors in deciding whether force applied in a given situation was reasonable, among them being:

- the gravity of the misbehavior
- the age of the learner
- the sex and size of the learner
- the size of the person administering the punishment
- the implement used to administer the punishment
- the attitude or disposition of the person administering the punishment

What these criteria suggest is that corporal punishment must be used with extreme care. An incident in which a very angry, very large teacher used a heavy instrument on a small child would probably violate the definition of reasonable force.

Most laws relating to corporal punishment are state and local school district regulations. In recent years, several states have passed laws prohibiting the practice. In addition, many local school districts have established similar policies. Those states and districts that do not prohibit the practice usually have very strict guidelines concerning how corporal punishment is to be administered.

Teachers need to understand that the simple legality of corporal punishment in a state or local school district does not, by itself, protect a teacher from legal action. Citizens have a right to sue for redress if they believe the teacher has used corporal punishment carelessly or has exceeded the limits of reasonableness. In addition, a teacher could face possible legal action if the administration of corporal punishment aggravates a learner's health or medical problems, even if the teacher was unaware of the ailment.

In summary, corporal punishment in the schools remains controversial. Teachers who use it may face legal action even in those places where the practice is permitted. Many teachers feel that the risks of corporal punishment outweigh the benefits and have turned to other methods of discipline.

## Teachers' Legal Liability

In recent years, the incidence of litigation against teachers has increased dramatically. Some believe this has come about because of an erosion of public confidence in the schools; others feel that it has resulted because schools have become larger, which may make people feel that they are dealing with cold and remote institutions. For whatever reasons, teachers today are being taken to court in alarmingly high numbers. In thinking about protecting themselves against the possibility of becoming involved in a court action, two areas of particular concern to teachers are negligence and actions taken to report child abuse.

## Negligence

*Negligence* is the failure to use reasonable care to prevent someone from harm. There are three kinds of negligence: misfeasance, nonfeasance, and malfeasance. *Misfeasance* occurs when a person fails to act in a proper manner to prevent harm from coming to another person. *Nonfeasance* occurs when a person fails to act when it was his or her responsibility to do so and, as a result, someone is harmed. *Malfeasance* occurs when harm comes to someone because someone else has deliberately acted in an improper fashion.

Teachers and administrators regularly check playground equipment to ensure its safety. Legal liability problems can result if learners suffer injuries because equipment has not been properly maintained.

Misfeasance for teachers usually occurs when a teacher acts unwisely or without taking proper safeguards. The teacher may have had a worthy motive but still acted in a way that resulted in harm. For example, a teacher of very young children might ask a child to carry a glass container from one location to another. If the child falls and is cut, the teacher might be charged with misfeasance. The courts might deem it improper for the teacher to have asked a very young child to perform this kind of a task.

Nonfeasance incidents frequently occur when something happens during a teacher's absence from his or her place of responsibility. For example, a learner might be hurt when a teacher is out of the classroom and not available to supervise class members. A teacher who is away from an assigned area of responsibility on the playground might be charged with nonfeasance if a child is injured. Court cases tend to turn not so much on the issue of absence from the duty station as on the question of whether the absence was justifiable. If the teacher left the classroom to put out a wastebasket fire in a lavatory across the hall and, in his or her absence, a learner was hurt in the classroom, the courts might well decide that the fire situation represented a reasonable cause for the teacher's absence.

This teacher is carefully monitoring this student who is working with chemicals in the laboratory. This kind of professional attention protects teachers in the event of a negligence suit.

Malfeasance cases often involve circumstances in which it is alleged that a teacher has acted deliberately and knowingly to do something that resulted in a learner injury. For example, a litigant might contend that a teacher deliberately used too much force in breaking up a fight and, as a result, a learner was hurt unnecessarily.

Basic legal tests are often used in deciding teacher negligence cases. In general, courts want to know whether a reasonable individual with similar training would have acted the same way, and whether the teacher could have foreseen the possibility of an injury occurring.

## Reporting Suspected Child Abuse

Public concern for child abuse is growing. Today, all 50 states and the District of Columbia have laws requiring the mandatory reporting of suspected instances of child abuse. Because teachers have prolonged contact with children, they are deemed to be in a position to note instances of child abuse. Therefore, many state laws require teachers to report child abuse when they see it. Under mandatory reporting laws, teachers who fail to report suspected child abuse can face both criminal and civil charges.

Teachers should know that a high level of suspicion is not required for reporting suspected child abuse. The terms used to describe grounds for reporting suspected cases include such phrases as *reasonable grounds, cause to believe,* or *reasonable cause to believe.* This means that a teacher does not need to know beyond a reasonable doubt that a child has been abused. If there is some reasonable suspicion that an injury to a

*"Mr. Shapiro has got to stop reading newspaper reports of teacher-liability suits."*
Courtesy of Ford Button.

child is not the result of an unavoidable accident, the suspected abuse should be reported.

All states have provided a form of immunity from lawsuits for reports of child abuse that have been made in good faith. This offers some protection for the teacher who is fearful of a lawsuit brought by the child's parents. When teachers act reasonably and in good faith, the law typically shields them from liability. If, however, it is demonstrated that the teacher's report was filed with some malicious intent or in bad faith, the teacher may well face legal action.

## Key Ideas in Summary

- Teacher certification is a function of state government. Many states have arrangements that will allow people who are certified in one state to qualify for certification in another.

- Teachers' conditions of employment are governed by the contracts they sign. A contract is a legal document that places obligations both on the teacher and the employing district. When being considered for positions, prospective teachers

**Table 18-1**
Summary table: Legal concerns of teachers

| Topic | Key Points |
|---|---|
| Conditions of employment | |
| • Teachers' certification | This is a state function; reciprocity agreements exist among many states. |
| • Hiring process | Questions asked in employment interviews must have a demonstrable relationship to the position. |
| • Teachers' contracts | Legally binding, written documents that spell out the obligations of teachers and their school district employers. |
| • Testing for AIDS and drug abuse | School districts generally must demonstrate a "compelling interest" in information yielded by any tests they require. |
| • Loyalty oaths | In determining their legality, courts tend to consider contents of oaths and specificity of language found in the oaths. |
| Teachers' rights | |
| • Personal lives | Restrictions may be imposed that differ from those imposed on people in other occupations; generally, districts today attempt to place fewer restrictions on teachers' private lives than they did in the past. |
| • Freedom of association | In deciding cases involving freedom of association, courts have tended to consider whether the association impaired the individual's teaching effectiveness. |
| • Personal appearance | Courts have generally supported the rights of school districts to establish personal grooming standards for teachers. |

**Table 18-1**
*continued*

| Topic | Key Points |
|---|---|
| Teachers' rights (cont.) | |
| • Lifestyle issues | In making decisions involving lifestyle issues, courts have tended to consider the degree to which the teacher's lifestyle influences his or her ability to discharge professional responsibilities effectively. |
| • Immoral and unprofessional conduct | A difficulty courts have faced is that what is immoral or unprofessional in one setting may not be so viewed in another; cases have tended to focus on the relationship of the teacher's behavior to his or her ability to teach and remain credible in the community. |
| • Criminal conduct | Teachers *may* face dismissal for conviction of a criminal offense or even for indictment on a criminal charge; however, actual decisions tend to vary depending on the special circumstances of the individual case. |
| Instructional conduct | |
| • Grades and statements about students | Courts have tended to view teachers as grading experts and have been generally reluctant to overturn grades unless there is evidence that they were given capriciously or in bad faith; defamatory comments in learner records or letters of recommendation may provide grounds for a successful libel suit against the teacher who made them. |
| • Academic freedom | Courts have tended to support teachers' rights to introduce material relevant to what is being taught, appropriate to learners' age and maturity levels, and not likely to interfere with the educational process. |

**Table 18-1**
*continued*

| Topic | Key Points |
|---|---|
| Instructional conduct | |
| • Copyright law | Use of much print and video material is governed by the fair use doctrine, which provides clear guidelines regarding what kind of use is acceptable without permission from the copyright holder; computer software is not covered by the fair use doctrine. |
| • Freedom of conscience | Courts have generally frowned on efforts of teachers to impose their own religious views on learners; decisions in many other kinds of freedom-of-conscience cases have varied, depending on the specifics of the individual situation. |
| • Excessive use of force in discipline | Teachers may use reasonable, but not excessive, force in disciplining learners; factors considered in determining whether force applied is reasonable include the gravity of the misbehavior, the learner's age, the learner's sex and size, the size of the person administering punishment, the sort of implement used, and the attitude of the person administering the punishment. |
| Teachers' legal liability | |
| • Negligence | Teachers can be found guilty of three categories of negligence: misfeasance, nonfeasance, and malfeasance. |
| • Reporting suspected child abuse | Teachers have a legal responsibility to report instances of suspected child abuse; failure to do so may result in legal action against the teacher. |

generally can be asked only questions that have a demonstrable relationship to the job for which they are applying.

- Teachers, for the most part, have been found to have the same freedom-of-association rights as other citizens. In general, courts have decided against teachers most frequently when there has been compelling evidence that their associations have impaired their teaching effectiveness.

- In the area of personal appearance, courts usually have supported the rights of school districts to establish dress and grooming standards for teachers. Such standards have tended to be overturned most frequently when teachers have successfully argued that these regulations were unreasonable or were interfering with racial pride or academic freedom.

- Court decisions relating to teachers' personal lives and lifestyles have been mixed. In general, the courts have found that teachers, because of the special nature of their work, can be held to higher standards of personal behavior than the citizenry at large. With respect to such personal issues, such as homosexuality, court decisions have varied—many judgments have been based on evidence of the degree to which teachers' behaviors have undercut their credibility or otherwise interfered with their ability to discharge their professional responsibilities.

- Attempts to dismiss teachers because of alleged immoral behavior have sometimes been supported and sometimes overturned by the courts. Decisions have resulted from circumstances unique to each case and the nature of the community where the behavior occurred.

- In cases regarding academic freedom, the courts generally have supported teachers' rights to introduce content relevant to their teaching assignments. On the other hand, the courts have not been sympathetic to cases involving teacher attempts to convey content bearing little or no relationship to their assigned courses.

- For the most part, courts have been reluctant to overturn teachers' grading decisions, as they have tended to view teachers as experts. Grading decisions that have been overruled usually involved situations where the grades resulted from capricious or arbitrary grading practices.

- There are strict guidelines that teachers must follow in using copyrighted material of any kind. The fair use doctrine allows some limited use of copyrighted materials in the classroom, but any use beyond that requires teachers to obtain permission from the copyright holder.

- Corporal punishment has been declared not to constitute "cruel and unusual punishment" as that phrase is used in the U.S. Constitution. In cases involving the appropriateness and legality of corporal punishment, the courts often have considered the gravity of the misbehavior, the age of the learner, the sex and size of the learner, the size of the person administering the punishment, and the attitude of the person administering the punishment.

- Teachers may be sued for negligence if they fail to discharge their duties in a responsible manner. The three major categories of negligence include nonfeasance, misfeasance, and malfeasance. Teachers may also be subject to legal action if they fail to report suspected child abuse.

## Review and Discussion Questions

1. Why is it important that teachers know something about legal cases pertaining to schools and teaching?
2. What are some patterns that have been revealed in loyalty oath cases involving teachers?
3. What are some examples of situations in which dismissals of teachers relating to their associations with certain groups or people have been upheld by the courts?
4. Has it generally been considered legal for courts to require teachers to meet certain standards of personal appearance?
5. What are some topics that the courts have considered under the general heading "lifestyle issues?"
6. Why have courts sometimes experienced difficulty in resolving cases involving alleged immoral conduct of teachers?
7. Should conviction of a felony be sufficient evidence of immorality to justify dismissal of a teacher? Why or why not?
8. Should there be any limits placed on the kinds of content teachers are allowed to introduce to their learners?
9. To what extent should authorities, other than the classroom teacher, be able to change an individual learner's grade?
10. What are some variables that courts have often considered when making decisions in corporal punishment cases?

## Ideas for Field Experiences, Projects, and Enrichment

1. Find out the requirements for teacher certification in your state. Are there several kinds or classes of teaching certificates? If so, what are the qualifications for each, and what kind of authority does each confer? You may wish to talk to people at your institution's certification or placement office. As well, your

instructor may be able to suggest other information sources. Share your findings with others in your class in the form of an oral report.

2. Invite a representative of a local teachers' association, for example a local unit of either the National Education Association or American Federation of Teachers, to come to your class to talk about the issue of teacher liability. Ask this person to discuss the kinds of protections these groups make available to protect teachers against liability actions.

3. Invite a personnel director from a local school district to visit your class. Ask this person to comment on the kinds of questions that can and cannot be legally asked during an interview.

4. Obtain a sample teaching contract from a local school district. Review the contract to identify the conditions of employment and those areas where clarification might be needed.

5. *Phi Delta Kappan* is a leading professional education journal. Each month it includes a feature focusing on legal concerns of educators. Read several of these features and prepare a short report for your class on what you have learned.

## Supplementary Reading

Fischer, L., D. Schimmel, and C. Kelly. *Teachers and the Law*. 2d ed. New York: Longman, 1987.

Francis, S. N., and C. E. Stacy. "Law and the Sensual Teacher." *Phi Delta Kappan* (October 1977): 98–103.

Myers, J. E. B., B. G. Epley, and P. G. Nakaue. "Responding to Child Abuse: Critical Issues for Education and Their Counsel." In T. Jones and D. Semler. *School Law Update 1986*. Topeka, KS: National Organization on Legal Problems of Education, 1986, 203–21.

Sametz, L., and C. S. McLoughlin. *Educators, Children, and the Law*. Springfield, IL: C. C. Thomas, 1985.

*School Law News*. Capitol Publications, Inc., Suite G-12, 2430 Pennsylvania Avenue, N.W., Washington, DC 20037.

*West's Education Law Reporter*. West Publishing Company, 50 West Kellogg Blvd., P.O. Box 64526, St. Paul, MN 55164-0526 (annual editions).

## References

*Board of Trustees of Compton Junior College District* v. *Stubblefield*, 94 Cal. Rptr. 318, 321 (1971).

*Burton* v. *Cascade School District Union High School No. 5*, 353 F. Supp. 254 (D. Ore. 1973).

*Clark* v. *Ann Arbor School District*, 344 N.W. 2d 48 (Mich. App. 1983).

Committee on the Judiciary. *H.R. No. 94-1476*, 94th Congress, 201 Sess. 68-70 (1976).

*Dike* v. *School Board of Orange County, Florida*, 650 F. 2d 783 (5th Cir. 1981).

Fischer, L., D. Schimmel, and C. Kelly. *Teachers and the Law.* 2d ed. New York: Longman, 1987.

*Golden* v. *Board of Education of the County of Harrison*, 285 S.E. 2d 665 (W. Va. 1981).

*Hoagland* v. *Mont Vernon School District No. 320*, 623 P.2d 1156 (Wash. 1981).

*Ingraham* v. *Wright*, 430 U.S. 651 (1977).

*Katz* v. *Ambach*, 472 N.Y.S. 2d 492 (App. Div. 1984).

*Kenai Peninsula Borough of Education* v. *Brown*, 691 P.2d 1034 (Alaska 1984).

*Kimble* v. *Worth County R-111 Board of Education*, 669 S.W. 2d 949 (Mo. App. 1984).

*Kingsville Independent School District* v. *Cooper*, 611 F.2d 1109 (5th Cir. 1980).

*Lesley* v. *Oxford Area School District*, 420 A2d 764 (Pa. 1980).

*Morrison* v. *State Board of Education*, 461 P.2d 375 (Cal. 1969).

*Palmer* v. *Board of Education of City of Chicago*, 603 F.2d 1271 (7th Cir. 1979), cert. denied 44 U.S. 1026 (1980).

*Parducci* v. *Rutland*, 316 F. Supp. 352 (M.D. Ala. 1979).

*Patchogue-Medford Congress of Teachers* v. *Board of Education*, 505 N.Y.S. 2d 888 (N.Y. App. Div. 1986).

*Petit* v. *Board of Education*, 513 P. 2d 889 (Cal. 1973).

*Ross* v. *Springfield School District No. 19*, 691 P.2d 509 (Ore. App. 1984).

*Russo* v. *Central School District No. 1*, 469 F.2d 623 (2nd Cir. 1972), cert. denied, 411 U.S. 832 (1973).

*Sarac* v. *State Board of Education*, 57 Cal. Rptr. 69 (1969).

*Sullivan* v. *Meade Independent School District, No. 101*, 530 F. 2d 799 (8th Cir. 1976).

*Thompson* v. *Southwest School District*, 483 F. Supp. 1170 (W.D.M.O. 1980).

*West Educational Law Reporter.* St. Paul, MN: West Publishing Company, 1977, and supplement, 1985.

*Yang* v. *Special Charter School District No. 150* , Peoria County, 296 N.E. 2d 74 (Ill. 1973).

# Chapter 19

# Learners' Rights and Responsibilities

• • • • • • • • • • • • • • • • • • • • • • • • • • • • • • • • • • •

## Objectives

This chapter provides information to help the reader to

- define the doctrine of *in loco parentis*.
- identify changes over time in how our society has viewed the schools.
- explain components of due process as it applies to learners in the schools.
- point out some learner rights in areas concerned with matters of conscience.
- describe some rights and limitations that apply to learners in the areas of free speech and expression.
- identify some legal standards that apply to search and seizure in school settings.
- describe some reactions of the courts in cases that have involved learners' personal appearance and dress.
- point out some provisions of the Family Rights and Privacy Act.

# Focus Questions

1. How have changes in society's view of the relationship between young people and the schools changed the legal rights of learners?
2. How have changes in the *in loco parentis* doctrine altered the relationship between teacher and learner?
3. Why is the *Tinker* v. *Des Moines* case considered a landmark in the area of learner rights?
4. What are some features of the substantive and procedural components of due process that must be observed in situations involving school learners?
5. What requirements are often imposed by states before authorizing the operation of nonpublic schools?
6. What are some kinds of things that court decisions have suggested administrators might legally censor from school publications?
7. What legal tests often are applied to determine whether a school search was reasonable?
8. What have been some patterns of court decisions in cases involving learners' personal appearance?
9. What trends have emerged in recent years regarding rights of pregnant learners to attend school?
10. Under what circumstances might a teacher face legal problems related to a violation of the Family Rights and Privacy Act?

· · · · · · · · · · · · · · · · · · · · · · · · · ·

# Introduction

Over the past few decades, many courts have considered learner rights cases. In some instances, decisions have acted to clarify and expand learner rights; in others, decisions have reflected inconsistent patterns. The net result is a confused hodgepodge of information relating to the appropriate legal relationships between school officials and learners.

It is important for teachers to have some basic understandings of issues related to learner rights. Courts typically do not accept ignorance of the law or ignorance of appropriate legal precedent as acceptable defenses when teachers are hailed into court because of an alleged violation of a learner's rights. This chapter provides information that illuminates some principles related to the legal appropriateness of various learner, teacher, and administrator actions.

## Changes in Society's View of the Child in School

The traditional legal doctrine governing the relationship of the school to the child was known as *in loco parentis*. According to this doctrine, the school acted "in place of the parent." This meant that the school and its designates (administrators and teachers) were free to treat young people much as they would be treated by their parents. Common-law precedents relating to the parent–child relationship were extended to the school.

For example, children cannot take their parents to court and demand a hearing on the grounds of a disagreement over some parental directive. Parents are legally defined as having a custodial relationship with their children. Under *in loco parentis*, this same custodial relationship was vested in the school. Buttressed by this legal doctrine, school officials did not have to justify actions taken against young people who were judged to have broken school rules and regulations. Just as the young person could not sue a parent, so, too, under *in loco parentis*, the young person (or his or her legal representatives) could not sue the school.

The *in loco parentis* doctrine began to crumble in the early 1960s, when a number of human and civil rights issues captured public attention. Efforts to extend full constitutional privileges to all racial groups prompted people to become interested in whether constitutional guarantees really apply to everybody or only to "some everybodies." University groups were quick to speak out against institutional practices that seemed to deny students the same constitutional protections they would enjoy if they were not enrolled in institutions of higher learning. Finally, an increasing public suspicion that the government was not being responsive to the general public will concerning the Vietnam War led to a closer scrutiny of all traditional sources of authority. In this context, it was only a matter of time before questions began to be raised regarding the *in loco parentis* relationship between school officials and school learners.

Some critics of *in loco parentis* charged that the doctrine represented an outdated view of how society viewed its young people. Historically, the doctrine had evolved because of changing conceptions of childhood. Indeed, the whole idea of there being a time called *childhood* that was distinctly different from *adulthood* has not always been accepted. Many years ago, children were viewed as miniature adults. Little thought was given to the long period between helpless infancy and the time a person became a contributing member of the adult community. In times when all family members had to work to maintain the household, full adult rights were extended to children at a very early age.

As the years went by and western societies delayed the time of a person's initial entry into the work force, the concept of childhood gradually developed. With increases in technology, the number of years between a person's birth and the time he or she would assume the work burdens of an adult increased.

In a sense, schools might be considered to have evolved as "holding institutions" for young people who had no real economic function to perform until they reached a certain level of intellectual and chronological maturity. These nonworking children could not be kept at home, as that would interfere with the work efficiency of adult family members. Nor could they go to work, as there was no economically efficient return from their labor. The solution was to send them to a special institution, the school.

Early schools were different from today's public schools. Many of them were very small and were clearly institutions of the local community. The ability of local leaders to hire and fire teachers ensured a congruence between instructional practices and local values. Given the kind of person likely to be hired as a teacher, parents were not at all reluctant to accept the school as a surrogate parent for their children. If the economics had been right, many parents would have enjoyed having their children at home as contributing workmates. But since this was not the case, parents willingly turned them over to the school and the teacher, an institution and an individual they expected to stand *in loco parentis*.

Since schools were seen as holding institutions where young people could be sent until they were mature enough to do "real work," public expectations of the schools were not high. As a result, teachers and administrators were likely to be as prized for their close reflection of community mores as for their contributions to the academic development of learners.

Given the view that academic learning was not particularly important, no great efforts were expended to keep misbehaving learners in school. Schooling was regarded as a privilege to be enjoyed by those who could live by the rules, not a right that society felt was owed to all young people. And, since schooling was not a right, learners were not viewed as having any legal recourse for challenging decisions to remove them from school when they violated the rules. The doctrine of *in loco parentis* ensured that expelled learners had no more right to take such a decision to court than they had to take their own parents to court for insisting that they perform certain household chores.

The view of schooling as a privilege rather than a right started to unravel when critics began to point out that literacy had become necessary for survival in our society. Given the need for an educated population, it was illogical to argue that public school, the best available mechanism for promoting literacy, should be viewed as something other than a right to which all young people were entitled. As this view became more widespread, more and more challenges to the *in loco parentis* doctrine began appearing on court dockets. Box 19–1 examines the privilege–right issue in further depth.

BOX 19–1
## ATTITUDES TOWARD SCHOOLS AND LEARNERS

During earlier times in our history, schooling was considered to be a privilege. Since a privilege does not come to a person as a right but rather as a result of having met certain conditions, learners in those days who were expelled from schools had little recourse to challenge such actions.

Recently, there has been a trend for schooling to be viewed as a right. A right entitles the holder to certain legal protections. With regard to schooling, there has been a tendency to extend to learners the same constitutional protections enjoyed by all adults. This has meant that a decision to expel a learner from school must be done in such a way that his or her due process rights are observed.

*What Do You Think?*
1. Should schooling be viewed as a privilege or as a right? Why?
2. Do you think there should be some outer limit of educators' authority over learners in schools? If so, what should this outer limit be?
3. Do you think that 25 years from now there will be more public sentiment for viewing schooling as a privilege or as a right? Why do you think so?

In *Dixon* v. *Alabama State Board of Education* [294 F. 2d 150 (1961)], the court ruled that a tax-supported public education had become so fundamental that it should be regarded as a "substantial right." This important shift in the legal view of education as a right rather than a privilege carried with it important constitutional implications. The U.S. Constitution protects certain rights of citizens. Among these protections is a requirement that "due process of law" be observed in situations that could result in the loss of a right. "Due process" requires that people threatened with the loss of a right be provided with information such as the nature of the charges against them, the identity of their accusers, and other protections, including the right to be represented by counsel. Beginning with the *Dixon* case, there has been a continuing trend to extend due process rights to learners in the schools.

In addition to due process guarantees, other court decisions have had the effect of extending to school learners privileges granted to citizens under the Bill of Rights. A landmark decision of this kind was the famous case of *Tinker* v. *Des Moines Independent Community School District* [343 U.S. 503 (1969)]. In the *Tinker* case, the Supreme Court struck down a school district rule banning the wearing of arm bands as a gesture of protest against the Vietnam War. Holding the rule to be an illegal restraint of freedom of speech, the Court pointed out that constitutional guarantees do extend to learners in school.

The decision in the *Tinker* case prompted much debate in educational circles. Some teachers were confused regarding exactly what authority did remain to them in the area of controlling learners. A few people saw the *Tinker* decision as an interference in the school management process that could undermine the smooth functioning of the educational program. Others drew different conclusions from their review of the *Tinker* case. In their view, the Supreme Court had done little to undermine the real authority of school officials. Instead, these people saw the Court as confining its concern to the *processes* followed by school officials in exercising their authority. In the view of educators who viewed the *Tinker* decision positively, the effect of extending rights enjoyed by adults to school learners provided educators with an opportunity to develop procedures that would enhance public confidence in the schools. Not only would these procedures be constitutional, but they would also blunt the criticism of people who felt that many actions of school authorities were arbitrary and irresponsible.

## Due Process

Several references have been made in this chapter to "due process." Although most people have a general feeling that due process is designed to ensure that people receive fair treatment in an adversarial situation, the specific implications of due process are less well-known.

Just as students' rights must be respected, students, too, must learn a healthy respect for the law.

In general, there are two basic parts of due process. The first, the substantive component, includes the basic set of principles on which due process is based. The second, the procedural component, consists of the procedures that must be followed to ensure that due process rights have not been violated.

## The Substantive Component

It is important for teachers to be familiar with some fundamental principles associated with due process. The substantive component of due process can be thought of as including the following principles:

- Individuals are not to be disciplined on the basis of unwritten rules.
- Rules are not to be vague.
- Individuals are entitled to a hearing before an impartial tribunal.
- The identity of witnesses must be revealed.
- Decisions are to be supported by substantial evidence.
- The hearing can be public or private, depending on the wishes of the accused.

In times past, educators sometimes overlooked one or more of these principles. For example, some administrators failed to specify rules out of a fear that a set of written regulations would undermine their flexibility to respond to problem situations. Furthermore, many rules and regulations that *were* written were couched in such vague terms that people could not easily determine whether or not they were in compliance.

In the days when the courts were not insisting on due process guarantees for school children, there was a general reluctance to release witnesses' names to young people who were charged with violating school rules or regulations. There was a fear that such a release might result in witnesses being intimidated and that, in future cases, people would hesitate to come forward with information.

It is doubtless true that the necessity to protect the due process rights of young people has increased the work of school administrators and has somewhat reduced their flexibility. On the other hand, given the amount of documentation that now must support charges, there probably has been a healthy reduction in the number of miscarriages of justice in cases involving young people and school authorities.

## The Procedural Component

The procedural component is concerned with the procedures that must be followed to ensure that principles of due process will be observed. In general, the procedural component of due process includes the following:

- Rules governing learners' behavior must be distributed in writing to learners and their parents at the beginning of the school year.
- Whenever learners have been accused of a rules infraction that might result in a due process procedure, the charges must be provided in writing to learners and their parents.

- Written notice of the hearing must be given such that there is sufficient time provided for learners and their representatives to prepare a defense. Usually, the hearing must be held within two weeks.
- A fair hearing must include these features:
  - right of the accused to be represented by legal counsel
  - right of the accused to present a defense and introduce evidence
  - right of the accused to face his or her accusers
  - right of the accused to cross-examine witnesses
- The decision of the hearing board is to be based on the evidence presented and must be rendered within a reasonable period of time.
- The accused must be informed of his or her rights to appeal decisions.

These procedures require a heavy investment of time by school personnel. Their complexity probably has done much to ensure that fewer capricious charges are made against young people today than in times past, when it was not necessary to follow due process procedures. Box 19–2 considers several views of this issue.

## Nonpublic Schools

In recent years, legal issues concerning the relationship of the child to the school have continued to evolve. For example, all states now have compulsory attendance laws. Today it is widely acknowledged that educated citizens are productive citizens and, hence, the entire society has a vested interest in ensuring that all young people receive educational services. Therefore, school attendance has come to be defined as a duty. Compulsory attendance laws have overwhelmingly been upheld when they have been challenged in the courts.

The need for young people to attend school, however, does not necessarily imply a requirement that they attend public schools. Parochial and private schools have long played a role in the education of our nation's young people. Home schooling (an arrangement whereby parents teach their own children at home) is another educational option that is available in some places.

Individual states tend to have their own regulations governing the operation of nonpublic school alternatives. These regulations often specify requirements associated with the curriculum to be taught, teacher qualifications, and health and safety standards. In general, they seek to ensure that young people who go to a nonpublic school will receive an education that is at least equivalent to what the state requires its public schools to provide.

There have been many court cases focusing on the issue of what constitutes "equivalency." Many of these have involved situations where parents have sought to educate their children at home. In an Illinois case, the Supreme Court of that state upheld the rights of parents to teach their daughter at home. In its decision, the court ruled that, while state law required all children to be educated, it did not specify the place and particular manner of their education. The court further went on to note that

BOX 19–2
# DUE PROCESS AND PROBLEM LEARNERS

In recent years, because courts have acted to define public education as a right rather than a privilege, the due process clause of the Constitution has been extended to protect learners in the schools. This means that learners in the schools are entitled to the same protections extended to adult citizens when they are charged with violations of rules or regulations.

*What Do You Think?*

1. Some people have said that the courts' extension of due process rights to school learners has tied administrators' hands. As a result, they argue, administrators are increasingly reluctant to do anything about problem learners in their schools. How do you react to this allegation?

2. Other people argue that extension of due process rights to school learners is one of the best things that has ever happened to education. For the first time, these people contend, school learners do not feel that they will be treated arbitrarily or capriciously. As a result, there has been a reduction in the numbers of problems between learners and school authorities. How do you react to this view?

3. When they first read about due process requirements, some people maintain that "it certainly doesn't work that way in my school district." How is it possible for some school district officials to have paid little attention to due process requirements?

the conditions of instruction in the home were consistent with the state's standards for private schools [*People* v. *Levisen,* 90 N.E. 2d 213 (Ill. 1950)].

In a Maine case, a court ruled that the state had the right to impose reasonable standards on parents seeking to educate their children at home. When the parents in this case refused to submit their home schooling plans for approval, their children were declared to be truant when they did not present themselves at the local public school [*State* v. *McDonough,* 468 A.2d 9787 (Me. 1983)]. Similarly, a Kansas court found that home schooling that was unplanned or unscheduled and taught by a mother who was not certified did not meet the legal requirements for an "equivalent education" [*In re Sawyer,* 672 P.2d 1093 (Kan. 1983)]. In general, the ability of private and home schools to meet compulsory attendance standards depends on the individual state's laws and on how the courts have chosen to interpret the equivalent education requirement.

## Freedom of Conscience

Controversies in this area have centered around several key issues. Among them have been concerns related to the teaching of certain content, objections to require-

*"You can stop worrying about those angry phone calls from my teacher. I've been suspended from school indefinitely!"*
Courtesy of Ford Button.

ments for learner participation in ceremonies involving saluting the flag, and disputes relating to the issue of free exercise of religion.

## Objections to Curriculum Content

In general, the courts have agreed that learners can be excused from certain parts of the academic program if they have religious or moral objections to what is being studied. Two issues have often been considered by judges in deciding cases of this kind. The first relates to whether the subject being objected to is deemed essential for citizenship. The second issue concerns the degree to which schools have a right to make and enforce regulations to ensure the efficient and effective operation of schools. Court decisions have tended to focus heavily on the specifics of the situation being litigated.

Several cases have been brought by people who have objected to the teaching of evolution. In Arkansas, the state legislature at one time passed a law forbidding schools in that state from including evolution in the prescribed curriculum. The Supreme Court ruled this law to be unconstitutional on the grounds that it violated the First Amendment clause relating to the establishment of religion [*Epperson* v. *State of Arkansas*, 393 U.S. 97 (1968)].

In some places, there have been attempts to force the schools to teach "creationism" or "scientific creationism" along with evolution. These efforts have generally been found to be unconstitutional on the grounds that creationism is a religious belief and thus requiring it to be taught would violate the First Amendment's establishment-of-religion clause. On the other hand, at least one court has implied that creationism could be introduced in a social studies class provided it was described simply as a belief held by some people [*McLean* v. *Arkansas Board of Education*, 529 F. Supp. 1255 (E.D. Ark. 1982)].

### Saluting the Flag

In general, the courts have agreed that learners can refuse to salute the flag because of religious or moral convictions. The courts have decided that a refusal to salute the flag does not constitute a serious threat to the welfare of the state; hence, the state has no compelling interest in ensuring that every learner does salute the flag. In the absence of this compelling interest, the courts have given precedence to the individual moral and religious principles of learners. The courts have also ruled that a learner cannot be required to stand or leave the room while others participate in the flag-salute ceremony [*Lipp* v. *Morris*, F.2d 834, 836 (3d. Cir. 1978)].

### Religious Observances

Contrary to some popular opinion, the courts have not required that religion be completely excluded from public schools—it is permissible for learners to study about religion in such courses as comparative religion, art, music, and social studies. To be legal, the study of religion must take place in such a way that lessons do not advance or inhibit a particular religion. For example, a school musical group may perform compositions with religious themes so long as the primary purpose is secular, not religious.

Cases involving school prayers have been heard by many state courts, but decisions have not followed a predictable pattern. In an Iowa case, the courts determined that prayer at a graduation ceremony was unconstitutional because the primary purpose of the practice was viewed as being religious [*Graham* v. *Central Community School District*, 608 F. Supp. 531 (S.D. Iowa 1985)]. On the other hand, a Michigan court determined that prayer represented only a solemn opening for a graduation ceremony—a practice with a long tradition—and therefore served a purpose that was at least as much secular as it was religious. Hence, this court ruled the prayer to be permissible [*Stein* v. *Plainwell Community Schools*, 610 F. Supp. 43 (W.D. Mich. 1985)]. See "What the Experts Say" on the question of whether prayer clubs in school are legal.

---

WHAT THE EXPERTS SAY

*Should learner prayer clubs be allowed to meet in schools?*

Experts Lawrence Rossow and Nancy Rossow (1990) have studied the question of whether it is legal for school authorities to grant permission for high school prayer clubs to meet in school buildings. The issue turns on the question of the maturity level of secondary-school learners. The basic question is: "Can high school students understand that their school is not endorsing religion if it allows religious activities on school property?" (Rossow and Rossow, 1990, p. 207).

The Rossows (1990) have suggested that those who have commented positively on maturity levels of high school students have tended to compare their levels of maturity with much younger elementary school students. On the other hand, those who have commented negatively about high school students' maturity levels have tended to compare them with college and university students and with adults.

Before the early 1980s, most court decisions disallowed student religious activities in schools. A potential change in this pattern was observed after 1983 when the school board in Williamsport, Pennsylvania, denied a request by a student prayer club to meet in a school room. This ruling was challenged on the ground that it violated students' free speech rights. The case went to court.

In its decision, the court ruled in favor of the school administration, holding that constitutional prohibitions against establishment of religion took precedence over students' free speech rights (*Bender* v. *Williamsport Area School District*, 563 F. Supp. 697 [E.D. Pa. 1983]). The decision took into account the students' levels of maturity, and it reflected the view that high school students were not yet mature enough to grasp the point that authorization to meet did not imply school endorsement of a particular religion.

The *Bender* decision was appealed. The U.S. Court of Appeals for the 3rd Circuit reversed the lower court's ruling, arguing for the maturity levels of high school students and for the supremacy, in this situation, of students' free speech rights over concerns related to the establishment of religion.

At this point, the Williamsport Area School District appealed the decision to the U.S. Supreme Court. In 1986, the Supreme Court ruled that the U.S. Court of Appeals had had no jurisdiction in the case and should never have heard the appeal of the original *Bender* case. The effect of this decision was to declare null and void the decision of the U.S. Court of Appeals for the 3rd Circuit and to let stand the original *Bender* case decision (which supported the ban on meetings of high school prayer groups in school buildings during the school day).

As Rossow and Rossow (1990) have noted, in its decision the Supreme Court did not directly address the issue of high school students' maturity and the legality of allowing high school buildings to be used for prayer group meetings. How the High Court would rule on such a case is still open to question. The action of the U.S. Congress in passing the Equal Access Act of 1984 may have laid the grounds for further potential legal action that in time may result in a definitive Supreme Court ruling on this issue.

The Equal Access Act guarantees access to space within all public schools receiving federal funds of any kind to all groups, regardless of their political, religious, or philosophical nature. This seems to guarantee access to religious organizations such as school prayer clubs, and it clearly represents a view that high school students are mature enough to understand that allowing prayer groups to meet in the school is not endorsing a particular religious point of view.

## Freedom of Speech and Expression

A number of court cases have considered issues related to freedom of speech and expression. The rule that the courts have followed in determining whether freedom of speech and expression may be abridged by school authorities seems to be that abridgment is proper only when such speech or expression can be shown to result in a serious disruption of the learning process.

For example, in one case a school regulation banning the wearing of protest messages by learners was challenged. In this situation, because administrators and other witnesses were able to cite a number of specific incidences of violent disruptions involving fights between different ideological factions in the school, the court let the school regulation stand. The wearing of messages had been shown to interfere with the school program, and the rule was regarded as a legitimate exercise of administrative authority.

A number of cases have focused on the rights of expression of learners who have written material for school newspapers and journals. Generally, these publications enjoy the same legal protections as the adult press. Numerous cases have come to court involving attempts of administrators to suppress the publication of these materials because of an alleged use of "improper" language. Generally the rule here, too, has been one of establishing a convincing connection between the contents of the newspaper or journal and some documented disruption of the educational process. It is legal for administrators to screen content, provided that they can prove that this screening is necessary to prevent disruption and that it is not simply used to suppress content that might prove politically embarrassing to the school.

## Search and Seizure

The Fourth Amendment of the U.S. Constitution protects individuals against unreasonable search and seizure. Recent concern about drug abuse and crime in the schools has brought forth numerous challenges to the rights of school officials to conduct searches.

Two general principles govern the right to search: probable cause and reasonable suspicion. *Probable cause* means that evidence of wrongdoing is sufficiently convincing to strongly support the view that a party is guilty of illegal behavior. Often probable cause requires the testimony of a reliable witness. Probable cause normally is required before authorities will issue a search warrant. It is a very strict standard.

*Reasonable suspicion* is a much less stringent standard, requiring only that there be some reasonable suspicion that someone is guilty of an offense. Typically, this is the standard applied when school authorities decide that a search is warranted. More specifically, school authorities apply two other guidelines: (1) the expectation of privacy and (2) the potential intrusiveness of the search. A search to be conducted in an area in which the individual has little expectation of privacy does not need as much justification as a search in an area in which an individual has a great expectation of privacy. For example, little expectation of privacy is associated with a school desk, which is public property. On the other hand, a purse is a personal possession and, logically, a person might have a higher expectation of privacy regarding its contents.

In general, the issue of intrusiveness has to do with the degree to which a search might have to come into close contact with a person's body. The closer the search comes to the body, the more intrusive it is. The most intrusive search of all is a strip search.

When considering whether any kind of search is appropriate, school officials often apply four basic tests. The first concerns the thing or object to be found. The greater the potential danger to the health or safety of learners in the school, the greater is the justification for the search. A gun or a bomb poses an immediate and serious danger; on the other hand, a stolen CD player may offer little immediate threat. Hence, school officials might need a great deal of evidence to establish the likelihood that the object would be found before they would authorize a search.

A second test relates to the quality of the information that has led to consideration of a possible search. The reliability of the people reporting the information must be assessed. Several reliable individuals who divulge similar information provide a more defensible ground for a search than a tip from an anonymous caller.

The third test concerns the nature of the place to be searched. If this is an area where there is a high traditional expectation of privacy, school officials will want very solid information before authorizing a search. However, they might be willing to authorize a search based on less convincing information if the search is to be conducted in an area, such as a school locker, where there is little traditional expectation of privacy.

This dog is sniffing for drugs.

The fourth test focuses on the nature of the proposed search itself. If searches of individuals are to be conducted, authorities will want much evidence before giving their approval. The age and sex of the person to be searched is also often a consideration.

In summary, case law in the area of search and seizure does not provide absolutely clear guidelines to educators. Because of this uncertainty, teachers probably should not attempt searches on their own initiative. Responsibility for authorizing searches should be left in the hands of those school administrators who are in a position to check their legal position with the school district's legal counsel. This chapter's Case Study provides an example of how tricky a search situation can be.

CASE STUDY

## *To search or not to search?*

**Ms. Shin is a sixth-grade teacher in a large middle school.** This morning, she noticed several boys loitering in a back hallway of the school building. Ms. Shin knows most of the students in the school, and she recognized them as members of one of the seventh-grade classes. One of the boys seemed to be taking something out of a backpack and giving it to the other students in exchange for some money. Ms. Shin strongly suspects that she was witnessing a drug transaction. She walked quickly toward the boy with the backpack, wondering whether she should search it.

*Do you think Ms. Shin should search the backpack? Would her observations convince a court that her actions were justified in the event the student or his parents challenge their legality? What alternative actions, short of conducting a personal search of the backpack, might be open to her? What do you think the appropriate course of action would be in this situation?*

### Personal Appearance of Learners

Decisions in court cases centering on learners' appearance have not reflected a consistent pattern. For example, federal appeals courts in the First Circuit, Fourth Circuit, Seventh Circuit, and Eighth Circuit have all declared that an individual's right to establish personal grooming standards is constitutionally protected. On the other hand, courts in the Fifth Circuit, Ninth Circuit, Tenth Circuit, and Eleventh Circuit have declared that no such constitutional protection exists and thus courts should not interfere with school officials' attempts to establish grooming standards for learners.

Cases where individual grooming rights have been upheld have been decided on several grounds. In one instance, the First Circuit Court of Appeals held that the Fourteenth Amendment establishes a "sphere of personal liberty" for every individual that can be restricted only when its exercise interferes with the rights of others [*Richards* v. *Thurston*, 424 F.2d 1281 (1st Circ. 1970)]. In another case, a principal had argued that hair length of male students needed to be regulated for reasons of health and safety. The court rejected this argument, noting that no compelling argument had been made why a similar requirement should not also restrict the length of girls' hair [*Crews* v. *Clones*, 432 F.2d 1259 (7th Circ. 1970)].

Courts that have ruled that grooming standards for learners do not violate any of their important rights have argued that the right to an individual grooming style is a minor and relatively insignificant issue. Consequently, some judges have suggested that the courts should not waste time considering such matters and that school district officials should feel free to establish certain grooming standards.

The issue of dress codes for learners has also come in for some attention in the courts. In some cases they have been held to be constitutional, and in some cases they have been found to be unconstitutional. Those that have been ruled unconstitutional have been found to be unreasonable, capricious, arbitrary, and little related to the educational process. On the other hand, codes designed to prohibit unsanitary clothing or the wearing of other articles that might pose a health hazard (or in some other way interfere with the educational process) have been looked on more favorably by the courts. Box 19–3 asks you to consider some questions related to learners' personal appearance at school.

## Marriage and Pregnancy

Until relatively recent times, schools routinely excluded pregnant learners whether they were married or unmarried. One rationale for these policies was that teenage marriage should be discouraged and that the presence of pregnant learners in school would promote an unhealthy interest in early matrimony. Some people also thought that married girls might be prone to talk with others about the more intimate aspects of their

---

### BOX 19–3
# HAIR LENGTH AND DRESS CODES

The Supreme Court has never rendered a definitive decision in a case involving male hair length in public schools or one involving proper school attire. Place-to-place regulations in these areas vary widely—some state courts have made decisions on one side of these issues; other state courts have held on the opposite side. No final judicial solution seems in sight at this time.

*What Do You Think?*
1. Should schools have strict regulations regarding male hair length and learner dress? Why or why not?
2. Did the schools you attended have such regulations? How well were they received? How did you feel about them?
3. Should school authorities spend time worrying about male hair length and learner dress codes? Why or why not?
4. Courts judge many school regulations in terms of whether they are essential to the smooth functioning of the educational process. In your opinion, are male hair length regulations and dress codes necessary to prevent disruption of the school program? Why or why not?

marital relationships, thereby exercising a "morally corrupting" influence over other young people. The moral corruption argument was particularly common when rationales were built in support of excluding unmarried pregnant learners from school.

In recent years, the courts have tended to make decisions designed to protect the rights of all learners to complete an education. There has been a trend to support the idea that school policies denying pregnant learners the privilege of attending school undermine these learners' potential to acquire the knowledge they need to support themselves and their dependent children. Though practices vary, most districts today make provisions for pregnant learners to continue their educations.

### Family Educational Rights and Privacy

Beginning in the 1960s and continuing into the 1990s, there has been a growing concern over potential misuses of all kinds of records, including school records. For example, some people have worried that a young person who had difficulty with a teacher in the early elementary grades might be stigmatized throughout his or her entire school career by records suggesting that the individual was a troublemaker. Concern about possible misuse of records helped ensure passage of the Family Educational Rights and Privacy Act in 1974.

This act required schools to provide parents free access to any records on their children. Furthermore, learners over age 18 and those in postsecondary schools gained the right to view these records themselves. The act also restricted how schools could distribute these records. Before the act was passed, it was customary for many schools to release these records on request to government agencies, law enforcement agencies, and others. Now, with the Family Educational Rights and Privacy Act, schools are allowed to release records only after strict guidelines have been followed.

This act has implications for future teachers as they seek initial teaching positions. Usually, in preparing placement papers for teacher candidates, personnel at the college or university placement center will ask whether individuals wish to have an open or closed file. If an open file is chosen, the candidate retains the right to read everything that goes into it. If a closed file is chosen, the candidate waives the right to see what is placed inside.

People who write recommendations usually are notified by the placement center whether a candidate has opted for an open file or a closed file. Some professors and others who write recommendations hesitate to provide them to undergraduates who have opted for an open file. Furthermore, some school district personnel people tend to look differently at placement files that are open and those that are closed. Rightly or wrongly, some of them feel they get a more honest appraisal of a candidate's strengths and weaknesses in a closed file.

••••••••••••••••••••••••••••••••••

## Key Ideas in Summary

- Traditionally, the legal doctrine governing relationships between school authorities and learners was *in loco parentis*. In essence, this doctrine implied that the legal relationship between school and learner was much like that existing between parent and child. One implication of this doctrine was that learners did not enjoy the full rights of citizens and could not take school authorities to court to protest decisions. This doctrine began to break down in the 1960s, and today most rights enjoyed by citizens in the general public are extended to school learners.

- A number of First Amendment guarantees have been extended to school learners. A key case in extending Bill of Rights guarantees to learners was *Tinker* v. *Des Moines Independent Community School District* [343 U.S. 503 (1969)]. In this case, the Supreme Court acted to establish the principle that guarantees free speech should be extended to learners in the schools.

- Today, due process guarantees apply to learners in the schools. Due process is designed to ensure that people are treated fairly in adversarial situations. The substantive component of due process references the basic principles on which due process is based; the procedural component outlines procedures to be followed to ensure that due process rights have not been violated.

- All states have compulsory school attendance laws. These have nearly always been upheld by the courts in the few cases where they have been challenged. However, compulsory attendance laws do not force parents to send their children to public schools—home schools, parochial schools, and private schools are usually considered legal alternatives, provided that they can establish that they deliver an education that is at least equivalent to that provided in the public schools.

- A number of issues related to freedom of conscience have come before the courts. Among topics litigated are concerns related to the teaching of certain content, objections to learner participation in flag-saluting ceremonies, and disputes concerning the issue of free exercise of religion. In arriving at decisions, the courts have tended to weigh heavily unique dimensions of the specific situation under consideration.

- School-related issues of freedom of speech and freedom of the press have frequently come before the courts. In general, the courts have extended the same protection to learners as to adults, unless school officials have been able to show that the practice to which they have objected clearly disrupted the educational process.

- In considering the appropriateness of searches of learners and their property in schools, the courts have tended to consider the expectation of privacy and the intrusiveness of the search. In general, the less the expectation of privacy and the more distant the search is from the body of a learner, the more willing courts have been to support the search authority of school officials.

- Court decisions in cases centering on the question of learner dress and appearance have not reflected a consistent pattern. In some cases, the judges have argued that there exists a constitutionally supported right to establish personal

**Table 19–1**
Summary table: Learners' rights and responsibilities

| Topic | Key Points |
|---|---|
| *In loco parentis* | This is the legal doctrine that, in years gone by, defined legal relationships between learners and school officials. Essentially, this doctrine denied learners the right to sue schools for actions taken against them in cases involving school regulations. This doctrine has now been generally overturned; today's learners generally enjoy the full constitutional protection of rights enjoyed by all citizens. |
| Due process | These are legal procedures that must be observed to ensure respect of the rights guaranteed by citizens under the U.S. Constitution. Court decisions have had the effect of extending due process rights to school learners. |
| Nonpublic schools | Compulsory attendance laws do not necessarily require learners to attend public schools; states may authorize alternatives such as parochial, private, or home schooling, provided that there is a demonstrated equivalency of quality. |
| Freedom of conscience | Court cases in this area have focused on such issues as objections to certain required content, objections to saluting the flag, and concerns relating to religious practices. Decisions have tended to be closely tied to the situations under consideration. |
| Freedom of speech and expression | In general, the courts have extended rights of freedom of speech and expression to learners. However, the courts have been willing to uphold administrative decisions restricting these rights when their exercise has been definitely shown to interfere with the educational process. |

**Table 19–1**
*continued*

| Topic | Key Points |
|---|---|
| Search and seizure | Courts have been willing to accept a standard of reasonable suspicion in supporting decisions of school authorities to conduct searches. In general, searches supported by the courts generally have tended to be of areas characterized by little expectation of privacy and of a nature that minimized intrusion on the person being searched. |
| Personal appearance of learners | Court decisions related to this issue have reflected an extremely mixed pattern. Generally, there has been a willingness to uphold restrictions imposed by school authorities when personal practices of individual learners have threatened the health and safety of others or have clearly interfered with the educational process. |
| Marriage and pregnancy | At one time, many schools required pregnant learners to leave school. Today, most schools make provisions for them to remain. |
| Family Educational Rights and Privacy Act of 1974 | This act makes school records pertaining to their children available to parents and to learners over age 18. It also establishes guidelines regarding the general dissemination of information in learners' files. |

grooming standards. In other cases, the courts have declared that no such right exists. Those dress codes that have been most frequently supported have established a clear connection between the regulation and learners' health and safety.

- In years gone by, schools almost routinely forbade pregnant learners from continuing their enrollment in school programs. In recent years, however, there has been growing approbation for the idea that no learners, even those who are pregnant, should be denied an education. Part of the logic supporting this view has been that pregnant learners should not be denied access to knowledge they will need to support themselves and their children.

- The Family Rights and Privacy Act of 1974 established very strict rules regarding distribution of information in learners' files. Further, learners' parents are guaranteed access to the files, and the files are open to learners themselves who are over age 18 or enrolled in a college or university. Part of the impetus for the passage of this legislation was a concern that negative information in learner files was needlessly stigmatizing some individuals by giving teachers and others a negative mind-set regarding these learners' behavior patterns.

## Review and Discussion Questions

1. How has the doctrine of *in loco parentis* changed in recent years?
2. Do you agree with the decision rendered in the *Tinker* case? How might you respond to people who suggest that this decision encouraged learners to defy teachers and administrators?
3. What is due process? How would you distinguish between the substantive component and the procedural component of due process?
4. What kinds of general requirements do states usually impose on private schools before authorizing their operation?
5. Under what conditions have the courts sometimes agreed to support a parent's request not to have his or her child exposed to certain content taught in the school program?
6. Under what conditions have courts sometimes supported decisions of school administrators that have acted to limit learners' rights of freedom of speech?
7. What does the issue of expectation of privacy have to do with a court's likelihood of supporting a school official's decision to order a search?
8. Why do you suppose that court decisions in cases involving learners' grooming standards have not reflected a consistent pattern?
9. Should learners who are pregnant be allowed to remain in school? How does your personal reaction square with what courts have said about this issue in recent years?

10. Why is it important for teachers to be familiar with the provisions of the Family Rights and Privacy Act of 1974?

····································

# Ideas for Field Experiences, Projects, and Enrichment

1. Invite to your class some teachers who serve as advisors for school newspapers, literary magazines, yearbooks, or other publications. Ask them to comment on issues associated with monitoring the content of learners' writing, and whether they are provided with any guidelines from their school district, professional organizations, or other groups regarding censorship of school publications.

2. Interview several teachers about any concerns they might have regarding rights and responsibilities of learners. Do any of these people feel that recent court decisions have made teaching more difficult? If so, in what ways?

3. Review several recent copies of professional education journals, such as *Phi Delta Kappan* or *Educational Leadership*. Look at articles focusing on legal issues in education, prepare summaries of several that discuss court actions in areas related to learners' rights, and share them with others in your class.

4. Organize a class debate on one of the issues introduced in this chapter. For example, you might wish to debate court actions related to such areas as grooming and dress codes, providing instructional services to pregnant learners, or censoring learner publications.

5. Invite a local school administrator to visit your class. Ask this person to describe how dismissal actions in his or her district are handled in a way that preserves the due process rights of affected learners. Also inquire about how other court decisions have influenced school policies and procedures.

····································

# Supplementary Reading

Connors, E. *Student Discipline and the Law*. Bloomington, IN: Phi Delta Kappa Educational Foundation, 1979.

Fischer, L., D. Schimmel, and C. Kelly. *Teachers and the Law*. 2d ed. New York: Longman, 1987.

Hammes, R. "*In Loco Parentis*: Some Considerations in Teacher/Student Relationships." *Clearing House* (Summer 1982): 8–11.

Menacher, J., and E. Pascarella. "How Aware Are Educators of Supreme Court Decisions That Affect Them?" *Phi Delta Kappan* (February 1983): 424–26.

Rossow, L. *Search and Seizure in the Schools.* Topeka, KS: National Organization on Legal Problems of Education, 1987.

....................................

# References

*Bender* v. *Williamsport Area School District,* 563 F. Supp. 697 (E.D. Pa. 1983).

*Crews* v. *Clones,* 432 F. 2d 1259 (7th Cir. 1970).

*Dixon* v. *Alabama State Board of Education,* 294 F. 2d 150 (1961).

*Epperson* v. *State of Arkansas,* 393 U.S. 97 (1968).

*Graham* v. *Central Community School District,* 608 F. Supp. 531 (S.D. Iowa 1985).

*In re Sawyer,* 672 P. 2d 1093 (Kan. 1983).

*Lipp* v. *Morris,* 579 F. 2d 834, 836 (3d. Cir. 1978).

*McLean* v. *Arkansas Board of Education,* 529 F. Supp. 1255 (E.D. Ark. 1982).

*People* v. *Levisen,* 90 N.E. 2d 213 (Ill. 1950).

*Richards* v. *Thurston,* 424 F. 2d 1281 (1st Circ. 1970).

Rossow, L. F., and N. D. Rossow. "Student-Initiated Religious Activity: Constitutional Argument or Psychological Inquiry?" *Journal of Law and Education* (Spring 1990): 207–17.

*State* v. *McDonough,* 468 A.2d 977 (Me. 1983).

*Stein* v. *Plainwell Community Schools,* 610 F. Supp. 43 (W.D. Mich. 1985).

*Tinker* v. *Des Moines Independent Community School District,* 343 U.S. 503 (1969).

# Author Index

# Subject Index